Buddies Afield
Hunting and Fishing With Great Dogs Across North America

James L. Mauney

Lewiston, Idaho

Buddies Afield
Hunting and Fishing With Great Dogs
Across North America

Copyright © 2009 by James L. Mauney

All rights reserved, including the right to reproduce this book,
or portions thereof in any form or by any means, electronic or mechanical,
including photocopying, recording, or by any
information storage and retrieval system, without permission
in writing from James L. Mauney or his designee.

James L. Mauney
25914 Coyote Grade
Lewiston, Idaho 83501

Library of Congress Control Number: 2008943373

ISBN: 9780972609531

Published July 2009

Edited and Published in the United States of America by:
Wm. Harold Nesbitt
Crossing Trails Publications
4804 Kentwood Lane
Woodbridge, VA 22193
http://www.crossingtrails.com

Cover illustration from a painting by Diane Mazy of one of the author's favorite dogs, Rock Honeybear of the Yukon.

This book is dedicated to my dog buddies who have been central characters in many adventures afield and to my father and mother, Reverend Jesse Lloyd and Eloise James Mauney, who provided early encouragement for my interest in nature and dogs.

Buddies Afield

Eloise and Rev. Jesse Lloyd Mauney, the author's parents, at Harbor Mountain Lookout above Sitka Harbor, AK in 1970 with Big Ben and Kent.

Foreword

My early adventures afield were often shared with junior high school buddies. My first adventures afield with four-footed buddies began several years later with the acquisition of my first hunting dog, a Chesapeake Bay retriever I named Storm. Some 45 years later, one of those junior high buddies, Harold Nesbitt, inspired me to write this book.

Growing up in the early 1950s, I was not entertained by TV but by radio programs such as Gunsmoke, The Lone Ranger, Sergeant Preston of the Yukon, and Frank Buck's Bring 'Em Back Alive. Sources of written inspiration included Robert Ruark's "The Old Man and the Boy," Mark Twain's "The Adventures of Huckleberry Finn," and Hemingway's "The Big Two-Hearted River." I also avidly devoured many stacks of outdoor magazines including Field and Stream, Sports Afield, and Outdoor Life. In those days outdoor magazines contained many adventure stories and were not merely the accounting of how to, where to, and when to.

My earliest childhood friends always included a family dog. There was Hercules, a Boston bull terrier that was a family member for 13 years, and a collie called Pauper, a family member for 15 years.

I entered grammar school in the rural community of Pineville, North Carolina with some reluctance. I hated to give up my free lifestyle and be separated from my childhood playmates who were most often African-American kids who lived across a nearby field. My local hero was an elderly graybeard of the African-American community. As livestock manager for a local farm, he was very knowledgeable in the ways of animals and small boys. I was never prouder than when, on occasion, he permitted me to join him on the front seat of his wagon, pulled down Main Street by mule team.

As was true of many young boys of that era, my father taught me to safely handle and shoot a single-shot .22 rifle. My interest in the outdoors and hunting and fishing did not necessarily coincide with that of my parents. However, they were always supportive of me in my interests. I have wonderful memories of early Christmases; memories of fellowship with family; good times; gifts shared; and festive meals. Major Christmas presents from my parents would greatly influence my later life. Most memorable were a BB rifle, a real longbow and arrows, and for my 12th

Christmas, the most memorable and influential of all—a J.C. Higgins bolt-action 20 gauge shotgun.

Early on I was afflicted with chronic asthma that severely curtailed my physical activities and limited my participation in sports. Perhaps partly as a result of my affliction, I have always been independent and something of a loner. During my formative teenage years, fall would find me hiking steep Appalachian slopes in pursuit of squirrel, rabbit, and the ever-evasive southern ruffed grouse. In summer, I could be found fishing along Reems Creek for trout, at Dockery's farm pond for bass, or at Weaverville's Lake Louise for sunfish. In the dead of winter, Bill Hart and Harold Nesbitt were my companions and competitors in trapping the local wetlands for muskrats. Our take gave us some welcome pocket money.

One summer in the early 1950s, my cousins Bill and Charlie and my brother Gene and I were visiting grandparents in Frederick, Maryland. We entered a kid's fishing tournament held on Frederick's Color Lake. When the day was over, and somewhat to the resentment of the local youth, we outlanders walked away with several top prizes.

My cousin Bill was the more effective fisherman. I only managed to rival him in numbers of fish landed because my limited social skills kept me from being as successful with (and distracted by) girls. Looking back on those days, it seems that often when we teamed up, misadventures soon followed. A typical example occurred on a summer day near Weaverville, North Carolina. After of a day spent raiding cherry trees and fishing Lake Louise, we were anxious to make it home for supper. A shortcut across a cow pasture was too tempting to pass up. We had ducked under a barbed wire fence and we were crossing the pasture when a belligerent bull took exception to our trespass. He "treed" us in the loft of an old barn where we spent a couple of long, anxious, thirsty hours. The bull finally lost interest and wandered off, permitting our escape.

While a student at Oakboro High School, I was introduced to my first real wing shooting. My companions most often were Jimmy "Moto" Davis and a couple of the Hatley boys. Our quarry during September was often the mourning dove. I don't recall us ever killing many birds. One fall Jimmy decided to improve his score with a 10 gauge shotgun but I don't believe this strategy resulted in more birds brought to bag. In later years Jimmy downsized to a 20 gauge and became an outstanding wing shot.

During a December hunt in West Virginia, I bagged my first bobwhite quail. Taking a cock quail on the wing convinced me that my shooting skills were taking a turn for the better.

By the time I graduated from Oakboro High school I was pretty much committed to spending life in association with the outdoors and creatures wild. I then entered North Carolina State University, where I majored in

Foreword

Wildlife Biology (Harold Nesbitt was a fellow wildlife student there). The summer of my graduation, I landed a job with the U.S. Fish and Wildlife Service in Alaska. Before the summer was over, I was to see a great deal of the great land that is Alaska. That summer's experience instilled in me forever afterwards a love for wild places.

The acquisition of my first hunting dog, and shortly thereafter my first good shotgun (a Charles Daly Superimposed), inspired me to become an avid bird hunter. A career move to Alaska gave me the opportunity and motivation to develop as a hunter of big game.

I learned as a young man that my only hope for a normal, enjoyable life was for me to subdue my asthma. My hope for accomplishing this was to maintain myself in good physical condition. My activities afield have served that end.

The adventures related in this book occurred as written. There has been no attempt on my part to exaggerate harvest success or feats of my dog buddies. A few names of people and places have been changed for the protection of their privacy. Due to the passage of years and limitations of memory, the sequence of some events may not be recorded entirely as they happened. Professional journals and harvest records maintained through the years proved handy in the recollection of events. Had I paid more attention to my mother (who was an English teacher) and father (whose livelihood as a Baptist Minister was dependent on a command of the English language), this book would have perhaps been more literate.

If these stories give experienced outdoorsman a few chuckles and stir up memories; if this book provides inspiration for the increased use of hunting dogs and therefore a more efficient harvest and the conservation of game; and if my adventures afield inspire some young person to enjoy some of the many opportunities to be found in sports afield, my efforts in this accounting will be justified.

No one adventure in this account is particularly remarkable. However, when taken as a whole, I believe it to be a unique accounting of the variety of experiences afield available to one man and his canine buddies in the late 20th. and early 21st. Centuries in North America.

James Lloyd Mauney

Buddies Afield

After a long hike up Triple J Mountain of the Mentassa Range, AK in 1989, author James L. Mauney rewards Jay with a much needed water break. This peak was named by local Nabesna Indians for this day's climbers: Jim, John Terry (who took this picture), and Jay.

Contents

Foreword ... v

BOOK I — Alaska Days

    Chapter 1 – Wrangell Mountains Ram ... 1
        Dall's sheep hunting in the Wrangell Mountains, 1972

    Chapter 2 – Caribou Are Curious Critters ... 7
        A subsistence hunt for caribou in the Jack Lake Country, 1973

    Chapter 3 – Red Coats In The Highlands ... 11
        After August blacktail bucks in SE Alaska, 1968-1971

    Chapter 4 – Falling For A Goat ... 25
        To Baronof Island for Rocky Mountain goat, 1969

    Chapter 5 – Alaska Potpourri ... 33
        Hunting game from snipe to hair seal, 1969-1978

    Chapter 6 – Hello Dolly ... 49
        Catching sea run Dolly Varden trout in SE Alaska, 1971

    Chapter 7 – Little Norway For Ducks And Salmon ... 53
        Waterfowl hunting and fishing near Petersburg, 1973

    Chapter 8 – Goats Don't Come Easy ... 61
        A too successful Rocky Mountain goat hunt, 1974

    Chapter 9 – Tebay Rainbows ... 69
        Rainbow trout are a bonus in Tebay country, 1974

    Chapter 10 – Sheenjek Combination ... 75
        Hunting grizzly and moose in the Sheenjek Wilderness, 1977

    Chapter 11 – Yukon Monarch ... 79
        Anvik River yields a trophy moose, 1976

Buddies Afield

Chapter 12 – Cold Bay Welcome ... 89
Alaska Retriever Club hunts geese at Izenbek NWR, 1978

Chapter 13 – Grizzly Don't Fetch ... 93
Grizzly encounters enliven a duck hunt, 1978

Chapter 14 – Rude Awakening ... 99
A grizzly spices Anvik River fish camp life, 1978

Chapter 15 – Raining Ducks And Geese ... 105
Fall at Pilot Point results in great waterfowl hunting, 1979

Chapter 16 – Kodiak Harvest ... 111
To Kodiak Island for great black-tailed deer hunting, 1981

Chapter 17 – Springtime Hooters ... 119
After blue grouse in the rainforest near Skagway, 1982

Chapter 18 – Blizzard Birds ... 127
A ptarmigan hunt becomes a struggle for survival, 1985

PHOTO GALLERY

Chapter 19 – Photos Of Buddies And Hunts ... 137

BOOK II — Trips Outside Alaska

Chapter 20 – Nothing Could Be Finer ... 145
Fall hunting and fishing in North Carolina, 1970-1980

Chapter 21 – You Bet 163
Wagers won and lost hunting South Dakota pheasants, 1980

Chapter 22 – Perro Grande ... 167
Dove hunting with Rock in Mexico, 1982

Chapter 23 – Florida Outback ... 173
Winter retriever training and hunting in Florida, 1984

Chapter 24 – Washington Combination ... 181
After deer and geese in NE Washington State, 1988

Chapter 25 – A Bull In The Brush ... 187
A most memorable Idaho trophy elk hunt, 1989

Contents

Chapter 26 –   Idaho Mixed Bag   . . .   191
                A red-letter day for waterfowl and quail, 1989

Chapter 27 –   Perfect Hunts   . . .   197
                Idaho hunts of filled limits and no unretrieved cripples, 1989

Chapter 28 –   Bank Shot   . . .   201
                Chasing chukars, the masked bandits of upland birds, 1990

Chapter 29 –   Special Memories of Simba   . . .   207
                Sharing life with my most outstanding dog, 1991-2001

Chapter 30 –   Chukar The Hard Way   . . .   219
                Earning a "game bird from Hell," 2001

Chapter 31 –   The Devil's Backbone   . . .   225
                Hunting upland birds and waterfowl in Snake River country, 2002

Chapter 32 –   Afield In The New Century   . . .   233
                Late season hunts for upland birds and waterfowl, 2001-2002

Chapter 33 –   Passage Of The Seasons   . . .   245
                Recent hunting is bittersweet with aging friends, 2001-2003

Chapter 34 –   Some Fall Firsts   . . .   273
                A young dog and a senior hunter share some hunting firsts, 2003

Chapter 35 –   Season's End Waterfowl   . . .   295
                The best waterfowling arrives with the New Year, 2004

APPENDIX

Chapter 36 –   Prepping Buddies For The Field   . . .   309
                Proper preparation means greater enjoyment afield

Chapter 37 –   The Cast Of Canine Characters   . . .   317
                Great dog buddies, with descriptions by their owners

Jim Mauney with companions Rock (foreground) and Jay and some very nice Idaho steelhead taken in 1990.

List of Illustrations

Author's parents, Rev. Jesse Lloyd and Eloise Mauney . . . iv
Author and Jay share water on a high Alaska ridge . . . viii
Author with Rock and Jay and Idaho steelheads . . . xii
Rock Honeybear of the Yukon with Dall's sheep trophy . . . xiv
Kent relaxes at end of Baranof Island, AK blacktail hunt . . . 10
Hunting Buddies Winston Hobgood and Kent with grizzly . . . 74
Rock and emperor geese taken at Cold Bay, AK . . . 88
Honeybear's Yukon Jay and a large king salmon . . . 104
Author, dogs, and salmon; author and dogs climb ladders in NC . . . 138
Jim's mom, Eloise Mauney, with Simba, Tip, and Jay . . . 139
Diane Mazy with her dogs; Jay helps pack out a caribou . . . 140
Judy Mauney and dogs; Jim fully armed; a hunting dog family . . . 141
Author's first geese; Rock and blacktail; AK All-breed Trial . . . 142
Rock retrieves salmon; good fishing; dogs on a ski trip . . . 143
Gene Mauney and Bill Hart in NC . . . 144
Genie Riis and Al Roggow after a fine SD pheasant hunt . . . 162
Jim and Rock are south of the Border for doves . . . 172
Jay with results of a mixed bag hunt for geese and deer . . . 180
Jay relaxes at end of a hunt for a nice bull elk . . . 186
Five hunters, three dogs, and filled limits . . . 196
Simba, Jim Mauney's favorite dog . . . 206
Little Abbie with a big Idaho pheasant . . . 218
Bill Conner, Wily, and Jim Mauney with mixed bag of ducks . . . 272
Author working with Abbie and Wily on retrieving basics . . . 308
Rock shows great form as he starts a retrieve . . . 316

FC AFC Rock Honeybear of the Yukon was an excellent field trial dog and also a fine companion on many hunts such as this one in 1976 that resulted in this Dall's sheep in the Wrangell Mountains, AK.

Book I – Alaska Days

Wrangell Mountains Ram

Dall's sheep hunting in the Wrangell Mountains, 1972.

I pulled on hiking boots, hastily stashed my hip boots, and shrugged into my backpack. I was embarking on my first hunt for a Dall's sheep ram, one of North America's top trophy animals. The clear eastern horizon gave the promise of a bluebird day and temperatures that would later make for unpleasantly warm hiking.

I had spent the past couple of months talking to guides, studying the topographic maps, hiking, and getting to know sheep country. My hiking had included prime sheep habitat in the Alaska, Mentasta, and Wrangell Mountains. My body and feet had toughened.

With sheep season imminent, I decided to hunt an area in the Wrangell Mountains. After leaving my truck on Nabesna Road, an initial crossing of Jack Creek was required to reach my chosen hunting area. The creek was running very high from recent rains. I had no wish to start the trip with wet boots, hence the need for hip boots. Crossing the rain-swollen creek while remaining dry was not easy. Neither would be the next few hours of hiking the steep, rough terrain under a heavy backpack. There would be no human trails. I could follow game trails when they ran in the right direction.

My backpack contained the gear and food for a week's survival in the mountain wilderness. A small mountain tent would provide my shelter. My strategy was to get into the high mountain valleys above the timber line to establish my base camp. From the base camp I would hunt the surrounding country. So today was for walking and exploring, with the hunting season to began tomorrow. "Heel up now boys," I urged Kent and his son Big Ben. If I got lucky, my big yellow Labs would function as pack animals and help me pack the meat out of the mountains.

The hike in from Nabesna Road began at an elevation of around 3,300 feet. Good sheep habitat would be found at 2,000 feet higher. The initial pitch up from the creek was through scattered black spruce trees. Red squirrels chattered at being disturbed by foreign intruders. Under foot, old moose spoor was abundant as this was moose winter range.

Buddies Afield — Alaska Days

Breaking out of the timber, I paused for a breather while gazing at the spectacular scenery. Nabesna Road curving along Jack Creek through the Nabesna Valley showed far below. The sheer, cathedral-like cliffs of the Wrangells rose precipitously to the east while to the north, the colorful Mentasta Mountains rolled to the northern horizon. The roar of Jack Creek could no longer be heard.

The 50-pound pack on my back did not make for carefree hiking. Each step upward required considerable effort but I was young and in very good shape. Stands of alder blanketed the terrain and had to be skirted or crashed through. I had picked a tentative destination that lay some eight to ten miles south of Nabesna Road after much study of topographic maps. Determined, I continued on and up. The hours dragged by. During early August in the North Country, the days are long. There would be plenty of daylight for walking today and for hunting in the days ahead.

Well above timber line I took a break and a long swig of water went down wonderfully. A piercing whistle suddenly shattered the quiet as we were noticed by a hoary marmot. I got out my binoculars and studied the mountain slopes to the east. Snow patches on sheltered slopes reflected white in stark contrast to the green of surrounding sheep pastures. Slides of rock and talus showed on steep, unstable slopes.

There! A mile or so away and 2,000 feet higher, those moving white specks were sheep! I counted over 90 animals. These were likely lambs, ewes, and young rams. The big old boys would be in small bands or solo.

Studying the terrain surrounding the gamboling sheep, I chuckled to myself. These sheep had chosen their pasturage wisely. Thousand foot drop-offs fell sharply away from their pasturage on three sides. The only possible approach to the herd was across the summit. I could see no cover there. Their sharp eyes would detect any suspicious movement in plenty of time for them to reach safety in the cliffs. They were safe from predators.

I had reached a brook that flowed and gurgled out of the high country. The going was no longer so steep. There were game trails here along the creek bottom. In some stretches the going was across open terrain and walking was on good, solid ground or gravel. But then thickets of alder or willow intersected our passage and had to be bulled through.

Caribou and moose spoor was plentiful among the willows—some of it quite fresh. Ground squirrels chattered from the rims of their burrows. Massive excavations marred some slopes where a bear had been at work seeking a snack of squirrel. Confident that my dog companions would let me know of a grizzly's presence, I saw no need to worry.

But I jumped to sudden alert when spooked by guttural cries and a thrashing in nearby brush. A family of 10 to 12 ptarmigan flushed from the

Chapter 1 — *Wrangell Mountains Ram*

willows ahead of the dogs. The birds were in brown and white transitional plumage. "No birds today boys," I noted as I called the dogs to heel. "We are after serious critters this trip."

The brook decreased to a trickle. Ahead an almost flat area of grassy hummocks stretched west and south into the distance. Indian cotton waved in the breeze from the hummock tops. I sighed in resignation. With cliffs to the east, I would be forced to cross this nightmare of sponge-like terrain. I slogged ahead, often teetering on one hummock while trying to step to the next. Quite frequently, my boots would slip and my next step would be into ankle-deep, icy water. And there were mosquitoes and biting gnats in abundance. In the distance I saw a caribou bull running crazily across the tundra. He was trying to escape the biting bugs.

Finally, the marshy area lay behind me. We were now far above the timber line. I directed my steps along a gurgling brook that emerged from a beautiful little mountain valley. Scattered dwarf willows followed the watercourse. Fresh sheep droppings appeared as I ascended into a bowl among craggy peaks. I would make my base camp here.

The day was getting short. I quickly pitched my tent and rolled out ground cloth and sleeping bag. The dogs were fed. A cup of hot tea with a shot of peach brandy for sweetener was sipped as dinner cooked. I snacked on pieces of pepperoni while some dehydrated chicken soup thickened with additional Minute Rice boiled on the pack stove. Teeth brushed and exhausted, I crawled into my sleeping bag. The loaded rifle was carefully placed within reach. A big dog lay curled on either side. They would alert me to unwelcome visitors in the night. I could sleep well tonight.

Next day dawned fair and full of promise. Sheep season was open. I was impatient to get on with the hunt. After a light breakfast of oatmeal and dehydrated fruit, I packed gear for the day's hunt. I would travel light. Water, bread and cheese for lunch, a box of ammunition, knives, meat saw, a flashlight, and clothing for layering as temperatures fluctuated were included in my pack.

As the day progressed, we covered many miles of country, pausing frequently to glass ahead. Sheep were occasionally seen in the far distance. Most of the sheep we spotted were lambs and ewes. By mid-afternoon temperatures were soaring. My companions and I were not the only critters suffering from heat. Caribou were lying down and also standing on high snowfields to cool off and to escape insect pests.

On a typical day, I hunted from dawn to sunset. With the arrival of midday, I paused for a snack and maybe a brief nap on a bed of moss. The days passed quickly. For the first several days I enjoyed beautiful weather. Then the rain and fog rolled in. Hunting during the bad weather was at a reduced level and effectiveness. Under Alaska law a legal ram must have horns that complete a three-quarter curl. I had seen few harvest-sized rams.

One day I spotted a nice ram. But I could approach no closer than 500 yards or so. I knew from many successful alpine deer hunts in southeastern Alaska that my rifle, a .308 Norma Magnum, was very dependable out to 300 yards. Out of frustration, I had go at the ram. The distance was just too great and my shot fell far short.

After several days of hard hunting, my grub was starting to run low. I was shedding pounds and I tightened my belt. Hunting the high country effectively required many calories of energy for both my dog critters and me. I would be forced to retreat before our food supplies were completely exhausted. I was facing the end of an unsuccessful hunt.

As I returned to camp that evening, a young bull caribou materialized from out of nowhere. He passed me at a gallop. Caught unaware, I failed to get off a shot. I was mentally kicking myself. But then a second bull showed and this time I was ready. The lung-shot bull ran a short distance and piled up. With a good supply of fresh camp meat, I was back in the sheep hunting business. The dogs would dine on scraps and I would eat the choice cuts. I cached the boned-out meat in a snow bank above camp.

The next morning I continued the hunt as I moved farther into the mountains into new country and I began to spot rams. But the rams spotted were either unapproachable or my stalks unsuccessful. The new terrain was wonderful, with superb scenery. Pika could be heard chattering among the rocks of the stable slides. Ground squirrels were abundant and one morning Kent caught a careless individual. As daylight faded to evening, I watched a lone wolverine hunting down-slope. Wildlife watching was fascinating but I was in the mountains for a ram and time was running out.

The days and miles covered mounted up. Most of my previous alpine big game hunting had been in southeast Alaska. Due to prevailing rainy weather, standard hunting footwear in the southeastern rain forests was usually of rubber. I had naively worn my southeastern Alaska deer boots on this hunt. The sharp rocks encountered crossing slides and talus slopes had cut and slowly destroyed my boots. This footgear would not last for many more days of hiking.

I eventually found my way into a high pass through the mountains. My topographic maps showed the pass to be 5,500 feet in elevation. Peaks immediately around the pass climbed to about 9,000 feet. Tanada Lake reflected in the distance. At the apex of the pass I came across scattered chunks of a crashed aircraft and camping gear. Some brave sheep hunter had "bought the farm." The accident appeared to have occurred a couple of years earlier. Landing and takeoff from this rough terrain would have been

Chapter 1 — *Wrangell Mountains Ram*

very, very tricky. Possibly the aircraft had had some mechanical problem, but the crash was most likely pilot error for attempting to land here.

I salvaged camping gear from the crash site. A large stew pot and other aluminum utensils stashed under a rock cairn would come in handy when hunting this area in future years.

By late afternoon I had wandered some four or five miles from my base camp in my search for rams. Here at last I found many sheep grazing the surrounding slopes. Some of these sheep were rams with heavy horns but I had arrived too late in the day for hunting. As I turned to retrace my weary route to camp, I saw big rams standing on outcroppings of rock profiled against the darkening sky. Before dawn tomorrow I would pull my camp and return here for my final days of hunting.

By midmorning the next day I had reached the high pass. My tent was quickly pitched in the shelter of a large boulder. My last day of hunting now began in earnest. Sheep frequently move within their range. They also rest up during the heat of midday. That certainly proved true this day. During the day's hunt I encountered numerous ewes and small rams but no trophy animals. As the sun set, I despondently returned to my camp. This would have to be my last day. My rubber bottom boots were literally in tatters. My food supply was essentially out except for some caribou meat. After nine days of very hard hunting, I was physically exhausted. In the morning I would head back to Nabesna Road as a very frustrated hunter.

I had almost reached the tent when suddenly in the west a white shape materialized like a ghost in the waning light. Almost as an afterthought I picked up and focused my binoculars. His big, curling horns were framed against the darkening skyline. I was looking at a very nice ram. He was standing on a slope about 100 yards up from the valley bottom.

The range was extreme—I estimated it as 400 yards plus. This would be my last chance. I slid my pack onto the top of a nearby boulder to give a solid rest. The Leupold 2-7 power scope was cranked up to its maximum power. I focused on the ram, then raised the cross hairs about the height of the sheep above his shoulder. I slowly squeezed the trigger and the still evening was shattered by the rifle's roar as in the gathering darkness flame belched from the rifle's muzzle. The distant sheep ran out of sight over the ridge. I had blown my chance; it was a slim chance, but a chance, and I had missed.

Camp was quiet and cheerless that night. After hastily snacking on some cold slices of caribou and a few morsels of bread, I crawled into a damp sleeping bag to doze fitfully for a few brief hours.

By dawn, I was up and moving with the tent down and gear ready to pack out. I reran last night's shot over and over in my mind. The ram had taken off very fast. Did he stumble? Could he have been hit? I had no expectations and no enthusiasm for the climb, but I would have to take a look. As I topped the ridge, the dogs surged excitedly ahead. There he was! A big, beautiful, full-curl Dall's sheep ram. The shot had been true. He had traveled only a few yards.

Calming down from the thrill of a successful hunt, I faced the ordeal ahead. The sheep would be carefully caped-out for mounting. The meat would be completely boned-out. My pack would then weigh more than 100 pounds with the horns. The dogs would take turns packing 30 pounds of meat and gear. Big Ben, a tremendously strong and tall dog, would pack the bulk of the miles back and Kent would relieve him. The hike out would be over some 12 miles of rough terrain. A long day, encompassing eight to ten hours of extreme exercise, faced us.

Sheep hunting is addictive. Time would reduce the memories of the pain endured on that first sheep hunt. Future Augusts would find me and my companions once again tramping wild sheep pastures in the Wrangell, Mentasta, and Brooks Ranges.

Caribou Are Curious Critters

A subsistence hunt for caribou in the Jack Lake country, 1973.

In the weak dawn light I stood on the cabin deck with my binoculars pressed to my eyes, slowly glassing the distant frost-burned tundra. Mount Sanford dominated the southwest horizon. Towering to more than 16,000 feet, the mountain's ice cliffs were awe-inspiring. Today I was looking for caribou. Movement would reveal their presence.

Three hundred feet below the cabin Jack Lake lay still and steaming in the frosty air of late September. Ice was forming in the shallows. The far lakeshore was fringed with stunted black spruce. Timbered draws radiated up from the lake into the treeless tundra. Sugarloaf Mountain rose starkly from the tundra to a flat 5,500 foot summit. The Tanada Mountains pierced the atmosphere to the southwest reminding one of shark teeth. In future years this land would be included in the new Wrangell–St. Elias National Park. Hunting opportunities here would then cease.

Suddenly my eyes picked up some movement in the middle distance. A gleam of white disrupted the brown background as sunlight reflected off white manes. A band of caribou moved in the stillness. I counted six or seven animals. Though the animals were over a mile away, I was certain that I could detect the flash of antlers. I could imagine steam rising from their nostrils in the frigid air. There were likely to be some good bulls among these animals. The caribou were feeding, constantly moving toward the horizon. They disappeared into a depression or draw, only to reappear.

Hunting these animals would be a physical challenge. There were no roads and no trails across the tundra. Walking would be much like trying to progress uphill across a sponge. The terrain included hummocks of grass interspersed with water. There would be small ponds to skirt. I was in good shape, toughened by a summer and fall of hiking and hunting the Alaska Range, Mentasta, and Wrangell Mountains. Packing out with meat would be an ordeal but I would give it a go.

Time was of the essence if I wanted to catch the caribou. The farther the chase, the longer would be the trip back. I made up my mind that I would set a reasonable maximum limit of maybe two miles on the distance I would pursue the caribou.

I quickly assembled my backpack, loading emergency gear, knives, and trail snacks. There was no need to pack pounds of water. Plenty of water would be found in the tundra. The dog pack I had acquired from the

Buddies Afield — Alaska Days

Kluane Indians was loaded. I picked up my .308 Norma Magnum and heeled my big yellow Labs, "come on Rock and Big Ben—the hunt is on!"

A few mallards flushed from the lake's inlet marsh as we skirted Jack Lake. I crossed the inlet on a beaver dam that bridged little Jack Creek. Arctic grayling spooked in the crystal clear creek water. "It would sure be easy to catch some fish today," I thought.

We proceeded to work our way across the tundra, climbing steadily. Whenever possible, I would pick out well-drained gravel outcroppings for good footing. Dense clumps of the heavily laden low-bush blueberry were scattered across the tundra and reflected purple in the early morning light. Bearberry leaves carpeting the tundra had been burned scarlet by frost. We were in for a bluebird day and temperatures were climbing. Reaching a tundra brook, I called a halt for a water break as I pulled off my windbreaker and wiped sweat from my eyes.

Refreshed and cooled by icy water, the dogs and I hastened forward and upward. Suddenly, the dogs became very excited and dashed into a clump of alder. A covey of brown and white ptarmigan exploded into the air with guttural utterances of indignation at our disturbance. "Heel Rock, heel Ben. We are not after birds today. I need some serious camp meat." My supply of mountain sheep was running low.

Almost two hours of tramping had passed. The morning was getting short. We should have spotted caribou by now. Maybe they had left the country. Caribou can easily and quickly cover many miles. I would tramp a little deeper into the tundra. Topping a ridge, I spotted movement in the distance. The caribou were at the base of a hill about a quarter-mile ahead. I dropped to the ground and fished the binoculars from my backpack. This band of animals was all bulls. There were a couple of really nice racks in evidence. Before the rut caribou tend to separate by sex. When rut-driven, these bulls would no longer be on friendly terms and fighting over cows would be the order of the day.

The animals continued to move. There were few good prospects for a stalk but the only wind was in my favor, blowing toward me down the escarpment. There was essential no cover to conceal my approach. The vegetation underfoot was no higher than would be found on a golf course. I would have to attempt closing on them by using the rolling terrain to my advantage whenever possible.

Gradually the distance was closed but we were getting farther and farther into the wilderness. I guessed that Jack Lake lay three miles behind me now. I would not be willingly packing meat much farther.

I peeped cautiously around the base of a low-lying ridge. The caribou were there. They were only about 400 yards off but too far away for sure

Chapter 2 — *Caribou Are Curious Critters*

shooting. I needed to close the distance. There was no good approach, no vegetation or rise of land to hide my movements.

I pulled off my backpack. "It's now down and dirty, dogs" I muttered under my breath and calmed them quietly, "Easy, easy." I dropped to my hands and knees and started crawling forward. I found a very slight depression and advanced deliberately. The dogs crawled at my heels.

Slowly, painfully the distance was closed to 300 yards. A couple of the bulls looked intently in my direction. Then they began shifting restlessly. With a good rest, I could shoot effectively from here. I slowly arranged my backpack as a shooting platform and pushed my rifle into place. The bulls were definitely watching us now. I looked for the biggest bull in the herd.

The caribou began moving. Unbelievably, they were moving toward us. Caribou are curious animals. They were trying to figure out what the devil we were. They would then attempt to get downwind of us. They approached to 150 yards and stopped—plenty close enough.

I aligned the cross hairs of my Leupold scope on the shoulder of the largest bull and gently squeezed the trigger. Following the crash of the rifle, I heard the bullet slap home. The bull dropped in his tracks. His spooked companions stampeded for the horizon.

The elation of the moment was short lived. "The excitement is over, dogs. Now the work begins." I resigned myself to the ordeal ahead.

I paused for a lunch break and a drink of water from a nearby spring. The next two hours were spent carefully boning-out meat. My backpack was eventually crammed full of prime cuts. The load would weigh 100 pounds plus. The Labs, having gorged themselves on meat scraps, lay curled in nests they had dug into the tundra. Veterans of many hunts, they quickly adapted to life in the wild. Their contentment would be short-lived. The dog pack was loaded with 30 pounds or so of meat.

I could pack no more weight. With regret, I would leave the nice caribou rack on the tundra. I was basically meat hunting. In the spring, ground squirrels would gnaw the antlers and utilize the minerals. "You are first Big Ben." He stood stoically as I loaded him.

I sat down and buckled into my pack. My rifle served as a crutch as I struggled to my feet. We had a long, long trail ahead of us but tonight there would be feasting. Another good and memorable day afield with best friends had passed.

Big Ben relaxes at the successful end of a 1968 black-tailed deer hunt with owner Jim Mauney on Baranof Island, AK.

Red Coats In The Highlands

After August blacktail bucks in SE Alaska, 1968-1971.

My favorite fall pursuit during my years as a resident of Sitka, Alaska was hunting buck black-tailed deer above timber line. When deer season opens on August 1, the bucks' antlers are covered with velvet and they are dressed in reddish summer coats. Late summer finds the bucks enjoying a life of comparative ease. They spend their days browsing on lush alpine vegetation, lying around chewing their cud, and sleeping on sunny slopes. Their preferred habitat is along fingers of timber penetrating the alpine. Their range extends from the big timber upward to include much of the alpine zone. On southeastern Alaska's Admiralty, Baranof, and Chichagof Islands, the alpine zone begins at an elevation of around 1,500 feet and extends upward to just below the bare rocky summits and snow-capped peaks of goat country (3,000 to 5,000 feet).

Summer deer grow fat, storing up reservoirs of energy that will be sorely needed in the late fall rut and during late winter when snows accumulate at lower elevations. Island deer face no serious predators other than the rare human packing a rifle and seeking fresh venison. The only resident large carnivore, the brown bear, may take an occasional fawn but presents no real threat to the deer population. *Ursus horribilus* has little hope of catching a healthy, mature deer.

My official excuse to my bride for hunting the early season was to provide the homestead with some fresh venison. The real reasons, I had to admit to myself, were much more complex. In a good year and the right location, there was an abundance of game animals to see: deer, mountain goat, and with luck maybe a brown bear. Eagles and ravens frequently ride air currents playing off cliff faces.

The natural environment of the black-tailed deer's summer habitat is spectacularly beautiful. The lower alpine is frequently covered with a rug of deep, green moss. Small stands of stunted cedar dot the lower landscape. In larger basins crystal clear ponds and blue lakes occupy depressions. Rivulets of water generated by heavy rains merge into roaring streams to cascade down the mountains and over falls. Among the sea of peaks, hanging glaciers may show up as a blinding white or subtle blue. Far below water of the open Pacific or saltwater fiords reflect light on sunny days.

Buddies Afield — Alaska Days

In southeast Alaska the year's best weather may occur in August. Days are frequently heralded in as the sea of mountain peaks lying in the east are turned to scarlet by a rising sun and are ushered out by blood-red sunsets over the Pacific.

By September and October serious rain and windstorms roll in from the Pacific with increasing regularity. Deer, and deer hunters, do not want to be caught above timber line when storms roll in. As the fall progresses, snow starts to accumulate in the high country. Hunted and hunter limit their activities to timbered slopes and finally, if the snows accumulate to great depths, the beaches.

Looking over a large number of blacktail bucks always gave me hope of finding that trophy buck, the classic double-Y, five-by-five. However, it was not until some years later that I took such a buck. That animal was taken on Kodak Island. During my southeast hunts I did see many nice bucks and took some nice 3x3's and 4x4's. A big southeastern buck will probably weigh less than 150 pounds. Boned-out, the hunter has about 60 pounds of meat to pack off the mountain.

I impatiently waited out foul weather by studying topographic maps, discussing alpine hike/hunt areas, going over gear, and planning. The country I would tramp was true wilderness. One hunting area I sometimes accessed involved struggling uphill across the tangled hell of a clear-cut, but once across one was plunged back into a wilderness of old-growth spruce and western hemlock. You might say wilderness hunters in southeast Alaska were spoiled. I came to regard my trip as almost tarnished if I came across the faint tracks of another hunter. In all my time above timber line, I never saw a human hunter who was not in my party.

During my initial exposure to high country hunts, I had learned some lessons the hard way. The hunter venturing into high country should first get into good physical shape to avoid suffering from miles of walking steep terrain and possibly dangerous falls. For the unaware, dehydration could be a dangerous problem when venturing into alpine areas lacking in water or snow.

As the August 1 opener approached, I assembled gear and sighted-in a recently acquired flat-shooting magnum rifle in .308 Norma caliber. My excitement and anticipation grew as the date approached. I seemed to be alone in my excitement. Few other southeast nimrods were at that date even thinking about deer hunting. Most deer hunters would not hunt until after the snows of November and December pushed the deer down the mountains. My partners for this hunt would my dogs Big Ben and his father Kent. They were company and bear protection, and they could be drafted as pack animals.

Chapter 3 — *Red Coats In The Highlands*

I planned my opening hunt for the north end of Kruzof Island. I hunted this area the previous fall with partners John and Larry. We had seen many deer. Quite a few of these were bucks; a couple sported outstanding racks.

The initial hunt had been squeezed into one long day. A trip by boat of some 30 miles took hunters up a fiord (part of Alaska's famous Inside Passage) between Baranof and Kruzof Islands to reach our hunting grounds. Traveling cost us a couple of hours hunting time in the morning and a couple of hours in afternoon. Fortunately, during August in Alaska the hours of daylight begin in the very early AM and end in late evening.

The weather was for bluebirds. As the day passed and we climbed, the temperature climbed. Once on the ridgeline we encountering many does and fawns. Deer spoor lay abundant. Following a series of mild winters the deer population had reached a high level.

Much to our discomfort we found the upper ridge devoid of ground water. We had packed no water.

John surging ahead of us ascended into a picturesque alpine basin. He had come across a band of bucks, downed a nice animal and was busily dressing and boning-out the buck when we came up. Larry and I, with energy running low and suffering from thirst, continued hunting. We finally settled for packing-out one nice buck between us. As we butchered our animal, another buck of identical size came walking up a well-worn game trail nearby. "Go on get out of here before I change my mind and fill my tag," Larry shouted, sending him running.

Some years later I was to hunt with John and friend Bob from John's big inboard motorboat. During this classic December hunt deep snows had pushed deer out of the high country down into timber just above sea level. Before leaving the vessel for a morning hunt John would toss a baited shrimp pot overboard. Come nightfall we would dine on prawns, crab, and grilled venison loins.

This solo hunt of the Kruzof alpine deer paradise would be different I promised myself. I planned to camp overnight and give myself plenty of time to find a real trophy buck.

The weather cooperated as the day dawned fair. The hour-and-a-half run up the Inside Passage was scenic but unremarkable. We arrived in our quiet bay as planned during a mid-afternoon low tide. I carefully anchored the boat. Plenty of daylight remained for the hike up the mountain to timber line and setting up camp before dark.

I groaned as I shrugged into a 30-pound pack. This was too much weight for my liking in view of the coming ascent. The pack contained only the bare essentials for an extended hunt above timber line. Essentials included: a 10 foot by 6 foot plastic sheet for shelter, several feet of 1/8 inch nylon string, 1/4 inch thick Insolite ground pad, sleeping bag, polyester vest and undershirt, nylon windbreak jacket, matches, fire starter, ammo, binoculars, pocket 35 mm camera, Buck skinning knife, bone saw, food, an alpine stove, flashlight, topo maps, water jug, and toothbrush.

After a grueling, seemingly never-to-end climb through virgin, moss-hung rain forest, I arrived at timber line. A short exploration turned up a more or less flat area of ground covered by grass near a cold water spring for my campsite. The basin, likely home of big buck deer, would be about a half-hour hike up the mountain from the campsite.

Camp was pitched as shadows lengthened. A standard southeast Alaska hunting castle was constructed by tying the plastic sheet to convenient brush. The resulting shelter, open on three sides, provided minimal but often essential shelter from the elements. The scanty shelter did have some advantages. It was light in weight for packing and could be left behind stashed under rocks if space and weight became a consideration, as it would if meat was obtained. Three open sides would give a rudely awakened camper an almost unrestricted view of his surroundings. He could hopefully bring his rifle into play before a big, brown, furry visitor seriously damaged his anatomy.

I kindled a small campfire to disperse shadows and also to discourage unwanted visitors in the night. The dogs munched hungrily on Purina Chow. With luck, tomorrow they would gorge on venison scraps. I sipped a hot cup of tea sweetened by peach brandy, my boots off and tired feet toasting in the heat thrown by our cheerful little fire. I enjoyed an appetizer of cheese and bread as my dinner of dehydrated soup fortified with Minute Rice heated on the pack stove.

Crawling wearily into my sleeping bag I discovered, as is usually the case, the ground underneath my back to be nowhere near as level as it had appeared when the pad was unrolled. "Oh well," I comforted myself, resting tired muscles. The night would not last long. Rays of dawn would streak the eastern sky about 4 a.m., and I would be up and away.

There was much tossing and turning during the night. There were tense awakenings when a dog on guard duty growled or barked at unknown night noise. Some hunters are reputed to tie their rifles to an arm or leg when sleeping out in grizzly country. The theory is that in case a sudden attack catches the hunter asleep, he will not be separated from his rifle. I thought it unnecessary to go to such extremities with dogs along.

The unwelcome screech of an alarm brought me out of a troubled sleep. I peered out at a dark landscape. The eastern sky was brightening. Breakfast was hot tea sans sweetener and a pastry. The pack was lightly

Chapter 3 — *Red Coats In The Highlands*

loaded with the bare essentials for hunting. I picked up the rifle and called, "Heel Kent. Heel Ben."

We headed up the ridge with our steps illuminated by flashlight. Finally, there was enough daylight to pick out surrounding objects and features of the landscape.

Just as I arrived at the high basin's rim, the sun crept over a high ridge rising to the east. The basin's slopes were illuminated as if by a dazzling spotlight. Moving, reddish forms stood out against green vegetation. Deer! A small herd of 12 to 15 animals browsed or lay resting and soaking in the warmth of early morning sun. Most of the animals were within 100 to 200 yards of my observation post. Several bucks sported obviously substantial antlers.

I dropped down, pulling Ben and Kent with me, and crawled behind a large boulder for concealment. The dogs sniffed the air, quivering with excitement of the chase and the hot scent of game. Off came the backpack and out came the binoculars. My hands shook as I focused on the animals. Several of the bucks sported nice racks but one was outstanding. Heart racing, I carefully arranged the backpack as a firm rest and got into prone shooting position.

Suddenly, the deer were on their feet, alert and shifting nervously. Some gazed in our direction. There seemed to be no wind to carry my scent but something had spooked them. Before I could bring my rifle to bear, the animals began moving in a milling herd. The deer reached the far edge of the slope and paused, trying to locate the cause of their alarm. A few more steps would carry them into a stand of spruce.

The distance was all of 400 yards. I held high above the big buck's shoulder and slowly squeezed the trigger. The boom of the big magnum shattered wilderness silence. Deer scattered to the winds except for the large buck. He fell, then rolled a short distance down the slope. I sprang to my feet in elation. "Come on boys we have our work cut for us now. Let's go check out our trophy."

The dogs dashed ahead to scent-out and worry the deer. I approached the animal reverently and called the dogs off. The buck's velvet-covered antlers were unusually heavy and broad for a Southeast Alaska blacktail. His rack was a 4x4, with all tines sprouting from main beams. He was my largest southeast deer.

I bent to the task of gutting the animal and boning-out meat. The dogs gorged themselves on meat scraps. The last task was to make handy with bone saw and collect my trophy antlers. The trip out was an ordeal, as expected, but there was inspiration to quicken my steps. A hot shower, cold beer, and warm arms would welcome the successful hunter home from the hills. Tomorrow, we would dine on venison liver and onions. There would be an abundance of chops and steaks for future barbecues.

A couple of years had passed. Winter before last had been a hard one with late winter-early spring snows accumulating to four or five feet. The local deer population had crashed. Thousands of starving deer had perished feeding desperately on kelp along rocky beaches. The prospects for deer hunting this fall were none too good.

This was to be my last fall as a resident of southeast Alaska. My full-time work commitment was over for now. I planned to spend a lot of time hunting and fishing in the month ahead before heading south for the winter. My brother Gene would fly up from Washington State to join me in some wilderness adventures. The weather forecast for the week following Gene's arrival was not promising. Fair weather was to be interspersed with rainy days. We decided to limit our initial ventures into the high country to day hikes along the island's limited road system. Day hikes would give our bodies a chance to harden for serious expeditions of several days duration.

Our first hike was a well-used trail that followed upstream along beautiful Indian River. My Volvo station wagon carried us to the trailhead just at the city limits. The trailhead's elevation was maybe 100 feet. Our three dog companions included my two yellow Labs and Ivan, Gene's Norwegian elkhound. For two hours we hoofed the increasingly faint trail under a canopy of magnificent virgin spruce and hemlock. The dogs, frisking along unrestrained, were having a high old time investigating scents. As we gradually gained elevation the surrounding precipitous mountain slopes closed in. Finally, the trail petered out altogether. Studying a topographic map and the surrounding slopes, we spotted a ridge that appeared to give a route into the alpine zone. Onward and upward we puffed.

We reached the final fringe of timber to confront a nearly vertical slope tangled with salmonberry and devil's club. The alpine zone was tantalizingly close, but reaching it would be quite an ordeal. As we studied the discouraging slope, Gene touched my arm and quietly whispered in my ear, and pointed. "There's a buck."

Sure enough, the red coat of a nice buck stood out from the vegetation maybe 150 yards up the slope. He leisurely browsed the lush growth.
The deer was not a trophy but we were basically meat hunting. I was operating on the philosophy that a bird in the hand is worth several in the bush.

Chapter 3 — *Red Coats In The Highlands*

A spruce provided a convenient rifle rest. At the crash of the magnum, the buck fell in his tracks to be held in place on the steep slope by clutching vegetation.

The fun was over. We left rifle and extra gear at the timber line and worked slowly, painfully up to the kill site. Gene helped me shift the carcass as I cut and boned. The heart and liver were carefully removed and put on a moss covered rock. The dogs devoured tossed scraps of venison. With the competition for fresh meat, they were no longer buddies and snarled at each other. Ivan, though much smaller than either Lab, was determined to hold his own. We tied them apart. Big Ben carried an entire boned-out hind leg to his assigned place.

Finally, the butchering was over and I began to load the meat. The liver was missing. I spied the last chunk of the carefully saved delicacy disappearing down Kent's throat. "You sorry SOB," I shouted my displeasure. "You had plenty of meat of your own." I guess I could not blame him too much. The liver was on the ground in easy reach and like me the dogs considered it a special delicacy. There would be no venison liver and onions for dinner tonight. We would have to settle for broiled backstrap.

Our pack spent the next couple of days resting around the homestead and dining on venison and fresh fish from Sitka Sound. The TV menu was very limited in our village in those days. Evening entertainment was often reading and talking over old times.

"You know Gene, we have come a long ways in time and distance since our boyhood days in North Carolina."

"Yes I wouldn't have missed out on the many places traveled and experiences lived for anything. Sometimes one has to wonder if we are as happy living away from family though. Mother and J.L. are looking forward to having us home this winter."

"I'm very much looking forward to reuniting with family again for a while. The Old Man was personally tied to his profession, but he was always supportive of us in our interests. I think my most formative years were those as a teenager in the Blue Ridge Mountains of North Carolina. I will always remember the many days spent fishing the local waters and hunting the hills for squirrels and grouse. I sure would have loved a true hunting dog companion. Old Pauper, our collie, was a wonderful family dog but he headed for home when the shotgun went off.

"You were always into fishing but never were a hunter. My teenage friends Bill Hart and Harold Nesbitt were good companions afield. We were kind of rivals trapping muskrats for pocket money. As I recall we sold the muskrat pelts for $2 to $3 each. Seemed like substantial money to a boy in the 1950s. The problem was we never caught many.

"Clark Pennel our principal at Weaverville Jr. High, did not believe in sparing the rod but he understood his boys. He gave us all the day off on the opening day of trout season (April 1). Few boys would have reported in anyway. As we teenage boys grew older there are more and more diversions in the fall from hunting and fishing—football, girls, cars, girls, and finally college and coeds. Unfortunately, given the many diversions boys sometimes lose interest in field sports all together."

Evening stars showed through scattered clouds as I fell quiet. After the several days of little exercise, we were restless and more than ready for more adventures afield. We then discussed possible hikes.

"My first visit up here, we hiked the Lucky Chance Mine country above Silver Bay. The landscape there was an alpine fairyland of moss covered slopes broken by deep blue alpine lakes. I kept hoping to find some gold-containing quartz around the old mine shafts," Gene remembered.

"That has got to be some of my favorite hiking country. The old timer who owns the claims can really tell some tales. He has always readily given me permission to use the old mine trail for access to the high country."

"That first time in was sure some ordeal. The first mile through heavy timber was OK excepting a blow-down or two. Then we broke timber line and found the first quarter-mile of trail taken over by salmon berry, alder, and devil's club. Breaking trail was a nightmare. You did take a nice little buck when we finally got into the alpine."

"Yeah I remember the ordeal of cutting our way to open up that trail, foot by painful foot."

"I have taken a couple of deer from the Lucky Chance country through the years. I don't think that there is a particularly heavy population of deer in that area though.

"Judy went on a hunt in that country with me one time. I was proud of her making it in all the way. I am sure that it was the longest, hardest hike of her life. We made camp on a picture perfect, moss-covered bench above timber line overlooking Silver Bay. A ring of rocks had been placed for a campfire some years back; we were not the first to camp there. Judy found a can left behind by earlier campers. It was perforated by rather large tooth holes where a grizzly had crunched it. She was exhausted and the weather was deteriorating. The threatened presence of bear was the final straw and she freaked out. I don't think she ever got over me taking her there. I looked around a little for deer, but with rising cold wind and rain, the deer

Chapter 3 — *Red Coats In The Highlands*

had sought shelter below timber line. We toughed out the night and hiked out at first light."

Gene and I decided to tackle a steep trail up the backside of Harbor Mountain for a day hike. After too few hours of sleep, we rolled out to face a cloudless dawn.

The trail proved to be well marked but very, very steep. After two hours or so of trudging uphill we broke out at the timber line. From an elevation of sea level, we had ascended to 2,500 feet and then to 3,000 feet. A well-used game trail meandered across deer meadows interspersed at points by stunted spruce. Scattered over the meadow were small pools of water. Harbor Mountain's summit in the distance included a series of cliffs to 4,000 feet. To the west, the volcanic cone of Mt. Edgecumbe rose from the open Pacific. Waves broke as white foam around the multitude of islands and reefs of Sitka Sound. Waters of the Inside Passage running north mirrored sunlight.

"What you say we take an early lunch break and soak up some scenery. I want pictures." Gene suggested.

I readily agreed and we shrugged out of our packs. With photos taken and lunches devoured, we lay in the shade of a small hemlock, resting on deep moss.

I sighed, "Guess that I'm supposed to be looking for a buck up here. Wrong time of day for deer to be out. In this bright sunlight they won't be moving much. Let's see some more country anyway."

We strolled leisurely over the park-like meadow approaching the mountain's sudden ascent to its summit. The bench ended and fell into the void as a series of cliffs.

The binoculars hanging around my neck came into play as I glassed vast spaces of beautiful but vacant terrain. My attention came back to nearby surroundings. Glancing down a draw immediately below I came to immediate attention. A nice buck was bedded down on a grassy bench 100 yards down the slope. He leisurely chewed his cud and gazed drowsily into the void. The cross hairs of my Leupold scope came to rest on the buck's neck. At the shot he slumped and lay without moving.

Back at the homestead that night we discussed our successes. I had shared our wealth of meat with a friend's large family.

"We have earned our deer but we have also been very lucky. We hit the weather right and maybe found deer where we shouldn't have. You'll get the idea making meat in this country is a sure thing."

"Now I know better than that," Gene protested.

Felling confident, I ventured, "well, how about we do a little fishing tomorrow to relax. Then, in a couple of days, we will try a little hike into mountain goat country."

But our expedition up Bear Mountain into goat country turned into a fiasco of survival against the elements. We returned home considerably subdued.

After a couple of days spent resting and drying out, we headed north along the Baranof Island coast. The weather was wonderful for the hike up to timberline deer country. However, as we pitched camp with the sun setting over the Pacific, we looked out on an endless sea of low-lying fog. We woke to a gray, cheerless world. Visibility was limited to a few yards. The hours dragged by as we waited around camp, hoping the fog would lift. The dogs were bedded down and comfortable and showed little inclination to move.

Finally, after a cheerless lunch, I suggested, "how about we pack it in." I heard no protests from my brother.

As we proceeded down the mountain, a dark shape wearing a rocking chair of antlers emerged from the fog to trot unhurriedly across the path immediately in front of us. I quickly worked the bolt to chamber a round but was too slow. The big buck disappeared into the fog. "Damn, I would have liked to have had a crack at that buck," I lamented. We trudged on down the mountain.

Our next big expedition was into the high country above Nakwasina Bay. I had hunted this country before. This was good goat and deer range. Several years back I had shot a beautiful trophy billy out of a herd atop the ridge. Thinking the animal down for keeps I tried to figure a safe way across an almost vertical snow chute. My partner was more daring than I beat me across and found the goat back on his feet. At his shot, the goat fell down a 2,000-foot cliff. An attempt to find his carcass was futile.

Gene and I then struggled up the first thousand vertical feet of slope through a clear-cut logged area. The slash and downed trees constantly presented barriers to forward progress. Finally, we were into big open timber. As we hiked upward, another half-hour passed quietly. Frequently we crossed or followed game trails worn into the mountainside by generations of deer, goat, and bear.

Calling for a break, Gene looked around puzzled. Dropping my pack I realized something was wrong. Ivan was missing. Gene began calling softly and then loudly. Finally he was shouting and whistling at the top of his voice. No Ivan appeared. We waited, becoming increasingly uneasy.

"That common Norwegian Luffer Boy SOB," Gene gave vent to his frustration. "He must have taken off on a scent trail."

Chapter 3 — *Red Coats In The Highlands*

We waited another half-hour. The sun was beginning to slant down in the western horizon. We needed to move up or down.

"What do you want to do? We either go up and pitch camp or go back down to the boat."

"Let's go up" Gene decided. "I don't want to cross that logging strip with night coming on. Maybe he will trail us up. If he catches up with a brown bear and picks a fight that's just too bad."

We pitched a cheerless camp that night. Even the Labs seemed subdued. Over some painkiller, Gene's worry showed through. "Are there a lot of grizzly in this valley."

"I have to be honest. This valley contains a couple of major salmon streams. Bear are attracted to salmon. One of the biggest brown bear I know of was taken at the foot of this mountain. He squared out at over 11 feet; that is 11 feet long and 11 feet wide. One thing you don't have to worry about, with his fur coat Ivan will not sleep cold. He will miss his supper though."

We woke to a smoldering campfire and no Ivan. I made a halfhearted effort of glassing for a buck. Gene was no longer into the trip.

"Let's pull camp and head down," I suggested.

Gene fed Kent and Ben the chow he had packed uphill for Ivan. "No need to pack it back down the mountain."

Heading back down the ridge we left the open country behind and approached broken timber. I glanced over a drop-off to my right and came to a surprised halt. A nice buck was browsing at the cliff's bottom.

The deer was less than 100 yards away, almost straight below us. I quickly got into a sitting position with my pack as a rest. I seldom take an offhand shot at game. I carefully aimed at the buck's neck and squeezed the trigger. The roar of the shot echoed off of the surrounding mountains. I watched as the buck dashed off.

I shook my head in amazement. "Did you see that miracle of that dead deer running off? Just as well," I made light of my disappointment. "I didn't really want to pack a deer back down and across that clear-cut."

Thinking about the shot, I knew I had failed to allow for a rifle's tendency to shoot high on steep downhill targets. Our harvest success had definitely taken a turn for the worse.

As we approached the boat, the brush suddenly erupted and Ivan trotted out, wagging all over. "You sorry son of a gun. I should kick your tail good for you." Gene disguised his relief.

Several days later our luck changed and we came home with my third buck of the season. I really did not need more venison but friends did.

A spell of nice weather rolled in with the daytime skies a clear "Carolina blue." The temptation was too great. "It might be a long time before I get to hunt Southeast blacktails in August again," I pled my case to Gene. "What do you say we give it another go."

Gene was agreeable, "might as well take advantage of this good weather and head out in the morning. We are rested up and our gear won't take much time to get together."

Shortly after sunrise we pulled out of Crescent Harbor. A faint crescent of moon faded in what promised to be a clear sky. The sea lay quiet as a millpond. Mewing of gulls broke the morning quietness as the light rapidly improved. Avoiding rocks and reefs while underway was no longer a problem. I pushed forward on the throttle.

After a 20-minute run, we arrived in a beautiful little bay. Our expedition would be along an alpine ridge lying to the west. The hike from sea level to the alpine was the standard ordeal. Reaching the last fringe of spruce we cast about and located a flat, grassy area for our camp. There was a spring of water nearby. With camp established and a supply of wood gathered for campfires, we headed out.

The ridge rose in a series of benches toward sharp, bare mountain peaks. We moved upward, unhurriedly soaking up the morning sun and appreciating the breathtaking scenery. From time to time I would stop and glass promising terrain. With pleasure, I noted abundant deer spoor.

Gazing toward the open Pacific we were disturbed to see an endless wall of low clouds advancing that obscured Sitka Sound and its multitude of low islets.

"Do we go on or head down," Gene asked.

"Probably just low-lying fog which won't reach this elevation," I said with hope in my voice.

Our ridge merged with others and ascended more steeply. About an hour into our hike the ridge narrowed to rocky boulders strewn in a knife-edge formation. The drop-off on either side was sheer. Scattered clumps of wind-brutalized cedar clung tenaciously to the mountainside. A misstep here would be fatal. We stepped cautiously.

Wisps of fog had reached and began to blow across the ridge. The mist thickened to clouds rapidly blotting out the sun. Temperatures plummeted. We paused to pull on windbreakers. Moisture beaded on the dog's coats and our clothing.

"We had better head down," I observed the obvious. We started down, but it was too late. Visibility quickly fell to yards and then to feet. Our disorientation was complete. "We had better hold up," I called a halt. "It

Chapter 3 — *Red Coats In The Highlands*

would be very easy to make a misstep. Even if we could descend safely we would never find the camp in this soup."

"This is as good a spot as any," Gene agreed.

We had reached a small, moss-covered piece of slanting earth among the rocks. It was vitally important now to conserve body heat. We lay down with our canine buddies alongside. We alternately dozed off to awake and attempt find a more comfortable position on the six-foot-wide ridge top. Sometime during hours that dragged by, I dug out my camera and took a candid picture of Gene lying between Ben and Kent. Unknown to me Gene took my picture with Ivan lying alongside.

Dozing fitfully, I had nightmares that I was again in a small bush aircraft. We were over a fog-shrouded earth. The Pacific Ocean and peaks of the Coastal Range lay hidden below. The fuel gauge was bouncing on zero. The pilot searched vainly for a way down. The minutes crept by with agonizing slowness. The downside of our predicament was not pleasant. Would we miss Baranof Island altogether and run out of gas over the endless Pacific, or would we descend blindly into the side of some mountainside? Finally there was a break in the clouds, a chance for survival and we took it.

I awoke. As in my dream, the fog enveloping the mountainside had thinned. A light rain fell. We climbed stiffly to our feet and stumbled down the mountain. Finally our little camp came into view. What a welcome site it was!

I rolled out of my damp but warm sleeping bag next day at midmorning with little enthusiasm. A light rain was falling and the mountain peaks were laced with strands of clouds. Gene stirred and pulled up his stocking cap. "Are you going hunting today."

"I'll walk around for a couple of hours. I can catch glimpses of Mt. Edgecumbe and the Ocean. I don't think that we are likely to get dangerously fogged-in today."

"Put on the tea. I guess I'll walk along."

After downing cups of steaming tea and hot oatmeal we felt more cheerful though the weather showed little sign of improving. A sharp breeze assailed the ridge with a mist of rain and scuttling clouds.

We eventually worked our way up to and past the knife-edge on which we had been trapped yesterday. The peak's summit a quarter-mile ahead was sometimes visible through swirling clouds.

"I think it's about time to head down," I conceded. "No sensible deer would be moving around up here in this weather."

I glassed what I could see of the upper mountain slopes one last time. Through the eddying mists a whitish patch looked unnatural against a brown and gray background. I adjusted the binoculars finely. Branched antlers came into focus. A buck was bedded down with head up, white throat patch showing.

The buck was a long 300 yards or more away. Given the weather conditions the shot would be difficult. I got into a firm, prone shooting position utilizing a boulder and my backpack for a rest. I wanted no wounded animal to follow. My target was the buck's white throat patch. I turned up the variable scope's power to 7X.

Shortly after echoes from my shot had died away, I knew that my deer hunting season was over and a most memorable fall it had been.

Looking back, maybe the best part of the year's adventures in the high country was sharing experiences and memories with my brother Gene and with our dog buddies.

Falling For A Goat

To Baranof Island for Rocky Mountain goat, 1969.

My feet suddenly slipped on an almost vertical grass slope. Leaning into the slope that was slick from last night's dew for increased traction, I fell facing uphill. My body accelerated downward as if I were on a child's sliding board. Picking up speed, I tried digging into the slope with toes and fingers. My efforts were to no avail. A 100-foot plus precipice with a base of jagged rock rubble and certain death loomed immediately below.

The occasion was a mountain goat hunt in Alaska's rugged coastal mountains. This was not my first goat hunt and the dangers normal to such hunting were well known to me. Descending wearily after bagging a goat, I had in my haste unwittingly misjudged the safety of the terrain. I faced paying the ultimate price for my error.

My hunting buddy, Tom Schwantes, and I had eagerly planned this goat hunt from assembled topographic maps and discussions with other goat hunters. August deer hunt season had drawn us to Baranof Island's alpine fastness in pursuit of bucks in velvet. These early hunts had conditioned us to hiking and packing in the high country. By October, with our limits of black-tailed deer in our respective freezers, we were anxious for a goat hunt.

The coastal mountains of Baranof Island are not physically very high. The maximum elevations are only around 7,000 feet. The average peak crests out at about 4,000 feet. However, these mountains rise abruptly from the Pacific and are pretty much vertical. As a consequence, there are relatively few practical routes for the hunter to safely reach the alpine zone. This zone is favored by goats and generally starts at the 2,000 foot level. Access routes that do exist tend to be very challenging physically.

Weather in southeast Alaska is always a consideration when venturing into the high country. The west facing mountain slopes get 90 plus inches of precipitation yearly. Some east facing bays and slopes are even wetter. Most precipitation falls in the fall and winter months, with October one of the wettest months of the year. Termination dust (snow) begins to accumulate on the high peaks in October. As fall advances in lower elevations rain and fog are the rule rather than the exception. To enjoy a safe and successful hunt in the high country the hunter must hope for an unusual period of good weather days.

Finally, there was a break in the October rains with the forecast calling for several days of clear weather. We hastily arranged time off from work. Supplies were assembled for a three or four day hunt. Tom and I concurred on our route into the high country. We planned to hunt an area of high goat abundance.

In southeast Alaska the road system is extremely limited. Local hunters rely largely on their boats for hunting conveyance. My 16-foot boat would convey us around Sitka Sound to Katlian Bay and our "trail head."

The night before the hunt I slept fitfully in anticipation of the morning's adventures. There is no more beautiful and spectacular country than the alpine zone of southeastern Alaska. The ground underfoot is frequently covered with a carpet of moss four inches or more deep. There are jewel-like lakes, plunging waterfalls, hanging glaciers, points of timber, vertical cliffs, and spectacular views of the surrounding Pacific Ocean. By October our quarry, the mountain goat, would be sporting long and luxurious fur coats that would make outstanding rugs and trophies.

Judy, my loving bride, was much less enthusiastic about the coming goat hunt. She was not adverse to a beautiful goat rug but she knew about goat hunts in the Alaska wilderness and such dismal possibilities as falls from cliffs and grizzly encounters. She had expressed her feelings. "Please be careful. I am too young to be a widow. Sometimes during hunting season I feel almost like one now." I had promised to be careful.

The day dawned with bluebird weather. There was no significant wind from the west. Our hunt was on. Judy drove me and my gear two blocks to Crescent Boat Harbor where Tom was waiting. A bachelor, he patiently endured our domestic farewells. Kent, our yellow Lab, leaped eagerly from the station wagon. Kent would go with us as pack dog and camp guard. Brandy, our big black lab, would stay and protect her mistress and the homestead. My skiff was quickly filled with gear and passengers. The Pacific was calm and rippled gently, reminiscent of a big millpond. Passage to our destination went smoothly.

Arriving at Katlian Bay, I sought and found a sheltered cove for anchorage. The half flood tide was ideal. Our use of tide charts had been worthwhile. Tom and I unloaded gear, backpacks, and rifles as kelp stalks and fucus floats squished and popped under our boots. Our hunting gear formed a small mound on the rock-strewn beach. Roars of sea lions as they fed on herring echoed from seaward. Mallards talked along the tidal flats. Kent was busy marking territory but showed considerable interest in the latter "No bird Kent. Today we are after bigger game today," I told him.

In southeast Alaska extreme tidal fluctuations of 20 feet or more make anchoring a boat for beach access a unique challenge. A man does not want his boat to go high and dry to then be beaten into pieces on rocks by the flood tide. Beaching a boat at high water could mean the hunter returning at low water might not get under way until another flood tide could float his boat. And anchoring too far from shore during a low tide could render the boat inaccessible

Chapter 4 — *Falling For A Goat*

until the tide again ebbed. While a man could always swim for his boat, I had learned by bitter experience that swimming in the frigid winter North Pacific was not a welcome pastime.

By trial and error and observing other hunters' anchor tackle, I had devised my gear and strategy. My anchor gear consisted of pulley, snap swivel, Danforth anchor, and 200 feet of 3/4-inch nylon line. We carefully arranged this gear and gave the boat a shove, a tricky tactic. We both heaved sighs of relief when the process went smoothly. The anchored boat bobbed gently on small waves. The heavy anchor line was secured just above the high tide mark to an immense Sitka spruce.

As the beach steamed with warmth by the sun and fertile sea smells enriched the air, Tom and I inspected our full packs. With sleeping bag, insulated pad, tent, jacket, foul weather gear, and food, mine topped out at around 40 pounds. Tom's was considerably heavier. A strapping 6-footer weighing in at over 200 pounds, Tom prided himself on his packing powers. Rumors were that some of his hunting partners had been known to salt his packs with beer and canned goods in an attempt to weight him down, hoping they could thereby keep up with him. They of course would volunteer to help him dispose of the excess cargo when the campsite was reached.

I held Tom's pack for him to shrug into. "Heavy pack Tom. You wouldn't have a couple of cans of beer in there would you?"

"You bet" he assured me. "More than a couple. This promises to be a hot day and there is long, dusty hike of six miles or so to base camp. I think a cold one or two will be called for by our campfire tonight. In case we make meat tomorrow, we will surely need refreshment to celebrate."

Our initial hike followed a well-worn game trail. The trail followed a tiny stream and skirted between a heavily vegetated low hill and a steep mountain slope. We had used this trail to access deer hunting country on numerous occasions.

"Bears like to lie in the thickets along that ridge to our left when sleeping off a meal of salmon," I reminded Tom as I was loading my .308 Norma Magnum with 200-grain Sierra hand-loaded rounds.

"I will be ready for any eventuality," Tom remarked as he loaded his .338. "I notice you are packing a new rifle."

"This magnum gives me a little more firepower than my .30-06. I will tell you the story of its acquisition later. You are a reassuring companion to have along in bear woods. Kent will work ahead of us. He knows about bear. There will be no bear surprises with him along."

We progressed upward through towering virgin Sitka spruce. Sunlight filtered only dimly through the closed canopy. Dense clumps of alder interlaced with devils club, the bane of hikers, grew where giant trees had fallen to open the canopy. Stands of young, head-high spruce reduced visibility in places to just a few feet. High bush cranberry and blueberry bushes grew in abundance. These plants are a favorite winter deer food and their fruits are favored grizzly food.

Fresh mounds of bear scat decorated the middle of the trail. Kent's hackles stood erect. A moist area in the trail showed huge footprints. Water was still filling the indentations. Tom and I chambered rounds. Kent took the lead as we moved cautiously ahead. There was crashing as a heavy animal spooked.

About a mile from the beach, we broke through a dense stand of alder onto an old logging road. We would follow this road into upper Katlian Valley. In rocky stretches, the road was open and broad. In more earthen stretches, rapidly growing alder had closed passage to a single-file trail. We pressed on, covering the miles without incident.

There was a welcome pause beside a small freshwater stream for a midday snack and water break. The valley had narrowed noticeably and sheer mountain slopes closed in. We were not far from our intended campsite.

"It sure doesn't take long for alder to grow and take over a road," Tom observed.

"Damn alders," I responded, thinking of the many miserable hours I had spent battling through alder thickets. "They are one of my least favorite plants. They will make this road impassable within a very few years. They are of no use as deer food. They do provide shelter for critters. They are also useful for smoking meat and fish."

Occasionally, a small stream crossed the old road. During logging operations these streams had flowed through culverts. With logging operations over, the culverts were pulled and the road was officially closed. We crossed several such stream channels with no problem. We had walked several miles. Tom would never admit he was getting tired. We arrived at one such stream that was a little broader than most, with steep banks. I jumped across, having to stretch my short legs to clear the potential trap.

As Tom crossed, he came down hard with an exclamation of pain. "Damn. I think I may have turned my ankle. I caught it on a alder root and came down wrong. As you said, damn alders anyway!"

"Your 60-pound pack didn't make your landing any softer. Sit down and take off your boot. Let's look at your ankle."

With boot and sock removed, Tom's ankle already showed signs of swelling and discoloration. "Doesn't look good for you to go goat hunting, Tom. Probably we should head on back to the boat."

"No I don't think so. It's no more than another mile to our camp. I can take it easy tonight. Probably will be OK tomorrow. Besides, I am not up to hiking back to the boat tonight." Neither of us wanted to give up the hunt we had planned so long. I suggested, "It's your call Tom."

Chapter 4 — *Falling For A Goat*

We proceeded slowly, with Tom limping painfully up the trail. Finally, we arrived just before sunset. The site was in a fringe of big timber right at timber line. The valley essentially ended there. The terrain veered sharply up mountain slopes on three sides. Towering cliffs ruled out further progress without some serious mountaineering. A brook trickled merrily nearby. Giant spruce and hemlock shut out the setting sun. A huge overhanging boulder sheltered an area of ground. The boulder's underside was smoke blackened where fireplace rocks had restrained campfires of hunters in years past.

Sighing with relief, we slipped out of our packs. Kent busily scratched himself a nest among pine needles and leaves and settled in with a low sigh.

"You roll out your sleeping bag and pad, Tom, and take it easy. I will round up a supply of wood and get a fire going."

A fire was soon blazing as the night closed in. Tom lay back on his bag with his boots off, sipping a cold one. His ankle was now swollen obviously. I popped open a beer for myself as I rustled up some supper. I told Tom, "I wish we had some aspirin for you to take."

"I'll make it," Tom insisted. "Tell me about your new rifle."

"I attended a meeting in Prince Rupert, British Columbia this spring. While there, I made the mistake of going into a gun shop. I fell in lust with this English made rifle with a blond stock and wound up its new owner. I thought the price in view of exchange rates was a heck of a bargain. But I had the Devil's own time getting it into the U.S. through Customs. The real trouble started when I came home with my new acquisition. Judy informed me in no uncertain terms that we needed no more blondes in the family. She and two yellow Labs were enough. Finally, I convinced her that my .30-06 was just not heavy enough for safety in the woods. I needed a magnum for grizzly protection and for tough mountain goats.

"I may have jumped out of the frying pan into the fire with my strategy. Now she is afraid for me to run around in the bear woods. The problem has become particularly acute since that Fish Bay grizzly did in the old logger. Would have been nice to have you along on that posse but that was just before you became a Fish and Game Agent."

"That hunt would have given me an excuse to buy myself a .460 Weatherby like Cliff packs. I heard that the going on that hunt was real spooky."

"Yeah, packing a .44 Mag. on my hip and a .350 Mag. rifle, I felt really under-gunned. At the kill site we found blood up to 6 feet high on tree trunks. I think that we were kind of lucky not to have found that bear. We both know that bullet placement and not strictly caliber size is key to clean kills. But when a grizzly unexpectedly charges you in thick cover from five feet or so, effective bullet placement may be hard to come by. Some fellows prefer a shotgun for close-up defense."

A couple of beers were now under our belts and we were feeling less pain. The conversation continued as I fed Kent and prepared our dinner. As an old man of 29, I felt qualified to give Tom (a youngster of 21) advice about life. "Tom, a young bachelor like you had better think twice before jumping into the blissful state of matrimony. Choose carefully. If you don't, there will likely be no more new customized Weatherbys bought and your time in the woods will be cut back. Maybe a man should stick to strictly functional guns and women. There would be a lot fewer upkeep problems."

"That may be true but you don't strictly practice what you preach, Jim. Your tastes don't seem to be satisfied by function alone. Your bride is a beautiful woman and you have some quality firearms."

"By gosh you are right on both counts, Tom. I will tell Judy what you said. She will be flattered. I don't regret marriage. However, most women do think somewhat different from us. I have had a woman look at beautiful wood in my shotgun and customized .30-06 stock and inform me that it was a shame to waste such pretty wood on a gun."

We quickly got back to hunting—a subject with which we both felt more comfortable. "You have quite a reputation as a deer hunter, Tom. You manage to keep your family stocked with venison most falls. Thankfully, we each took our bucks above timber line this August. Prospects look poor for this year's winter deer hunts following last spring's population crash."

"Yeah, judging from the number of deer I saw during my August hunts, prospects for beach hunters look grim this year," Tom concurred. "Very few deer survived the heavy spring snows. Extended seasons and drastically increased bag limits came too late."

"Sport hunters took all the meat they could use and lost interest in further killing. I took 10 deer myself. Rumor has it that you took twice that number. It probably would have been most humane to shoot more starving deer but few of us have the stomach for that. Besides, in Alaska we have laws against the waste of game."

"You and I have had a good hunting year starting with our spring Chichagof Island bear hunt," Tom remembered.

"That was a memorable hunt, Tom. Our bear made a beautiful trophy. Jonas Brothers of Denver did a fine job on the hide. Well, we better hit the hay. Hopefully, your ankle will be OK in the morning."

I awakened at first light as the sun struggled over high peaks to our east. Tom was already up and moving. He had a fire blazing, but he was limping badly.

"There's a goat at the head of the valley above the point of timber on our left, no more than a half-mile from camp." He handed me the binoculars. "That goat should be easy to bag." Sure enough a goat was feeding along the

Chapter 4 — *Falling For A Goat*

valley's uppermost slopes. As we watched, the goat was working his way upward and leisurely ascended a series of outcropping cliffs.

"There will be no goat hunting for me today," Tom admitted with regret. "I need another day's rest in camp. I think you should give it a try. Looks like a three to four-year-old. Should be prime eating. I could use some fresh meat for barbecues."

"Are you sure, Tom? I will feel awful bad hunting and having to leave you behind in camp. Let's have a hot drink and think about it," I suggested.

It was finally agreed that I would try for the goat. I would hunt up to the base of the cliffs where I would wait in cover for its possible reappearance. Stunted hemlock would provide cover. An earlier inventory of our equipment revealed one serious omission. We had brought no line for safe climbing and lowering of meat-filled packs. I promised Tom and myself that I would not ascend the cliffs by myself..

"If I am successful, Tom, half of the meat is yours. Do you want the horns or the hide?"

"I opt for the horns," he chose.

"Well, before we can divvy that goat up, I guess I had better get up the mountain and bag him. See you later, Tom."

"Good luck, Jim."

By midmorning, Kent and I had ascended from the fringe of timber into the alpine. Watching the cliffs for a conspicuous patch of white or suspicious movement, I carefully worked upward. I held up short of the cliffs. A flat rock within a stand of small hemlock provided me a ringside seat. Kent dug into the moss for a snooze. I put my pack aside. The mountain face rose unbroken above.. The goat was feeding or lying up on the outcrop's summit. I would wait.

Finally, with midday approaching, my patience ran thin. Not planning on a long hunt, I had brought no lunch. Out of curiosity I left my stand, deciding to check out the cliff's face. I found it broken into a series of rock shelves. These shelves could be ascended separately.

Exercising questionable judgment, I continued upward. At first, the going was easy but gradually ascending became a challenge. I had to boost Kent upward where he could gain no footholds. I found myself climbing hand over hand, carefully considering placement of hands and feet. The point had been reached and passed where descending would have been more dangerous than continuing upwards. Panting and shaking from exertion and tension, we at last reached a small plateau.

Small clumps of stunted cedar grew here and there. Underfoot, a deep rug-like cushion of moss quieted our footfalls. The goat, startled by our sudden appearance, rose to his feet among some cedar. He fell at the heavy rifle report .

My joy at the hunt's success was short-lived. "What do we do now Kent? Without ropes, there is no way I can make the descent with 80 pounds or so of goat meat on my back.. I sure could use Tom's help now," I admitted to myself. There was just one way to get the goat down. I would shove him over the cliff. This tactic started things in motion. As the goat rolled toward the cliff, Kent figured dinner was making an escape. He charged forward in pursuit. Panicked, I shouted, "Kent, heel! Kent, heel!" Reaching the last fringe of cedar at the cliff edge, he halted. The goat hurled into space to hit rocks far below with a crash.

More than somewhat shaken, I began to descend. I followed a somewhat different route from that of my ascent. As is usually the case, this proved to be a mistake. We reached a nearly vertical grass slope. Tracks showed goats some times crossed here, avoiding some bad rocky pitches. Kent, with his four-footed-drive, scampered across the grassy slope with no apparent difficulty. Trying to ignore the sheer drop yawning below, I began crossing. Suddenly, I was off my feet and sliding. Efforts to stop the downward plunge were failing.

Rushing toward the abyss, I instinctively made a grab for a scrawny bush and the bush held! My feet dangled at the cliff edge. I lay there shaking, clutching the bush for dear life. My rifle was strapped over my shoulder, and though banged around, it was OK except for some new scratches on the stock. I gratefully studied the scrawny but tough little bush to which I clung. My savior was an alder!

I slowly recovered some courage. I had gotten myself into a bad spot and there was no one except me to get myself out. Crawling on all fours, I managed to work my way off the grassy slope. Once off the slope, I regained my feet. The rest of the descent went painstakingly slow but without incident.

Following a short search, with Kent's nose leading the way, we found the goat. One horn was missing, broken off by the fall. The body was beaten-up, with bones obviously broken. Skinning, butchering, and boning-out meat took me several hours. I saved the pelt and also found the missing horn. Finally, trophies and all salvageable meat was in my backpack. I stumbled into camp exhausted as the sun sank with a red glow behind peaks to the west.

Tom was waiting. "I have been worried about you. I have been anxious ever since your shot from the cliffs. From the size of your pack, it looks like we have ourselves some goat meat." Tom was now moving easier on his sore ankle and he helped me take off my heavy pack.. Tomorrow, we would make a slow pack out back to the boat and return to Sitka.

"You look a little peaked. You had better have a cold one," Tom offered.

As we sipped our brews, I related the day's hunt, concluding, "you know, I never thought that I would owe my life to an alder bush, but I do now."

Alaska Potpourri

Hunting game from snipe to hair seal, 1969-1978

Fairplay Rocks

August and September hunts for Dall's sheep, caribou, and black bear in Alaska's Wrangell Mountains and the Alaska Range were history. Waterfowl hunting for mallards collected jump-shooting the Mineral Lakes had followed. Now it was mid-October and time for upland bird hunting.

I told myself, "I am prepared. Bring on the birds. This hunt, I will not run out of shells." My expectations were to encounter the droves of rock ptarmigan reputed to inhabit the environs of Mount Fairplay.

Running out of shells when hunting ptarmigan seems to be a common problem. A year earlier, my brother, Gene, and I had departed Haines in October, heading for points south. The Haines highway summits in British Columbia's White Pass, midway between Haines, Alaska and Haines Junction, Yukon Territory. Miles and miles of extensive alpine zone are ideal ptarmigan habitat. After considerable searching I finally located and purchased an alien bird-hunting license at a province highway camp.

After setting up a hasty tent camp, my Labs (Ben and Kent) and I took to the hills. We worked along patches of stunted alder that is called buckbrush locally, and climbed steep slopes that otherwise were cloaked only by low vegetation and moss. As the day passed, we found and flushed willow ptarmigan in great numbers. My shooting was not bad. The daily bag limit was 20 birds, and the possession limit was a multiple of that number. My supply of shotgun shells was exhausted before noon of the second day's hunt.

Gene and I drove north toward Haines Junction, hoping to re-supply with ammunition there. No such luck. More than 100 miles of bad gravel road to Whitehorse had been covered before shells were found. In those days before the Trans Alaska Pipeline, very little traffic was encountered on the Alaska Highway. We retraced the route back to White Pass a few days later. While we were absent, a series of Pacific storms had moved in. With the weather deteriorating, few birds were found in the high country. Besides, it was no fun tramping the open country in wind, fog, and a mixture of snow and rain. The trip south was resumed.

Buddies Afield — Alaska Days

Some years later I would again run out of shotshells when hunting ptarmigan. That hunt took place after a hike of five miles from Nabesna Road into the Mentasta Mountains Lost Lake area. Running-out of shells little affected success of that hunt. By the time my shells were exhausted, I had harvested 18 willow ptarmigan and a couple of spruce grouse.

My thoughts reverted back to the Mt. Fairplay hunt. A fish and game biologist acquaintance stationed in Tok assured me that rock ptarmigan were super abundant in the Mt. Fairplay country. Before heading out, I made sure I had an abundant supply of 12 gauge no. 6 shotgun shells.

From Tok, I drove east along the Alaska Highway and then turned left heading north up the Taylor Highway. My coolers contained an abundant supply of grub, including a large section of prime moose backstrap. A young hunter gave me the prime meat after Kent found his downed but "lost" moose.

Winter snowstorms would soon close Taylor Highway. I encountered only an occasional camper driven by moose or caribou hunters. No other bird hunters were in the vast country so I faced no competition.

After ascending a last long grade, the road broke out of the scraggily stands of gnarled black spruce into an alpine wonderland. Except for the occasional patches of low bull brush and willows, the vegetation we would hunt was no higher than the mowed grass encountered on a golf course. The day was overcast but the subdued sunlight seemed to enhance the vegetation's red and purple colors. As was the norm in this country, a sharp, cold wind blew constantly.

Nearing the highway's summit, I found and pulled into a gravel pit. The pit had been dug during highway construction. Its surrounding high banks would give my rig some protection from the buffeting wind. A campfire would provide warmth and cheer during the long nights but at this site above timber line wood was in short supply. I finally scrounged up enough dry alder and willow for a small blaze.

As sunlight faded behind scudding clouds dominating the sky to the west, the high, snowy peaks of the distant Wrangell and Alaska Ranges lying to the south faded from sight. Valleys dark with evergreen forest lying far below our high elevation were swallowed by the encroaching night. Our fire snapped and crackled, holding the wilderness night at bay. Kent contentedly munched a dinner of Purina Kibbles. I prepared my own dinner, cheered and warmed by a cup of hot tea spiked with brandy.

"We will find some birds in the morning Kent," I promised him. "Your son Big Ben would love to be here with us." Thoughts turned to our missing partner whose life was taken by a speeding car. I blamed moisture forming in my eyes on wood smoke.

Chapter 5 — *Alaska Potpourri*

With dinner over, I snuggled under two sleeping bags. The clouds had thinned and Northern Lights were putting on a spectacular display. "Much better than TV for falling asleep," I thought before dozing off.

We rolled out to a morning of deep cold. Though the temperature was well below freezing, the gusting wind had prevented frost formation. After a hasty breakfast, I quickly assembled gear for a day of tramping the high country. Kent was more than ready to hunt. I slipped into a light backpack and shouldered the over-and-under shotgun.

Not far up a steep slope, its surface more rock than vegetation, Kent became birdy. Studying the ground as we moved stealthily upward, I observed chicken-like droppings. Kent suddenly sprang ahead and the air was filled with the raucous sounds of flushing ptarmigan. A single bird fell to my shots. I studied the plump, two-toned bird Kent delivered to my hand. It was in transition brown-and-white plumage. At this date, white predominated. I noted the rock ptarmigan were somewhat smaller than the willow ptarmigan I was accustomed to hunting in the Wrangells.

During the remainder of the day, we covered miles of alpine country. Sometimes after descending into a ravine, or when climbing a slope, we found small groups of birds that were not enthusiastic about flying. Kent was released to force the flush. Close flushes provided me with the opportunity for doubles. Sometimes we encountered vast flocks that flushed from a ridgetop well out of shotgun range. By the day's end, I estimated we had moved no fewer than 200 birds. Our take, though short of a limit, was more than adequate for a number of tasty, future barbecue dinners.

Fatigued from a long day of tramping over steep terrain, we arrived back at camp in the gloom of late afternoon. A fire was hastily kindled. My entree of ptarmigan breasts basted with barbecue sauce grilled over glowing wood coals as I sipped "sweetened tea."

The next morning we rolled out to spitting snow. The ground and surrounding mountain slopes were quickly turning white. Walking and hunting steep mountain slopes slippery with snow would be an invitation to disaster. Driving the steep, narrow mountain road slick with snow could soon become impossible in my two-wheel-drive Volvo station wagon.

"Time to head south, Kent," I told him as I hastily packed. "Maybe we will find some ruffed grouse in Carolina." We were soon under way for points far south. Our Fairplay ptarmigan hunt had been a good final chapter for a fall in the North Country.

Buddies Afield — Alaska Days

Turnigan for snipe

The first hard freezes of late October had arrived in the Anchorage area. Fall's first light snowfalls, locally called termination dust, had deepened and were working down the slopes of the Chugach Mountains. Waterfowl hunting had wound down for the fall. Sandhill cranes had long since departed for points south. Except for a few stragglers, most geese and ducks had departed interior Alaska for warmer climes.

Earlier in the fall Larry Heckart and I had hurried a bunch of cranes south. One day during the peak of wildfowl migration a fog shut off the passage through the Chugach Mountains Portage and Turnigan Passes. Migrating wildfowl had stacked up. With Rock at heel, we hiked along railroad tracks that skirted Placer River. Several miles into a mountain valley we stumbled on a gigantic flock of the huge cranes. As they soared away with a deafening din, two stayed behind for us to pack out.

Soon it would be time for snow sports and evenings spent reading and remembering by a roaring woodstove. Today though, there was still some feathered quarry to pursue.

I pulled my truck into an overlook across from Potter Marsh Wildlife Sanctuary to glass the Anchorage tidal flat. Vast expanses of flats had been bared by the falling tide. Tide tables showed that on this morning the tide would fall to minus levels. The clear, frosty morning was a welcome change from recent days of mixed snow and rainstorms. The mewing of gulls and calls of ravens scavenging the flats echoed from along the receding water edge. A pair of bald eagles screeched from the bare limbs of a giant spruce snag. Prospects for today's outing received sudden encouragement. A troop of small winged creatures darted from over the tops of surrounding spruce and cottonwood trees to the north and dropped into the salt marsh.

Our game of choice this beautiful day would be the Wilson's (or jack) snipe. Locally, snipe hunting was one of our few opportunities to get a taste of upland game hunting ahead of a dog. With their erratic, zigzag flight, snipe are very, very challenging targets for the wing shooter.

The small birds when dressed out yield only a breast to broil for the successful hunter's dining. Four to six snipe are generally required for each diner. To procure a mess of birds, the hunter could expect to expend lots of shells.

"I think that in view of those newly arriving snipe our timing is good for today's hunt." Rock listened to me attentively. Then he began whining, eager to be off. I thought that the young Chesapeake, recently a first-time father, was not acting in a dignified, fatherly manner.

Chapter 5 — *Alaska Potpourri*

I dumped a box of no. 8 shotshells into my vest pockets and picked up my Charles Daly over-and-under. As a second thought, I added a bottle of water to the game pocket of my vest. The day promised to warm up quickly and there would be no fresh drinking water on the flats suitable for man or his furry companion. "Let's get moving," I encouraged Rock. "We need to get our birds and get out. The tide will come flooding back in again in about four hours."

After we descended the bluffs and broke through a last fringe of cottonwood trees, the real work began. To reach open low rushes and open flats, the preferred habitat of feeding snipe, we had to break through a hundred yards or so of tangled, head-high reeds interspersed with small pockets of water and tidal gullies. The going was slow and frustrating. Just keeping my balance was a challenge. Some of the water pools, evidently of low salinity, were covered with a skim of ice.

Rock left my side to charge through the swamp. High reeds swayed in the direction of his departure. His effort put up two mallards that became airborne with indignant squawking. I whistled Rock back to my side. He gazed at me with his beautiful amber eyes and brow wrinkled in question. You could almost hear him asking. "I did my part. Why didn't you shoot?"

"I'm not geared up for ducks today, Rock. The light 8's I am carrying would likely only cripple large birds. Time for you to heel up and hunt close. No sense wasting energy."

As we hacked our way through the vegetative barrier, I remembered back to the fall waterfowl opener on September 1. We had hunted this same marsh then and there had been many ducks. A lot of hunters had convened on the marsh from Anchorage in the early morning. There was much shooting. Unfortunately, many of the hunters were afield without dogs and they had lost many ducks that they downed in the high tules.

My duck hunt that day was finished early. My limit of seven birds was in hand and included mallard, pintail, and a couple of baldpate. Through my four-footed companion's heroic efforts we had left no cripples behind. I left to a much less exciting afternoon. I would report to the office for an anticlimactic afternoon of paperwork. Our exit from the marsh took us back through the high reeds. My thoughts were interrupted when Rock left my side and vanished into the tangle of vegetation.

I had thought to myself, "now where did that curly son-of-a-gun go?" I shouted and blew my dog whistle. "Come on—we are through hunting."

Rock reappeared and presented me with a green-winged teal lost by some long departed hunter. "Good work, Rock." I dispatched the crippled bird. I do not believe in wasting game resources and started to add the teal to my bag. Then the thought occurred. "What if I get checked?" As Rock investigated other scents, I left the excess duck in the marsh. It would provide a meal for a mink or otter. This proved to be a good move. When I arrived back at my truck, a federal game warden was waiting to check me.

Today, once we were free of the shoreline vegetation, we began our snipe hunt in earnest. Stretches of firm mud provided pleasant walking. The going became tentative when I found it necessary to cross boggy areas. Rock surged across such areas easily to emerge covered and dripping a gray coating of mud. I stepped carefully, trying to avoid icy water slopping over the top of my hip boots. Bubbles of hydrogen sulfide gas rose in my steps.

"For sensible folks, this is not the environment for a Sunday afternoon walk. Maybe we should have gone to church," I thought to myself, cursing as water slurped over the top of my left boot. But we soon found snipe, lots of snipe. And for a change my shooting success on this species was very pleasing.

Rock would work a piece of preferred vegetative cover and snipe would emerge to dart away with their peculiar rasping sound. Usually we flushed singles, but sometimes doubles, and infrequently a congregation of six or more birds took to the air.

After completing a neat double, feeling very good about my shooting prowess, I sent Rock in search of the second bird. I felt then like blowing through my barrels in triumph.

Rock soon flushed another snipe, which I promptly missed with both barrels. My ego deflated somewhat until I completed another double.
We emerged from the marsh before noon—tired, muddy, and thoroughly soaked, but "happy as hogs in slop." My game vest contained few unfired shells, but it sagged with a limit of snipe.

"What a beautiful day for a walk in the marsh. Let's head for Indian. You need a cleansing swim in a clear creek before you can lie beside the woodstove. I sure need a shower before lunch. I think that this afternoon I will hit the old Birdhouse Bar for a cold one or two. If my luck holds, maybe there will be a flight of stewardesses in," I told Rock.

Two Time Bear

Escaping the frigid air and the threat of snow in interior Alaska, Kent and I arrived in Haines. The Gulf of Alaska weather seemed almost balmy in contrast to our recent environs. The Chilkat Valley was basking in an unusually nice spell of late Indian Summer. Giant cottonwood trees, which filled the river valley, were still in full leaf. Even at this late October date their leaves were only slightly tinged with yellow. However, about 2,000

Chapter 5 — *Alaska Potpourri*

feet up the towering mountain slopes, the frost-nipped alpine reflected bright reds and yellows. Flocks of bald eagles worked the Chilkat River's braided channels, dining on the abundant spawning chum salmon.

My second morning in the valley, I was welcomed into the home of good friend Norm Blank and his family. After a wonderful lunch featuring smoked red salmon sandwiches, I hit Norm with my plans. I was anxious for a goat hunt while the fair weather held.

"I'm not going to have time for a goat hunt this fall," Norm said with some regret. "I spent too much time this fall chasing a moose I failed to bag. Now I'm tied up on a construction job."

"I'll give it a go myself then. Maybe I will hike into the high country up the old trail across from the old moose check station."

"That trail is mighty steep," ventured Norm. "Let me see your topo map and I'll show you another possibility for a hunt."

Later, as I took my leave, I requested, "If I don't show up in about four days, send out the rescue party."

"Keep a watch out for bears at night," Norm warned. "They seem to be unusually plentiful this fall."

By mid-afternoon, Kent and I were huffing and puffing up a very, very steep trail. The 50-pound pack on my back seemed to get heavier with each step. I was fully equipped to hunt the high country for two or three days. "I don't see how the trail to my originally proposed hunt area could have been any steeper," I grumbled to myself.

After an hour-and-a-half of toil we approached timber line. A struggle through a final barrier of almost impenetrable, twisting alder brought us to open alpine slopes that climbed steeply upward to the ridge summit. I shrugged out of my pack with a groan. Kent and I flopped down in agreement. It was high time for a rest and water.

My game plan was to ascend to the ridge summit and pitch my base camp there. I would then hunt along the surrounding ridges and peaks.

There are always some doubts when first hunting unknown country. I worried to myself, "sure hope that we can find good water for camping tonight. Otherwise we will be on scanty rations. On the bright side, I'm sure that with this fine weather we will have a beautiful night above timber line. I hope the northern lights are out."

As we rested in the sparse, alder-thrown shade, I pulled out my binoculars and began scanning the surrounding high country. A brief but thorough search showed no living white patches. I was lowering the binoculars when a large, black form in the middle of an alder patch on the ridge adjacent to us caught my eye. That black patch sure seemed out of place. As I continued to watch, I was sure that I detected movement. The binoculars were quickly brought into play and revealed my suspicions to be true as a large black bear came into focus.

I did some quick rethinking. I was not certain of finding a goat. The black bear fall diet in Alaska includes vast quantities of berries. A fat fall black bear can make wonderful eating. In hunting I have always gone by the philosophy that a bird in the hand is worth two in the bush. I reached a quick decision. I would go for a bear rather than a goat.

Getting into a prone shooting position, my backpack made for a firm shooting support. The distance was an estimated 300 yards. My .300 Magnum was loaded with 200-grain, flat-shooting Speer handloads. The cross hairs of my Leupold came to rest high on the bear's shoulder. The light rifle roared and recoiled sharply back into my shoulder. The bear tumbled downward and was caught by intersecting alders. There was no movement.

Kent started to dart forward almost at the shot. "Heel Kent. We need to check out that big, black critter very cautiously."

Very slowly and carefully I made my way up and across a precipitous slope connecting the ridges. "Sure a good thing this slope is bone dry today," I thought, "or there could be a repeat of my last, almost disastrous Baranof goat hunt."

We closed on the bear and there was no movement. I delivered an insurance shot and Kent rushed in to worry our trophy. I made no effort to check him.

Pack and rifle were put aside. I made my way through intervening alders to the bear with some difficulty. The bear was a nice fat boar and in good coat. It was well he hung up on the alders, or on this slope he would have rolled for hundreds of feet down the mountain. Such a fall could have ruined hide and meat. My best efforts to drag the bear from the alders were of no avail. The bear was too heavy and entangled. How the Devil do I go about skinning and butchering an animal in the middle of an alder patch? I soon found out how the work would be accomplished. The answer was very slowly, painfully, and carefully. Finally, my pack was loaded with boned-out meat and hide.

Kent and I paused for a snack and also chugged down most of our remaining water supply in preparation for the coming ordeal of descent. The Chilkat River gleamed far below. The sun was beginning to dip toward the jagged peaks of the Kicking Horse Mountains. There was no time to tarry if I were going to make it to the road before dark. I struggled into the pack's straps and then used my rifle as a crutch to gain my feet with the 100-pound load. My steps were slow, and deliberate as we went

Chapter 5 — *Alaska Potpourri*

down. A fall on these steep slopes would result in unpleasant damage to my pack and body.

I arrived back at Norm's long after sunset, sweaty, dusty, blood-spattered, and completely exhausted. The family was surprised at my early return but they welcomed me back.

"From your bloody clothes I would say you either killed something or you are hurt bad," Norm greeted me.

"I took a nice black bear Norm. I'd like to keep the hide but I will split the meat with your family."

Norm agreed, "seeing as how I didn't bag a moose this fall, we could sure use the fresh meat."

"You need a shower," Pat suggested. "I will heat up a couple of bowls of my homemade soup and bread for you."

The next morning was passed cleaning and hanging the meat, dressing, stretching, and salting down the bear hide. That afternoon I rested as sore joints and muscles recovered from my hunt. I called up the local fish and game officer, an acquaintance of some years, and made an appointment to have the bear hide sealed the next morning.

Jack admired the hide as he sealed it. "Nice black bear and a good job skinning. Will square out about 6 feet, 1 inch."

No separate permits were required for black bear hunting in Alaska in those days. But after sealing the hide with a metal tag, Jack pulled out a duplicate second tag. "Now I just need the skull."

"You what," I stammered. "I didn't know regulations required that a black bear's skull be brought in for sealing. I had no room in my backpack and didn't want the skull anyway. The bear was taken while goat hunting and the skull was left 2,000 feet up the side of a steep mountain."

Jack looked at me in a seriously and steady gaze. "You had better find that skull."

"God, I hate climbing that mountain again. I haven't yet recovered from the first time."

"Just think," Jack permitted himself a small smile. "You are lucky. You are going to get to have two hunts for that bear."

"I will head back this afternoon." I relented. Something told me that before this was settled, the bear would have his revenge.

Sitka Sound Seal

By mid-February, outdoor activities in southeast Alaska were limited and most hunting seasons were long over. Occasionally, there was good snow for cross-country skiing. Some brave souls trolled among the islands for feeder king salmon. But for most of us, recreational activities were limited to inside sports. Our very limited TV programming had little to offer. Luckily, I enjoyed reading and my wife was good company. Time passed pleasantly enough. However, someone inclined toward outdoor sports eventually becomes maxed-out on even the most intriguing indoor winter activities.

For the last week we had experienced unseasonably cold, clear weather for southeast Alaska. A very heavy snowfall followed by hard rains just before the cold front moved in had rendered the snow's surface a soggy consistency that subsequently froze as a hard crust. This ended prospects for cross country skiing. The eventual impact the deep, crusted snow had on local deer herds would be disastrous.

One frigid Saturday afternoon, my dogs (Kent and Ben) and I hiked up beautiful Indian River. The going was not bad on the crusted snow. But occasionally a booted foot placed carelessly on a soft patch of snow resulted in a plunge to the knee. The still backwaters of the river were iced over. Occasionally, old deer spoor was seen frozen into the icy snow. After covering about two miles, my need for exercise was satisfied. We paused beside a deep, crystal clear pool.

I just happened to have a training bumper with me and I decided to have some fun with the dogs. Carefully edging my way out on a rock outcropping overlooking the pool, I threw the bumper. Big Ben plunged into the pool with a tremendous splash, went under, and came up to retrieve the bumper. Kent was next.

The dogs alternated retrieves. The day's high temperature was to reach only 10 degrees F. Now in the late afternoon, the temperature had started to plunge downward. The dogs' water-soaked coats froze between dives and were soon crackling with ice. I directed successive retrieves from higher and higher up the overhanging boulder. For his final dive, Kent was a good six feet above the water.

Kent launched eagerly. I was standing to his left with my shoulder just even with his hurtling body. I felt a bump and then I was airborne and plunging into the 32-degree water. Kent and I rose to the surface sputtering and raced for the icy bank. Kent packed his bumper. Big Ben was sitting on the bank watching our antics curiously.

I yelled, "time's wasting let's head for the homestead" as the dogs and I broke into a brisk trot. In a short while, my outer clothing was frozen and crackled at every step. Young dogs and young men recover quickly. In a few days we were restless and eager for another outing.

Chapter 5 — *Alaska Potpourri*

Earlier that winter I had secured some light, 110-grain bullets for loading a quantity of .30-06 hulls. I zeroed my rifle with the light loads. The recoil was inconsequential compared to the heavy deer/bear loads I usually hunted with. This load was developed with seal hunting in mind.

Through the late 1960s, resident hunters, regardless of race, were permitted to harvest seals for their meat and or hides. Tanned seal hides made wonderful trophies and beautiful garments. For liver gourmets, seal liver is outstanding.

The typical hunting shot at seals was from an unstable boat with a seal's head bobbing 200 to 300 yards away. There tended to be many misses for every seal harvested. I had thusly taken an occasional seal incidentally to a deer hunt.

Seals can be very curious critters. One morning while sea duck hunting, I had watched in fascination as a young seal curiously watched the dogs' water antics and swam to within 15 feet of the beach. The dogs were also curious about the strange animal and wanted to follow him into the surf. Maybe tolling with a dog would work for seal as it did for waterfowl. But although Labs are wonderful swimmers, the sea is a seal's element. A seal might not welcome canine company.

One evening I popped the question, "Judy do you mind if the dogs and I take the boat and go seal hunting this Saturday. I would like to collect a couple of hides so Mary B. can make me a vest. A vest would match with your beautiful parka."

"I'm tired of you moping restlessly around the house. Go."

"You are welcome to come along."

"Boating at these zero temperatures has zero appeal. Just don't try winter swimming again."

Saturday morning dawned cold and clear. By the time I finished a hearty breakfast, the sun was well up. Judy drove us to Crescent Boat Harbor. Our first task of the day was to de-ice the boat. I scraped the windshield to remove heavy frost and lit a gas torch to aid in unthawing my steering system. Finally, we chugged slowly out of the harbor. As would be expected no other boater was about.

We exited the harbor to a calm Pacific. Not the slightest breeze rippled its placid surface. The rocky shore was caressed by a gentle offshore swell. I steered north for the Inside Passage. The day's strategy was to hunt along the heads of some bays just off the river mouths and tidal flats.

Arriving at Katlian Bay, I turned toward the snow-painted mountains towering at its head. I soon began hitting skim ice, which yielded only grudgingly to the boat's hull. Deeper into the bay, the ice thickened. River discharged fresh water was floating and freezing on top of the bay's salt water. Breaking ice was not good for the boat's hull. Throttling down, I crunched a circle back to my entrance path.

"Let's try Nakwasina Bay fellows," I told the dogs as I headed our skiff north. We arrived at Nakwasina Bay's south entrance. A short way into the bay ice barred further passage. I steered back to the saltwater of the Inside Passage, which was kept open by surging tides, and turned north once more. We would try the bay's north entrance.

A mile or so into the bay's northern pass, we reached a small, rocky island surrounded by huge exposed boulders. My original hunting plans would have to be altered due to the ice. The thought occurred that the boulders might make a good location to wait in ambush for cruising seals. I pulled alongside a low, relatively flat boulder. Its surface, exposed by the low tide, was slick and algae covered but would provide us with a platform for landing and its bulk would shelter the boat from tidal surges. Once among the boulders, I studied the surfaces with great interest. Abundant droppings served as fertilizer for the abundant growth of marine plants.

"Could the droppings be those of a seal," I wondered. (I later realized that we had stumbled upon a marine mammal resting area.) I directed our party over low boulders and upward to boulders that rose above the high tide line. We settled down to wait on a smooth and dry granite surface.

The morning warmed and passed pleasantly. Ravens talked as they worked nearby rain forest clad slopes. From seaward came screams of feeding gulls. Suddenly the calm water's surface was shattered as several large brown heads appeared. I heard sharp expulsions as big animals cleared their lungs and gulped down fresh air. Sea lions! I wanted no close up encounters with them and I was not anxious for the big animals to haul out on the rocks we occupied. To my relief, they moved on down the bay.

The noon hour arrived and I broke out our snack lunch. Though our breaths were still visible as steam in the subfreezing air, the sun seemed warm. We reclined almost comfortably and dozed on our rocky perches.

A low whine brought me to attention. The two yellow dogs were watching the bay intently. I followed their gaze and discovered a mottled brown-and-black head bobbing about 100 yards out. A seal had come to call. A low growl rumbled in Ben's throat. "Quiet now, dogs" I soothed them.

My backpack came in handy as a shooting platform. A couple of minutes later I was aboard the skiff and heading out for the day's first harvest. This day's venture had already proved a success.

Two more hours slid by. The brief winter day was coming to an end. The tide had turned and was now in full flood. Our original landing would

Chapter 5 — *Alaska Potpourri*

soon be inundated. As we prepared to pull out, I spotted a second seal. The animal would pass us maybe 250 yards out.

At my shot, the animal appeared fatally hit as it threshed the sea's surface. But my arrival for the retrieve was too slow. The animal sank in a cloud of blood. Prepared for such eventualities, I broke out a line with grappling hooks affixed and brought it to the surface.

A short time later the dogs and I were on the miniature, rocky beach of a nearby island. I hastily snapped pictures as the dogs curiously sniffed the seal. Then the real work began. Seal are difficult to pelt out, but I bent cheerfully to the task. I had taken two magnificent hides for my vest. There would be plenty of seal liver to sauté with onions for future dinners. A warm house and an understanding woman would welcome successful hunters home from the field. We had stolen a wonderful day from the clutches of an Alaska winter.

White-out Ducks

I peeked out the front door into the night. The living room light was reflected back to me by swirling snow. New snow had accumulated in the yard and on the porch to a depth of a foot or so. A quick glance at the thermometer showed the mercury holding steady at 32 degrees F, perfect for a serious snowfall. I had scheduled the day away from work, planning for a duck hunt. Like the legendary postman, I was not to be easily swayed from my mission.

As I put warm clothing, shells, and shotgun together, Kent stretched and yawned. He eagerly anticipated the coming hunt. Big and black Brandy was very heavy in her advanced pregnancy and could only lie there and watch our preparations. She eyed me pleadingly. Guiltily, I tried to avoid her eyes. She had not had opportunity for a day afield of late. This was the last week of the year's duck season. Christmas was only a couple of weeks away. She needed a treat. Finally I relented, "Okay you can go." Brandy's heavy, otter-like tail thumped the floor happily.

"I'm taking Brandy," I called into the bedroom.

My bride moaned sleepily from the bed. "What? Are you sure? She is only a few days from whelping."

"I'll take good care of her," I promised. A note left on the kitchen table gave the day's destination as nearby Aleutkina Bay.

I left the house with Labs at heel and shotgun over my shoulder. No traffic stirred. Judy would need the car to get to work later in the morning. The walk to Crescent Boat Harbor and my boat was not a long one. As we walked toward the harbor, the snow thickened noticeably. Muffled by the falling snow, the clanging of a bell buoy far out on Sitka Sound added to the hour's loneliness.

My first task upon reaching the harbor was to shovel the boat free of snow. Boats moored nearby rode deeply under the weight of the new snow. I got the boat under way in a quiet world. As I exited the harbor, the snow seemed to fall ever more heavily. The boundaries of my world seemed to contract and close. I began to have serious doubts about the day's undertaking.

Flashlight in hand, I dug out a marine map to determine a compass bearing from the harbor to the mouth of Aleutkina Bay. We chugged slowly, and blindly, forward. My prayer was that the dash-mounted compass was accurate. The run to the bay's entrance was about three miles. If I steered the boat too far to the west I could easily wind up on one of the many treacherous reefs that dot the Sitka Sound.

The other worry, which nagged in the back of my mind, given the zero visibility conditions, was the possibility of collision with a large fishing vessel. Knowing that fishing seasons were generally over, and that surely no sane fisherman would be out in this weather, diminished this worry.

"I guess it's a good thing your mistress didn't realize how bad the weather conditions were today," I told the dogs. "If she had looked out the front door we wouldn't be going hunting. Come to think about it," I reflected wistfully. "Being back in bed cuddled up to a warm body would not be at all bad this morning."

Since my fiasco of hunting during a raging Pacific storm back in October, I had been under "orders from headquarters" not to go hunting in bad weather. The mishaps of that hunt came back to mind as I prepared the boat. Despite small craft weather warnings prior to that October hunt, I succeeded in battling the waves to the head of Katlian Bay. There I found quiet anchorage in a small, sheltered cove at the bay's head. By the time the dogs and I hit the duck flats, the wind was blowing at gale force. Gusts of 50 to 60 mph threatened to topple me from my feet. But the ducks and geese were in! The birds were reluctant to take to wing. When airborne, they blew backwards. Jump-shooting quickly brought two large, dusky Copper River Canada geese and several mallards to bag. As the wind continued to increase, I decided the better part of valor would be to head for the barn.

Four-foot to five-foot waves rolled up the bay with their tops churned to white foam by the raging wind. The 16-foot Glasspar, a good boat in reasonable sea conditions, was not adequate against what we faced. Every wave was breaking over the bow and sending spray into the boat. If one roller broke over the stern and drowned the motor, we would be in serious

Chapter 5 — *Alaska Potpourri*

trouble. The dogs could probably swim to the beach, but I would never reach the beach.

We finally beat our way out of the bay to face a raging North Pacific. Before we could reach shelter in the lee of seaward islands, we faced two miles of open ocean. Huge, white-crested rollers moved unimpeded toward land as far as the eye could see. Alaska Lumber and Pulp Co. maintained a station at the road's end. There, I steered the boat into the welcome shelter provided by protective log booms, tied up the boat, and called Judy for a car ride home. I retrieved my boat the next day.

I sure hoped today's hunt would not repeat that October disaster as the boat idled toward Aleutkina Bay. Finally, and much to my relief, the bluffs marking the bay's entrance were dimly visible off either bow. Covering the three miles had taken the better part of an hour.

The ebbing tide was approaching low water. I beached our boat in a foot of water. Planning ahead for a flooding tide, I hauled anchor and line far up the beach. As I tramped the tidal flats, kelp floats popped crisply under the soles of my hip boots. The rising sun lighted our white world but little. The boat, less than 100 feet away, was invisible.

I threw six decoys into a nearby tidal gut. The dogs and I stood around, making no attempt at concealment. We were concealed enough by the storm. I did not really expect any duck would be foolish enough to fly today. I also had not bothered with packing buckshot. No brown bear in his right mind would be out and about.

I blew into my duck call a couple of times and was shocked when a mallard answered. Moments later the dark form of a low-flying duck materialized. The point-blank shot was no challenge. It was Brandy's turn to retrieve. She splashed happily through shallow, snow-clogged sloughs. Thus encouraged, we continued our hunt.

Big Brandy was having a ball. During a recent physical examination the veterinarian had weighed her in at over 110 pounds. Her physical attributes of unusually long and dense hair coat, thick hide, and her tremendous body size made her the toughest cold water dog I have ever known. She routinely swam the cold Alaska bays for recreation.

A second duck was collected for Kent to retrieve. The boat drifted slowly closer on the flooding tide. I was shocked to see that 10 inches or so of new and heavy wet snow had already accumulated on the boat's bow and canopy. I scrambled to relieve the boat of the crushing weight.

We had been on the beach for a couple of hours when I heard the unexpected sound of an idling boat. "Surely there is not another dad-blamed fool out in this weather," I thought.

The approaching boat put up a couple of mallards. The ducks made the mistake of checking out the decoys.

Finally, the outlines of a boat were visible through the blizzard. The boat was a familiar black-and-white 21-foot Glasspar. Larry and Fred, my buddies from work, were on her deck.

"What in the Devil are you doing out boating on a day like today?" I called to them.

"Judy called the office worried. We came out to see if you are OK," they responded.

"I'm fine. Just shooting some ducks. Like shooting fish in a barrel in this weather. I'm about ready to head in though. I appreciate you checking on me."

Fred just shook his head and steered back for open water. The snowfall was finally slacking.

Some years later Fred and his son lost their lives in a boating accident to Alaska's cold waters.

Through the years I have many times taken more ducks in a day's shoot than the three birds I took home that day. The extreme circumstances made that hunt memorable.

Three days after our hunt, Brandy delivered a beautiful, healthy litter of five yellow and four black pups. One of these pups I named Big Ben. He was to become my inseparable companion. Some years in the future, I would gun the Copper River Flats with Ed Brostrom over another of the pups. But when destinations and our lives took us away from our life on Baranof Island two years later, Brandy would not be with us. The big dog that so loved water tragically lost her life in Indian River when she was swept over river falls.

Hello Dolly

Catching sea-run Dolly Varden trout in SE Alaska, 1971.

My light spinning rod throbbed with the pull of yet another heavy fish. The fish slowly surrendered to relentless rod pressure and I worked it into shallows where, feeling gravel, it spooked in a final desperate run. Finally subdued, a beautifully marked sea-run Dolly Varden slid onto the gravel bar. Ben, my big yellow Lab, grabbed the fish in his powerful jaws and gently delivered it to my hand. I paused to admire the fat, 2-1/2 to 3 pound fish. We needed fish for smoking. I was not playing catch and release this day, so I brought into play a fish persuader. A couple of blows to the head and the fish lay still to be added to a growing pile.

"Good boy, Ben. You're up next, Kent." I promised his father as I cast again and was soon fast to another fighting Dolly. As I played the fish, there was loud splashing 40 yards downstream, evidence that my brother Gene was also into fish.

The fall harvest season had arrived for residents of southeast Alaska. I had been spending much time afield with my dogs during the past month experiencing Alaska hunting and fishing to the fullest. My time afield helped to ease the pain of a recently dissolved marriage and the decision to at least temporary pull up stakes in Alaska. I planned to head south to sunny North Carolina and spend the winter with my family. Making a break with people and places that have become so much a part of one's life is never easy.

My brother, Gene, had flown up from Washington State with his Norwegian elkhound (Ivan). He had recently been working with the Quinault Indians on Washington's Olympic Peninsula. Having spent time logging in the rain forests of Washington, he soon proved to be a good companion to have along on wet Alaska wilderness adventures.

I had committed to a study involving moose during the September hunting season near Haines. Following the study, I would head my station wagon south. There was a plan in the back of my mind to sample upland bird and waterfowl hunting in the Yukon and British Columbia while en route. These plans were to eventually come to fruition. Meanwhile, we were enjoying the beautiful Pacific coast of the Alexander Archipelago to the fullest.

Much of August had been spent hunting Sitka blacktail bucks above timber line among the Baranof Island crags. My brother was not a hunter but he joined me to experience the country and watch wildlife. Generally, these hunts included two days and one night afield. The dogs accompanied us as welcome companions, pack animals, and bear alarms. With the limit of four bucks harvested, activities had turned to less demanding recreation, mainly fishing and hiking.

There had been one long, long hike with too little water across Kruzof Island to and around the summit of Mt. Edgecumbe after a too-late night of hitting the bars. This hike, in weather atypically warm for southeast Alaska, turned into something more than an ordeal for me. Dehydrated, I was prostrate with heat sickness by the time the summit was achieved. I began to fear that I would need a medical evacuation. But after some sleep and rest, I was able to hobble the long miles back to the boat.

One sunny day we undertook a 3,000-foot climb up precipitous Bear Mountain in pursuit of goats. Arriving above the timber line, we spotted a band of goats frolicking over distant craggy peaks. With night imminent, a raging storm moved in. We struggled to make a survival camp under the protection of weathered, stunted cedars. Our sleeping bags were pitched under a thin sheet of plastic that provided partial refuge from the wind that lashed out with rain and sleet. The narrow shelter was open on three sides and was crowded with two humans and three dogs trying to stay dry and share warmth. From our bags we prepared a hasty meal of condensed soup and rice. Warm food and shots of Schnapps revived our spirits. A magnum rifle lay by my side. It was very unlikely that any self-respecting grizzly would be abroad on a night like that on a storm ravaged mountain peak. The largely sleepless night crept slowly by. In the early morning, we were subdued as we headed back down the mountain.

Another day we enjoyed very exciting bottom fishing in Sitka Sound. Gene, Montana Bob, and I soaked herring on the sea floor while occasionally drinking a cold one. The kicked-back fishing ceased when Gene's heavy rod bent almost double. After a long battle he brought his catch alongside. A chicken halibut of about 20 pounds had taken his bait and a huge cod had in turn grabbed the halibut. Unfortunately, when we attempted to net the pair, the cod let go of his oversized meal and escaped by sinking into the briny depths.

Today, for a change of pace, we had chosen to ignore the obvious choice of fishing Sitka Sound for salmon or halibut. Instead, we departed Crescent Boat Harbor in search of stream fish. Our plans were to run to Nakwasina Bay and explore stream tributaries to the bay. Runs of pink and chum salmon would be over but we just might find silver salmon.

The day was typical of fall in southeastern Alaska. Clouds shrouded the surrounding mountains and a light mist of rain fell. Rain slickers and

Chapter 6 — *Hello Dolly*

hip boots would be standard outer gear. The Labs paid no attention to the rain. They eagerly ran down the dock to the boat, but Ivan, not a water dog, was not very enthusiastic.

No wind disturbed the rigging of the many boats tied in their berths. We exited the riprap surrounding the harbor to a sound that lay quiet. A regular pulse of gentle velvety swells rolled in from the open Pacific.

"With no wind, we should have good boating today," I concluded as designated guide. "We will make a day of it. I hope to fill up a cooler or two with fish for smoking. You have the lunches in your pack?"

Arriving in Nakwasina Bay, we chose to explore the northernmost and largest of its tributaries. The tide book showed tidal fluctuations this day would be minimal. The tide would soon turn to flood. These conditions would greatly simply the usually complicated anchoring process. We worked the boat to a point just inside the river's mouth, not far below the average high tide line. Stepping into the shallow water, I pulled up my hip boots. Barnacles on moss-slicked rocks crunched underfoot as I carried the anchor 60 feet or so up the beach. The dogs anticipated high adventure ahead and eagerly sprang from the boat.

Gene shrugged on his day pack and exited the skiff, tackle box and rod in hand. I unzipped a rifle case and quickly loaded the .30-06 with 220-grain solids. I reminded Gene, "With the dogs there is little likelihood the rifle will be needed today. "However, when on a salmon stream, a man had best be prepared for any eventuality. There are some mighty big brown bear in this valley. One 11-footer was taken here."

Light pack loaded and rod in hand, I splashed up the creek. By the time we had traveled 50 yards we were above the normal high tide line. As we continued to move upstream, we splashed through a couple of minor, shallow pools. No fish were in evidence and I began to doubt my wisdom as a guide.

Rounding a bend, we were confronted by an extensive pool. This pool was about 100 yards long and up to 40 yards wide. Both banks were heavily vegetated. Grasses, alder, and willow grew in tangled profusion. A wide gravel bar lay along much of its north bank. Water depths dropped rapidly into deep blue shades along the far bank. There was little current, but the water seemed to shift unnaturally. Clipping on Polaroid lenses, I intently studied the pool's depths. Long silvery shapes were distinguished. Excitedly I exclaimed, "We are into fish!"

Gene elected to fish the tail of the pool while I started fishing its upper reaches. With our first catch, I realized our quarry was the sea-run Dolly Varden trout that spend much of their lives at sea, fattening up there on abundant marine organisms. Opportunistic feeders, they frequently follow salmon runs into spawning streams where they dine heavily on salmon caviar. Later in the fall, the Dollys work their way upstream to complete their own spawning rituals. Unlike salmon, they may live to return to the sea and complete their life cycle many times.

As a proven major predator of juvenile salmon, a bounty was paid for Dolly tails in pre-statehood Alaska. There was also a bounty on bald eagles during that period. Thankfully, with statehood, most bounty systems were abandoned. In those early years of Alaska statehood, limits on most wildlife were generous. At the time of this fishing trip, there were no possession limits on Dollys.

I had early on discovered that sea-fattened Dolly Varden, very rich in oil, made wonderful smoked fish. An acquaintance in Sitka did a superb job of custom smoking fish on shares.

As the afternoon faded into evening we had fish on constantly. Finally I eyed our take and realized that our catch was more than adequate. There were fish for frying, fish for baking, and lots of fish for smoking. I called, "Ben and Kent. Come here!" I needed their leads to string fish so we could pack our catch back to the boat. Working steadily, I soon had our fish strung. Fish tails dragged the ground with strings at shoulder height.

Gene was still casting downstream. I watched as he hooked another good fish and played it intently. After some time, I realized something was wrong. The fish was not coming in. Maybe it had wrapped itself around a root or log. Gene carefully worked his way into deeper water to the area where the fish seemed to be holding.

For long moments Gene stared intently into the water lapping around his hip boots. Finally he reached into the water and scooped out a very large Dolly. Shaking his head, he carefully removed the spinner's hooks from the fish's mouth. After holding the fish upright facing into the current for a spell he released it. Gene waded his way upstream to me, shaking his head as he took down his rod.

I greeted him, "I am surprised that you released that last fish, Gene. He was a nice one. But we have plenty to take home."

"I still cannot believe what I just saw," Gene said in amazement. "That fish had grabbed onto a tree root and was holding on with his mouth so that I couldn't reel him in. That's a smart fish. No way could I kill him."

Little Norway For Ducks And Salmon

Waterfowl hunting and fishing near Petersburg, 1973.

Fall hunting in the Wrangell Mountains was over. In Alaska's interior, freeze-up was imminent. As October passed and storms rolled through the mountains, the snow line descended lower and lower. I had better options than to winter in the frozen land. I hit the road for warm climes much farther south. My faithful yellow Lab, Kent, was my companion. We had lost his son, Big Ben, the previous winter to a speeding car.

Opting for the easiest route south, I headed my truck for Haines. From Haines, I would take the Alaska State Ferry to Prince Rupert, British Columbia. Numerous cruises over the years had shown the ferry system to be a pleasant way to bypass about 1,200 miles of snowy Alaska Highway. From Prince Rupert, all the main roads across Canada had been paved in recent years. And taking the ferry there was always the chance that I would get lucky and meet an interesting passenger to share the trip.

As we drove the Alaska Highway, skirting the south shore of Yukon Territory's Kluane Lake, curtains of Northern Lights undulated in the dark night. Hours and many weary miles later the road reached its highest summit. Just short of the summit a big bull moose charged out of the alders and trotted unheedingly across the road in front of the truck. I slammed down on the brakes and steered toward the opposite shoulder. After barely missing the rut-crazed animal, I took time to calm my nerves.

The road quickly lost elevation and followed the glaciated Chilkat River seaward. The many mammoth cottonwood trees on the river's banks were for the most part still in full green leaf stage. I spent two good days with the Blank family. Norm Blank ran a commercial gill net operation at the time and fished mainly for red salmon. He had a custom smokehouse and cannery. He and his wife processed his catch and their smoked reds made for true gourmet eating. Norm was one of the more successful local moose hunters. On occasion, he went after mountain goats. For years we had planned to make a goat hunt together, perhaps giving it a try that fall.

The night after I arrived, heavy precipitation developed as a cold front moved in. We were mauled by an unseasonable blizzard. By dawn of the next day, many of the cottonwood trees were shattered and devastated by a crushing, 20-inch blanket of snow. I caught the next ferry south.

Buddies Afield — Alaska Days

My first port of call was Sitka, the beautifully located ocean-side town on Baranof Island. The land surface of Baranof Island is almost wholly part of Chugach National Forest. I had lived there for four years in the late 1960s. I have many good memories of Sitka and the Baranof Island environs. I had been involved in a mostly happy marital relationship there. Many days had been spent afield with my Labs. There were mountains to climb in pursuit of deer, goats, and blue grouse. Many miles had been covered by boat, hunting ducks and geese and fishing. Negative memories still lingered of a marriage deteriorating and a Lab drowning

A friend, Chuck Schwantes, and his wife, Terry, still lived in Sitka. His brother (Tom) was a renowned deer hunter with whom I had hunted on several occasions. Tom, a wildlife enforcement officer, was now assigned elsewhere. Chuck invited me to stay at his place for a day or so.

"How's the deer hunting this fall, Chuck" I inquired. I knew by experience that hunting success for black-tailed deer in southeast Alaska was highly variable. In years of peak abundance, hunting was fantastic. Heavy snow winters gave disastrous winter kills and population crashes.

"Not so good, Jim. Populations still have not recovered from a couple of hard winters. I have not been out yet this fall. I will hold off on my hunting and see if we get a heavy snow late in the season to concentrate deer in the low country. Terry and I could sure use some fresh venison. Why don't you get us a deer?"

After a night of the usual October rain, the morning dawned fair. Across Sitka Sound fresh snow showed on the upper reaches of Mt. Edgecumbe. I decided to hunt the forest immediately behind Chuck's house where heavily timbered terrain sloped gradually uphill for a mile or so before beginning the precipitous climb toward Harbor Mountain.

I still-hunted stealthily through the virgin rain forest. A dense, springy rug of moss cushioned my steps. Some of the giant Sitka spruce were 6 to 8 feet through at the base. Dim shafts of sunlight filtered through the dense canopy overhead. Kent, my pack animal, stuck close at heel. It was always reassuring to have a watchdog on duty when a man was dressing-out a deer in grizzly country. Fallen ancient giants created breaks in the forest canopy. Here, with increased light penetration, dense thickets of high-bush blueberry, cranberry, alder, and Devil's club thrived.

I had been hunting for a couple of hours when I started noticing fresh deer droppings. Kent inhaled the warm scent and quivered in excitement. I moved forward, carefully placing each step. A twig broke just ahead and I froze behind a spruce. A nice fork-horn buck stepped into sight. I raised my .30-06 and rested the cross hairs of the Leupold behind his left shoulder. The distance was only 30 to 40 yards and the scope was set on

Chapter 7 — *Little Norway For Ducks And Salmon*

2X for close-up shooting. The buck was bowled over by the impact of the 180-grain bullet. Chuck, Terry, and I would share some venison.

My next ferry stop was at the quaint seaside fishing village of Petersburg, known locally as Little Norway. Many of the local fishermen were of Norwegian decent. They joked that "no white men live in Petersburg, just Norwegians and Indians." My friend and former co-worker, Norm Johnson, lived in Petersburg. With blond hair and blue eyes, Norm's Scandinavian ancestry was obvious. He fit in well.

For years, Norm had regaled me with stories of the legendary water fowl hunting to be had on the nearby Stikine flats. I was in no hurry to get south. It was high time for me to hunt with old Norm.

The ferry docked in the early morning. I reached Norm at his office by phone. After greeting, Norm asked the hoped for question. "Can you stop off for a few days? How would you like to go duck hunting? I am setting up a trip to the Stikine Flats. We are leaving out of here by boat Friday and will hunt through a long weekend. I have a Forest Service cabin reserved in a prime spot. Northern birds should be in. Four of us are going but I may be able to squeeze in one more body and of course a good duck dog."

"Norm, I am easy. You talked me into it," I allowed. "I need some other activities to fill up the next two days. Any suggestions?"

"Come fall, there are many opportunities for hunting and fishing around these parts if you don't mind a little rain. Let's get together at the small boat harbor this afternoon. We will take the Glasspar out and drag some herring for king salmon. You can bring the beer, Budweiser."

Later that day, we were cruising in Norm's 18-foot cabin boat not far off the beach. Village houses rising picturesquely among spruce trees were at times obscured by a light mist. Piers jutting out from shore dripped in a steady, light rain.

"Sure is a nice afternoon, Norm," I said. "All we need now is a couple of king salmon. What are our chances? How has the deer hunting been?"

"There are a few feeder kings hereabouts all winter. The black-tailed deer population is down on the Island this winter. There is a better chance of success in fishing than in hunting deer locally."

Our conversation was rudely interrupted by the scream of my assigned reel. Opening another cold one would have to wait. I lunged for the rod and set the hook as line peeled off the big Penn reel.

"Hold on!" Norm shouted, shifting the motor into neutral. "You are into a nice one." The fish fought deep and hard. Finally, he was alongside. Norm was handy with the net so I swapped the rod for a fish billy. After a couple of blows to the head, the fish lay quietly for us to admire. The beautiful, silver-dollar-bright king would go 30 pounds or better. Sea lice clinging to its body ahead the anal fin attested to high salinity levels.

"Lots of good eating there," said Norm as he slipped the fish into a cooler filled with ice. "Now I need a cold one. How about some barbecued salmon for dinner tonight?" We shook hands and then opened refreshment.

"A salmon barbecue sounds wonderful. All of this southeastern Alaska liquid sunshine has the fishing competition holed up at home or in the bars." I gloated. "As far as I am concerned, this is a fine afternoon."

"What have you been up to this fall?" Norm wanted to know. "Hear you are into some kind of camp up north. You able to get in any hunting and fishing?"

"My partner, Rudy Gray, and I are trying to get a summer camp for teenage boys going. We have some land and a cabin site on Jack Lake in the Wrangells. The scenery is spectacular. I would not be surprised if some day that country becomes a national park. Unlike Denali Park in the Alaska Range, there are almost no tourists in the Wrangells."

"Fishing for Arctic grayling can be fantastic. I have stood in one place with fly rod and dry fly, catching and releasing 100 grayling up to 18 inches. Financing our camp operation has been problematic. I may have to go back to work." (A few years after this conversation the Wrangells were included in the new Wrangell – St. Elias National Park. As of this writing in 2004, tourists for the most part had not discovered this park.)

"As for hunting, this fall I hunted sheep, black bear, ducks, ptarmigan, and the occasional rabbit," I added.

"Jesus H Christ!" exclaimed Norm. "I am stuck here working for a living. How about moose?"

"Generally, a moose is too much meat for me. I did befriend a young moose hunter this fall. We shot a bunch of snowshoe hares together. I wanted some rabbit for camp meat and he wanted some to take back to Anchorage. One evening, he showed up at camp all down in the dumps. He had shot at a moose just at dark in a stand of burned timber. He thought his shot was good but he searched until dark and found no moose. It was really nasty going in the burned area. We found the moose with old Kent the next morning before it could spoil. It was a nice young bull of about three years and prime for eating. I helped him butcher and pack out. He gave me a big chunk of backstrap."

As we fished on, Norm asked about my plans for the winter. I told him, "I plan to winter in the Carolinas. I need to spend some time with my folks. Believe it or not, there is now a ski industry in the southern Appalachians. I have a seasonal job there. Maybe I will cross tracks with a ski bunny or two. For sure, I will hunt some ruffed grouse and bobwhite

Chapter 7 — *Little Norway For Ducks And Salmon*

quail and woodcock in the Sandhills. I will hit the Carolina beaches for a spring break before returning north."

"You single fellows have girls on the brain." Norm kidded.

"Well I know some dirty old married men, the present company not excluded, who also do not look the other way when a cutie walks by," I retorted back.

A shrieking reel interrupted our banter! Norm had a fish on. It was my turn to man the net. After another hard fight, his salmon was in the boat and on ice. The second fish also went 30 pounds and was almost a twin of our first fish. Captain Johnson grinned over his salmon, "we have done well and I don't know about you but I'm getting chilled. Besides, we have run out of beer. What you say we head in." The cold and dampness were taking their toll.

"I'll drink to that," I finished off my beer. "Is the fishing always this good here?"

"Not always. Sometimes I get skunked. Sometimes it's much better."

As we went back to the harbor, Norm gave me some options for the next day. "I have to work the next two days but there are a couple of possibilities for you. There is a minus tide about sunrise in the morning. You can drive out the road and hunt along the flats above town. You might pick up ducks or maybe geese. Or, you can take my small skiff across the bay to Petersburg Creek. Some very nice steelhead are running up the creek now. You might tie into one of them."

"I think that I will try for birds tomorrow. We just had an outstanding day of fishing. Kent and I need some exercise."

The next morning I was up early. The flats had to be hunted during a low tide. In southeast Alaska, tides can fluctuate over 20 feet between high and low. When I got to a jumping off point, the falling tide had exposed extensive tidal flats. The upper flats were fringed by high marsh grass while the lower flats were bare mud and gravel, with an occasional rock outcropping. Guts (channels) carved by water flow traversed the flats. Strands of broken kelp lay at random. As I moved forward, fucus floats popped under my boots.

I had covered about a half-mile when I rounded a clump of towering marsh grass and heard geese talking. I stopped to listen; they were on the ground and not far ahead. I quickly removed duck loads from my shotgun and chambered copper-coated number 2 shot. I cautiously peeped through the nearby cover. Heads bobbed as big birds grazed and shuffled across the flats. They were within range.

I stepped out and the startled geese threshed into the air. The Charles Daly Superimposed swung true. At the double shot, two big geese crashed to the ground. Kent charged out to retrieve and deliver the nearest goose. He was quickly back and after the remaining bird. The geese were dusky Copper River Canadas. They would easily weigh over 12 pounds each.

"Kent, old man," I told him, "I have my hands full with a goose and shotgun. You are going to have to pack your bird back to the road."

We headed back, quickly heating up from exertion. It was a bluebird day and not exactly ideal for waterfowl hunting. Kent panted around his mouth-full of goose.

Over breakfast the next morning, Norm and I discussed steelhead fishing. "What kind of tackle do you have?" Norm inquired.

"I thought that I would use my 6 weight fly rod. I have some wet flies. My leader material is 6 pound test."

"Kind of light," observed Norm. "If the flies don't produce, try tipping them with these." He handed me a small jar of home-cured salmon eggs. "The creek will be high. You may have to use some split shot to get down to the fish. Me, I would use 10 or 12 pound test leader. I would be glad to give you some."

As a youth, I had gotten into fishing for large fish on very light tackle. I had landed and released some very nice large mouth bass on 2-pound test leader. To my later regret, I declined Norm's offer of heavier leaders.

When I arrived near the creek mouth, the tide was at mid-ebb. I took time to anchor the boat out from shore. It would go high and dry. I would have several hours of fishing before catching the next tide out. A light rain was falling. I grabbed my shotgun for bear insurance and picked up my fly rod. Kent was eager to go and charged ahead. I was reassured by his companionship. No bear would surprise me.

After a couple of hours of fishing, I had found no fish. Rounding a bend, I came to a long, deep pool with a gravel bar that offered a good fishing approach. The far bank was sheer. Strands of high grass trailed from the bank into the current, and brush projected over the lower pool. A snag could be seen just beneath the surface.

I added to the appeal of my fly with salmon eggs and made a cast into the upper end of the pool. The fly, weighed by a split shot, sank quickly. The line drifted toward a deep eddy, hesitated, and then moved against the current. I quickly raised the rod and struck.

A huge silver fish leaped out of the water! Time passed as the fish surged up and down the pool, leaping and turning the water to froth. I cautiously played the fish, controlling pressure on the line by thumb and index finger. Twice, I managed to turn the steelhead away from the brush and snag. Kent watched the action in fascination.

Chapter 7 — *Little Norway For Ducks And Salmon*

I had had the big fish in shallows twice and I saw him clearly. In this stream, steelhead were known to reach 18 pounds or more. My fish showed huge and sea bright in the dim sunlight. A wide pink bar ran his length. I led the big fish in slowly once again. Now he was now almost within reaching distance. How I wished for a dip net. Applying cautious pressure, I rolled the fish over on his side and worked him into the shallows. I saw the fly hooked in the corner of his jaw. It could pull out at any time! I noted with desperation the frayed leader. The fish, feeling gravel scrape his side, gave a final desperate surge and the leader parted. I cursed and watched as my trophy swam slowly back into the pool depths.

"Let's go home Kent. Today our luck ran out. It sure was exciting though. Tomorrow we will chase some ducks."

The Forest Service cabin was located on a small, heavily wooded island just off Stikine flats. The cabin's roof and surrounding trees all supported a heavy growth of moss. Even the woodshed was covered.

The flats were accessible by foot only during moderate to low tides. When a high tide of frigid water surged in, a man did not want to be caught attempting to cross the intervening tidal guts. We anchored in deep water on the bay side of the island as daylight was failing. Rain fell heavily. We unloaded our gear and provisions hastily. Raucous quacking echoed along the flats as flocks of ducks appeared out of the sunset to converge on the flats. The northern mallards were in!

The next three days were a storybook waterfowl hunt. We crossed the flats to hunt between tides. We jump shot for the most part. We hunted singly or in pairs along the flats skirting potholes of water. As we slogged along, mallards feeding and resting in the marsh vegetation sprang into the air. Many of the birds flushed in good shooting range as singles, pairs, or small bunches. The copper-coated lead no. 5 shot we used in those days was very effective. I recall few cripples or lost birds. Limits were generous: eight birds a day with a three-day possession limit. Most of the ducks brought to bag were mallards but an occasional gadwall was taken. Either sex birds were legal game but for the most part we selected big red-legged, greenheads. Kent worked hard and efficiently and our carrying straps filled.

Even on the Stikine Flats it is a rare occurrence when a man hits the birds and hunting conditions just right. Three of our party of five hunted hard, spending hours each day tramping the flats. Norm and his son, Roy, and I were serious hunters. Roy was in his late teens, and he and I made a good team. We would angle into promising spots from converging directions. Kent was then sent in for the flush. Roy proved himself to be a good wing shot time and again. Sometimes we had one bird down, sometimes four or five. Two of our party did not tramp far across the flats or spend much time away from the cabin.

Dark brought to a close a typical day of outstanding hunting. We sat around the roaring woodstove, warming up and sipping cool refreshments. A hissing Coleman lantern lighted the cabin as highlights of the day's hunt were rehashed. Plans were made for the morrow. Norm's old black lab female and yellow Kent had been fed and were contentedly drying beside the stove. Wind whistling through the spruce seemed to shake the cabin. Rain came down in sheets. Dinner was a pan of duck giblets smothered in onions, served with a pot of boiled rice.

The three days of memorable hunting passed quickly. My shooting was quite satisfactory and the dog work was wonderful. By the evening of the last day, our duck limits were for the most part filled. Our ducks had been drawn and hung in long strings between the eves of the woodshed.

The hike back to the cabin the last afternoon was made in haste. The tide was rolling up tidal guts, threatening to block our retreat. As we hastened toward safety, vast flocks of geese materialized. Honking, milling geese circled and settled along the flats. Deep, dark water from the encroaching tide now surrounded our island. The geese were safe from us. We thought longingly about hunting geese in the morning but other duties called. There were offices to go to, a school to attend, and a ferry to catch.

Back in Petersburg, I prepared to drive aboard the ferry. "Sure enjoyed the hunt Norm. Best sustained duck shoot I have ever been on. You are an outstanding guide. I sure would have liked to have landed that big steelhead though. By far the largest steelhead I have ever had on a line."

Norm agreed. "We had an outstanding duck hunt, no doubt about it. Maybe the next time you stop by, we can hit the Stikine for geese. When you go after a big fish, be sure you use a leader that is up to the job."

In the late afternoon, I was on the southbound ferry. Regulations required that Kent make the trip in the truck below decks. I took myself to the ship's bar for a cold one and my good luck continued. I found a lovely and interesting lady who continued the trip to Alberta as my companion.

One never knows what the future holds. Norm and I never did get to take that Stikine goose hunt. By the next fall I was back working full-time and I also had some social commitments that seemed important at the time. Norm, still in his 30's, was taken away by a failed heart.

Goats Don't Come Easy

A too successful Rocky Mountain goat hunt, 1974.

The timing was right. Norm and I were finally going to make our long talked about goat hunt. The area around Haines, Alaska basked in a most unusual spell of Indian Summer. I was migrating south from Nabesna Road after a summer and early fall in Alaska's Interior. My travels would take me much farther south for the winter, but I was in no hurry to go south as long as there was hunting to do and the weather continued fair. Norm had caught up on work around his family's custom salmon cannery and was ready for a hunt.

On my first evening in Haines, we were discussing hunting over a couple of cold ones. Norm's moose hunts that fall had not produced.
"We could sure use some fresh meat," admitted Norm. "Moose didn't cooperate over at the cabin this fall. Prices of beef are high at the local markets. Besides, wild meat is generally better quality. I have a couple of days free. Maybe we should make our long talked-about goat hunt. Not near as much meat as a moose but a goat of up to about six years can be prime meat before the late fall rut."

Toughened by an early fall of sheep and caribou hunting, I was more than ready for another excuse to climb a mountain. I was quick to agree with Norm we should go for a mountain goat.

"Norm I have made four successful goat hunts thus far in my life. I've found myself risking life and limb on every hunt before getting down with the meat, hide, and horns. Something always seems to go amiss up in the goat cliffs. Seems easy for things 'to go to Hell in a hand basket' when a man has a 100-pound pack on his back and he is struggling down a mountain."

"We will use more strategy on this hunt. I know of a little known trail into some good goat country. The trail up is steep but safe if a man watches his step. Once on top, the going is good, water is abundant, scenery magnificent, and finding a good campsite will be no problem. We will shoot only one goat between us. Splitting up the meat will make packing no problem. Patrica will look after the girls and the homestead. I assume that you will take Kent with you."

I liked Norm's reasoning. Norm was a strapping 6 feet tall and hardened by a summer of commercial fishing; he could pack a hefty load. As a younger man, he had been quite the goat hunter.

"Sounds good to me, Norm. If we get lucky, you can have most of the meat for your family. I have a long drive across country facing me and I cannot transport a lot of meat. I will opt for the hide. With frosts at night in the high country, the hair should be long and the hides should be getting prime about now. Kent can help pack meat if necessary. He will warn us of any unwelcome brown visitors in the night. Too bad I lost Big Ben last winter. He could really pack a load."

"The loss of Ben was tragic. There could well be bears working the alpine for berries. You can have the horns and the hide," agreed Norm. "And the first shot."

That evening, we carefully went over gear and got our packs together. We planned to travel light and fast. Foods were chosen for light weight and ease of preparation. An ultra-light two-man tent would provide night shelter. We would pack little water. Norm knew from experience that there were springs and runoff from snowfields in the high country we would hunt. A small mountaineering stove would permit us to have hot meals and tea. We discussed packing only one rifle but finally decided we would each carry. I would hunt with my .308 Norma Mag. Norm would hunt with a .270. Norm added a flashlight to his pack for good measure.

"Don't forget your toothbrushes," Patricia reminded us as she made sure that we were well stocked with delicious smoked salmon and her homemade oatmeal cookies.

"My toothbrush is in my pack," I assured her. "I consider a toothbrush and toothpaste to be essential equipment for overnight hunts."

But the best laid plans do go awry. Developments the next morning held Norm in town until mid-afternoon. "We will still have plenty of time to hike in this evening and set up camp," he assured me. "We will start hunting at first light tomorrow and should be able to cover a lot of country in a day. The weatherman says clear weather will last at least a couple of more days."

Norm arrived home in the afternoon. My truck was loaded and we headed up Alaska Highway 7. This road connects the coastal community of Haines with the northern interior. Glacial, braided channels of the Chilkat River, a major migratory corridor of fall dog (or chum) salmon flowed on our left. Precipitous cliffs of the Chilkat Mountains rose abruptly to our right. Many bald eagles perched in riverbank cottonwood trees. They were resting and drying their feathers after fishing the river. Other eagles soared and rode thermals off rocky cliffs. Across the river, the spectacular spires of Kicking Horse Mountain stabbed the western sky.

Chapter 8 — *Goats Don't Come Easy*

We arrived at an obscure pullout. Norm found the concealed trailhead behind some brush. "This was an old prospector's trail," he informed me. "Let's hit it," he urged. "It only hurts a little while."

We quit procrastinating and shouldered our 40-pound packs. As promised, the trail was steep. We puffed along, climbing steadily under towering Sitka spruce and western hemlock. The light beneath the closed canopy of rain forest was gloomy.

"About how far is it to where we will set up camp?" I finally asked.

"I guess about 1-1/2 miles. If we keep moving we should break timber line in an hour or so."

As we ascended, I noted very old blazes on trailside trees. There was no sign of recent human use. Spore of game including bear and moose was evident. We paused occasionally for water breaks.

As we gained elevation, the tree height decreased. At about the 1,500 foot level, approaching the alpine, we encountered more and more stands of alder. Finally, we stumbled out of the brush onto an alpine bench where we arrived in a spectacularly beautiful fairyland. Here and there clumps of dwarf cedar survived the harsh environment. The moss under foot was 6 to 8 inches deep. Below us, the mountain, except for the heavily wooded ridge we had ascended, descended precipitously in a series of sheer cliffs to the river. Braided channels of glacial water gleamed in the last rays of sunlight. Far to the south a vast sheet of reflected light marked the sea. A rapidly setting sun bathed the stark peaks to the west with crimson light. The mountain we were on rose in a series of benches broken by rock slides to a rounded summit.

We hurriedly pitched the tent and set up camp. Kent, a very tired Lab indeed, sighed as he curled up in a nest scratched into the moss.

"I don't think a man is going to need much of a ground pad. With this moss under our bags, we will think we are sleeping on feather beds," I ventured.

"No rain tonight," predicted Norm. "I think I will sleep outside the tent under the stars."

"I think I will join you, Norm, we can put some of our gear in the tent in case there is a dew. I will keep rifle handy at my side just in case. There was much bear sign among the blueberry bushes right at timber line."

"I don't plan to sleep too far from my rifle either. How about some smoked salmon sandwiches for dinner to go along with that soup you are putting on?"

I busily filled our cups with boiling tea and located my small flask of peach brandy. "Help yourself to the sweetener," I passed the bottle.

Kent munched away on his dinner of Purina Chow.

"Doesn't get much better than this" Norm sighed.

We were reclined in deep moss, munching our salmon sandwiches, spooning up hot soup, and sipping fortified tea.

"Agreed. What a spectacularly beautiful location for our camp The hike in was worth it whether we make meat or not. We could see Northern Lights tonight."

When darkness concealed the landscape, it was time to brush teeth and hit the sack. We looked forward to a spectacular hunt the next day. As we crawled into our sleeping bags, Kent snuggled up to my side.

"It's going to get quite cool tonight with this clear weather," Norm suggested. "We will probably wake up to frost. Kent, you stay alert and let us know if we have shaggy visitors."

During the night, I awoke from my slumbers to a spectacular display of lights undulating overhead. I woke Norm, "Norm, look at the display."

"Spectacular!" We watched silently until dozing back to sleep. Kent seemed unimpressed.

We rolled out of our snug bags just as the sky behind mountains to the southeast turned gray. A heavy blanket of frost blanketed moss, tent, and bags. We fortified on hot chocolate and pastries, while Kent breakfasted on Dog Chow. Norm finished first. "Time to saddle up. Our bags will dry out when the sun comes out. Hope our camp has no untimely visitors in our absence."

"There is always a chance of that in bear country," I agreed. "But I have seldom had bear problems in my wilderness hunts."

"Must be karma," suggested Norm. "Given all the time you spend out in bear country."

"I do kind of consider the grizzly my totem," I admitted. "Let's go find ourselves a goat."

Shrugging into greatly lightened and now halfway comfortable packs, we picked up our rifles. Norm led off with a brisk, carefree walk.

As different tracts of terrain came into view, we stopped and glassed for suspicious white patches against the various greens and grays of the mountainside. Spectacular drifts of last winter snow survived in draws and shaded areas.

We had traveled not much more than a quarter-mile from camp and the sun's first rays were just peeping over the mountain's crest when my binoculars picked up series of suspicious white shapes framed against a green background of moss. "Goats!" I exclaimed. "A whole herd of them."

I handed Norm the binoculars. He studied the animals carefully.

"Some nice goats in that bunch. We can get up on them, I do believe. They must be a mile or so away as the raven flies. I know this mountain. I say

Chapter 8 — *Goats Don't Come Easy*

we head up the way we are going another half-mile or so. We will reach the ridge top and then circle back above them."

"How many did you count, Norm? I counted at least 10."

"I counted 10 myself but there could be more we can't see from this position."

We headed out at an accelerated pace and quickly gained elevation. Cresting out, we circled in the direction of the goat pasture. The sun was now well overhead and there was no noticeable wind. We reached and crossed a vast field of snow. The snow was packed and firm under our boots so that crossing was a delight, with footing excellent. We paused at its summit for landscape pictures.

The ridge rose to a crest that eventually descended in the direction we had seen the goats. We covered a mile or so, gradually losing elevation. More than an hour had passed since our initial sighting. Would the goats still be where we had spotted them? If they had moved, could we find them?

We peeped cautiously over a rise. The goats were there; some were browsing, some were lying down. They were only 500 or 600 yards away. We agreed to try closing the distance to 200 yards or less for certain shot placement. I wanted to spend some time studying the herd to pick out the largest billy.

Our progress was carefully kept behind rock outcroppings. We closed to a sharply rising rim of rock. Hopefully, this ridge would cover our final approach. On its crest we would be in good shooting position. As we reached the ridge, Norm and I had a hasty, whispered conference. "You go ahead and take first shot. I will back you. Remember only one goat," Norm summed up the situation.

Now on hands and knees, I moved intently upward. Just below the crest of the ridge, I carefully removed my backpack. With rifle in hand, I then wiggled forward. Kent stayed below, as I had commanded, quivering with excitement.

Topping the ridge, I moved up behind a boulder, brought up the binoculars, and cautiously peeped ahead. The animals were still there! They were completely unaware of the presence of human predators. I could now count 12 animals. Long, white guard hairs rippled in a gentle crosswind. The goats were slightly downhill and about 100 yards away. I studied the herd and picked out what I believed was the largest billy.

From behind the boulder, I motioned Norm up. He ascended very cautiously. I pushed my backpack into place and slid my alpine rifle on top of it. Reflecting on the tranquil scene, I had regrets that we had come to kill. But the excitement of the chase was present and we had come for meat. There would never be a better chance. I settled into place for a steady prone shot and looked over. Norm was in place and set. I nodded.

I brought the duplex cross hairs of the Leupold scope to rest on the front shoulder of a magnificent billy and slowly tightened up on the hair trigger. At the thunder of the rifle, there was mass confusion. Goats seemed to be stampeding everywhere. I was conscious of the boom of Norm's rifle.

My goat, hit through the shoulders with a 200-grain handload, had fallen in his tracks. I leaped to my feet and slapped Norm on the back. "We did it. What a storybook goat hunt!"

I was surprised at Norm's seeming lack of enthusiasm. "I backed you up," Norm said. "But the goat ran off."

"No. Norm, you are mistaken. Our goat is lying there, he's not moving a muscle."

Norm looked, then he said in a somewhat puzzled voice, "Oh. You are right. In the confusion of the stampede maybe I shot at another goat. I sure hope that I missed."

There was a thoughtful silence. Kent was whining at my side, eager to close on the kill.

Norm and I exhausted our film supply taking pictures of our billy for posterity. Then the work began. We carefully skinned the goat, taking care that the hide came off intact. The meat was boned out. Kent dined on the meat scraps. My final effort was to remove the horns.

Norm was uncharacteristically silent. Earlier, he had walked to the edge of the drop-off where several goats had disappeared. He saw no sign of animals there.

"Let's have a snack and a drink of water before we head back to camp," I suggested. "Our packs aren't going to be bad at all with one goat split two ways. I can't believe that I'm having such an easy goat hunt."

After our break, we shouldered the now substantial packs and headed down. Below the kill site extensive cliffs separated us from camp. The wise choice was to circle back the way we had come.

An hour or so later we had worked our way down from the summit and were skirting along cliffs below the kill site. Raven talk and cries came from up a steep, rocky draw where the black birds seemed concentrated. Studying the overhanging cliffs, we spotted three to five of the big birds riding the air currents, descending into and then ascending from the draw.

"Are you thinking what I'm thinking, Norm." I finally could no longer ignore the evidence.

"Yeah. I am afraid those birds have found themselves some meat. I guess we had better go up and have a look-see. Why don't we leave your

Chapter 8 — *Goats Don't Come Easy*

pack here with the meat, hide, and extra gear? I'll take my pack and rifle. All you need to bring is bone saw and knife. I think our easy goat hunt may be over."

We began to climb slowly and methodically upward into the steep draw. Loose rocks frequently went crashing downhill, dislodged under our boots. Our energy level was ebbing and the day was no longer so sparkling.

Kent suddenly surged forward, then halted and began pawing among boulders. In the lead, Norm spotted white hair and called back, "Yep. Our easy goat hunt is over."

We tiredly boned out our second goat. Norm's pack was filled when he decided, "I'm not taking hide and horns. We will be doing well to make it down with the meat from this goat plus the hide and meat we already have from the first goat."

"It's too bad to leave your trophy hide and horns behind, Norm, but you are probably right about the maximum weight we can pack off this mountain."

We descended the unstable draw slowly and painfully. Norm packed the goat and I packed Norm's rifle back to where we had left my pack.

Just before sunset, we stumbled back into the camp we had vacated early in the morning. The sleeping bags and tent welcomed us and looked very appealing. I quickly dropped my pack and lay down in the soft moss.
"I am about exhausted, Norm. I'm sure glad the day's work is over. We can take our time and we will have all day tomorrow to pack out."

Norm hesitated, "I hate to tell you this but I've got to get back tonight. I have some business at the lumber mill first thing in the morning. I can head down and drive your rig home and pick you up tomorrow at the trailhead."

"If you have to make it down tonight, I will stick with you. We started this hunt together and as far as I am concerned we will end it together." I was not too happy about developments. "I wish that I had known that we had only one day for our goat hunt. Maybe I would have exercised good judgment and gone fishing. I have been this route before. Though one hunt was actually successful, rushed goat hunts in this country somehow always become an ordeal. Given the hour, by the time we break camp and repack, we will be faced with making most of the descent in the dark. That will be a dangerous undertaking with 100-pound packs on our backs."

"Thankfully, I have a flashlight. Let's load up, eat something, and rest for a half-hour before heading down."

"I sure hope that you have good batteries. The descent will probably take us a couple of hours."

"I am sorry for the way things worked out" Norm apologized.

"You don't need to apologize. We had a wonderful hunt and we both got goats. We will remember this one for a long time. You may have to help me down though."

"We will help each other," promised Norm.

The trip back down the mountain on the precipitous, rocky trail with one flashlight was a nightmare. Tree roots reached out to catch weary feet of top-heavy hikers. Only our hands holding on surrounding trees, and the support by a partner, prevented serious falls. But finally we were down.

Two weary, successful goat hunters returned to Haines, hot showers, and a cold beer or two.

Late the next afternoon, Norm and I were standing in his backyard drinking frosty cocktails and watching eagles soar off the face of Mt. Ripinsky. The fresh goat meat hung in Norm's cooler. A beautiful hide lay salted and curing. I proudly examined our trophy horns. The women of the household were inside making final preparations for a sumptuous dinner of celebration.

"Well, we did it," sighed Norm as he turned goat backstrap on the barbecue grill. "I'm getting too old for goat hunting. I think that I will hunt goats no more."

"We had a great one, Norm. The country we hunted is the most beautiful imaginable. I agree with you about killing goats though. From now on, my hunts for the high climbers will be with camera only. Film, although not very nourishing, sure is a lot lighter to pack out."

Tebay Rainbows

Rainbow trout are a bonus in Tebay country, 1974.

We were fishing beautiful Tebay Lake, high in Alaska's spectacular Chugach Mountains. We had arrived a few days earlier by a Beaver plane on floats. The hour-long flight out of Cordova and up the Copper River had been spectacular. Below our craft the glaciated river raged, while craggy mountains laced with glaciers lay off the wing tips. Our party consisted of Rudy, our organizer; Herb, the cigar King from Tampa; three teen age boys from Chicago; me; and old Kent, my yellow Lab.

Rudy, as organizer of Arctic Bound Camp, was exposing urban boys to a variety of wilderness experiences. We other hangers-on were along to help out as needed and also get in some wilderness rainbow trout fishing.

Mountains sloped sharply down to the Tebay Lake system on all sides. Most of the terrain was covered by dwarf alpine vegetation or was bare rock and rock sides. Mountain goats occupied the upper, moss-covered slopes, with some seeking refuge atop the cliffs. Stands of stunted black spruce occupied both the upper and lower portions of the basin. Our camp was nestled amid a sparse stand of spruce, just up the lake from the lower lake's outlet.

The camp was spacious for such a wilderness setting. It included three log cabins, a boat dock, storage shed, smoke house, and (of great daily importance) a snug outhouse. I noted with more than passing interest that steel bars studded with sharpened spikes protected the heavy planking of the cabin's main door. The varnished wood beneath the protective bars was marred by deep claw marks left by a bruin that had come calling. The main cabin included kitchen, dining, and lounging areas. There were a couple of side rooms for gear, supply storage, and bunking. Heating was by a strategically located woodstove. The two small, outlying cabins were used as bunkhouses.

I elected to occupy one of the outlying cabins with Kent. As I entered the cabin to roll out air mattress and sleeping bag, I noted the door to be none too substantial. There was no evidence of bear visitors but I would sleep with rifle handy the next few nights.

A mound of supplies accumulated on the dock as the Beaver was emptied. The aircraft roared off in a shower of spray and quietness again pervaded the wilderness.

All hands worked hard to pack gear and supplies up to the cabins. Then, the boys could wait no longer. Seizing spinning rods, they were out on the pier and casting into the deep, cold, crystal-clear water. Soon, their excited shouts shattered the wilderness stillness as they hooked and played hungry, wild rainbow trout.

"They are really into fish, Rudy. Fishing here must be as good as you promised," I could not help but observe.

"Lots of fish in these lakes. They are not really fished much. At this elevation in Alaska, lakes are only ice-free three or four months a year. Only way in here for fishing is by aircraft on floats. The rainbow run mostly 10 to 16 inches, but there are lots of them and they like to cooperate by biting on whatever you throw at them. We had better go check on the lads."

The boys had found and quickly figured out the function of the live box that was tied alongside the pier's end. Peering into the box, I saw an abundance of wavering forms.

"I caught the biggest. I bet he will go 18 inches!" Bruce, the oldest of the boys, could not help bragging some.

"OK fellows. You have done good. Catch one more fish each and call it quits for today," instructed Rudy. "It's almost dinner time and some fresh trout to eat tonight will be wonderful. Knock a dozen or so over the head and clean them. Jim here will show you how. Tomorrow, we will launch the two skiffs and explore the lakes."

As the boys finished fish-cleaning chores, Herb, Rudy, and I sat on the cabin's porch with before-dinner cocktails and watched the sun torch the rugged peaks piercing the western sky. Dinner that night was festive as the hungry crew quickly consumed mounds of fried trout.

During the days to follow, trout would be a staple in our diets. We had fried trout, trout baked in tinfoil, and alder-smoked trout. Trout was fried with eggs for breakfast and there were cold trout sandwiches for lunch. One evening, I made up a wonderful fish stew. On another evening I volunteered to cook trout in a batter recipe from accomplished Norwegian chef, Arnie, that I got while on a cruise aboard the Paragon. The boys liked this method of preparation best of all.

One morning, we made an early departure and rowed the boats the length of the lower lake, going through a connecting channel and into the upper lake. I found myself manning a set of oars for the mile-long trip when a strong headwind blew up and made quite a workout. We arrived in the upper lake and found the effort was worth while. Few human fishers visited the upper lake. We manned our rods and were quickly into rainbows. If anything, they averaged larger here than in the lower main

Chapter 9 — *Tebay Rainbows*

lake. I caught my largest fish of the trip, a beautiful, heavy fish that went about 20 inches. After a lunch of sandwiches, we voyaged back down the lakes. The wind had died down. For the return trip, I gladly relinquished the boat oars to strong teenage arms.

For a variety of experiences, we tore ourselves away from fishing for day hikes. One such day we hiked down the outlet of the lower lake to a series of falls that served as a check on upstream salmon migration. At the foot of a spectacular falls, I found the toothed jaw of a big fish. It was evidence of a salmon whose migration was blocked.

One sunny afternoon the boys, Kent, and I took a skiff across Tebay Lake for a hike up the mountain slopes. We chose a ridge that ascended brush-free from the lake into a towering peak. The climb was a very challenging scramble up a moss-carpeted slope. Mountain goat droppings were abundant as we ascended. I pointed out some fresh grizzly scat to the boys. With responsibility for the boys' safety, I was assured by the weight of the .338 rifle I was packing. After an hour or so of steep climbing, the younger boys were running out of steam. We had reached a bench with deep moss cover.

"Let's take a water break and get out your candy bars." My suggestion was met with sighs of relief. The crew quickly sprawled out on the vegetative carpet, unlimbered their water jugs, and munched their Babe Ruth and Hershey bars.

We rested quietly for some minutes. My suggestion that we continue upward was met with more than a few moans, but soon we were all on our feet and heading upward.

Another half-hour passed as we toiled upward. We finally reached the summit of our ridge. The view was spectacular. A sea of mountain peaks ranged to the east and west. The camp cabins on the opposite bank of the lake far below appeared as dollhouses. The crew sat and drank in the scenery, and the feeling of attainment was strong.

Bruce summed it for the boys as he opened his canteen. "So this is what it is all about."

"Yep, this is what it is all about," I agreed.

The day following our alpine hike, the crew slept in. At midmorning, Rudy announced brunch. The boys came sleepily into the main cabin as it became toasty from the roaring woodstove. They quickly perked-up over steaming mugs of hot chocolate and heaped plates of bacon and blueberry pancakes.

"Life can't be all recreation. We need to rustle up firewood today to replenish our dwindling supply," announced Rudy.

"How about that huge old snag below camp, Rudy," I inquired. "It would fall right by the lake and we could load it in a boat for packing back to camp."

"I have looked at that one before. The way it is leaning, I have my doubts it would fall clear of the lake. We will go have another good look at it though."

When we got there, we studied the big old spruce from all angles. "I believe it will fall clear Rudy," I said.

"Go ahead and give it a try," Rudy said, as he handed me the chain saw. He then climbed the bank and took off his hat, laying it on the ground. "There's your target. Bet you can't hit it."

The saw roared as I notched and cut. Finally, the tree swayed and toppled to the ground with a huge crash. A corner of Rudy's cap was under the tree.

"Almost a bull's eye," judged Rudy. "We'll call it a draw, OK? Hand me the saw and I'll get started chunking it up. You boys can load the boat and get wood to camp. Then you can build up your muscles as you split with the maul."

Feeling pleased with my work, I busied myself trimming off branches with the ax.

Our last full day in camp got interesting. In the late afternoon I was busily reeling in another good rainbow when my fishing revelry was rudely interrupted. Rudy, also reeling in a good fish, had sidled up to me and bumped me hard with his shoulder. I was puzzled at this turn of events and started to loudly express my confusion. Rudy placed a finger to his lips to indicate the need for silence and nodded his head repeatedly up the beach. I noted old Kent standing a few feet away, drawing in big draughts of air and peering intently in that direction. Glancing up beach, the cause for the distraction from fishing became very obvious. Well short of 100 yards away, a very large Toklat color phase boar grizzly was ambling along the beach, coming our way! We had not expected bear company and were unarmed; the .338 was back in camp, 100 long yards away.

The bear came on. Kent was now quivering in excitement. The bear was probably still unaware of our presence. Rudy and I quickly pulled in our fish. We ignored our fish stringer, already heavy with trout, and we quickly freed the two fish. Our options were limited. The closest trees for climbing were back near camp.

Rudy moved close to me and whispered, "leave everything and let's get the flock out of here." We dropped our rods and I followed Rudy in a dash back up the beach for the safety of four solid walls and the insurance

Chapter 9 — *Tebay Rainbows*

of a .338 rifle. "Heel Kent," I urged him as I took to my heels. Happily, the bear evidently elected not to follow us.

During our pre-dinner cocktails that night, we related the day's bear adventure to our young companions. One bear tale led to another. No one would venture far from shelter that night.

Later, with tooth brushing out of the way, I reinforced the flimsy door of my cabin with a strategically propped chair. A rifle and a flashlight lay near at hand. As the night passed, I tossed restlessly in my sleeping bag. My dreams became nightmares of blood-streaked tree trunks once encountered on Baranof Island. I was again on a posse after a man-killer grizzly. Suddenly, the bear charged out of a thick stand of head-high spruce at point-blank range. I struggled to align my rifle with the bear. My hand then touched and locked on warm fur. I sat up screaming and threw something soft and warm across the cabin.

Then I came back to reality. Kent was at my side, looking at me in alarm. I groped for the flashlight and its beam showed the door was still firmly shut. There had been no bear. My flashlight showed the still warm body of a vole (small, mouse-like mammal), lying against the cabin wall where I had flung it. This little mammal was my "grizzly."

We found the rods the next morning where we had dropped them. But the string of fish was missing.

Jim Mauney took this picture as hunting pards Kent and Winston Hobgood admire the big grizzly shot by Winston on the Sheenjek River, AK in 1978. After the drying period, the bear's skull was measured and certified for the records book.

Sheenjek Combination

Hunting grizzly and moose in the Sheenjek Wilderness, 1977.

We had procrastinated long enough. I gripped my rifle firmly and then looked at hunting buddy Winston Hobgood. "Are you ready to bite the bullet. Night is coming on fast." We were faced with entering dense brush to possibly face a very big, and very mad, wounded grizzly.

Winston stubbed out his cigarette, then ground it beneath his boot and picked up his rifle. "Yeah, I guess. Ready as I'll ever be."

"Hie on Rock," I urged my Chesapeake. "You learned lots of tricks on driving bear from old Anvik River Brute. Now find us a bear."

We were on the Sheenjek River, far above the Arctic Circle. The final leg to our destination was reached by bush plane from Fort Yukon. Fall was advancing into winter. Still pools of the river were frozen. Soon the Porcupine and Yukon Rivers to which the Sheenjek is tributary would be turning to ice.

We had flown miles up the Sheenjek looking for good moose and salmon habitat. I was inventorying the river's salmon population and looking for tagged salmon. The moose was for me. Abundant salmon would indicate prime feeding for grizzly. Winston had talked of wanting to bag a grizzly. We flew over and passed up several promising areas. Some areas had to be ruled out by lack of aircraft access. The area we sought had to be in proximity of a gravel bar that could be used as a landing strip. We finally found a likely bar among the braided river channels.

The landing went OK. We quickly unloaded our gear. Our pilot did not wish to linger as the brief Arctic fall day was fading fast.

"Good luck," he wished. "The temperatures are falling. Going to be cold. The mercury will drop well below zero tonight. See you in about three days."

With night imminent, we hastily put up a tent. The next important task was to round up a huge stack of firewood. Fortunately, finding wood was no problem. Much driftwood had been deposited along the bar by spring floods. We were soon sipping hot tea sweetened with Schnapps and toasting in warmth of a blazing fire as Northern Lights played overhead.

"Listen to all that splashing from the creek," I remarked. "This is a major spawning area for fall Yukon chum salmon. I bet that there are grizzly and wolves nearby. Our pack dog might have to be a bear dog before the trip is over."

Buddies Afield — Alaska Days

Rolling out in the frosty landscape of early morning was hard. Embers of last night's fire still smoldered. Breakfast was hot tea and oatmeal. We went over plans for the day.

"You know," admitted Winston, "I have made up my mind I would not mind taking a nice grizzly."

"I guess a man is entitled to one," I allowed. "I took a beautiful bear from Chichagof Island several years back. All I want is a good eating bull moose. But if we come across a bear and you want him, I will back you."

"We are not too far from the foothills of the Brooks Range and could run across caribou," Winston added to the prospects.

"Some prime caribou meat would make a very welcome addition to my freezer," I allowed.

The short day passed quickly. We learned the country that seemed so open from an aircraft was in fact very difficult to hunt. Dense stands of alder and willow fringed the gravel bars. Back from the river, black spruce grew in profusion. Within the spruce stands there was a lot of blow-down. The going was hard and noisy.

"It's going to be hard to get up on a moose here," concluded Winston.

"I haven't seen much fresh spoor," I admitted. "The only moving wildlife I have seen is a lot of spawning salmon and the many ravens that are dining on spawned-out carcasses. I think we are here in time for winter." Ice flows were becoming abundant in the rapidly freezing river.

The day was waning as we approached a large, still-open-water side channel. Several springs moderated the water temperature, keeping it from freezing. This was the prime habit salmon sought for spawning, and they were very abundant and active. Gravel bars were littered with partially eaten salmon carcasses. Many had obviously not died natural deaths. As we advanced, we could see that in some places fresh salmon blood coated the rocks. Rock was now very alert, smelling the air and watching the brush. He started to surge ahead.

"Heel up here now, Rock. I think that we have a bear very nearby."

Suddenly, there was a crash in the brush just ahead. A big, dark boar grizzly surged into sight. He stopped on the bank about 50 to 60 yards ahead. He looked in our direction as we froze in place.

"There's your bear," I whispered to Winston. "Take him if you want."

Winston raised his .270. His weapon would suffice with perfect bullet placement but was surely not the caliber of choice for a big grizzly. The rifle crashed and the bear charged ahead. My philosophy is that as long as a bear is moving you keep shooting. I raised my .308 Norma Magnum and took a backup shot. The grizzly crossed the stream throwing up a geyser of water. He was quickly up the far bank and out of sight in brush.

Chapter 10 — *Sheenjek Combination*

"Now we have our hands full," I groaned. "Quite possibly a wounded grizzly is waiting for us in the brush and night is coming on."

"I'm sure that I hit him good but maybe not good enough," worried Winston. "Want to go after him now or wait until morning?"

I pondered the decision. "If I have to worry about going after that bear in the morning there will be no sleep tonight. Smoke a cigarette. We will let him lie awhile and then follow. I will send Rock ahead. Rock will let us know when the bear is close. A bear cannot catch a smart dog unless the dog closes. Hopefully, Brute taught him well."

We worked the bolts of our rifles, making sure that the rounds were chambered. Crossing the stream was expedited with hip boots. Rock was unfazed by the icy water, reaching the far bank where he shook his ice-covered coat and a hail of ice crystals filled the air. We advanced slowly and methodically, with Rock leading the way. Every piece of cover ahead was carefully scanned in the failing light.

I recalled a similar situation a few years back on Chichagof Island. A brown bear had killed a logger and I found myself on a posse. I recalled human blood waist-high on tree boles at the site of the attack.

Rock disappeared into a particularly nasty piece of cover. There was no barking or growling. As we advanced, the yellow dog came into sight standing over a very still grizzly. Winston and I heaved sighs of relief. I heeled Rock and Winston put in an insurance shot.

There was much celebration around the campfire that night as the Northern lights played overhead. We knew the bear was big but did not realize how big until the skull was later measured for the Boone and Crockett Club big-game records. The bear missed making the all-time records book by a fraction of an inch.

"This will be my last grizzly hunt," I vowed. "I may hunt black bear again for meat but I never have and never will eat grizzly. If I chose to eat grizzly, then grizzly have every right to put me on their menu. Consider it superstition if you like, but I consider the big bear kind of my totem. I have seen what an enraged bear can do to a man. Grizzly have passed on a number of opportunities to take me. Grizzly and I from now on will have a kind of understanding of live and let live. Only reason I would shoot a grizzly from here on out would be a life-threatening situation for me or for a buddy."

Some years later, I got into semiserious wildlife photography. Among my favorite animals to watch and try to photograph were wild grizzlies. Time and again the big bear gave me breaks. J.T. of Hollywood fame was my partner on several such misadventures. We finally agreed that we were flirting too closely with an untidy and untimely end and gave up the sport.

The following day at our Sheenjek camp was one of much activity. The bear was carefully skinned, with the skin then packed the mile to camp. There was little time for hunting moose.

On our third morning, we slept in. Finally, the call of nature roused me from the warmth of my sleeping bag to face another frigid morning. After having satisfied bodily needs, I fetched my rifle and toothbrush from the tent. I leaned the rifle on a nearby log and proceeded to brush my teeth.

Bear hunter Winston was finally awake and he crawled to the tent door. I heard his frantic hiss and turned to see him gesturing down the open gravel bar. I slowly laid down my toothbrush and picked up my rifle. About 200 yards away a nice mulligan bull moose was gazing in our direction. He stood very near a heavy patch of willows and appeared to be about to bolt. A couple of steps backward and he would disappear. The magnum roared as Winston backed me up. The moose stood several moments longer, then walked a few steps forward to suddenly fall in his tracks. We had our winter's meat supply! We would have a full plane load for the morning's flight.

The rest of the day was spent dressing and packing moose meat. With two of us, the pack was an easy one of just over 200 yards along a frozen gravel bar. Rock was not needed for packing and had it easy. He gorged himself on moose scraps and defended the moose from the "camp robbers" (Canada jays). The two-year-old bull was in excellent condition as indicated by much internal fat. He would be prime eating.

That night we celebrated with a big bonfire, consumed the rest of our Schnapps supply, and dined on moose loin. Rock, having consumed pounds of meat scraps, had no interest in the Purina Dog Chow he usually loved, and he curled contentedly by the fire.

Yukon Monarch

Anvik River yields a trophy moose, 1976.

Stepping around a clump of towering willow, I froze in my tracks. Rock was heeled close at my side. A huge bull moose stood immediately ahead, glaring at us. No more than 30 yards of open ground intervened. I noted the awesome spread of his antlers. A cow standing 20 feet to his left shifted nervously. I had stumbled on moose in rut. The cow seemed ready to spook. The bull, however, was ready to take on unwelcome intruders who had interfered with romance. He pawed the ground with enormous hooves. A photograph I'd seen in a bush trading post flashed through my mind. The picture showed two intertwined skeletons and a mangled rifle. A hunter and a bull moose had done each other in.

At this point I believed it was the bull or me. Deliberately, I raised the 30:06 and brought the cross hairs of the Leupold scope to bear on his left shoulder. I did not wish to have a dying or wounded moose in my lap. My hope was for a shot that would break his shoulder, to anchor him in place and carry on into his vitals. The 220-grain hand loads in my rifle with were up to the job; but under pressure, was I? Bullet placement was critical. I slowly squeezed the trigger.

I had been delivered to the upper Anvik River by bush aircraft the previous afternoon. The area I had selected for a bit of moose hunting was extremely isolated. The Village of Anvik, our flight's origin, lay on the north bank of the Yukon River some 80 air miles to the south. The nearest human habitation was a homesteader's cabin about 30 miles downstream. A few miles downstream of the upper cabin was the Lavoi homestead, home of Anvik River Brute. Brute, a 120-pound white malamute, was renowned for routing both black and grizzly bears. He had taught Rock some of the finer points of bear chasing.

Our flight had proceeded upstream until the Anvil foothills rose in the near distance. During hunting season, the upper Anvik was accessible only by bush aircraft or jet boat. Access was further limited by weather and river water levels. Aircraft access was restricted to a few gravel bars, which at low water could function as landing strips. For all practical purposes, the human hunter seldom or never visited this area. There was limited winter access to this country by dog sled, snowmobile, or aircraft on snow skis, but only after sufficient snow cover had accumulated. This was long after moose hunting seasons were closed.

I knew firsthand of the big bull moose that roam along the Yukon and its tributaries. As a biologist for the State of Alaska, I had spent many hours flying this remote wilderness, documenting salmon populations. I had numerous opportunities to observe the area's major wildlife: moose, grizzly bear, and wolf. I had, on more than one occasion, observed bull moose with antler spreads greater than the height of a tall man.

One morning on the upper Koyukuk River we had flown over two huge, rutting bulls engaged in mortal combat. The country over which they battled was largely open, broken by an occasional clump of black spruce or willow. It appeared that an acre of ground had been literally devastated by their struggles. The ground had been pawed up and low vegetation shredded by their trampling hooves. As we circled low overhead, one maddened bull lowered his head, shook his six-foot rack of antlers at us, and seemed to dare us to land.

A big, angry moose of either sex is one animal a human should have respect for and approach only with caution. There are numerous records of humans coming out on the short end of the stick following their moose encounters.

One summer I conducted fieldwork in the Beluga area. While working the area, I was living with my dogs (Rock and Jay) in a duck-hunting shack on the Susitna Flats. I took great delight in watching the great variety and multitudes of waterfowl that stopped by en route back north.

Some of the area streams were famous locally for their king salmon runs that were handy to Anchorage-based fishers who arrived by bush aircraft. Pilots used gravel one-lane roads as functioning airports. There were no air traffic controllers. One afternoon as I was driving down a narrow road, I came on the scene of a recent tragedy. Two aircraft lay as scattered, shattered, and burned scrap. There had been a midair collision between a Cessna 185 and a Heliocourier. All involved died, including a father and his 13-year-old son.

There were no women or bars locally that summer to distract from a healthy outdoor life. A good book was entertainment during the brief summer nights. In my spare time, I did some running (with .357 Magnum in hand; bear and moose were plentiful); fishing for king salmon; and dog training.

I had learned the technique of packing heat when bush running from my fellow Fish and Game cohort Kevin Delaney. Some years down the pike my friend Mike from Anchorage jogged by a cow moose that was browsing along an urban bike trail. When he regained consciousness, he was bleeding profusely with his skull kicked in. He started packing a .44 pistol. The following spring he was again charged, but this time he shot the attacking cow.

While working in the Beluga area I set up a patterned field-trial-type water blind 300 yards down a long slough. When passing by the slough, I would stop and send my dog, Jay, on the long water blind. His job was to swim the length of the slough, pick up a plastic training bumper, swim

Chapter 11 — *Yukon Monarch*

back to me, and deliver the bumper to hand. If he had problems staying on line, I would stop him by whistle and direct him by hand signals.

Jay quickly mastered the blind. Late one afternoon he was performing his blind flawlessly, swimming down for the bumper and starting back with no directions from me. A little moose calf walked out on a point near which Jay passed. At first I thought it very cute as the calf watched the dog with interest. Then the calf gave a couple of bleats and the brush parted with a crash. Here came mother. Mother moose took a look at the dog swimming and said to herself, "Ha, now I have a wolf at a disadvantage. I am going to stomp him into the mud."

The cow plunged into the slough. The water reached only to the knees of her long legs. Jay continued to swim trustingly to me as the cow closed on him. He did not realize that doom was descending. He would have no chance. The distance was too great and the seconds too precious. I could never reach them. I said to myself, "what can I do?"

The truck was parked a few feet away. A loaded .357 Magnum pistol was on the front seat. There was not much hope of turning the cow and saving my wonderful buddy but I had to try. I made a dive for the pickup and came up with the pistol. The moose was closing rapidly. The two animals were moving and they were about 100 yards or more away. I shot quickly, at first trying to merely scare the cow. The bullet slammed the water in front of her. She was now practically on top of the dog and she paid no attention to the commotion caused by the shot. Alaska law does allow man to shoot wildlife in defense of his life and property. I had brief seconds for one more chance.

I took a two handed grip on the .357 Magnum and sighted on the moose's body. At the roar of the pistol there was an explosion of water down the slough. Both animals disappeared in cascading sheets of water. When the scene cleared, the cow had turned and Jay was still swimming toward me, still packing his bumper.

My trophy moose hunt was timed to coincide with the mid-September rut, which was late fall in the far North. The day we flew in was a beautiful, bluebird Indian Summer day. Willows following along the stream banks were golden in the late afternoon sun. Frosts had nipped open areas of tundra and clumps of ground vegetation reflected deep red and purple. There had been little precipitation of late and the river was in relatively low flow. The chances of finding an exposed gravel bar where we could successful put the Cessna 172 down were good.

The gravel bar we selected for our landing was in the vicinity of an old forest fire burn. The country opened by the burn would make for good walking and glassing. New willow growth, which flourishes in the years following a fire, would provide good dining for the giant browsers. The promising gravel bar was along the river's east bank. Low, treeless hills rose immediately above. My pilot brought the Cessna around for a closer look-see, making a preliminary pass or two. He then performed a touch-and-go to test the firmness of the landing surface.

"What do you think, Dale?" I asked anxiously.

"Kind of short but the surface looks OK. I believe I can get you in, and if the water doesn't rise much, out. Just don't shoot two moose," he joked.

"I know better than that. Let's give it a go then," I decided.

Considering the nature of the landing strip, our touchdown went smoothly. Anxiety of the landing behind, we taxied to the upstream end of the bar and hastily unloaded my gear. Rock, my faithful dog, was happy to once again have firm ground under his paws and he hastened to mark territory.

"I will see you in about three days if the creek don't rise. Good luck." With a roar, my transport back to civilized places was airborne in the gathering dusk. Dale was anxious to cross the intervening mountains and reach the Bearing Sea shore and Unalakleet before dark.

As I set up camp, I noted fresh grizzly scat and tracks along the bar. I hastily loaded the .30-06 with 220-grain solids and, as an afterthought, chambered loads of 00 buckshot in the Daly 12 gauge over-and-under. "Sure is good to have you along for companionship and to watch my back in case unwelcome guests visit camp, Rock."

With the tent up and sleeping bag inside and unrolled, I hastened to the next most important task of gathering a huge pile of driftwood and blow-downs for campfires. Frost was in the offing this night. The warmth of a fire would be most welcome and would also discourage visits from bears. One good thing about freezing temperatures is that there would be no annoying mosquitoes. During the summers, Yukon River mosquitoes and other winged pests could make life for warm-blooded critters a living Hell.

As the last light of day waned, I decided to make a hasty reconnaissance of the area. Shouldering my rifle and binoculars hanging from my neck, I climbed to the crest of a hill that rose to maybe 50 feet immediately behind camp. Just as I reached the top, my attention was drawn to a dark object breaking the light of the setting sun reflected from the river. I brought my binoculars to bear and caught my breath. A huge bull moose was up to his knees in the water, crossing a shallow section of the river. He was only about a quarter-mile downstream. As he crossed, his tremendous spread of antlers was silhouetted against the red and orange glow of the western sky. Reaching my side of the river, he disappeared into the deepening gloom. I hastened back to camp to kindle a fire and cook some grub on my Optimus stove. After Rock was fed, I calmed my excitement from seeing the big bull with a cup of hot tea made mellow with brandy. There was a very real possibility of encountering a trophy moose tomorrow.

Chapter 11 — *Yukon Monarch*

I awakened in the early morning light with embers from last night's bonfire smoldering in my rock fire pit. A pot of tea was put on to boil. The aroma of hot tea boiling over soon permeated the chilly air. Preparations were made in haste for the day's hunt. A lunch of cheese and bread and a jug of drinking water were included in my freighter pack. My equipment checklist included two knives, a sharpening stone, 20 rounds of rifle ammo, a meat saw, 20 yards of quarter-inch nylon line, a compass, matches in a waterproof container, and a nylon dog pack.. Rock munched on Purina Dog Chow for breakfast while I downed some instant oatmeal sweetened with jelly.

Picking up rifle and binoculars, I scrambled to the top of my observation hill. The sun had topped the eastern horizon and was beginning to melt the light frost that covered the ground. The sky was cloudless and only a light breeze stirred. In terms of weather, a nice day was in the offing. I glassed the extensive burned area to my south. Blackened boles of fire-killed spruce trees stood out in contrast to the frost painted new growth of plants and brush. In the distance, sun rays reflecting unnaturally from an object at the lower edge of the burn caught my eye. I focused my binoculars there. The reflection had been made by sunlight striking a huge set of moose antlers. Two moose came into focus. A cow and a bull were standing close together. My bull had found a cow. Their breaths were steaming in the chill morning air.

I pondered the possibilities for approaching my quarry. The moose were a long mile away as the raven flies. I would need to follow the riverbank south, skirting the burn. After traveling about a mile, I would cut into the burn and start a stealthy search for the bull. I hastened down to camp and shouldered my pack. "Heel, Rock.. You just may be in for some heavy work as a pack dog before this day is over."

I proceeded along the gravel bar almost at a trot. Approaching its lower extremity, I noticed quite a disturbance in a stretch of backwater. Ducks! The birds ignored me. They had obviously never been educated to the ways of human hunters. Having always heard that a bird in the hand was worth two in the bush I hesitated only briefly. I did not think it likely that distant shots would spook moose that were lovesick and unfamiliar with the threat of gunfire. Back to camp I hustled to swap rifle for shotgun and a hand-full of number 6's. Again approaching the ducks to within easy shotgun range required little stealth.

Five widgeon threshed into the air. Two shots shattered the morning stillness and two birds remained behind. Rock rushed in to make the retrieves. He hit the water in a shower of spray and quickly delivered the ducks to hand.

"Good work Rock." I patted his big head. "A good start and a good omen for the day. I will take these birds back to camp and swap guns again. It is time to get serious. Much more challenging critters await us."

I tramped downstream along the east bank of the river along a well-worn trail made by bear and moose traffic. I noted with more than passing interest the abundance of bear spoor and I was relieved to see that little of the sign seemed fresh. In this upriver open country the bear would be grizzly. Blacks do not compete very successfully with their larger and more aggressive cousins. I had no wish to face down or have to shoot a grizzly. Rock might well put a bear into flight but there was no sense pushing our luck. There was also some wolf spoor but we could expect little trouble from wolves.

The Anvik system includes one of the Yukon River's major salmon spawning grounds. During years of peak abundance, upward of 500,000 dog (chum), king, and pink salmon spawn in this system during June and July. Bear are drawn to the salmon feast from miles around. During the height of salmon spawning, bear constantly patrol and fish favorite pools and riffles. By the late fall, the summer-run fish had long since spawned, died, and been recycled into the environment. Now, the only salmon in the system were silvers spawning in select and unique headwaters. There were no such spawning grounds within miles of me. Most bear would have returned to the hills for the berry season, taking up a largely vegetarian life style. Of course, there was always the stray bear that may choose to work the river bottom.

I had been walking down the river about three-quarters of an hour and judged that I had covered upward of a mile. I worked my way through the fringe of alder, which grew as a thicket along the riverbank. Alder can grow to a height of 20 feet or so and the trunks and branches frequently intertwine. It had always amazed me that moose, with their widespread antlers, could move through the alder thickets with apparent ease. Escaping the alder, I made my way through the burn, trying to avoid or stepping over the trunks of downed spruce. No wind blew and the wilderness seemed very quiet. Only the murmur of running water and occasional call of a raven broke the stillness. I proceeded very cautiously now, placing each foot carefully to avoid breaking twigs underfoot. Clumps of willows interrupted forward vision. As I rounded a big clump of willows, there was my quarry! He was much closer than I had expected and in fact much closer than I would have liked!

The heavy rifle crashed. The bull was down! He was not moving. The cow stampeded. I could hear her crashing through the brush in her panic to escape the scene. Rock surged forward to check out the downed bull. I approached more cautiously, with a fresh round chambered. Only now did I realize what a truly mammoth animal this bull was. His antler spread was considerably greater than my height. Such an animal could be extremely dangerous when wounded. At close range, I carefully put another slug into his neck. Rock, reverting to wolf instincts, began to worry the dead bull.

Chapter 11 — *Yukon Monarch*

"Old boy, the excitement is now over. We have our work cut out for us," I proclaimed. I put rifle and pack aside. First it was picture-taking time and Rock posed proudly. Then the real work began. Butchering such a large animal single-handed proved to be a major undertaking. I could not pack the great weight of intact hind or fore quarters. I had to bone-out the meat. The trip back to camp would cover nearly a mile-and-a-half.. Fortunately, after plowing through a stand of alder, the going would be on easy walking terrain. I was in good, trail-hardened condition after a fall of chasing sheep in the Wrangell Mountains and would be physically up to the job ahead.

Legs and meat from the uppermost side of the moose were removed, then carefully boned-out and laid aside on brush to cool. The next task seemed to be impossible—turn the huge carcass over so I could butcher from the other side. The nylon line I carried in my pack now came in handy. I arranged a system of lines connecting the under limbs to surrounding fire-killed spruce and applied tension. With a couple of stout poles as levers, the job was slowly accomplished.

Air temperatures warmed up as midday approached. Insect life warmed by the sun emerged from shelter. Among their ranks, swarms of white socks, attracted by the fresh blood, gnawed on my exposed wrists, adding my blood to that of the moose. Rock dined on scrap meat until he could eat no more.

After several hours of struggling, butchering was finally completed. The big freighter pack was filled with 100 plus pounds of meat and Rock's pack was crammed with about 30 pounds of meat. The antlers were removed by knife and saw for packing. They would prove to be a load in themselves. When later scored for Boone and Crockett records, the spread exceeded 69-1/2 inches. The total score fell just short of making the all-time records book. I believe that this bull was very old and past his prime. Probably in his prime years his antlers would have exceeded, perhaps greatly, their dimensions of the last year of his life. In any event, he was a moose hunter's trophy of a lifetime.

The packing began with pain. Hunters in Alaska can tell if they have a heavy pack by the difficulty they encounter standing erect. If they must perform a "push up" by use of rifle or pole to gain their feet, they have a man-sized pack.. Utilizing this approach was the only way I could gain my feet for load after load. The weight of my pack approached my weight of 145 pounds.

For the first pack back to camp, I carried my rifle for bear insurance. By the second trip, I decided the eight-pound rifle was too much additional weight. I left my buckshot loaded shotgun at the end of the gravel bar just below camp. With the meat cached around camp, a fire was left burning. My rifle was left just short of the kill site. For the mile or so walk between these two points I trusted to luck and Rock that I would avoid trouble with grizzly. The packing proceeded like this for two days. By the end of the second day's packing, I was limping badly and Rock's feet were bloody. We had suffered enough. My last pack consisted largely of the mammoth antlers.

I figured that between Rock and I, we had packed out 500 to 600 pounds of meat. Authorities on butchering figure that only about 40 percent of an animal's live weight converts into boned-out meat. With my rough field dressing, it was unlikely this high a percentage of meat was saved. Projecting from this, my bull would have weighed 1,250 to 1,500 pounds on the hoof.

Arriving back at camp in the late evenings, the first task was to stoke up the campfire into a giant blaze. We had no wish to attract or feed meat hungry bears. Sore muscles and joints were permitted to relax in the warmth of the blaze. For me, there was a celebration drink of hot tea sweetened with brandy. Dinner was rustled up as the Northern Lights danced overhead.

I had carefully saved the liver to carry back to camp. The second night I planned to dine on liver and onions. Wrong! I learned after frying a skillet full of liver that it was inedible unless one was truly starving. The organ had become saturated with urine. The bull had obviously been attending cows for some time and herding animals in rut have rather kinky tastes. The uncooked liver was in fact so strong that Rock turned up his nose when offered a chunk. The liver was left behind when we vacated camp for the bears and ravens to enjoy. I would often dine on meat from this moose during the next year or so. Meat from the old bull proved flavorful but "about like chewing on shoe leather." For prime eating, a hunter should stick to shooting young bulls or cows.

The third night in camp we faced deteriorating weather. Rain developed during the night. As the rain pattered against my tent, I had visions of the river rising. I could not afford much decrease in the length of my impromptu landing strip and I tossed uneasily in my sleeping bag. Rock curled contentedly by my side. If the river rose much, there would be no landing with a fixed wing aircraft. It was a long, long walk to town from here. In fact such a walk was for all practical purposes out of the question.

Under such circumstances, a man really starts to miss the comforts of home. I recalled with longing my lovely blond girlfriend, Linda. She had made a sheep hunt into the high mountains with me the past August. Not only was she a constant delight to share sleeping bags with, she was most helpful in assuring the success of the hunt. A most unusual young woman, she pulled her share of camp chores and helped significantly in packing out our camp and sheep.

I was up early to face a foreboding and drizzly gray dawn. The river had risen a couple of inches vertically, and the length of the gravel bar had shrunk by yards. With more rain in the offing, camp was dismantled and gear packed for a quick departure. The early morning hours slipped by slowly.

Suddenly Rock was attentive and barked in excitement. He had learned from Yukon huskies to recognize an approaching aircraft motor. A short time later, I

Chapter 11 — *Yukon Monarch*

could hear our plane in the distance, working upriver searching for our camp. The pilot finally located our bar with the help of my violent waving. He made several passes to check out our shrinking landing strip. Finally he banked around and then touched down.

Dale shut off the engine and deplaned. "Getting kind of tight landing here. Wouldn't want to try it much shorter. Let's get loaded and get out of here."

Catching sight of the immense antlers and the pile of trash bag wrapped meat he exclaimed, "Good Lord, what a moose. We will never get all that meat, gear, you, and Rock out in one trip. I will have to fly at least two trips. Let's get to loading."

We quickly filled the aircraft. The great antlers could be put inside only with considerable difficulty.

"I'll drop this load at the Anvik airstrip. The Twin Otter to Anchorage will be in about noon. You should have time to make the connection. Hope the water rises no further."

Dale carefully taxied to the far end of the bar. With such a heavy load, he would need every available foot of runway. Fortunately, there was a head wind that enhanced lift. The engine roared in full power as he raced along the bar. Approaching water, he was suddenly airborne.

An hour later our air chariot of the wilderness returned for Rock our remaining gear, and me. We were on our way back to civilization. I watched with some nostalgia as the Anvik wilderness receding beneath our wings. A most memorable wilderness adventure was over.

There is an Alaskan saying: "There are many bold pilots; there are many old pilots; there are few old, bold pilots." My pilot for this hunt was bold but certainly not old and was, in my judgment, very competent. Two years later I learned that he lost his life in bad weather while flying over the Bearing Sea.

Buddies Afield — Alaska Days

Rock wonders why his master, Jim Mauney, is taking so long with this picture at the end of a hunt for emperor geese at Cold Bay, AK in 1979. It's time to get those tasty geese home!

Cold Bay Welcome

Alaska Retriever Club hunts geese at Izembek NWR, 1978.

The chartered Electra plane was filled with a boisterous group of 40 waterfowl hunters and 20 of their retriever buddies. The retrievers were under control in crates in the baggage area. The human contingent was not under much control at all. Two pretty stewardesses were kept very busy hustling cocktails to thirsty men. The girls artfully dodged poorly worded propositions and sometimes-straying hands. Duck and goose calls brought into play added to a general uproar. Members of the Alaska Retriever Club were on their way from Anchorage to Cold Bay on a wild geese chase.

The hunt organizer called for quiet and the din subsided somewhat for his message to reach eager ears. He happily passed along information that refuge managers had reported goose migrations were at their peak. He reviewed the list of waterfowl that could be expected in harvests. This list was extensive and included Emperor geese, Canada geese, brant, possibly snow geese, and several duck species. Total waterfowl possession limits approached a theoretically ridiculous total of 60 or so birds. He also reported there were large numbers of ptarmigan to chase over the tundra. Few of us expected or wanted to bring home that many birds. We were all anticipating plenty of shooting opportunities, but in fact most of us probably had not packed 60 shells. In closing remarks we were told, "the Izembek Refuge manager sent word to keep a watch over your shoulder. He said that there are some mighty big brown bear roaming around Cold Bay. They might not be adverse to confiscating a waterfowl dinner."

Private trucks had been leased to transport hunters to their lodging and then from their lodging to the fields. Lodging was an old and drafty, unlighted and unheated aircraft hanger. But at least with a roof over their heads wet hunters could crawl into their sleeping bags with dogs alongside. After a wet day, hunters and dogs would at least sleep dry.

The long flight out the Alaska Peninsula to Cold Bay seemed to pass quickly. By the time of touch down in Cold Bay, most of the hunters were well lubricated and feeling no pain. Maybe this was just as well in view of the weather and accommodations that greeted them.

I had relocated to the Anchorage area a few months earlier with my live-in companion, a young, blond Chesapeake Bay retriever named Rock. Rock's father (FC AFC CFC CAFC Chesdel Chippewa Chief) was an outstanding field trial champion. I learned early on that young Rock had inherited outstanding potential for competing in the field trial game as well as hunting. My fellow employee and buddy, Jim Riis, told me about the Alaska Retriever Club, so I joined it. My motivation was to meet fellows of similar interests and learn about advanced training for the hunting retriever. Needless to say, I eventually also became hooked on training retrievers for the field trial game.

By the mid-1970 years, a couple of the Alaska Club's members had become renowned nationally for their successes in trials. However in those days most of the clubs members were hunters who enjoyed good dog work and played the trial game largely for fun and only when there was nothing to hunt. Jim Riis and I came under this category.

Jim and I were very fortunate to get to know Al Roggow, a charter club member. Al never lost sight of the real purpose of a good retriever. His black Lab Field Champion Cookie's Anny Fanny could compete in trials with the best of them. She was also an excellent and accomplished hunting dog. Al always appreciated good dog work, whether in a trial or in the hunting field. He became more or less a mentor for younger club members including Jim and me.

During its early years, one of the most enjoyable events the Club sponsored was the annual expedition of members to Cold Bay. The first trip I went on, the cost to members was about 40 bucks a head, and dogs flew free. The second year the fee jumped to 50 dollars. At that time, the cost seemed pretty high to a working field biologist. These days, a similar trip would cost the hunter hundreds of dollars.

After a fitful night in the hanger sleeping quarters, not-so-enthusiastic hunters awoke in the blackness of a rainy predawn. There were more than a few moans from over-indulgences of the previous evening. Trucks soon arrived to haul small groups of hunters to drop-off zones. Hunters had not bothered to bring decoys. The hunting strategy was to study flight patterns of the geese, then occupy the right spot and so intercept subsequent flights. Shooting opportunities were largely limited to pass shooting.

The birds had been hunted little, and in the case of newly arriving young birds, never. Aleutian winds tend to blow from light gale to gale force, and as a result, moving geese tended to fly quite low over the barren tundra, well within range of the copper plated number 2's most of us used.

Jim and his dog Tie, Al and his dog Annie, and Rock and I were dropped off as a group. Al had hunted Cold Bay before. He generously consented to point us in the right direction. Keeping up with the spry senior citizen over the springy sponge proved to be no easy feat. Jim and I were 20 to 25 years his junior and we prided ourselves with being physically fit. But Al seemed to skim over the energy-draining terrain.

Chapter 12 — *Cold Bay Welcome*

Dressed in my rain gear and wearing hip boots, I found myself sweating profusely despite a chill wind and cold rain.

As we arrived on the banks of a hidden sough, the sun rose, turning clouds on the eastern horizon crimson. Geese could be heard talking in the distance. As we listened, their talking became increasingly restless and then the goose music became very loud as flocks took to the air. A series of shots rang out in the distance as shooting time arrived. Additional flights of birds spooked into the air. Their talk became almost deafening as flocks of birds were seen moving at all compass points.

"Set up here among the tules," Al suggested. "And get ready. I'm going to slip on around a ways and set up." He moved down the tundra.

A few minutes later, Jim whispered urgently. "Here they come." Four pairs of eyes were locked on a small flight of light colored birds headed our way. The two dogs shivered in anticipation. Then the birds were overhead. "Take them," Jim shouted.

We were up on our feet and our over-and-unders quickly emptied. Three geese remained behind, one falling on land and two into the lagoon. I sent Rock for a water bird while Tie made the short land retrieve. Tie then had the opportunity to take a swim.

After their delivery, our two furry companions indulged in enthusiastic shaking, sending torrents of water cascading off our rain gear.

Jim and I admired the beautiful birds. These were our first Emperor geese. The usual winter migration pattern for this goose species is to fly westward out the Aleutian Islands. Few sportsmen ever have opportunity to see the Emperor much less hunt them. One winter I observed a lost Emperor goose in Sitka, southeastern Alaska's old Russian capital.

As the morning passed. additional flights of light geese came into gun range and additional birds were added to our limit.

"I understand the young birds are excellent eating," commented Jim, "the old birds are reportedly somewhat indifferent on the table." We would experience the excellent eating qualities of these geese a few days later. Back in Anchorage, Jim's wife, Genie, roasted a young goose to perfection and served it with generous helpings of wild rice.

The second day of hunting, Jim and I knocked-off the pursuit of light geese along the lagoon early. We decided to hike and see some new country. Our walk took us to a high summit overlooking a bay. The only vegetation in sight was a carpet of tundra that crunched under our boots. The view in all directions was unrestricted and awe inspiring. We sat down to drink in the surrounding scenery. Far below, a dark, drifting shadow occupied the bay's center. As we watched, the shadow lifted from the bay, approaching us and materialized into Canada geese.

Buddies Afield — Alaska Days

The geese would fly low over our lofty perch if our good luck held. As the wave of geese approached, we hunkered low with the dogs shivering at our sides. Suddenly the geese were there and two hunters sprang eagerly to their feet. Shots rang out but were drowned by the wind. The broken flock flew on, leaving behind four of their numbers.

It was now time for dog work. Rock and Tie quickly completed their retrieves and waited eagerly for more of the work they so loved. Thus our first Cold Bay hunt ended on a triumphant note.

Our second venture to Cold Bay resulted in more Emperor geese bagged. At the day's end, we observed brant in some hunter bags. Jim and I decided we would try to add this species to our hunting experience.

The second morning's dawn found us hiking the tundra along an isolated bay. The wind whistled and gusted, threatening to build up to a full-scale gale. Jim observed, "this wind bodes well for brant hunting. It might make sitting out on open water uncomfortable for the birds. If we can find the right location, maybe some birds will fly over us."

Our explorations were fruitful. We found a point that projected between two large bays. The wind and a very high tide were favorable for pushing brant over us and a stand of tall cattails gave us concealment. Men and dog partners settled in, impatiently waiting for action.

Our wait was not long. Brant were talking restlessly, somewhere down the bay. The water, as revealed by the dim, early morning light, was tossed in wind driven whitecaps. Soon we spotted airborne birds moving in our direction. They were seeking a more sheltered resting area in the bay to our backs. Sometime later Jim composed a poem about the ensuing action. He penned the poem on the back of a beautiful photograph and presented it to me. The photo framed geese flying against a background of a full moon. On back of the photograph the poem began:

The brant came on
Wave after wave
Men and dogs were waiting
Shots rang out
Volley after volley
The harvest was begun

Grizzly Don't Fetch

Grizzly encounters enliven a duck hunt, 1978.

We were airborne in a high performance Heliocurrier equipped with snow skis. Winter had arrived with mid-October on the North Slope of the Alaska Range. The air temperature was not far above zero degrees F as the weak morning sun crept above the horizon. The flat light showed a landscape of snow-covered tundra and muskeg that was broken by green stands of spruce and brown clumps of leafless willow and alder. Peaks of the magnificent Alaska Range towered to the south.

Flying west from our takeoff at Clear, we reached the Toklat River and turned upstream, flying south toward the mountains. The river was running heavy with ice flows; the many side sloughs and ponds were ice covered. Moose tracks wandered seemingly at random in the snow. The prospects did not seem to be very good for finding open water and certainly not for the ducks we sought.

The Toklat has its origins in the ice-capped peaks of the Alaska Range close by North America's highest mountain, Denali (The High One). Much of this river's length would eventually be included in Denali National Park. The Toklat flows into the Kantishna, which is tributary to the Tanana, which then merges with the mighty Yukon. After some 900 miles, greatly diluted Toklat waters empty into the Bearing Sea.

The Yukon River system is home to some of the Earth's major salmon populations. Yukon salmon include the renowned king and chum, and lesser numbers of the pink and silver. Chum salmon, locally called dog salmon, have two distinct runs: summer and fall. Adult salmon generally use the highly glaciated main stream only as a migratory corridor. The returning fish instinctively seek out the clear water tributaries.

Fall chum salmon enter the lower Yukon in August to begin a long migration up the river. Some of these salmon swim over 2,000 miles before reaching their ancestral spawning grounds in the late fall. Salmon spawning in Alaska's fall often encounters winter weather conditions and reproduction is successful only in spring or up-welling warm water areas. Though winter air temperatures may drop to 50 below, waters of these spring areas are a constant 38-40 degrees F and remain more or less free of ice. We were seeking a major such "warm water" area on the Toklat.

Suddenly, off the ice-jammed main stem of the river, we spied areas of open water, steaming in the icy air. The pilot brought the plane around to fly over it. Heavy game usage was obvious, with many tracks of moose, wolf, and grizzly in the snow. Salmon in the thousands were observed spawning in ice-free tributary waters. The roar of the plane's engine at tree top level flushed ravens from the spruce; and yes, large numbers of mallards were spooking from the water! These hardy mallards represent one of the northern-most wintering populations of their species in North America. This area presented the only opportunity for taking waterfowl in Alaska's interior during winter.

After a few passes, we located a gravel bar suitable for touch down. Gusty crosswinds ("willa-wawas") out of the Alaska Range sometimes make landings and takeoffs hazardous to health. As we made the final approach, I recalled an earlier reconnaissance trip to this area. There were some very anxious moments then as our Super Cub was caught in a strong downdraft during takeoff.

Today's landing was routine. Safely on the ground, we then assisted our pilot to quickly unload supplies for several days' stay. We three (J.T., Tyler, and me) would be joined by Dimitri and the remainder of our gear on a second flight. Among the most important items of personal equipment were our 12 gauge shotguns and a supply of duck loads. Also included in our shotgun fodder were some 00 buckshot and rifled slugs. These were for chance, close-up encounters with predators much larger than we were.

Two essential members of our party were the Chesapeakes, Rock Honeybear of the Yukon and his son Rock. Rock, some years down the pike, was awarded the titles Field Champion and Amateur Field Champion for successes in trials by the American Kennel Club. During hunts for *palomas* in Mexico, he was affectionately titled the *perro grande* by village children. At the time of this hunt, though only four years old, he was a veteran of many hunts and wilderness adventures. In addition to natural retrieving skills enhanced by training, Rock had learned the finer points for dealing with bears, including grizzly, from a big Yukon malamute by the name of Brute. Rock also had had lots of retrieving experience for his age. Our friendly pilot cheerfully wished us good luck; "have fun. I will be back in three days, weather permitting."

Bitter experiences had shown us that in winter in Alaska, a "weather permitting schedule" could be an indeterminate number of days. Bill, our pilot, cranked the motor and after a brief warm-up, he lifted off with a roar and a storm of sand and fine snow. He was heading for shelter and warmth in Fairbanks. We cleared areas of light snow to put down ground cloths, tents, and finally sleeping bags on top of self-inflating air mattresses.

We then rounded up a huge pile of downed trees and driftwood for the very essential campfire. A roaring fire would be most cheerful after a cold

Chapter 13 — *Grizzly Don't Fetch*

day afield. Its warmth and light would permit us to enjoy our cups of hot chocolate or tea sweetened with peppermint Schnapps or maybe brandy as our supper cooked. Wet and freezing bodies, dogs, and clothes would dry in its warmth. Hopefully, the fire would prevent uninvited night visitors.

Finally settled in, we were ready for serious endeavors. We pulled on hip boots, heeled the dogs, and headed out. Slowly we worked open water areas hoping to jump ducks. Heavy cover consisting of alder, willow, and spruce hugged the watercourses. Game trails, deeply worn into the landscape, wandered in and out of the cover. Away from the water, trees were replaced by large expanses of open tundra.

Salmon, heavily engaged in spawning, were observed stacked in the clear, shallow waters. Pool water levels bulged as salmon shifted up and down the stream in great numbers. The stream bottom was often covered with pink, water-hardened salmon eggs. These eggs had been dug up to perish as one salmon nest was superimposed on another. Spawning fish were too numerous for the available spawning habitat. Melodies from gorged and happy water ouzels filled the air as the birds emerged from walking the stream bottoms where they were feeding on salmon caviar.

Around favored spawning pools and riffles, the snow was crimson with salmon blood. Salmon carcasses, partially eaten, were often stacked in windrows. They had been killed and discarded by grizzlies and wolves. In the face of such overabundance, the predators were selectively dining on the eggs, which they seemed to prefer. Even the ravens were highly selective, consuming only choice portions. One fall during a flight over an area of such abundance, in the very remote Yukon Territory's Fishing Branch, I had the good fortune to be witness as bears and wolves fed on salmon practically shoulder to shoulder along a gravel bar.

Winter storms would bury many of the excess dead salmon under four to five feet of snow. These carcasses would later be dug up by hungry wolves, foxes, and wolverines in the late winter to provide food at a time of severe scarcity. Resident Canada jays, ravens, and golden eagles would also benefit from this late-winter food source.

Occasionally, we jumped small bunches of mallards. We targeted the male greenheads only. The dogs worked enthusiastically despite the low temperatures, picking up all the birds we splashed into the river and then delivering them to hand. In the subfreezing air, the dogs' coats were soon matted with ice. This icy armor made crackling, tinkling noises as they moved. Waterfowl limits in the far north were generous and our take was rapidly mounting.

In a large, deep pool the two brilliant fish stood out among the many calico chum. Green heads and red bodies identified them as spawning silver salmon. Arctic grayling were no doubt scattered there too, feeding among the salmon, but they were obscured by the salmon multitudes.

Days are very short at this latitude during the winter. The time was only mid-afternoon by watch but darkness was rapidly approaching. It was time for camp and a fire. I took a shortcut through a stand of spruce that was intermixed with cottonwood, birch, and aspen. Rock became birdy. There was the thunder of wings from a ruffed grouse! I swung the Browning superimposed and at the shot, a grouse tumbled. Rock quickly completed the retrieve. A brief hunt followed and a second ruffed grouse was added to the bag. Just before exiting the stand of timber, we flushed a brace of spruce grouse (locally "fool hens"). One fell to the shot. Roast grouse would be a welcome addition to fireside dining. We continued to camp, looking forward to warmth, food, and companionship.

A fire was lit and stoked to a blaze while the dogs were fed. Our dinner cooked as our cups of hot chocolate and tea, greatly enhanced by ethanol sweetener, were downed. We warmed to the occasion with memories of this and other day's hunts. Some of the most entertaining memories and conjectures had to do with Bird Creek, Alaska's internationally infamous watering hole and our neighborhood retreat, the Birdhouse Bar. There, the faithful bartenders served abundant liquid refreshment accompanied by an unlimited supply of jokes and pranks. The patrons, including on memorable occasions an abundance of snow bunnies and stewardesses, would be whooping it up. (Young men were sometimes unsure whether they were hunter or hunted.)

Previous camping experiences in grizzly country had made us very cautious. As we turned in, loaded shotguns lay at our sides. The dogs, now for the most part dry, curled up at the bottom of our sleeping bags. But sleep was fitful. We were often awakened by dog barks and growls. Ice chunks crashing in the river and sheets of ice shifting and shattering were, to the imagination, caused by big, long-clawed feet.

We rolled out with the delayed arrival of daylight. The fire had died to coals. Enthusiasm, like the thermometer in the zero degree air, was at a low ebb. A light skiff of snow had fallen during the night. We noted with more than passing interest the fresh wolf and bear tracks immediately around camp. The fire was quickly rekindled and we breakfasted on hot chocolate (without the benefit of "sweetener") and hot oatmeal. Cheered by the food and our anticipation of the day ahead, we then prepared our sandwiches for lunch.

We decided to again cross the frozen main channel of the river. This proved difficult. The fluctuating water levels had shattered the sheet ice, leaving leads of open water. Carefully picking an area of solid ice, we

Chapter 13 — *Grizzly Don't Fetch*

crossed the river. Some salmon moved in shallow riffles, their backs out of the water, with icicles hanging from their dorsal fins.

During our explorations down stream, we came across some moss-covered, dilapidated cabins. Sheltered in a stand of heavy spruce, these cabins were probably way stations on the old Iditarod trail. The site choice was no accident. Salmon were an important source of food for humans and dog teams. Old-timers, becoming bored by a steady diet of moose, salmon and sourdough bread, also likely shot some ducks.

As the morning passed, we worked back upstream. It doesn't take mallards long to wise up. Fewer ducks were jumped than during the first day's hunt and there was much less shooting. The birds taken were shiny and handsome, in full winter plumage with legs vividly red. Later cleaning revealed the very fat birds had been dining on salmon caviar. Much to the dismay of hunters who prefer birds with vegetarian diets, these birds would prove very poor table fare.

Toward evening, I observed a flock of about 20 mallards flying and circling on the far side of the river. They appeared to pitch in beyond some deciduous timber. The day was waning, with little shooting time left. It did not take me long to decide that I would cross the river and pursue them.

Arriving at the main river channel, I could not find a good place to cross, so I took a chance. Rock and I began to cross on marginal ice. The water hissed as it flowed below us. There was a splintering crash as we broke through the ice and plunged in. I was in the water up to my waist but there was no immediate danger. The river was shallow. Rock scrambled up and out the far bank. Freezing water added another coat to his ice armor. With some choice expletives warming the frosty air, I broke the ice as I crawled out to join my dog. I then pulled off my hip boots, poured out ice water, and wrung out my socks. My shotgun had been partially immersed and I wiped it free of a thin ice coating as I broke it open to remove and check both loads and barrels. Luckily, the barrels were ice-free.

My clothes were crusted with ice from the waist down. Good, heavy wool outer garments with polypropylene layering underneath had slowed the water penetration. The sun was still above the horizon and the air, even though only about 15 degrees F, seemed almost balmy. Camp was only a mile or so away. Being young and no doubt foolish, I decided to press on. "Rock, come on," I encouraged, "let's go find those birds."

Now creaking and crackling at every step, we passed through timber. Ahead, across the rocky, barren flood plain, there was an open water area where there should be ducks. We stealthily drew nearer. There was little to no vegetative cover. The trees we passed were now a hundred or so yards behind us. By crouching low, my silhouette was obscured. I did hear some considerable splashing upstream. I thought to myself, "one of my partners must be upstream bird-dogging for me."

Suddenly spooked mallards quacked as they sprang into the air. Five birds in a bunch were headed downstream straight toward me. I dropped two of the oncoming birds with the under barrel of my Browning. I thought to myself that I would give those survivors "what for" going away. But a trigger pull produced no disturbance to the air other than some exclamations from me. The firing pin for the over barrel was frozen.

As Rock completed the first retrieve of the double, I ejected the spent shell and loaded another round. There were many more birds somewhere close. In response to the continued loud splashing, I moved forward for a better view upstream, expecting to see one of my human partners.

I was rudely surprised. Two grizzlies were my bird dogs! Having ventured out in the fading daylight, they were busily fishing a spawning riffle about 50 yards away. The shotgun blast had not disturbed them. One bear was a beautiful blond with chocolate feet (known in Alaska as Toklat color phase), and the second bear was a dark chocolate color. That dark bear started my way, no doubt to investigate the finer aspects of duck retrieving. He was getting much too close.

That bear obviously had never learned to honor a retrieve. That being the case, I doubted that he would deliver to hand (and might even bite the hand). We would not attempt to find out. No doubt that remaining duck would be a welcome hors d'oeuvre with their chum salmon entrees.

No tree was handy for climbing. No bear could catch Rock unless he found it necessary to stand in my defense. A determined bear would have no problem catching me. Rock might turn one bear, not two.

In my opinion the two-shot shotgun is barely adequate against one grizzly; a one-shot shotgun measured by the same standard would be nowhere near adequate for the current grizzly situation. I deemed it wise to vacate the scene as discretely as possible.

Rock was intent on retrieving that second duck. "Forget that damn duck! Here comes the bear! Heel! Let's do like mother duck and get the flock out of here." I told him. Clutching the icy shotgun, with Rock at my heels, we beat a hasty retreat that quickly became a rout and finally an all-out run. As far as I know, the bears made no attempt to catch up and deliver my duck to me.

Rude Awakening

A grizzly spices Anvik River fish camp life, 1978.

The grizzly still came on! The crazed animal had taken three rounds of 00 buckshot and was still coming strong. In desperation, Jerry worked the action of the Remington 870 shotgun. There was one more chance and he would make it good. Focusing on the bear's open mouth, he pulled the trigger. There was a sickening click. The gun was empty!

When summer arrives on Alaska's salmon streams, life becomes frantic. Salmon in multitudes arrive at their ancestral spawning grounds, the end of their life cycle near. Their final acts are those of reproduction: digging nests, mating, and spawning. Creatures great and small are drawn to this surge of life from the sea. Salmon provide a yearly nutrient boost essential to many life cycles. Large carnivores drawn to the feed include wolves and black and grizzly bears.

The Anvik River is a clear-water tributary of the Lower Yukon River. This river is a major salmon spawning destination. During peak return years, upwards of 500,000 summer chum, and several thousand king salmon return to this system. Lesser numbers of pink salmon join the summer rush. Silver salmon follow in the fall. Within the stream and following the salmon, vast numbers of voracious aquatic predators gather in spawning areas. Their numbers include some Artic fish. Arctic grayling and Arctic char feast on salmon eggs. Within the side sloughs, northern pike lurk, ready to spring on passing juvenile salmon.

People of the Yukon are heavily dependent upon the river's salmon for subsistence. Fish catches above subsistence needs are harvested for sale and barter. Most human harvest is by the gill net fisheries at the Yukon's mouth. Lesser numbers of salmon are taken by fish wheels at sites along the river's mainstream. There is relatively little human fish harvest within the spawning tributaries, which are generally too remote and inaccessible to draw the attention of humans.

The success of salmon returns to major spawning grounds is important information needed for fisheries management. The Alaska Department of Fish and Game, responsible for the management of the State's fisheries resources, has enumerated salmon on the Anvik since Statehood.

During the exploratory years, estimates of relative salmon abundance were made from aircraft. The Department established a seasonal salmon counting station on the Anvik in the early 1970s. The original site was some 80 miles upstream of the Anvik's confluence with the Yukon. At the site, a weir was erected to channel salmon for visual counting. During the brief Arctic night, counting was made possible by a generator powered light system. By the late 1970s, counting had evolved to a sonar system.

Dense vegetation consisting of spruce, cottonwood, willow, and alder cover much of the lower Anvik's banks. Away from the river, permafrost underlies much of the land and the terrain is much more open. Trees surviving here are largely scattered stands of stunted black spruce. The Yukon is notorious for its bloodthirsty hordes of insects: mosquitoes, white socks, black flies, and the no-see-ums. These critters are especially abundant in vegetative cover. Wildlife trails abound in the timber and in brush. Frequent users of these trails include black and grizzly bear.

As water levels fall following snow melt and runoff in the late spring, expansive gravel bars are exposed along the river. Camping on open gravel bars diminishes probable encounters with wildlife. On these bars daytime breezes and a benevolent sun can thin the insect armies. Unwelcome four legged critters approaching camp are also easier to spot on the open bars.

At the Anvik River fish camp, our crew bunked in small, individual tents. They kept their sleeping tents carefully zipped to exclude most of the winged hordes. Wall tents were used for cooking and storage of supplies.

During summers, the only access to the upper Anvik is by riverboat or by bush aircraft. A skilled and bold pilot can land his aircraft on a gravel bar at low water. Even riskier, a floatplane can land on some stretches of the shallow river.

Jerry and Sally Lavoie left the Midwest behind to homestead on the Anvik. They cleared five acres of land and built a beautiful log cabin. With much work, they grew a very nice greenhouse garden. Among vegetables they grew were cabbages, potatoes, onions, and lettuce. The nearest small village (Anvik) is some 80 miles down-river. A winter trap line produced some fur they sold for subsistence money. They used a team of sled dogs for running the trap line.

I met Jerry and Sally my first year on the river. In time, they were recruited to join the biological crew. They welcomed the chance to earn a little cash, hard to come by on the river.

Early on, I became acquainted with their huge white malamute, Brute. Only about four years of age when we first met, he was already locally famous. Tremendously strong and weighing in at about 120 pounds of bone and muscle, he was an experienced and skillful fighter, and the undisputed, ace-high pack leader. Though much larger than the current size favored for Iditarod dogs, he was eventually to be on Jerry's race team for the Anchorage to Nome run. Brute was the only dog given the run of

Chapter 14 — *Rude Awakening*

his homestead. Stories of the big wolf dog chasing bear were numerous. Initially I was somewhat skeptical of these stories.

The bear most dangerous to man is generally the bear surprised at close quarters. While living in southeast Alaska, my yellow labs Kent and Big Ben prevented several such surprises, thereby preventing unwanted close-up encounters with grizzly.

One fall morning in Southeast Alaska I awakened before dawn looking forward to the day with dread. At daylight, I was airborne and a posse member, flying out in search of a man killer grizzly. At the attack site there were splashes of the victim's blood that could be seen on tree trunks 6 feet above ground. A bear-wise dog would sure have been a comfort as we struggled through head-high spruce thickets. Unfortunately, Big Ben had been left at home.

In many places, the cover was literally as thick as hair on a dog's back. The old logger had been taken in similar cover. He had surprised a bear at close quarters, thereby provoking an attack. We were heavily armed. I had a .350 Remington Magnum in my hands and a .44 Magnum on my hip. My partner was packing a .458 Winchester Magnum plus a sidearm. If we stumbled on a bear in this cover, there would be likely be time for one shot. If the worst happened, it would be a case of hoping your partner could pry the bear off your back.

My young Chesapeake, Rock, accompanied me to the Anvik River. In time he would be a famous Field Champion and hunt many species of game with me across the breadth of North America. In Mexico, village kids would call him the *perro grande.* As a young dog of about 85 pounds, Rock was no match for Brute. The big wolf dog did not take long to dominate. In time they became buddies and Brute passed on to him some of the finer points of routing bear. In the years to come, Rock's protection of me saw me through many misadventures.

And then one morning all my reservations about Brute's skills as a bear dog were dispelled. The day before had been our last day of the salmon counting season. A chartered plane landed with food and refreshment. It was time for a party. Afterwards, a partied-out crew crashed in the Lavoie's homestead cabin for what little was left of the night. Early that morning, I was awakened by incessant barking. No one else stirred. I turned over, trying to go back to sleep but the barking continued. For me sleep would not come.

In a fog, I made my way to the front door. Gazing through the door window, I witnessed an amazing scene. Shuffling down a path from the woods was a huge Toklat-color boar grizzly (blond with chocolate legs and feet). He was headed for the cabin and garden. The way was not being made easy for him. Old Brute was working him. Brute made short, swift charges at the bear, barking furiously. As Brute approached, the bear would rise, towering to over 9 feet on his hind legs. Brute would then unhurriedly trot back down the path toward the cabin. The bear would shuffle forward. Brute would charge again barking furiously. This scene was repeated over and over and over. Finally the bear had enough. Getting into the garden was too much of a hassle. He was not all that hungry for salad. With Brute continuing to harass him, the grizzly headed away.

I have always prided myself in maintaining clean camps. We had no wish to litter the wilderness and surely did not want to attract bear. All trash from the Anvik camp was burned and buried. During the salmon spawning season, bear were for the most part too occupied with dining on fish to be interested in human camps. We seldom had bear problems. But then our luck with bear changed.

That summer I had spent little time on the Anvik. I had no chance to bend a rod in the river's huge grayling and char and enjoy a few quiet evenings with the crew around a campfire. The Yukon was big country for me to cover and there was all that paperwork in Anchorage. Stories about bear activity around camp began to reach me.

Pausing during aerial salmon surveys, I made a quick stop by camp. A young grizzly, probably three or four years old, was hanging out there. Bears of this age are generally the ones that get into trouble with humans. The crew told stories about sightings and of a near encounter by the outhouse. Several times, shots had been fired into the air to spook the bear. The bear was becoming acclimated to human activity. I checked the garbage pit and confirmed that all trash was burned.

Each of the crew's sleeping tents was furnished with a pump shotgun. Shotgun magazines were to be kept fully loaded with four shells, usually a combination of 00 buck and rifled slugs. A .338 Winchester Magnum rifle was kept in the mess tent.

Jerry was getting a dog team together for an Iditarod Race. He had 12 dogs and would need more. The dogs, except for Brute, were kept staked out on a large gravel bar about a quarter-mile below the main camp. Brute had the run of the camp, and that freedom proved invaluable when he was able to save both Jerry and Sally from a determined bear.

It happened one morning as the counting season was drawing to a close, Sally rolled out early as was her custom. She went to the cook tent and heated up some coffee. After finishing her cup of coffee, she picked up a shotgun and headed down to feed the dogs. Jerry had been on night duty and was sleeping in. Sally reached the dog team and began preparing dog food. A large tub of fish and rice was put on to cook over hot coals.

Chapter 14 — *Rude Awakening*

Cracking brush on the far riverbank drew Sally's attention. A grizzly stood watching her. The bear started across the river. Sally picked up the shotgun. She was more than competent with firearms, but she had no wish to face down a grizzly. She hastily retreated. The bear crossed the river and was followed her! The tethered dogs went wild, screaming, barking, and lunging to the ends of chains.

Reaching camp with the bear following, Sally shouted in desperation for Jerry. Groggily shaking sleep out of his eyes, Jerry tumbled out of his sleeping bag and staggered out of their tent.

"Jerry, a bear is following me," Sally screamed. She thrust the shotgun into his hands as the bear charged. Jerry quickly fired three shots. The bear was pumped on adrenaline and would not go down. Jerry worked the action a fourth time and pulled the trigger only to have the firing pen fall on an empty chamber. "Damn," he exclaimed. He realized too late that the gun had not been fully loaded and was now empty. There was to be no fourth chance. Aghast, Jerry and Sally were frozen in place. Desperate thoughts flashed through their minds. The fury was almost upon them. There was no escape! The bear was mortally wounded and bent on a final act of revenge.

Suddenly there was a new roar as 120 pounds of white fury savagely launched and tore into the bear! The bear was diverted as Brute saved the day by turning him! Jerry and Sally now had another chance.

Jerry dived into the tent and came up with his .44 Magnum. The bear was pursuing Brute in vain, stumbling and obviously very sick. Jerry got close and a shot to the head finally ended the bear's struggles. It was all over but the later nightmares.

Brute would eat very well that night. He could even occupy Jerry's bed if he so wished.

Jay (full name Honeybear's Yukon Jay) poses with a very large king salmon caught by his owner Jim Mauney in Alaska in 1984.

Raining Ducks And Geese

Fall at Pilot Point results in great waterfowl hunting, 1979.

On a fine October day, an Alaska Airline jet delivered a party of six waterfowl hunters to King Salmon. The party included five humans and one canine. After landing, we received our cased shotguns that had been stowed in the forward cabin by a friendly stewardess, then we hurried to make our next connection. A chartered Beaver floatplane was ready to carry us on the final leg of our journey. Our destination was the remote location of Pilot Point, on the north shore of the Alaska Peninsula that projects into Bristol Bay.

The weather rapidly deteriorated after we left King Salmon. Our flight took us through rainstorm after rainstorm. Cloud shrouded peaks of the Alaska Peninsula were sometimes visible below us. A white surf line marked the meeting of storm tossed waves with the rock cliffs.

Finally, we were circling our destination. The sun was obscured by fast moving, scudding clouds. Below us, dimly visible in the limited light, lay a watery and windswept world. The island was sliced by inlets and broken by small ponds. The highest visible vegetation consisted of tall grass and rushes that were tossing in the wind. Two tiny and seemingly dilapidated gray cabins broke the natural landscape. We were to find another party of hunters already occupied one cabin. The other would provide shelter for four of our party during the next few days.

Our relief was great when our transport touched down, tossing up sheets of water. Rain pushed by the gusting, roaring wind rattled off our aircraft. Our outer gear of hip boots and rain jackets would be of immediate use in unloading our supplies. When our pilot killed the roaring engine, we became aware of the music of talking geese that filled the air. Small bunches of ducks swept by. A volley of shots echoed from down the island. Evidently we had spooked birds into shooting range of the occupying forces. Someone quipped, "it's raining ducks and geese."

"Let's get this gear put away," Larry urged. "I'm ready to put some lead into the air."

After packing our gear and supplies up from the lagoon, Larry, Tom and I quickly packed the gear into the small cabin while Lou and Mike searched for a small, high-and-dry piece of ground on which they could pitch a large tent they would use.

Buddies Afield — Alaska Days

We entered our new "home" through a loosely fitted door. The 8 x 10 foot interior sheltered a rough table and a set of bunk beds on opposite walls. But the steady dripping of slow water leaks was hard to ignore. A mixture of mud and water covered much of the floor. Outside, the wind raged and rain rattled on the cabin's roof and walls. Rain draining from the cabin's roof was directed into an open 50-gallon drum. This rain water would be our drinking water.

Back outside, we struggled to help our partners erect their tent in the gusting wind. The ground underfoot seemed to be more water than land.

"Maybe we should all crowd into the cabin" suggested Tom. "It's not much, but I think that in this weather it is a Hell of a lot better than a tent."

"We will be OK in our tent," insisted Lou.

With the tent up, we all became impatient to put some geese in the bag. "Let's head out and catch the afternoon flight, I suggested. "Rock is eager to fetch some birds."

We split up and headed into the marshes. Our strategy was to observe goose flight patterns and place ourselves into position for effective pass shooting. There were many geese and there was no need to sky bust birds; many flew into lethal range of the copper-coated-lead no. 2's and BB's.

Lou had hunted the Point before. He knew the terrain and where he could hunt effectively with his shotgun of choice, a side-by-side 20 gauge. He needed to catch birds coming over very low; and with no dog, his geese would have to be dropped into light cover to prevent loss. He and Mike quickly disappeared to his sites.

Tom, Larry, and I hunted more or less together. Rock had his paws and mouth full, so to speak, retrieving geese for the three of us. The daily goose limits were generous and possession limits were three daily limits.

Some two hours later with night descending, we gathered back at camp. We were all packing geese.

"You did all right with your little side-by-side, Lou," I commented, observing his limit of geese.

"The 20 works OK on geese if a hunter picks his shots," Lou said.

"Let's get out of this rain and get some dinner cooking. Looks like Rock is more than ready to dry out." Tom observed.

"We all need to dry out and my watch shows that it is now well into the cocktail hour," I agreed.

A lantern illuminated the cabin's small interior as Rock munched happily on a pile of dry Kibbles. Dinner slowly simmered on a Coleman stove. Sometimes a particularly vicious wind gust rattled the cabin and found cracks for admission. The camp stove's fire dimmed and flared in response to the windy gusts. I judged the humidity of the steaming interior

Chapter 15 — *Raining Ducks And Geese*

had to be approaching 100 percent. The closed atmosphere seemed almost toasty. We discussed the day's shooting over chilled beers retrieved from the porch.

After a couple of cold ones, Tom suggested, "Let's go check and see how old Lou and Mike are making out in the tent."

We pulled on rain jackets and trooped out to visit our partners. Mike unzipped the tent flap and we peered curiously into the lantern-lighted interior. Dinner was simmering on a camp stove. A low corner of the tent sported a pool of water. Two sleeping bags were rolled out and crowed on a very limited dry area. A large jug of red wine sat uncorked and looked to be considerably diminished. Lou sat contentedly plucking a goose. The open entrance flap admitted gusts of wind on which goose down eddied, falling between gusts like gray snow.

"Too bad you didn't arrange to get that other cabin," I ventured.

Lou, a good organizer of expeditions, had made the arrangements for this hunt. Some years in the future he would set up a wildlife photo safari to East Africa in which I was fortunate to be a member. On this safari I was to learn the pursuit of birds and mammals with a camera and telephoto lens could be just as challenging and rewarding as their pursuit with rifle or shotgun. However, my retrievers never did come to that point of view.

My comment seemed to rub Lou the wrong way. "Mike and I are doing just fine in this tent. Huh, Mike?"

Mike just grinned good-naturedly. "Shooting is good and I'm OK."

"Hey speaking of arrangements, you still owe 50 bucks from that time we entertained the blond and brunette sisters from Kodiak," Lou quickly reminded me.

"Yeah, I am really in your debt for that outing. But I don't think we entertained so much as we were entertained. I never have figured out if they were really sisters or if they were even from Kodiak."

"Did I ever tell you about running into the blond sister again?"

"I haven't ever heard that story before," Tom cut in. It was obvious that Larry and Tom were eager to hear the details of how I came to owe Lou 50 bucks. The conversation level deteriorated rapidly after that, bringing laughs all around.

Through chattering teeth I finally ventured, "I don't know about you fellows but I can think of better places to tell war stories than standing in pouring rain."

Returning to our cabin in the darkness, we passed the neighboring cabin. A large, brown form huddled on the front porch completely exposed to the elements. The hunters had apparently refused to share their shelter with their Chesapeake retriever.

Inside our cabin, Rock was curled in a dry corner shivering slightly in his sleep. His fur would more or less dry overnight and he would be ready for more action in the morning.

"I cannot imagine how some hunters could be so thoughtless as to hunt their dog hard all day in this weather and then make him spend the night outside." I voiced my indignation once inside. "I don't care how big and tough they are, any dog has a limit of how much exposure to cold water and weather he can endure."

"Pretty poor sports," agreed Tom.

"Some fellows shouldn't have a dog," Larry allowed.

We rolled out next morning in the blackness of predawn. Water was quickly heated and hot beverages and pastries cheered the crew. Rock, now dry to the touch, munched contentedly of a fresh supply of chow.

As we pulled on our damp, soggy rain gear and our hip boots, Tom expressed a premonition, "we are really going to get them today, fellows."

Action started early as the eastern sky began to brighten. Sunlight tried to penetrate the racing clouds and rain fell only lightly. As Lou and Mike quickly disappeared to some secret destination, three large white birds materialized from out of the mists. I realized too late that these were not seagulls or swans. They were snow geese.

The snows were low enough but too far away for either Larry or I to attempt shots. Tom, some 50 yards away, would perhaps have a chance. His ability at making long pass shots was legendary. We were soon to witness shooting that justified the stories we had heard. His 12 gauge boomed three times and three snow geese dropped from the sky. Rock got into the action as he rushed to retrieve a goose from the high grass.

Rock delivered the bird to me as we made our way over to Tom. To my amazement, Tom already had the other two white geese in hand. The big brown dog from the other cabin stood at his side.

"Some shooting, Tom. I see you have made a friend."

Larry observed, "you sure didn't need any help from us to bag those."

"First white geese we have seen here. I had to show you fellows how it is supposed to be done. This is a nice dog," Tom said as he patted the dog's head. [Those three geese were the only white geese we saw during our entire hunt.]

"Too bad his owner doesn't seem to think so," as I remembered the dog shivering on the porch last night.

The rest of the day passed quickly as we tramped the marshes and selectively shot geese. By the day's end, the long strings of geese hanging along the cabin's outside walls were very impressive.

Chapter 15 — *Raining Ducks And Geese*

Rainfall had increased to a torrent as dog and human members of our party sought refuge under our meager but most welcome shelter. As we went inside, I couldn't help observing that the big brown dog still occupied his lonely, windswept porch.

Dawn of our third and last day to hunt promised slightly improving weather. As the morning passed, I seemed to be in the wrong place at the wrong time to bag the remaining geese of my possession limit. I returned to the cabin for a welcome noon lunch break. Tom was back with his limit of geese and Larry was one bird short of his.

After lunch, Larry studied a sack of plastic duck decoys he had put into our supplies. "You know, I think I have enough geese. I think that I will have a fun change-of-pace and set up for some of those greenheads that keep flying over."

Tom allowed that he would join in the duck project. "I'll show you how we blow a duck call in the Dakotas."

As we headed out to hunt, Tom steered by the neighboring cabin to pet the brown dog shivering on the porch. As we walked away he angrily voiced our thoughts, "I wonder if they are even feeding him. Anyone ever meet up with those people?" We all concluded that we had seen little of the mysterious hunters.

"I haven't heard them doing much shooting. Maybe they don't like getting wet," I observed.

"But they sure don't seem to mind their dog being wet and coming down with hypothermia or pneumonia," Larry concluded.

I helped my partners pitch decoys onto a nearby pond. A stand of high grass provided them with a makeshift blind. I told them, "good luck and have fun. I need to bag three more geese. Any ducks you can't reach in your hip boots, just leave them. I will then swing by later with Rock and pick them up for you."

That afternoon my luck and positioning in regards to goose movement improved. My Browning Superimposed accounted for the remaining birds of my possession limit. Rock, as always, was happy to retrieve more birds.

We arrived back at the duck pond to see several birds floating on its placid surface. "Time for you to go to work and get wet sure enough, Rock." I sent the eager dog to work. He needed little handling on the short water blind retrieves. Soon all the ducks were in hand.

Larry informed me, "those retrieves were the easy part. I hate to tell you this but there is a crippled goose in the marsh on the far side of the pond. He came down hard, I thought, but evidently was only winged and crawled out on the far bank to disappear in the tules."

"How long ago did you drop the bird?" I queried.

"Oh, a half-hour or so. If you don't want to send Rock, I don't blame you. It's very unlikely the goose can be found. May have traveled quite a ways by now."

I knew that Rock had his work cut out. The pond was about 40 yards across. He would have to take my line across the pond. Once across, I would handle him to about the location the goose was last seen. From that point on, the retrieve would be entirely up to him. He would be out of sight in high vegetation and there would be no further handling. Rock was an accomplished field-trial dog but this would be a much greater test of dog ability than any Open Field Trial Blind. He was also a dog of considerable and outstanding hunting ability. We would have to give the retrieve a try. Rock hit the water and was soon across and on the far bank, but he could find no scent.

"Maybe the bird landed farther to the left," Larry wondered.

My come-in whistle brought Rock back into the water. A short whistle blast then caught his attention. I gave him a hand signal to the left and he swam along the bank for 10 yards or so. I stopped him there with another whistle and gave him a back signal into the marsh.

Initially, there was splashing and crashing as the powerful Chesapeake bulled his way through dense stand of tules. The sounds of his movements gradually disappeared in the distance. Then, the minutes dragged by as we waited for Rock's reappearance. "Do you think he is on a cripple," Larry wondered.

I confessed, "I really don't know. There is a lot of bird scent in the marsh around here." We became aware of renewed splashing among the tules as their tops swayed. Rock was returning. Finally, he burst through the wall of vegetation packing a big, live, very unhappy goose.

"All right, Rock," Tom cheered.

"I'll give him part of my dinner tonight," promised Larry. "That was an impossible retrieve and save."

I proudly took the goose Rock handed to me and affectionately patted his big head. "Just part of our standard service fellows."

The following morning we were back in King Salmon awaiting arrival of the Alaska Airlines flight that would take us back to Anchorage. Some blue sky showed through the clouds. We took advantage of the wait to pose for and take some end-of-the-hunt success pictures. Rock, apparently non-the-worse from his recent days of extreme exertion, posed proudly with hunters and birds.

Kodiak Harvest

To Kodiak Island for great Sitka black-tailed deer hunting, 1981.

I kept hearing tales of the abundance and good hunting for Sitka black-tailed deer on Kodiak Island. Tyler, my buddy of many an adventure (and more than a few misadventures), set up the hunt. Our mutual friend, Jay Massey, told us about successfully hunting Kodiak blacktails with a longbow. But he also told us candidly that he kept a .44 Magnum handy in case of brown bear trouble.

I had hunted blacktail on many occasions in Southeast Alaska. Tyler had never hunted this species and neither of us had been to Kodiak Island. This was be a new hunting adventure for us both. We were primarily interested in adding to our winter's meat supply, but we were not averse to bagging a nice trophy buck or two. During years of high abundance, the Alaska Fish and Game Dept. sets generous harvest limits for Kodiak deer.

Our hunt was to be strictly no frills, economy class all the way. The transportation to the city of Kodiak was by an Alaska Airlines jet. To reach the outback, Tyler had arranged for transport on a mail delivery/supply flight with one of the bush flight services. One of their amphibious aircraft would deliver us to a remote salmon cannery, which just happened to be in an area of high deer abundance.

Our mid-November hunt found the cannery closed for the winter. Only security and maintenance staff remained. Tyler had come prepared, including in our equipment an inflatable raft for us to use as transport from the cannery to the head of the bay. He assured me that it had few leaks. Propulsion would be by us wielding oars.

Kodiak Island is notorious for a wide variety of winter weather including rain and snow, and then more rain. An abandoned cabin was to be our shelter.

Having heard tales of waterfowl abundance along Island wetlands, we opted to pack shotguns as well as rifles. Rock, my reliable Chesapeake hunting companion, was included in the party. Hopefully, he would help retrieve some ducks and maybe serve as a pack dog for getting deer meat to camp. He was also a proven bear alarm.

Areas of high deer usage are also home for the legendary Kodiak brown bears (a larger version of the grizzly). Bear sometimes become conditioned to rifle fire during deer season so that a rifle shot becomes sort of a "Pavlov dinner gong" signaling fresh meat is available for the taking. When a bear starts visiting hunter kills, deer hunting can become very interesting and spooky.

Southeast Alaska hunters frequently use deer calls with success. I had seen knowledgeable hunters successfully use a willows leaf or a sprig of grass to call deer. The drawback with such techniques was that sometimes bear came to the call. On this Kodiak hunt, we were hunting late in the season and snow had begun to accumulate in the high country. Most grizzly would probably be snug in their dens but there was no need to ask for trouble. Tyler and I refrained from this methodology. For the most part, we would still hunt in big, open timber from beach to snow line.

We arrived at Kodiak on a clear, frosty November morning. My dog, Rock, was happy to abandon the kennel he had occupied during the jet flight. Our bush flight was scheduled for mid-afternoon, so we passed time by wandering around Kodiak boat harbor. An amazing variety of both commercial and sport fishing vessels filled most berths.

Finally, jump-off time arrived. We quickly loaded our substantial mound of gear into the bobbing float aircraft. Our plane (appropriately called a Widgeon, given its amphibious mode of operation) was vintage World War II but still very functional.. Entrance into the aircraft was gained from the top of its wings. The loading downward into the fuselage was reminiscent of climbing into a floating coffin. With the aircraft fully loaded, its cabin windows were partially immersed in water. Rock a veteran of many bush flights, made himself at home on top of a mound of gear and supplies. Tyler and I strapped ourselves in as best we could. Twin motors revved loudly, windows became obscured by foaming water, and then we were airborne.

The flight outward over Kodiak Island was spectacular. Steep, craggy mountains dropped down to jewel-like inlets. Giant Sitka spruce and mammoth cottonwood trees fringed the seashore and ranged up the lower mountain slopes. Timber line started a few hundred feet above sea level. Open grasslands and alpine zone were buried under a blanket of deep snow. Our low flight often skimmed the high ridges on which we sometimes spotted mammoth bear tracks.

Touching down at our destination, we felt a surge of anxiety as the aircraft settled in and bay water surged above the windows, cutting off visibility. Water also dripped from the ceiling and ran down the windows inside. I consoled myself that this water was probably only from condensation. For our pilot, the landing was, of course, only routine.

On land, the first order of business after unloading was to inflate our raft. Daylight hours during late fall days are short and the afternoon was well along. We were anxious to head up the bay to find our cabin before dark.

With Tyler manning the oars, we proceeded up the bay. Clouds building over mountains to our west obscured the sun. As we approached tide flats laid bare by the falling tide, we were thrilled to see clouds of waterfowl take to the air and mallards were prominent among their numbers.

Chapter 16 — *Kodiak Harvest*

Whistling wings of diving ducks disturbed the quiet atmosphere of the bay. One flight of old squaw ducks veered our way, so Tyler unlimbered his side-by-side. He wanted a nice drake of this species for trophy mounting. At the boom of his 12 gauge, a drake plummeted from the air. Rock bailed overboard into the frigid water. Breaking skim ice, he had hard going hard but soon he was back to the raft with the duck and ready to be pulled aboard. We cursed enthusiastically in the icy shower of salt water liberated by his shaking. Small bunches of goldeneye, old squaw, bufflehead, Harlequin ducks, and scoter continued to vacate our bay for safer environs. At Tyler's shot, many more puddle ducks had threshed into the air along the flats. They had abruptly and ominously departed our bay.

"Good shot Tyler," I congratulated him. "Good work Rock.. We could have done without the shower though. Prospects appear good for some waterfowl hunting." Little did we know that with many bays to choose from, and no other hunters to move them around, few birds would return to this bay where they had been disturbed.

Tyler admired his drake, smoothing its plumage. "A good start for our hunt. Let's find the cabin. Night is well neigh and it looks like rain; and most important, it's past the cocktail hour."

About a quarter-mile short of the tidal flats, we found our cabin hidden in the edge of big woods just above the high tide mark. The cabin wore a heavy layer of moss. To say it had seen better days would be putting it mildly. A light mist of rain began to fall as we packed gear up the beach.

We pulled the empty but fully inflated raft into the trees and secured it with a heavy line. In future years we would learn the hard way of a grizzly's tendency to play with rubber rafts as a retrieving dog would with a rubber ball. Such bear play can result in a raft becoming considerably worse for wear. Without the raft, we would have a long, tough walk around the bay and back to the cannery.

We were encamped by nightfall. A hissing Coleman lantern lighted our operation and a camp stove roared as it warmed water for tea, which flavored with brandy, would go down smoothly. Rain was coming down in torrents and was whipped by the rising wind to slash against the sides and roof of our shelter. Leaks began to reveal themselves with steady drips. We rearranged our gear and us to the few remaining dry areas. Spare pots and pans were placed under the worst leaks. Cocktails were sipped while Tyler prepared a hasty dinner.

Anticipating an early rise for the morning's hunt, pre-bedtime ablutions were dispensed with and we rolled into our sleeping bags early. Rifles, with magazines loaded, and flashlights were handy in case unwelcome furry visitors came to call. Rock, our bear alarm, curled up contentedly along my side. We slept well to a chorus of drips and howling wind.

We awakened to a very black morning. Outside, rain still fell, while inside the roof still leaked. With dampened enthusiasm, we rolled out of sleeping bags that were now damp.

"Hard to get enthusiastic this morning. I did my share of hunting big game in the rain while living in southeast Alaska. We have only three days to hunt, so I guess we better bite the bullet," I concluded.

Tyler was somewhat more enthusiastic and soon had the lantern going. "I want to bag a couple of big bucks today. Time to be up and about. Our water catchers are about to run over. We sure don't need any more rain."

Brief excursions outside answered the demands of nature. The wind had dropped and the rain was now mixed with snow. The predawn light showed an inch or so of snow covering the ground. Mountains rising above the bay to our east promised a late sunrise.

Inside the cabin, water was soon boiling and hot chocolate made. We then consumed a quick breakfast of oatmeal garnished with raisins, brown sugar, and dehydrated milk.

"We may just have ourselves a good tracking snow," I observed. "Could make for good hunting. What say we split up and cover different country until we learn our way around."

"Fine by me," Tyler agreed. "Which way do you want to hunt?"

"I think I will hunt up toward the tide flats at the head of the bay."

"I'll head out the other way" Tyler picked up his rifle, chambered a round, and shouldered his pack.

I was working my way slowly through the dark, dripping woods when suddenly, and not far to my rear, all Hell broke out. Shots from Tyler's 7 mm rifle shattered the early morning stillness. It sounded like a small war. Tyler was either into a herd of deer or in a losing battle with a bear. Since I had heard no screams, I assumed it to be the former.

As I worked my way forward, the light conditions slowly improved. I could now make out very fresh deer tracks in the snow. Some of the tracks were quite large. Suddenly, there was movement in bushes ahead and to my left. The light was still poor but good enough to reveal at least three deer. They surged forward, spooked. "Damn, I was moving too fast." Branched antlers flashed; at least one of the deer was a buck and a nice one at that. Swinging on the fleeing buck, I made a snap shot. Flying hooves continued to crash as sounds faded in the distance. As a rule, I do not shoot at moving big game animals. In my excitement I had violated this rule. I experienced a sinking feeling that I had a wounded animal on my hands. It was fully light now. I forged ahead and found the trails of the fleeing deer. Sure enough, drops of blood speckled the snow. Now I must correct my mistake. Rock heeled at my side as he eagerly snorted the warm blood scent and wanted to surge ahead.

Chapter 16 — *Kodiak Harvest*

It seemed that I followed the blood trail for hours and the morning was waning. In a couple of places the weakening animal had stopped to rest and blood had stained large areas of snow crimson

As the day aged and temperature increased, the snow melted away. Tracking became increasingly difficult for the human eye. In areas sheltered by large spruce, the vegetation was free of snow. The tracks I followed intermingled with those of other deer, so I let Rock take the lead. The deer had to be close.

We pushed noisily through some light brush. A large buck sprang from his bed but I brought up the rifle too late. Trailing was resumed. The buck, hard pressed by us, circled toward the bay. "Surely he won't try to swim across," I told myself. We were now following a well-worn game trail. Large tracks and drops of blood showed now and again in patches of snow as Rock trailed unerringly. The trail now lay just inside a fringe of big timber that followed the shoreline. Waves splashed gently against the shore, just yards away.

Then I spotted a grayish-white patch, which contrasted with the brown of a huge cottonwood tree trunk some 60 to 70 yards ahead. I brought up my rifle and scanned through the scope. A nice rack of antlers materialized. The buck stood watching his back trail. A nearby tree provided me a convenient rest for my rifle. The cross hairs of the Leupold came to rest on the buck's white neck patch. At the roar of the rifle, he dropped in his tracks. Rock and I trotted forward eagerly and found a very nice, mature 4x4 buck. He had fallen scant feet from salt water. I admired the unique and beautiful wilderness in which this magnificent buck made his last stand. I then paused for a moment of reflection. The killing of a beautiful animal was a time for some sadness as well as celebration.

"Thanks for helping me out of the spot I got myself into with this buck," I patted Rock as he worried the carcass. "You are sure entitled to your fill of venison scraps but for now you must stay out of the way. Your job is to watch my back as I do the butchering."

Dropping my pack, I took time out for a quick water and lunch break before getting to work. Gulls cried over the open bay. Ravens were talking in the timber. On Kodiak, as in southeast Alaska, ravens work the hunter deer kills. A rifle shot was their call to dinner.

The deer was carefully boned out and antlers removed. I struggled to my feet under my now heavy, man-sized pack. Heading out slowly, I stepped carefully under the heavy weight of the pack. "Let's find camp, Rock. You take the lead and warn me of any big, brown, four-footed critters who may want a share of our venison." Tyler and I would have new stories to tell over cocktails tonight.

I arrived back at the cabin to find Tyler, bloody to the elbows, busily butchering. The ground was littered with assorted pieces of deer anatomy.

"With all the shooting I heard I thought that we were being invaded but I see that you must have been thinning the deer population," I prodded him.

Tyler paused in his butchering. "I ran into a whole herd of deer not 200 yards from the cabin. By the time the smoke cleared, I had four on the ground: two nice bucks, a big doe, and a spike. The fun was over in a hurry. I have been butchering and packing meat most all day. I see you connected."

"You had some shoot. With a limit of five deer, you are almost through hunting already. I bagged a good buck but I had to work for him. I fear that with all the gut piles nearby and fresh meat at the cabin, any grizzly out and about will quite likely look us up."

"I am almost caught up here," Tyler said as he bagged the last of his venison. "I will hunt for an outstanding trophy from here on out. Maybe we should chase some ducks this afternoon."

Our venison chilled quickly in the cool air. It would be stored in large plastic trash bags for transport back to Anchorage. Full bags of meat were piled for storage against a side of the cabin and then covered with a tarp. The meat would freeze as temperature fell during the night.

As the sun fell toward the western summits, we manned our raft and crossed the bay for the tide flats. Captain Tyler manned the oars with a will. I played navigator, directing "hard to port, now starboard." Our non-too-subtle approach across the calm bay spooked a few mallards. A variety of sea ducks again flushed from the bay. We were not really interested in divers but they were taking no chances. A seal surfaced to curiously watch our antics. A pair of bald eagles circled the flats, screaming in the fair sky. The sun began to slide behind snowy ridges and night drew near. No mallards flew within gun range. We headed in without firing a shot. Despite the lack of waterfowl, we were not at all unhappy with the day's hunting.

That night, we celebrated with generous cups of "doctored" tea. I fried a mess of liver and onions for dinner, made gravy, and served it all over rice. Rock turned up his nose at an offering of Purina Dog Chow. He only wanted to sleep off a stomach stretched to capacity with venison scraps.

As we departed camp in the early morning, I elected to hunt higher up the snow-covered slopes. Tyler stuck to the heavily wooded low country. Ascending, I found the snow rapidly became deeper. At first deer, spoor was plentiful and fresh. Feeding deer had pawed patches of low-growing, lush vegetation free of snow. By the time I gained a few hundred feet in elevation, the tree line lay below and vegetative cover had diminished to brush dominated by alder. Snow reached to my knees and was rapidly getting deeper. As I ascended higher, there were fewer and fewer deer tracks. I actually entered low-lying clouds and a light snow fell. Hunting the high country was out of question. Besides, no self-respecting deer would be found in the high country on a day like this.

I dropped downhill and quickly came across fresh deer tracks. A short while later, a nice doe stepped from cover. She would do nicely for winter meat. A head

Chapter 16 — *Kodiak Harvest*

shot added her to my limit. I quickly dressed and boned out the steaming meat. Butchering finished, the hunt continued toward the bay's head.

The day was well along when I crossed a set of outsize tracks and excitedly took up the trail. Rock quivered with eagerness at my side. The deer's tracks ambled through the open forest, occasionally penetrating a thicket. As the cover thickened, I proceeded with extra caution, carefully parting limbs and brush in my path. My guess was that the buck was looking for a doe.

I had been tracking for about an hour and had covered maybe a mile when the forest opened. I broke into the open and discovered the buck had circled up the valley to approach the tidal flats. I scanned the flats and spotted a large buck walking slowly across. The buck paused to sniff the ground for doe scent and he occasionally lifted his heavily antlered head to look around in all directions.

This was the buck I was after. He paused about 200 yards away, easy range for a .300 Mag. A dead spruce beside the trail gave me a firm rest. The 200-grain Speer bullet took him through the left shoulder, passing through his body. At the impact, he dropped in his tracks.

I reached the kill site and admired a very nice 4x4 buck. As I lay rifle aside and drew my Buck knife, Tyler emerged from the woods. "You beat me to that buck," my partner admitted with some regret. "I saw him crossing the flats and was planning my shot. I will give you a hand getting him back to camp. Good shooting."

We turned to the task at hand. With two of us, the butchering and packing went quickly. We made it back to camp with both deer well before dark.

That night, as we rehashed the day's adventures, Tyler admitted to passing up several small deer in search of a big buck. I was in a very happy mood as I drank fortified tea and reflected on the classic hunt and nice buck brought to bag.

"How do the Kodiak bucks compare to those from southeast Alaska?" Tyler wanted to know.

"From the bucks I have seen, I would judge the largest Kodiak blacktails to be somewhat heavier than those from Southeast. Also, I believe the antlers are somewhat heavier for Kodiak Island bucks."

The next morning, we awakened to raging winds and rain. Deer would be laid up in such weather I assured Tyler. We spent most of the day huddled in our sleeping bags, trying to keep dry and warm. Restless, with our last day for hunting waning, we finally ventured out that afternoon. My excursion was not very determined and was brief. Tyler's was somewhat more determined and longer, but both yielded the same negative results. As suspected, no deer were moving that day.

That night, we relived our successful last hunt of the year. "We sure had a good hunt, Tyler. We are a couple of deer or so short of our combined limit but we have plenty of venison to take home. We will have to make another hunt for that classic 5x5, double-fork blacktail. I just hope aircraft can fly tomorrow. We have had a long spring, summer, and fall of working and hunting in the Alaska bush. The enforced chastity and celibacy are beginning to get old. I am about ready for a spell in the relative comforts of my place in Indian. Anchorage's temptations and our infamous neighborhood Birdhouse saloon need our patronage. I wonder if any visiting stewardesses have missed us."

"I'm sure they have missed us," observed Tyler. "They probably don't realize it though. I'm more than ready for some social life and a few cocktails."

"Maybe next time around we should try hunting a week or so earlier in the fall before snow covers the high country," Tyler suggested, formulating future strategy. "It sure would be nice to hunt the high, open grasslands and see a lot of deer. I guess bear problems would be greater earlier in the fall."

Our future Kodiak hunts would be conducted on open grassland country in early October and both of Tyler's conjectures proved to be true. We would also each eventually connect with our wished-for trophy bucks.

"Speaking of grizzly, remember the Fishing Branch? I sure enjoyed watching grizzly fishing. Remember the big blond boar that liked to wade for his salmon and the almost black boar that performed high dives to catch his fish dinner? We were too close for comfort a few times," I recalled.

"No place like the wilderness of the Yukon's Upper Porcupine for bear watching. With only a shotgun, I did feel a little under-gunned at times. We were lucky never having to shoot," Tyler recalled.

"A .338 would have been a great comfort at times," I agreed. "That day the sow with two cubs false charged you and Craig continues to give me nightmares. I had to watch helplessly from 150 yards away. I kept screaming, trying in vain to alert you. The roar of rushing water drowned my cries. The shotgun I was packing was useless at that distance. Still hard to believe that she turned back and you two never saw her."

Our plane pickup was on time. But in future hunts to Kodiak, we would learn that on-schedule aircraft pickups in the fall were the exception rather than the rule. The weather conditions were notorious for altering flight plans. On one hunt, as we lay in our tent awaiting pickup, we were lashed unmercifully with 80 plus mile-an-hour winds, rain, and snow. Only our combined body weight kept the tent from becoming airborne. We were remembered and rescued two days late on that trip. The delay was caused by our original pilot being killed in a crash during a storm a day or so after dropping us off.

Springtime Hooters

After blue grouse in the rainforest near Skagway, 1982.

The word "hooter" in springtime southeast Alaska's rain forests does not have the connotation that is popular over much of the U.S. these days. The word has no reference to human female anatomy. To the springtime Alaska bird hunter, a hooter is a male of the blue grouse species. The term "hooter" has reference to the male bird's springtime call. The hoot is the male's method of declaring his territory and also attracting hen grouse in the mood for romance.

The male's strategy is to fly high up into the branches of a giant Sitka spruce. From that lofty perch, he then proceeds to emit his deep, resonant, and throbbing call or hoot. His haunting calls echo down from the steep canyon walls, announcing his presence far and wide. The hooting call is described in Peterson's Field Guide as "… about one octave lower than notes of Great Horned Owl; ventriloquial."

The State of Alaska provides for a spring season harvest of this second largest member of the North American grouse family. Mature male grouse can easily exceed 2 pounds in weight. It is the hooting male grouse that is the objective of these spring hunts. You could say that this is a northern version of spring turkey hunting.

The blue grouse meat is both white and firm. This grouse can make for delicious eating whether it is saluted, baked, barbecued, or fried. A single grouse will provide ample meat for two diners.

Interest in hooter hunting and harvest is low. The local sportsmen find trolling for salmon or jigging for giant halibut is much easier and certainly more productive springtime sport.

Hooter hunting can also be physically challenging. Often, steep and cliff-studded slopes must be navigated to reach the hooter's perch. The number of vertical feet ascended and descended do mount up. A hunter's physical condition is quickly revealed. A careless ascent or descent can lead to life-threatening falls. Weather can be very disagreeable, with spring rain and snow showers. A hunter will often find himself confronted with an almost impassable alder thicket or patch of Devil's Club. Interestingly, an old legend among the Tlingit Indians has it that the brown bear like to frequent the area beneath a hooter's tree.

Bucking a Devil's Club patch usually results in the hunter's legs, arms, and crotch being perforated with nasty stickers. These, if not removed very promptly, fester. Wives or lady friends seem to delight in playing nurse to the agonized hunter with needles and forceps. Giggles frequently meet his groans of pain as they remove these stickers. The fairer sex generally seem to delight in this punishment for any man who chooses to spend quality time in such foolish pursuits rather than with them.

Hooter hunting involves both tactics and planning. First the hunter must reach some good grouse habitat. Finding suitable habitat frequently involves walking miles along a salmon stream that courses from a heavily timbered valley. The hunter must sharpen his hearing to detect hooting above the wind and the rushing water. Hoots echoing from surrounding mountain slopes can be very deceptive as to origin. The birds seek to gain maximum range and effectiveness by calling from great heights. The preferred calling perch is frequently in the highest spruce just at timber or snow line.

Often, a hunter will climb 500 to 1,000 feet up a mountain slope to no avail. The stalking hunter may determine en route that the call was actually coming from the opposing mountain slope. Arriving at the suspected call area, the hooting may have ceased. The bird may have found himself a hen, he be feeding, or he may have been spooked. There is little possibility of determining the location of a silent bird. The frustrated and tired hunter must then descend to the valley floor and start all over again, climbing up another mountain slope.

When a stand of spruce containing a calling bird is reached, the hunter must then determine which towering spruce has the bird. The hunter then moves stealthily around and among trees, searching methodically with his binoculars. The very observant, careful, and also lucky hunter will detect some out-of-place movement, or an unusual outline, among the high, leafy branches. Often the bird, well camouflaged in the uppermost branches of a giant spruce some 80 to 100 feet tall is never detected.

Mike, a friend living in Juneau in the late 1960s, was a serious hooter hunter who preferred to use a scoped .220 Swift rifle as his blue grouse weapon. He also packed a Smith and Wesson .44 Magnum on his hip for bear insurance. On more than one occasion, I saw him demonstrate his considerable skills with a sidearm. Mike hunted country inhabited mainly by black and not grizzly bear. A sidearm is far more suitable for defense against black bear than against grizzly.

I sometimes pack a sidearm for bear insurance, but I do have little confidence in a pistol as potent bear medicine. However, when close-up, a large-bore pistol is certainly more effective than throwing rocks.

An accomplished Tlingit hooter hunter acquaintance from Ketchikan claimed to be able to effectively call grouse in by mouth. I never saw this

Chapter 17 — *Springtime Hooters*

demonstrated in the woods, but his hooter talk certainly did sound very impressive in a village bar.

The hooter hunter's equipment is similar to that useful for deer hunting in southeast Alaska and may include these items: a good, water-resistant pair of binoculars for spotting birds; sturdy, lug-sole mountain boots, which can be lifesaving; layered wool and polypropylene clothing to repel moisture and retain body heat; a light daypack for carrying an additional jacket and/or rain gear, snacks, water jug, compass, knife; and binoculars, fire starter, and extra ammo. Birds brought to bag can be secured in plastic bags and then carried in the backpack.

My preferred grouse gun was a good quality 12 gauge over-and-under. Often, the only position for a shot at a bird will be far removed from his perch tree. For taking the big birds at 40-60 yards, I preferred 1-1/4 oz. loads of no. 4 lead shot. When hunting country populated with brown or coastal grizzly, shotgun charges of either 00 buckshot or rifled slugs (or a combination of them) are a great comfort to have handy. With a double, the hunter can quickly switch from bird to bear loads.

I always had a faithful retriever companion at heel to share the bird hunt, make difficult finds, retrieve birds falling into cover, and discourage bear surprises. Very occasionally, a dog will find and flush a blue grouse and present the hunter a true wing shot opportunity.

Hooter hunting can become highly addictive to a small percentage of hunters. I thought that I had long since kicked the habit; that my years of living and working in the Alaska interior where there are no blue grouse had helped wean me from this mad spring pastime. But my hooter hunt years in Sitka, and later near Haines, were haunting memories.

One April, my traveling companions and I found ourselves by chance in a remote valley above Skagway. Hooting birds were far from my mind. Cathy, my lady companion, was very pleasant company and was most men's concept of a "hooter." My faithful Chesapeake companion, Rock, completed our party. We had flown from Alaska to the East Coast for early spring with family. On the return trip, we deplaned in Seattle, where I took ownership of a new pickup, and then we hit the long dusty Alaska Highway for the return trip North.

A side tour took us over the Chilkoot Pass by way of the newly constructed Carcross (Yukon) to Skagway (Alaska) Highway. The scenery as the highway descends from the spectacular alpine of Bennett and Tushi Lakes to sea level at Skagway is awesome.

Just west of Skagway, we decided to drive a logging road that followed a narrow valley shadowed by towering Sitka spruce, western hemlock, and snow-capped mountains. The drive began in late evening, with the brief subarctic spring night soon to descend. Some miles up the road, we arranged a hasty car camp. I kindled a campfire as a mixed light rain and snow fell. We broke out our winter woolies. Nearby a stream, banks full with melted snow runoff, rushed and crashed. Robin and thrush were staking-out territories with evening songs. The sweet notes of a water ouzel emerged from the nearby stream. Mating season was under way. With some luck, we would hear the call of wolves during the night. But suddenly I was aware of haunting calls echoing from the surrounding slopes. Blue grouse!

It just so happened that I had my Beretta over-and-under, a supply of shells, and a current hunting license. A check of the hunting regulations showed grouse season was open. Rock needed exercise as did I. Our ferry reservations for Haines were still 24 hours away.

As we ate a hasty dinner in the fading light, I broached the possibility of a grouse hunt the next day. My arguments stressed the gourmet qualities of the well-prepared grouse. Further, I assured Cathy that this would be a unique opportunity for her to observe a wonderful bird in its natural habitat and add to her life list of birds. I explained that tours of Skagway and the luxury of hot showers and restaurant dining should be changed in light of this unexpected opportunity. If Cathy's acquiescence was somewhat less than enthusiastic, I failed to take note in my own enthusiasm.

During the night, rain and snow fell steadily. Pale early daylight broke much too soon. Precipitation had decreased to a light drizzle. There was no snow accumulation at valley level, but treetops piercing through cloud shrouded mountain slopes were festooned with new, light snow.

Using great will power, I rolled away from my warm companion and out from among the cozy sleeping bags. My movement awoke Rock, who stretched, yawned, and was then ready for adventure.

I lit the camp stove and then put water on to boil. A hurried breakfast of hot tea and oatmeal was prepared. Rock was given his morning snack of Purina as our trail gear was assembled.

"Time to rise and shine. Daylight's burning." I awoke Cathy.

She sat up with a sigh, peeping out the truck windows at a soggy and dreary landscape. Observing the liquid sunshine, she slid back under cover. "You go ahead and have a good outing. I think that in view of the weather, I will just forgo an outing today. I have a good book to read and will be just fine here in camp. I'll go next time."

"A shame to miss this opportunity to add to your life list," I suggested in disappointment. And unfortunately, as is so often the case in life, an opportunity missed frequently never occurs again. Cathy and I never did hike blue grouse country together.

Chapter 17 — *Springtime Hooters*

As on so many adventures afield, it would be Rock and I together in the wilderness. The hunt would prove to be no walk in the park, but would be a very successful and memorable one.

Small boulders provided steps across the nearby rushing stream to gain access to the forest. Once across the brook, we then plunged into and were quickly swallowed up by dripping rain forest canopy. The dim daylight became even gloomier. Patches of alder and Devil's club grew where the canopy had been broken and opened by a fallen giant tree. These natural torture chambers were carefully avoided. Avoidance is relatively easy when ascending but unfortunately not so easy when descending. Newly emerged skunk cabbage sprouted in the wet areas. Old moose spoor was in evidence as the slope grew steeper. We continued our ascent as grouse calls echoed more and more strongly from canyon walls.

Climbing upward, I sometimes found myself using hands as well as feet for stability. In such spots, I envied Rock's "four-wheel drive." I was thankful that my shotgun, equipped with a sling, could be carried over my shoulder to leave my hands free.

Then up ahead and above us, the air seemed to throb and swirl with the calls of a grouse. We were nearing timber line. All-encompassing canopy gave away to increasing alpine openings that were broken by fingers of last winter's snow. Slide areas were overhung by alder and Devil's Club. Pioneer clumps of tall spruce penetrated this zone, eventually giving way to stunted hemlock.

I looked out across the valley. The level of light had increased greatly and occasional breaks in eddying clouds showed patches of blue sky, spectacular views of the valley far below, and jagged mountain peaks. The precipitation had practically stopped.

I paused, puffing to catch my breath from the uphill climb. We had reached and were standing among a final stand of spruce. Grouse calls now seemed to come from all directions. The bird was somewhere in the tree right above our heads.

"Careful now, Rock," I quietly calmed him with my hand on his head. I did not want to spook the grouse before we could locate him and get into position for a shot. "Sit," I whispered to Rock.

Quickly, 00 buck shells were removed from my shotgun and replaced by no. 4's. I shrugged out of my daypack, carefully anchoring it against a spruce bole as I dug out binoculars. The final search began. Around and under tall trees we circled. I methodically examined by eye, and then by binoculars, one tree and then another. Possible sightings were scrutinized, evaluated, and eliminated. At times the hooting ceased and time seemed to drag. Had my quarry flown and escaped?

Finally, I decided that the grouse had to be in a tree among a group of three, but he was not to be spotted from below. I would have to move away from the call tree and find an open view through surrounding trees and alder. With luck and careful observation, I would spot the grouse's profile among the branches, silhouetted against the sky. My first attempt at long distance spotting was to the left of the suspected call tree. I found no break in the obscuring vegetation. The same proved true from up the slope. I checked my watch. The spotting stage of this hunt had already covered over a half-hour. In a final attempt, I decided to cross a slide area that was surrounded by thickets of alder and Devil's club. Bulling my way through the thicket, I winced as stalks of compressed Devils sprang up and struck home. Stickers drove through my clothes and into my skin. One crotch shot really smarted and I struggled to keep my curses just under my breath.

Now about 40 yards out and up, I finally found a silhouetted view of the suspected perch tree. I brought binoculars into play. Another chorus of hoots echoed on the otherwise still mountain air. There—I discerned movement among the topmost branches of the middle spruce. There was no wind to move the limbs. The outline of a big bird now became obvious. I considered my options. There would be no closer approach or better shot. I would have to try for him from here. I knew from experience that my shotgun and loads were up to the job.

I carefully drew a bead on the grouse and pressed the trigger. The 12 gauge's booming sound echoed and reechoed from canyon walls. A huge bird lurched from the tree in a wobbly, 100-yard flight down the mountain. There was a crash as he fell into a tangle of trees and brush.

My part of the kill was over. Rock did not hesitate. He disappeared downhill with a rush. I followed his descent, slipping, stumbling, and even sliding through alder and Devil's club. Now I could curse loudly when a stalk hit home. I emerged from the thicket to see Rock heading back to me. He had a very large bird in his mouth.

"Good boy Rock," I loudly praised him as he completed delivery. "You made a save on that bird and made the day."

We made our way back to the base of the spruce where my backpack had been stashed. "Time for a lunch break and some water."

We had munched snow through the morning to alleviate thirst. I put our prize bird away and dug out our lunch of cheese and bread for me and two dog biscuits for Rock. We shared water from a bottle and a candy bar.

Air temperature had warmed up considerably. As we ate and rested, I heard distant rumbling and then watched as one avalanche after another cascaded down surrounding mountain slopes. "A man wants to be careful what mountain slopes he is hunting in the early spring," I reflected.

Chapter 17 — *Springtime Hooters*

"What a beautiful day Rock," I exclaimed. With success assured and energy renewed, it was now easy to ignore the constant drip of water from moisture saturated vegetation. Maybe we were lucky to be afield in cool weather. I recalled hooter hunts several years earlier in warm May weather above Haines with canine companions Kent and Big Ben, his son. The mosquitoes had been atrocious then. My reflections on our wilderness surroundings were interrupted. I became aware of some renewed hooting. Another cock bird was calling. The calls were from nearby timber and towards the west, but at a slightly higher elevation. I told Rock, "we had our work cut-out for us on our first grouse. Let's go see if we can find an easy one."

We worked up and around the mountain slope. Rock was into scent checking now and he walked reluctantly at heel as the early afternoon slipped by quickly.

When we rounded a slight ridge, the hoots seemed very near. We continued and entered a stand of stunted spruce and hemlock bordering open alpine. I became aware of motion among the lower limbs of a stunted spruce. Astoundingly, a grouse was calling from only 10 feet up in the tree. I raised the shotgun and shot quickly. Rock retrieved and handed me the bird. I told him, "Almost too easy old man. I don't know about you, but after the first ordeal, I wasn't about to pass up an easy bird."

Pulling out my watch for a time check I was amazed to find the day had so quickly passed. "Time to head down, Rock. We are overdue. Our partner isn't going to be happy about missing out on Skagway."

"Funny," I mused to myself, "how members of the human population not seriously into hunting have a difficult time understanding how the passage of time is altered for the sportsman afield."

We quickly worked our way down the steep mountainside. Whenever possible, I steered our progress to open timber while Rock roamed ahead. Most bears were probably still in hibernation, so I was not really very worried about bear possibilities. My shotgun was loaded with birdshot, and the no. 4's would work on a bear that was very, very close. Acquaintances had proved that point while hunting duck flats in southeast Alaska. No distant bear should be shot in self-defense.

Rock was now working frantically, nose to the ground. The sudden roar of wings shattered the air as a grouse flushed from ground cover. I instinctively swung ahead of the fast fleeing bird and pressed the trigger. There was a shower of feathers and the grouse plummeted to the ground.

"We are quite the grouse hunters Rock," I told him as I relieved him of our third large bird. "We now have our limit. We have the makings of some prime grouse dinners."

We arrived back at the road and our truck bedraggled, tired, and wet. Cathy was waiting patiently and did not glance at her watch too pointedly. "I heard some shooting. Will we be having grouse dinner?" I opened the full pack and proudly displayed our trophies.

"Picture time," Cathy observed cheerfully and hastened to the truck for her 35-mm camera. Rock and I posed and she snapped enthusiastically. "Wonder if hearing a multitude of hoots and seeing freshly dead birds will qualify me to add this species to my life list?" she joked.

"You make that call, Cathy. Sorry that we are late for Skagway," I apologized. "We can shower aboard the state ferry. The galley will have wonderful seafood chowder and cold beer is plentiful in the saloon. I have friends in Haines that we will enjoy visiting tonight. We will save our grouse for fancy dining back home in Indian."

I then asked Cathy a very important question, "do you by any chance have a needle and tweezers in your gear?"

"Of course," she responded. "Why do you ask?"

"Well, I have this problem that I am going to need help with." I then explained my problem in graphic detail. I swear I saw a gleam in her eyes as she quickly agreed to come to my aid. "I sure hope that you don't hold a grudge about us being late," I told her. (If she did, I just might find out the hard way.)

Some years later, I had occasion to hunt flushed blue grouse in Idaho's high mountains. The fall weather was ideal and Rock's son, Jay, did an excellent job of flushing and retrieving the big birds. My limit of birds was taken on the wing. I cannot say that I remember the challenge and thrill of birds brought to bag on that memorable hunt to be any greater than that of springtime hunts for blue grouse in Alaska.

Blizzard Birds

A ptarmigan hunt becomes a struggle for survival, 1985.

Winter had arrived in Alaska's mountains. Snow eddied and swirled on a frigid wind and the treeless landscape lay under a wet, white blanket. Ice crunched beneath my boots. The sun was setting, unseen behind the Mentastas, and daylight was fading rapidly. My field of vision had diminished to a few feet. My clothing was wet and ice covered and my boots were wet. Walking failed to maintain warmth. There would be no surviving this night on the frozen tundra. Where was the trail? I must find it before dark. I must find the trail to return to the cabin and I must reach the cabin to live another day. I slogged on into the storm and gloom, with the dogs following, their icy coats crackling. The clock was running and it was the eleventh hour.

I had awakened in the early morning to loon music that rolled me out of bed. A fun hunt for ptarmigan was planned for today. The panoramic view from the cabin showed a brightening landscape, but the sky was heavy with clouds. The snow-covered peaks of the Wrangell Mountains rising in the east were obscured by haze. Below, Jack Lake lay still as a millpond, disturbed only by a swimming loon. Beyond the lake the escarpment of frost and frost-burned tundra was broken by an occasional draw as it climbed darkly toward the southern horizon. And Sugarloaf Mountain loomed gloomily in the foreground with its 5,500-foot summit showing a light frosting of snow. Jagged peaks of the Tanadas stabbed the clouds to the southwest. Only the lower, glaciated slopes of 16,000 foot Mt. Sanford were visible.

Exiting the cabin, I released the dogs for a romp. They were quickly across the porch and into the brush. The thermometer registered slightly above freezing. At my call the dogs returned to wait impatiently as I dished out their breakfasts. "You fellows eat up because you are going to work today," I warned them.

Hunting buddy Rudy called through the door. "Breakfast will be ready soon. How does pancakes and bacon sound? Water is hot. Come on in and fix your tea and put a lunch together."

I assembled a lunch of bread and cheese for us. A candy bar was added for desert. A couple of biscuits each would be lunch for the dogs. There was no need to pack water; there would be plenty on the tundra.

Buddies Afield — Alaska Days

We lingered at the table, discussing plans over a second cup of tea. "Have some more pancakes," Rudy urged me, heaping my plate. "You are going to need the energy."

"You sure do a good job on sourdough pancakes," I admitted. "You are quite the chef. Those Arctic grayling that you cooked last night were wonderful too."

"It was thoughtful of you to help me catch those grayling," said Rudy.

"The weather looks none too promising today. This will probably be my last chance for a hunt this year. One of the disadvantages of working for a living is the limited time left for hunting and fishing. Sure you don't want to go?" I asked.

"I think that I will stick around here," Rudy decided with obvious mixed feelings. "I am not much of a wing shot and besides, I have projects that need doing here. We are past due for a big snow. Most waterfowl except for a few divers left the lake for points south some time back. The trumpeters left two weeks ago. The loons will leave anytime now. When big snow comes to this country, man and wildlife are wise to move out or hole up. A couple of aircraft and their crews entombed on the ice cliffs of Mt. Sanford will attest to that. Remember our last sheep hunt together?"

Neither of us would ever forget that hunt. On opening day of sheep season, August 10, we had hiked 12 miles into the Wrangell Mountains, both of us groaning under 60-pound packs. Nearing our campsite at 5,500 feet, we had stumbled on a nice, nearly full-curl ram.

"Don't shoot Rudy," I had urged. "There are plenty of bigger sheep around and you don't want to end your hunt so quickly."

That night a blizzard rolled in. We lay in our tents as the storm raged for two days. Chances for a successful sheep hunt had fallen to just about zero. We fought the snow back to Nabesna Road, arriving at the truck exhausted and subdued. A week later, Indian summer arrived and melted much of the accumulated snow. Rudy had no more time for hunting. Duty called him north to his classroom in Bettles. But I had returned to the mountains. My perseverance was rewarded with a nice ram.

"I would like to have your company hunting today, Rudy, but you may be wise sticking to the cabin." As we talked, I glassed the open country that was across the lake for big game. "I don't see any big critters moving right now."

"In the not too distant future this country will be included in the Wrangell – St. Elias National Park," I commented. "My feelings about this are mixed. I would like the country protected as wilderness but park designation will end my hunting here. You think that Nabesna Road will

Chapter 18 — *Blizzard Birds*

become the three-ring circus that Denali National Park has become along its road system?"

"As we both know, there could be grizzly, caribou, moose, or wolves out of sight in any of the draws out there," Rudy observed "They could move into view at any time. The scenery here is every bit as spectacular as in Denali, but large wildlife is harder to see and the hiking is tougher. I think it will be some years before things change much here. You are very lucky to have memories of hunting this country as you did."

"We are fortunate that you homesteaded this land and we could build this cabin as a base of operations. The 3,300 feet elevation here is the upper limit for year-round human habitation in Alaska. Transportation of building materials and building on permafrost have been challenges. You have added on and made this a real home. There is no more spectacular view anywhere than from your deck in good weather. You have used this location to turn-on a number of city kids and lots of adults to wilderness values. My mother will always have fond memories of the time she sat on the deck and vicariously followed our caribou hunt by telescope."

"Thanks for the kind words, James. Your mother is a wonderful lady and is always a welcome guest here. Now, let's get to this morning's business. You plan to hunt up the big draw that empties half-way down the south shore. I will load you and the dogs in the skiff and run you across. This will save your having to cross Jack Creek, which is probably high now. Boating will also save you a couple of miles of hard walking around the lake. You just bring me back some birds."

I hustled my gear together. The going would be mainly uphill and very strenuous. Alaska days are short in the late fall. I would have no more than six hours of good daylight for hunting. I did not plan to hike more than a few miles, so I dressed light to keep weight down. My clothing, layered to prevent overheating, consisted of polypropylene underwear, wool pants, wool shirt, polypropylene vest, and finally my canvas-shooting vest. I packed a light nylon jacket in my game vest for use as a windbreaker or for protection if rain or snow developed. Light wool gloves and a wool hat completed my outfit. The heaviest items of my equipment were my Beretta superimposed shotgun and an ample supply of 12 gauge no. 6 shells. I believed survival gear to be unnecessary. The country was wide open and I knew it well.

"Time to bite the bullet, Rudy. I'll see you down at the dock."

My canine hunting companions, as on many other hunts, were the best. FC AFC Rock Honeybear of the Yukon was the veteran of our group. He, like me, though slowed by the passage of years and many, many hard miles covered, was always game for a hunt. His son, Honeybear's Yukon

Jay, who in future years would earn the AKC title of Master Hunter, was in his prime and eager to take on any adventure afield.

We loaded up the skiff, which with passengers and gear aboard, was filled to capacity. Jack Lake averages about one-half mile across and is miles three long. Its waters are very deep and cold, even in midsummer. Lake trout and burbot make their home in its icy depths. They could be dredged up by fishing deep. Arctic Grayling fed in its shallows, and on a good day, they could be fooled by a dry fly. Now approaching freeze up, the surface water temperature was nearing 32 degrees. Lake shallows were ice-covered in areas protected from the wind.

Jack Lake is notorious for strong midday winds, as some boaters had learned the hard way. As we headed across, the wind was picking up from the southeast, pushing up light waves. With our load, we did not challenge the open lake but hugged the shoreline. Our Chesapeake companions would not hesitate to swim the frigid waters for a duck; but Rudy and I had no desire for an icy bath.

The lakeshore rose abruptly from rocky beaches. A sparse forest of stunted spruce interspersed with occasional cottonwood and aspen grew immediately around the shore. We cruised along slowly as we watched the hillsides for big game.

Reaching our destination, we then quickly unloaded the boat. A small stream trickled into the lake from the draw where we had beached. A light rain had begun falling.

"Are you sure you want to hunt today?" Rudy asked.

I was eager to give it a go. "I don't plan to go far," I assured him. "I will stick to the draw. The gravel bed underfoot there will make for easy walking for me."

"When you do get back to the shore, shoot a couple of times," Rudy advised. "I will run over in the boat and pick you up. I hope you find lots of birds."

"Let's go, dogs, the daylight is burning. We have country to cover and we do not have much time to do it." The dogs did not need my urging and immediately they plunged ahead into the brush.

We quickly worked our way up through the fringe of timber. Canadian Jays (camp robbers) fussed at our intrusion. Snow buntings made rustling sounds feeding in the brush. The sound of waves and tinkling ice striking the lakeshore were no longer to be heard. Even the humming of Rudy's outboard crossing the lake faded in the distance. I heard no more loon call. Perhaps they had migrated? A red squirrel interrupted the quiet, adding to his winter cache of cones and fussing angrily at us from the top of a nearby spruce. We were headed for wilderness adventure!

Chapter 18 — *Blizzard Birds*

Moving up the draw, we steadily gained elevation and the trees were left behind. Woody cover was now restricted to banks and bottoms of draws. I negotiated dense stands of alder by following game trails. A dense stand of willows grew along the stream course and moose had heavily browsed them. Abundant moose and caribou spoor was on the ground. The surrounding hillsides were alpine tundra but the vegetation covering this tundra was no higher than on a well-tended golf course. I knew it was best to avoid certain lower areas; they were underlain by permafrost, marked by Indian cotton waving atop hummocks of vegetation. Terrain such as this conceals leads of open water.

Bear berries were abundant on the tundra. Low-bush blueberry bushes, growing thickly in sheltered areas, were heavy with frost wrinkled fruit. There was much good ptarmigan food here. There should be birds to take advantage of the feast.

The dogs were working very eagerly now. I soon spotted ptarmigan droppings in the willows. Now birds were running ahead of the dogs! Then, the air was full of brown and white forms erupting from the brush with angry, guttural mutterings! I swung ahead of a bird. At the boom of the 12 gauge, feathers filled the air and I swung on a second bird. The bulk of the large covey flew on up the draw.

"Good work Rock. Way to go Jay," I praised them as each delivered a bird. "A nice double and an excellent beginning for today's hunt. We will have lots more action before the day is over. There were over 40 birds in that covey."

I examined the birds. They were nice, heavy willow ptarmigan. One bird's plumage was winter white while the second bird's plumage was the transitional brown-and-white. Past hunts had taken me to the top of nearby Sugarloaf where I had shot rock ptarmigan. But clouds obscured that summit now. I would not hunt Sugarloaf today.

We hunted on. Singles, doubles, and a few large coveys of birds were found and flushed. Sometimes, a missed shot left me muttering but for the most part my shooting was good. These birds had obviously never seen a human hunter. Some would flush only when chased by the dogs. A good pointing dog would be a disadvantage today. The take and weight of birds in my game vest mounted. The limit for ptarmigan in Alaska was a liberal 20 birds in those days.

Occasionally, we came across the spoor of grizzly. In the brush we found the scattered bones and head of a very nice double-shovel bull caribou. This animal had probably fallen prey to a pack of wolves as a food kill. "I would have enjoyed bagging that bull," I thought. "Oh well, predators must eat too"

Buddies Afield — Alaska Days

The caribou skeleton brought back memories of a hunt here years ago. My companions at that time had been my yellow Labs, Big Ben and his sire, Kent. I had followed a small band of bull caribou far over the tundra. Catching up to them, I surprised the largest bull. With many pounds of meat to pack, the dogs were drafted into service.

I had learned to dog pack from Indians of Yukon's Kluane Lake. The villagers supplied me with my first dog pack, a heavy affair of canvas and moose hide. At the end of that hunt, I staggered under a 100-pound pack. My dogs moaned as they took turns packing 30 pounds each. Crossing the tundra under that overwhelming weight was really an ordeal but it was accomplished with the aid of good knees and a strong back (and perhaps a weak mind). I would not be tempted by such a feat again. Accidents had since taken their toll on my knees, and I hoped I was somewhat smarter.

The morning passed quickly as rain changed to a fine snow. My watch showed the time to be past midday. We found shelter from the cold, biting wind in the lee of a steep cut-bank. My improvised seat on a flat, smooth rock would keep me off the wet ground. A nearby pool of crystal-clear water would quench our thirsts. "Time for a break, dogs. We will have our lunch and count our take."

The temperature was falling as I slipped into my last layer of clothing. The bird count was a baker's dozen. We had enjoyed a very good morning. The number of shots fired and birds brought to bag were not too dissimilar. The dog work had been excellent. Finding, flushing, retrieving, and also occasionally chasing down a crippled bird had all been accomplished with some dispatch.

The rest was welcome and our lunch energizing but we did not linger long. Movement was necessary to maintain body heat. "Let's hunt a little farther, we are having too much fun to quit now," I voiced my feelings.

The upward climb gradually steepened. As we gained elevation, there were but few scattered clumps of willows growing immediately along the stream. The landscape was bleak tundra broken by rockslides. Ptarmigan were flushed occasionally but were difficult targets through the thickening snow. As a small bunch of birds flushed, flying to my left, the air over my head was filled by whirring pinions. I watched, fascinated, as a gyrfalcon closed on the fleeing birds. Prey and predator both disappeared over a low ridge. I wished him good hunting. I recalled another hunt that included a golden eagle's awesome stoop on flushed ptarmigan.

I paused, observing the landscape. The Mentasta Mountains rising north of Jack Lake were no longer to be seen through the thickening snow. Jack Lake and the surrounding band of dark green spruce showed only dimly in the distance. Only the lower slopes of nearby Sugarloaf were

Chapter 18 — *Blizzard Birds*

visible. The game vest sagged heavily from my shoulders. We were a bird or two shy of a limit but I had hunted enough.

The wind blew gustily and I doubted that Rudy could safely bring the boat across the lake as planned. If we cut across country, we could save several miles. Hiking the tundra would be tough but the total distance to cover should be only a couple of miles. We had plenty of time to complete the return hike before dark. "Time to head for the barn," I addressed the dogs. We headed back, losing elevation rapidly.

Snowfall was now very thick. The lake had disappeared, obscured by the shifting white curtain. The ground underfoot was white. This was a serious storm. Moist air from Prince William Sound had pushed north into the interior and collided with an Arctic front.

I was no longer able to get my bearings, but if I continued walking downhill to the north, I would reach the lake. I would then follow the shoreline around to the cabin.

In the whiteout, terrain and vegetation changes were not easily detected. I stumbled into wet areas and had no choice but to continue across. At first, I tried unsuccessfully to balance on hummocks slick with snow. The effort was futile. My boots became saturated and my pants soaked to the knees. Small basins containing tundra ponds materialized out of the mist. These basins had to be negotiated. The frozen, snow-covered ponds were to be avoided. The ice cover was thin yet and would not support my weight. Protected by high, steep banks, there was shelter from the wind in the bottoms of such bowls and the snow fell gently, generating a false sense of security. The urge to rest was almost overwhelming. It had to be resisted. Slipping and sliding downhill, and then struggling uphill, I experienced vertigo in the raging storm.

The afternoon had passed. I should have reached Jack Lake long ago. I should have reached trees. I thought wishfully about the compass I had left behind. I had packed no matches or lighter, but then there were no trees for a fire. The occasional bushes encountered were soggy with snow and would have been much too wet for burning.

If I did not make it back to the cabin tonight, Rudy would organize a rescue attempt. My Indian friends of the Nabesna Clan, Dick from Sportsman's Paradise Lodge, Bertrams from Silvertip Lodge, and the Ellis family would all turn out. But there could be no search efforts until the storm had passed. Staying put to wait out the storm, in my wet, inadequate clothing with no fire was not a viable option. Could I communicate to my dog companions my wish to return to the cabin? They could no doubt find the way. However, they expected me, as pack leader, to lead. Realistically, by the time they became hungry and cold enough to seek shelter I would likely not have the strength to follow. They would stay with me, sharing body heat to the bitter end. If it cleared tonight, I could navigate by the North Star but that was an unlikely event and it might be too late. If I was to get out of this situation I had gotten myself into, it would be my own doing and I must keep tramping.

To the east and south, unbroken wilderness extended for hundreds of miles. The Alaska Highway lay west of the Copper River, about 30 miles too far away. Realistically, my only option was finding Nabesna Road to the north. Thinking back, I was certain that my movements had been basically down hill. Likely, I had drifted southwest of Jack Lake. I recalled a tracked vehicle trail that accessed Tanada Lake from Nabesna Road. This trail left the road a couple miles west of Jack Lake and then ran south. If I continued descending to north or northeast, I should cross either Nabesna Road or the trail.

I chuckled to myself with one lighter thought. There was certainly no danger of an unwanted encounter with a grizzly tonight. No big critter in his right mind would be out in this storm.

After a seemingly interminable period of slow progress through the storm, I came upon an unnatural appearing bank. Was this bank formed when tracked vehicles cut into the tundra? Stooping low, I thought I could discern tracks showing faintly through a blanket of ice and snow. I turned to my right following what I hoped was a trail to the road. Time passed as we covered country. Finally, definitely discernible vehicle tracks appeared. Our footfalls broke through ice as we slogged through numerous bog holes marking the ATV trail. Were we heading north towards the cabin or south into wilderness?

Finally, the trail reached willows and continued through. "Hooray," I shouted into the storm. Night had arrived but we were standing on the Nabesna Road. I turned toward the east and Jack Lake Trail. The white, smooth road surface, outlined by dark brush, was easy to follow. I could now find my way by Braille if necessary. Only a couple of miles separated us from shelter and warmth. "We are on the beer and dog chow run now, doggies," I noted as I picked up the pace.

Arriving at Jack Lake Trail, we turned right, heading south. Finally, over the roar of the wind, waves were heard splashing in the night. We had reached Jack Lake. As we followed its welcome shore, I could smell wood smoke on the wind. We struggled up the final pitch of the trail as we surmounted a final hill. Light from the cabin windows reflected through the falling snow. The dogs surged eagerly ahead. Our disturbance when we reached the porch very soon had Rudy standing in the open cabin door. We had made it!

Chapter 18 — *Blizzard Birds*

"Wonderful to see you. Come in," he exclaimed. "I was worried." Studying me he noted, "You look to be in bad shape. Get out of those wet clothes and stand by the woodstove." He handed me a towel. "I have a stew on cooking. Don't worry about the dogs, I will feed them. Let me have your wet clothes I will hang them up to dry."

Bundled in dry clothes and dry slippers, I hugged the stove absorbing warmth. A steaming mug was thrust into my hands.

"Wonderful," I sipped appreciatively. "Hot buttered rum."

The storm raged through the night. I awoke in the midmorning, forced from my sleeping bag by the call of nature. The dogs stretched lazily. The light outside was dim and snow was still falling on a winter landscape. No stars would have been visible last night. No aircraft would fly the Wrangells this day. There would not have been a rescue mounted today.

Rudy was up and cooking as the woodstove roared. "How about eggs and bacon for brunch?" he asked.

"Great, I'll put the dogs out for a romp in the snow and make some snow yellow." The porch thermometer registered in the mid 20's.

"The tea water is hot. Pull up a chair. Toast will be ready in a minute." Rudy, always the gracious host, joined me at the table. "You might as well plan to stay here for a few more days. I am retired and have no place I need to go. You will not be driving to town until the roads are cleared Clearing will take a day or so after the storm has passed. Maybe Ellis will run his Cat down and clear Jack Lake Trail. I have plenty of food laid in. For entertainment, you can help yourself to my library. Judging by the weight of your game vest, you got lots of birds. I will broil up a couple apiece for us tonight. We can drink some of the beer you brought."

"Thanks for your most generous offer, Rudy. I accept. I will pass the time warm and contented. Your library must be the most extensive private book collection in the Wrangells. This company is the best."

"There was little I could do to help you after the storm moved in yesterday. Jack Lake became too rough for my small boat. I fired a couple of shots at dark, hoping to give you direction. You probably could not hear them above the wind. Would you make that hunt again?" he queried.

"The hunt was wonderful but the trip back was a frozen version of Hell. I expect it will be a while before I try such a hunt again and then only in good weather. I will also pack a compass, lighter, and fire starter. You know that this is one of my favorite places anywhere; but I wouldn't care to over-winter as you sometimes have. The winters would be much too long, cold, and dark. A good woman for company would greatly help the time to pass, but as we both know, few would be up for the experience."

Rudy grinned slyly, "I do have plans. I am returning to Thailand in the late winter."

"You old fox," I teased. "I might have known. I expect the late winter will find the dogs and me in Florida. You and I are getting to be a couple of regular snowbirds."

The storm continued to rage throughout the day and the temperature continued to drop, approaching zero.

Next morning, I was awakened by profound quiet. The wind had finally ceased. I glanced out to see stars shining in the southern sky. Overhead and in the North, the Northern lights played brilliantly and illuminated a frozen, snowy landscape. Jack Lake was frozen and snow covered, but the storm was over.

I snuggled back into my warm bag. My dreams of dogs flushing ptarmigan against Alaska's snowy mountain peaks faded to those of dogs sitting in a palm frond blind on Florida's Lake Okeechobee. In front of that blind, ring-necked ducks strafed our decoys. Those dreams would become reality as we traveled south where the dogs and I would enjoy many more adventures afield.

Photos Of Buddies And Hunts

Buddies Afield — Photo Gallery

(TOP) Jim Mauney's dogs accompany him on all outdoor adventures, even fishing trips such as this one that resulted in a nice brace of Alaska salmon. (BOTTOM) Jim gives Simba a helping hand in going up one of the 13 ladders on the Trail of 13 Ladders on Grandfather Mountain, NC that lead to a cave that prehistoric man once occupied. That's Wily watching from the top.

Chapter 19 — *Photos of Buddies and Hunts*

Mrs. Eloise Mauney, the author's mother, shown here in 1992 in Mission Valley, MT with three of Jim's dogs, Simba, Tip, and Jay.

Buddies Afield — Photo Gallery

(TOP) Ms. Diane Mazy, an accomplished artist as well as a hunter and Chesapeake enthusiast, with three favorite companions (Roby, Riffle, and Yeller) on a crisp Idaho day. (BOTTOM) Jim Mauney trains his dogs to help with the packing in and out on hunting trips. Shown here is Jay with a caribou that made some fine winter meals.

Chapter 19 — *Photos of Buddies and Hunts*

(TOP-L) Taken in 1968, Brandy, Kent, and Judy Mauney (author's wife at the time) at Totem Pole National Forest, AK. (TOP-R) A fully armed Jim Mauney in 1979, ready for bear or ? (BOTTOM) A 1984 family lineup of (l-r) FC AFC S&S's Sunshine Meg (mother); FC AFC Elijah's Sunshine Sally (grand-mother); FC AFC Rock Honeybear of the Yukon (father); and son Honeybear's Yukon Jay MH (Nat. Master Qualified).

Buddies Afield — Photo Gallery

(TOP-L) It was 1965 when author Jim Mauney took his first Canada geese at Kent Island, MD. (TOP-R) Rock is standing guard over a nice blacktail buck shot by Jim Mauney in 1977 on Kodiak Island, AK. (BOTTOM) Chesapeakes and their owners are ready for the Alaska All-Breed Trials in 1992.

Chapter 19 — *Photos of Buddies and Hunts*

(TOP-L) Rock shows the versatility of a well-trained retriever as his soft jaws deliver a large salmon to owner Jim Mauney in 1979. (TOP-R) Jim Mauney and Rock enjoyed a fine day on Alaska's Anvik River in 1979 as shown by very heavy results. (BOTTOM) While on a ski trip in 1982 to Twenty Mile Valley, AK, Jay and father Rock rest and talk it over.

Buddies Afield — Photo Gallery

It was May 2005 when Jim and Gene Mauney (on the left above; author's only sib) and boyhood friend Bill Hart (at right above) hiked the general area of Linville Gorge, NC.

Book II – Trips Outside Alaska

Nothing Could Be Finer

Fall hunting and fishing in North Carolina, 1970-1980.

Sugar Mountain Grouse

Rock and I had both gotten up for an early start in anticipation of a day afield. Night faded to a perfect fall morning with the air cold, clear, and almost intoxicating. Under the pale Carolina sky, fields lay nipped by frost. Leaves of oaks and maples illuminated by the morning sun glowed yellow and red. That great old song, "Nothing could be finer than to be in Carolina in the morning," had real meaning for me this October morning. We were off to pursue ruffed grouse in the Carolina Appalachians.

I had hiked and hunted this country and fished its streams for a considerable portion of my life. Through the years, both the countryside and I had seen many changes. In the near future there would be many, many more. Steep mountainsides would be cleared of pine and spruce for new ski resorts. River bottom hardwoods would be felled for additional golf courses. Alpine pastures and stands of beech trees would be altered with the insertion of new houses. High-rise housing units would tower to mar natural mountain contours. Ruffed grouse habitat and hunting coverts would be lost.

Early morning found me driving beside a gurgling mountain trout stream. The road had started out as a typical, winding and curvy two-lane mountain road. As the miles passed, we ran out of asphalt and the road quickly deteriorated. Finally, we were bumping up a steep, one-lane dirt track that twisted through encroaching "laurel hells." I carefully steered over or dodged large rocks that could rupture the station wagon's oil pan.

Rock was glad to reach our jump-off point. I was just relieved to get there. Puffing uphill, my efforts were made exaggerated by the thin air of 4,000 to 5,000 foot elevation. Young Rock eagerly explored the woods and brush for exciting smells, seeming not to notice the increased demands on his energy. Our path led us up the edge of an alpine meadow that then climbed to a high pass. Once there, we entered an open stand of beech trees that was broken by an occasional towering hemlock or white pine and bisected frequently by impenetrable stands of rhododendron. Searching among the beech, Rock became animated as he picked up fresh, hot bird scent. I shortly discovered chicken-like scratching and droppings among the forest litter.

Western and eastern grouse seem to be different classes of game birds when flushed. The western variety of grouse tends to fly into a tree and sit, curiously watching the hunter. This behavior results in many winding up in some hunter's skillet. The eastern grouse, when flushed, almost always flies off, dodging between trees and brush. Only a skillful or lucky wing shot will bring him to bag.

Having hunted ruffed grouse in Alaska and western Canada, Rock knew his game. As he worked a scent trail upward, my excitement began to mount. My anticipation was interrupted by the suddenly roar of wings and a flash of brown ahead. Rock had flushed a grouse. I swung my Daly superimposed as the bird dodged frantically through the timber and touched the trigger. An instant later I heard the thump of bird and ground colliding. Rock quickly completed the retrieve.

Glancing at my pocket watch I noted the morning had somehow slipped by. With a successful day assured, this was as a good time for lunch as any. I picked a moss covered rock for a seat and propped my shotgun against a forked tree. A nearby spring, its bottom glittered with sparkling quartz pebbles and iron pyrite rich sand, provided us with an abundance of sweet water. Several small larval salamanders were observed on the sparkling sand. For them, the spring's perpetually chilly water was home. I polished off a sandwich and Rock finished his dog biscuits in short order. The warm, sunny woods inspired a short rest. Rock scratched out a nest in the leaf litter and dozed fitfully, while I reflected drowsily in our pleasant surroundings.

My friend Bob, a rapidly rising young executive, unfortunately could spare little time for hunting. On a few occasions we managed to steal away for an outing on the northwest slopes of Beach Mountain. Our hunting partners were Rock and Bob's dog Gant, a son of Rock. We sometimes flushed grouse but as is so often the story of Appalachian grouse hunting, none fell to our shotguns.

That changed one evening as I drove the long, winding trail from the Blue Ridge Parkway to Bob and Theresa's sprawling mansion. As I rounded a sharp curve, a grouse scuttled out of the tract.

Chapter 20 — *Nothing Could Be Finer*

A little later, Bob and I were indulged in cold ones as I admired the latest new wing they always seemed to be adding to their castle.

I admitted, "I have been chasing grouse again but as usual with no success. I did almost hit a big grouse on the way in to your place."

"That is one smart bird. Gant and I often flush him."

I mistakenly took Bob's comment as a challenge. On the way back up the steep drive, I parked and took to foot with shotgun in hand and Rock at heel. We rounded a curve close to where I had flushed the bird earlier. Sure enough, the grouse had returned. He flushed and then fell far downhill among towering, alder hells. After a prolonged search, Rock trudged back up the hill to me packing the bird.

We returned to Bob's. "Here's your supper," I extended the grouse to him but he did not accept.

"Damn! That bird was a kind of pet. I didn't really want it killed. You take it home."

Somewhat as a truce I arranged a deer-hunting trip to a beautiful plantation just north of Charleston. We were there at my buddy Will's invitation to hunt among beautiful live oak, longleaf pines, and palmettos. Much of hunting hours were passed sitting and standing in spacious tree blinds. It was also a kick to follow white sand roads through stands of pin oaks hoping to jump a buck. Plantation regulations allowed for the harvest of bucks only. We saw several does but no mossy antlered old buck.

The trip was far from unrewarding. A midday expedition to the Sound with cane poles, a long-handled dip net, and chicken necks quickly produced a half-bushel of delicious blue crabs for steaming. There were evening trips to enjoy the excellent cuisine of Charleston, and there was a traditional southern oyster roast.

Rousing from my memories of those other trips, I found the woods far from quiet. Fallen leaves rustled as a squirrel or chipmunk searched for or maybe stashed acorns. Crows called in the distance. A large pileated woodpecker drummed on an old snag that rose far above the canopy. A deep throbbing drumming sound drifted down from an impenetrable laurel thicket from far up the mountain slope to bring me suddenly to full alert. A grouse was talking.

"Time for us to get moving, Rock. There are birds to hunt. The limit is three and we have only one in hand." I knew from past attempts that taking a bag limit of ruffed grouse in the southern Appalachians was about as unusual as finding "hen's teeth."

Our hunt finally carried us to the southeastern summit of Sugar Mountain. Here the rock outcroppings provided me with natural viewing platforms of the valleys far below. Farm houses appeared as miniatures linked by ribbons of road. Smoke spiraled upward from roaring wood stoves. Standing out in sharp relief from the green background, the brown and white cattle grazed a distant pasture. Surrounding mountain slopes, cloaked in brilliant fall foliage, were a riot of color.

Our progress continued along a sharp, knife-edged crest among wind stunted and twisted trees. We approached a tangle of wild grape and blackberry vines. I thought to myself, "this is a likely grouse cafeteria."

As expected, Rock found hot bird scent and wanted to surge ahead. "Easy, easy, Rock," I held him back.

I advanced cautiously and a grouse thundered into the air, flying straight ahead. I raised my shotgun. As I pulled the trigger, the grouse zigged and zagged. Somehow, I missed with both barrels and stood with my mouth open in disbelief and exasperation. Rock, also disgusted with my backup to his efforts, turned to glare at me disgustedly.

"Another miracle of a dead bird flying away just occurred." I made a feeble excuse to Rock. "It is too early to quit now. Let's see if we can find another bird."

The afternoon was waning. Earlier, we had found grouse that flushed wild. There had been no opportunity for a shot. We were again hunting in heavy timber. Descending a steep, rocky slope, I approached a break in the timber. The break turned out to be a recently cut right-of-way. We were following this trail when Rock darted into a rhododendron thicket.

Wings thrashed the air as a bird fought his way from the dense vegetation and broke free to fly down the slope. I caught sight of the grouse for an instant as it passed an opening in the foliage. I took a desperate shot. "Surely another miss," I told myself.

Rock, not so sure about my pessimism, disappeared below. I was astounded when a short while later he approached, huffing and puffing, and packing an unlucky grouse.

With a wonderful day behind, it was time to head back to the truck. As the sun's last rays illuminated the mountain peaks with an alpine glow, we arrived back at the steep meadow above our truck. A couple of old, gnarled apple trees gracing the meadow's upper slope were heavy with frost-nipped fruit. I paused to sample them. The apple proved sweet, delicious, and firm. Fruit was hastily loaded into my shooting vest until it was full and running over. Before good filming light faded I found time to photograph my mixed bag of ruffed grouse and apples.

Chapter 20 — *Nothing Could Be Finer*

Swamp squirrels

Rock and I had found no opportunity to tramp the fields with a shotgun recently. Rock was bored with the lack of action. Cousin Fred hit me with the idea of trying a pay-for-shooting type of establishment. I was easy to persuade. We would meet one morning at a commercial operation located in Carolina's upper piedmont. The day's game would be farm raised and planted quail and pheasant.

The day of our shoot arrived and we met as planned. We broke out our shotguns and I unloaded Rock. We walked the edge of a boom sedge field where Rock was released to hunt ahead.

A short distance into the field, Rock tensed and plunged into a high stand of grass and came out with a bobwhite. He delivered the live bird to me, which I dispatched and handed to Fred for stashing away. A short distance later this scene was again repeated.

"We're not getting much shooting Fred," I commented.

"Yeah but think of the ammo we are saving."

Eventually we each had shots at weakly flying quail that we added to our take. Then, Rock started working faster. "I think maybe he's on a pheasant. Let's follow him up."

We followed the eager Chesapeake maybe 50 yards farther where we approached a sparse clump of blackberry bushes. Rock lunged into the bushes and there were sounds of thrashing and a struggle. This time the proud dog delivered a very disgruntled and bedraggled cock pheasant. It was added to our bag. "Somehow this shoot is not working out quite like I expected," Fred admitted.

"The quality of hunting these pen-raised fliers compared to hunting wild birds definitely leaves something to be desired. Kind of like settling for second-best when you were expecting the real thing." I expressed our mutual feelings.

Fred was an experienced hand at hunting with beagles. On hunts together, he always seemed to be in position to intercept the dog-driven rabbit. When it came to fishing, I knew from firsthand observation that he more than held his own in numbers and size of fish landed.

"We can do better than this. You have a good mess of birds for dinner. Let's call this shoot. It reminds me too much of a deer hunt a year ago."

That last deer hunt had begun in swamp country of coastal Carolina. One early November morning found us parked at an access control gate of a large public wildlife management area east of New Bern. We studied the sandy road surface with more than passing interest.

"Lots of deer spoor here all right," I observed. "As you said there are lots of deer in this country. I wish we knew the layout of the refuge or at least had a map. Most deer hunters in this country hunt behind hounds."

"We can use big Ben and Kent. They are wonderful water dogs and I know that they have seen their share of deer killed." Fred suggested our strategy for the day.

"The Labs are good in trailing but will not bark on a trail. We will have to keep them in sight."

"No problem," Fred believed.

We shouldered our guns. I would hunt with my trusty .30-06 rifle. Fred was armed with a shotgun loaded with 00 buckshot.

I reflected a little late, "I sure wish I had brought hip boots, seeing that we are about to enter a swamp."

Walking the sand road, we progressed about a quarter mile into the swamp. Fresh deer tracks led the way. The dogs trailed eagerly but stayed obediently close in. Ditches half full of dark, peat-stained swamp water paralleled either side of the road, thus limiting our movements to the road. Less than a mile in, that access road suddenly ended, bringing our forward progress to a halt. "Now what?" I wondered.

"We need to get across the ditch and into the marsh. The deer are probably bedding down nearby."

"Crossing is no problem for the Labs, but I'm in no mood for a swim." We discovered that water in the left-hand ditch ended just ahead.

Fred was hot on the trail and not to be stopped by minor obstacles. "I'll try crossing." The brownish sand where Fred proposed a crossing was covered with small leaves and twigs. The crossing appeared firm enough, but strangely no deer tracks crossed here. "Why don't the deer use this crossing?" I wondered to myself.

Fred was making good progress until he started sinking. He tried to turn back but it was too late. His struggles served only to sink him deeper.

"What the F," He exclaimed and tossed his shotgun back to firm ground. "Help me get out of here."

"Hang on." With luck, I quickly found a long and stout fallen tree branch that I extended. With determined heaving, Fred was finally free of the quicksand. He stood on firm ground shaking, muddy to the waist and his enthusiasm for swamp hunting considerably dampened.

I suggested. "Four-legged critters can navigate this country with little problem but as you just found out humans can't. Let's bag this effort. We are supposed to meet your old man and my brother on down toward the coast this evening for some fishing tomorrow. I'm looking forward to

Chapter 20 — *Nothing Could Be Finer*

some ocean fishing. Maybe we can extend our trip to eastern Virginia. Friends near Franklin have deer dogs for hunting the swamps."

That evening we met Big Fred and my brother Gene. We enjoyed hot showers and a couple of cold ones in Big Fred's motel room. After a hot meal in the adjacent restaurant, cousin Fred and I were feeling much more optimistic.

Uncle Fred offered generously, "I know that you all have camping gear along but you all may as well roll out in my motel room for the night. An unseasonably hard freeze is supposed to hit tonight."

Young Fred was in an independent and pioneering mood and declined his father's generous offer. "I really want to camp out tonight in a field we saw near here if Jim will camp with me. Looks like a good deer area. We might wake up and find a big buck grazing nearby."

"At least with the cold there will be no mosquitoes," I said.

"You all should have your heads examined," uncle Fred suggested. Gene wisely opted to sleep in Big Fred's a warm motel room.

En route to the field, Fred and I passed a tavern. We looked at each other and by mutual consensus swung into the parking lot. Some liquid refreshment would help us face the cold night ahead.

The bar was crowed, noisy, and smoky and the jukebox blared. Fred, an attractive young man with a gift for gab, soon was on friendly terms with an attractive woman. As I pulled out, it was evident that he would not be going with me to that meadow.

In the wee black hours of the morning, my dog buddies launched from their nests, where they had curled tightly at my side, with barks and growls. A car was idling nearby with its lights shining on my station wagon. My left hand groped for a flashlight as my right hand found the cold form of my shotgun. I had put it along side my sleeping bag for just such possible emergencies.

"It's me," Fred called out from the car (his dad's). "I'm looking for my [blankety-blank] sleeping bag. Call off the bear dogs."

I later awoke to a frozen early morning world. Frost lay heavy on all exposed surfaces including our sleeping bags. My sleeping bag was an Arctic-rated Eddie Bauer down model and I had slept well. My yellow buddies were up and moving, eager to hunt. I hastily pulled on outer clothes while shivering in the frosty air.

As I attempted to rouse Fred I noted that he looked none too good. His face, I swear, was purple. His sleeping bag was only of light fiberfill. He did not need to go hunting on this cold morning. He needed warmth and sleep. I added my bag to his cover.

Buddies Afield — Trips Outside Alaska

Gray squirrels were chattering and moving as they fed in the nearby swamp. I shouldered my over-and-under, found a pocketful of number 6's in the truck, and replaced the 00 buckshot loads. The dogs and I were then on our way.

We moved stealthily along the field's edge where it bordered swamp. The logistical problem of how to retrieve downed game from a swamp without hip boots was quickly solved when I dropped the first squirrel. I had always trained and expected my retrievers to retrieve any variety of downed game, be it feathered or furred. Big Ben entered the icy water with a tremendous splash to return with a bedraggled squirrel. As he started to hand the squirrel to me, the still-live squirrel clamped down on Ben's nose, drawing blood with sharp incisors. Ben's powerful jaws clamped down in response. There was no more resistance.

Farther along the swamp, I spotted movement as another squirrel flattened against the bole of a water oak, attempting to hide among the leafless trees. Following the boom of the shotgun Kent had an excuse to swim. "You're up, Kent," I chuckled to myself with thoughts of the Far Side cartoon titled 'You're Up Red.' "Don't worry, Kent. The water is much too cold for gators."

Within an hour, with the hunt was over. The makings for a meal of southern fried squirrel with gravy were in the bag.

We all met at the restaurant where Fred and I were happy enough to warm up. The pups contentedly munched on Purina while humans enjoyed a big southern style breakfast of fried eggs, country ham, grits, redeye gravy, and plenty of biscuits. Big Fred, a traveling salesman of knives and fishing tackle by profession, as usual had a new wealth of jokes to share. He had a really good chuckle when hearing about the cold, frosty sleeping bag. "Freddy," he shook his head and came out with a typical Big Fred sarcasm. "If they stuffed all your brains into a peanut shell and shook it around there would be room for them to rattle."

My brother had heard about Fred's latest nighttime activities. "When are you gonna write your life story, Fred? It is sure to be a best seller. I understand you got material for another chapter last night. We're still betting that you will never pass away from natural causes. Probably will be from lead poisoning."

Anxious to hit the road for the coast, the crew was standing around our transportation, awaiting Cousin Fred who like his father he had a gift for gab. Young Fred finally showed up with the restaurant's cook, an African-American, in tow. "I want to see dem Alaska bear dogs Fred has been telling me about some kind of bad," our cook requested.

Chapter 20 — *Nothing Could Be Finer*

I let Big Ben and Kent out for him to admire. Kent was a well-proportioned 85-pound dog. His son Ben was huge for a Lab and topped out at about 110 pounds of muscle and bone.

"That young dog—he be awesome!" Our cook was duly impressed. "Wonder how would they like some bones?" he questioned.

"They would love some bones," I assured him.

The cook disappeared into the kitchen to reappear shortly with a large pail of chicken bones. Being young and uninformed about feeding chicken bones to dogs, I turned the pail over for them. As they crunched happily, their benefactor's eyes widened in delight. "Look at dem dogs crunching dem bones," he exclaimed.

"How would you like a mess of squirrels," I inquired.

"Captain, I would purely love a mess of squirrels. The wife and childrens loves squirrels. Don't have much time for huntin much anymore what with this steady cooking job."

"I just happen to have some squirrels for you. We are on our way fishing. You are welcome to them."

"Thank you. Thank you, Captain. Take care of dem bear dogs."

Big Fred was seldom in a hurry unless he was going fishing. Today he was ready to go fishing. "Time to head out. Load up."

"I bet there will be a babe wearing a bikini behind every fir tree" I sought to motivate the younger members of our party.

"Yeah right." When it came to prospects for hunting women, you couldn't fool young Fred. "It's November with a northeaster threatening the Outer Banks. No fir trees grow on the Outer Banks. The bikinis will be about as plentiful."

We arrived at the coast to find a storm moving in from the northeast as predicted. The surf was raging and the torrents of rain strafed land, water, and dwellings. There were few fishermen, the weather was too bad. But we discovered that the fish were plentiful and hungry. Our crew was in hog heaven. We fished mainly from one of the very long (one thousand plus feet) commercial fishing piers projecting beyond the crashing surf.

Our catch was varied and included mainly whiting, croaker, spot, and blue. Gene hooked into and, after a terrific battle with a light rod, landed a huge oceanic bonito. Few of the other fish landed were large. Most of the catch weighed in at less than a pound but their bites jerked the rods like an electric impulse. A fisherman hooking into a double or triple-header had his hands full. Our catch would be excellent eating when rolled in cornmeal, deep fried to a crisp brown, and served with hushpuppies, French fries, and coleslaw.

Buddies Afield — Trips Outside Alaska

Big Fred was the most tenacious fisherman in our crew. Neither wind nor rain could stop his fishing. I can still see him standing at a pier's end, buffeted by the wind and rain, cigar clamped between his teeth, happily reeling in fish after fish. Years later, I was to encounter a little old lady that was Fred's equal as a tenacious fisher. I met the spry, 88-years-young lady known locally as "Auntie" on Topsail Island's Jolly Roger Fishing Pier. Auntie was renowned for her fishing prowess. She fished mostly alone, and if the fish were biting, she sometimes fished all night despite howling winds and discouraging wind chill factors.

After leaving the coast, cousin Fred, Gene, and I later arrived at the Nottoway River's Battle Beach just north of the North Carolina and Virginia line. We made a brief stop at Bailey's Store just down the road. Our excuse for the stop was to purchase lunches of wheel cheese, saltine crackers, sardines, and soft drinks. As we munched and toasted by the roaring woodstove, we gazed at the numerous large whitetail racks gracing the store walls.

Over cocktails hosted by Ralph at Battle Beach, I admired again Ralph's outstanding whitetail mount. There was also the Dall's sheep from Alaska's Wrangell Mountains that I had given him mounted alongside. Somehow, the sheep looked out of place in the coastal swamp environs of eastern Virginia.

"The new restaurant you built from the old marina looks great, Ralph. I see that a couple of new houses are going up along the back lagoons where I used to frog hunt. The place is building up."

"Restaurant business is good and promises to get better. We have several more lots sold. Hard to stop progress. In a few years you won't recognize this place."

From my environmental perspective, what he said was unfortunately to prove right. I had fond memories of the area as I had know it in the early 1960s when it was almost wilderness. Some years down the road, Battle Beach would be just another high-end suburban residential area.

"You fellows want to go deer hunting the morning after next? We have a hunt organized in the Carolina big woods."

"You bet we do," Fred and I eagerly volunteered. Gene, who was not a hunter, elected to fish the Blackwater River.

Silvia observed, "I see you have a couple of dogs along. I hope they aren't like old Storm." She was remembering the day Storm, my first retriever, walked through the open door of her kitchen and made off with a freshly baked ham that sat cooling on the table. She had intended the ham for her family's Sunday dinner. That incident considerably diminished our popularity in the neighborhood for a while.

Chapter 20 — *Nothing Could Be Finer*

With Storm, a rawboned 90 pounds plus Chesapeake, there was seldom a dull moment. I drove a Triumph TR3 convertible in those days and Storm rode in the back seat. One day we took Cannon's Ferry across the Meherrin River to Tunis, a small fishing village on the banks of the broad Chowan River. A pack of deer hounds decided that chasing my small car down the dirt Main Street would be great sport. Storm decided to take exception to their sport, and he bailed out, rolled a couple of hounds, and routed the whole pack.

Another time Storm and I were visiting my parents in Newland, North Carolina, which at 3,000 feet is the highest county seat located east of the Mississippi. My minister father had become known locally as "the marry'n parson." I asked our old man (affectionately known as JL to his two sons), "how many couples do you reckon you have married?" He grinned and admitted that through the years he had gotten "a whole lot of people in trouble." During that visit, Storm took exception to the local neighborhood bully dog known as Killer. He rolled and then chased the 140-pound dog.

"How are Jim and Joe," I inquired to Silvia about the boys I sometimes felt I had helped raise.

"The boys have grown up. They have gotten to be quite the deer hunters. They are away attending college."

"How is your father?" Most of us addressed her father as Mr. Williams.

"Father passed away."

"I have fond memories hunting raccoons with your father one night. I remember riding the sand roads with Mr. Williams and Mr. Bailey in Mr. Williams' new diesel Mercedes. All were greatly enjoying listening to the hound music. Seems to me that some clear white refreshment was being passed around in a fruit jar. Don't recall whether or not we ever caught a coon."

Silvia assigned us bunking quarters in my old cabin down the beach from the main house in what she called Moccasin Hollow. Soon we cousins were rolled out in the cabin.

"Watch that back door Fred. It opens right over the river. The first step is a long one with a bath at the end. Fellows have been known to come close to taking the plunge after enjoying too much refreshment."

"This is a real neat location," Gene allowed after looking around. "I bet there's good fishing in the river."

"Fishing can be good for largemouth, bluegills, channel catfish, white and yellow perch, and anadromous species in the spring. Quite a run of herring and hickory shad migrate up these rivers. These southern coastal systems contain some of the greatest diversity of fish species to be found in the country."

"I bet a few girls have seen the inside of this cabin," observed Fred.

"A couple stopped in to see my etchings after a boat ride." I whetted his curiosity.

I was up the next morning before the sun topped the virgin stand of cypress towering in the swamps to the east. When I quietly slipped out the door with rifle in hand, no one else was stirring. A short walk brought me to an old logging road that ran deep into the swamps. I still-hunted, with my dogs at my side.

When a doe stepped quietly into the road a few yards ahead, the scope cross hairs came to bear behind her shoulder. But I was not motivated to squeeze the trigger; I was looking for a buck this morning. The dogs looked at me questioningly. I continued walking for another half-hour, enjoying sounds of the swamp's wildlife awakening. Finally, there was snorting and a heavy crash from brush nearby. My view of a fleeing deer was obscured by a tangle of vines and brush. I had missed my chance for this morning.

The morning for our deer hunt in the big woods dawned clear and cold. The hunt was well organized and each of about a dozen hunters was assigned to and dropped off at stands. Firearms on this hunt were restricted by club rules to shotguns. Shotguns are not my weapon of choice for big game hunting. The hound pack was released at the swamp's upper end, and deep baying soon shattered the morning stillness. The hounds had struck fresh scent. A shot or two rang out in the distance. After a seeming interminable period of time, sounds of baying and splashing approached my stand. The pulse rate picked up a notch. There was disappointment. Though many deer inhabited the drive area, on this day the number of hunters on stand greatly outnumbered the number of deer seen. A single small doe ran across the road midway between Fred's stand and my stand to disappear into the deep woods at our backs.

Back at the hunting lodge, we found a couple of small bucks hanging. As per club custom, these deer were butchered and each participating hunter was given a portion of venison.

The days of our mini safari were running out as I headed the rig south to drop Fred off at his home. Gene and I would then head for mother's home in western North Carolina. We had planned our travels to avoid the congested main roads, much preferring rural routes through picturesque coastal countryside. Several times while journeying through the country we saw groups of deer hunters on stand or en route to or from a hunt.

Chapter 20 — *Nothing Could Be Finer*

At one point, I was forced to brake suddenly and swerve sharply to barely miss a sow hog and her litter of young crossing our path. We began seeing loose pigs on a regular basis.

Fred had been very quiet since the last large group of swine we passed along the roadside. I thought, "wonder what he is scheming now."

"You know, I sure could some fresh ham," Fred revealed his thoughts.

As driver, I squelched his hopes. "I would like some good fresh ham myself, but there ain't enough time left in this trip to process ham starting out from scratch and there sure as the Devil ain't room in this station wagon for both me and a live pig. We have had a good trip. There is venison in our coolers and lots of fish were sent home with your father. Time to take it to the barn."

Bobwhites in the Sandhills

Most sport in the Sandhills area of North Carolina centers on carefully trimmed greens and a little white ball. Such luminaries as Bing Crosby and Bob Hope had played golf here. My recreational pursuit in this area was different. My two yellow Labs, Ben and Kent, and I found our sport in the rough. The sporting equipment I packed was an over-and-under shotgun.

In the Carolina Sandhills, winters tend to be very mild. The moderate climate has led to massive development and human population increases for the area. Sadly, the shopping centers, golf courses, suburban housing developments, and also changing farming practices all result in eliminating much wild quail habitat.

One November afternoon found my dog buddies and me hunting native bobwhite quail in the outback of a large farm carved out of longleaf pine, oak, and hickory forests. I had gained access to hunt quail on this farm by courtesy of my father who was both friend and pastor to the farm family. As he visited the family, I tramped around the farm's fallow land and cut-over woods. This farm's main money crop was chickens. At the day's end, father was sure to have a couple of chickens to take home. My day's take was much more in doubt and would for sure weigh considerably less than his.

Flushing dogs are not the classic breeds for bobwhite hunting. The purist would hunt behind a classic brace of setters or pointers. I had to insist that my Labs work close so that I would be in shooting position if and when birds were found and flushed.

The dogs became very excited as we worked a large field of broom sedge along a cut-over stand of hardwood trees. Their noses worked the ground, sucking up what to them was intoxicating bird scent.

Buddies Afield — Trips Outside Alaska

As they surged ahead, I urged "easy now, easy," and quickened my pace to close up ranks. Their increasingly excited casts showed that birds were now very close. Suddenly, there was an unnerving roar as a large covey burst into the air. The air seemed full of darting brown bodies. I swung on a bird flying straight away and pulled the trigger. He fell in a shower of feathers. My follow-up shot at a bird swinging back to the left also connected.

Kent and Ben quickly delivered the two quail to my hands. I paused to admire the handsome little birds, a male and a female. The male's sex was easily identified by the white head and throat markings, while the hen's markings were a more subdued cream.

"Good work, dogs!" I praised them. "That was a big covey. Must have been a dozen birds or so. I acquitted myself well with the Daly, if I do say so. I saw where a couple of birds pitched into that cut-over wood lot. Let's go and see if we can find a single or two."

We ascended a low hillside to search among piles of slash left from logging. A few small oak and dogwood trees had been left standing. The tangles of greenbrier thorns sometimes required us to pick our way so the going was sometimes slow.

The dogs found fresh scent around a pile of slash and brush. A small brown form roared unexpectedly to the air, then darting between trees. I somehow managed to miss the escaping quail with both barrels. We hunted on and closed on a small weed patch more cautiously. Then Kent hit scent and Ben backed him up. I closed in, carefully positioning myself for a clear shot. Ben plowed into the tangle of grass. As I was about to give up and call "no bird," a brown-feathered rocket streaked out. My shot connected. That quail had held really tight. My companions presented me with a second handsome male for the day.

The afternoon was waning as we worked back toward the farmhouse. We emerged through a thick stand of young longleaf pines and found ourselves in a high stand of broom sedge. I was taken completely by surprise when the day's second large covey thundered into the air. My first shot dropped nothing but pine straw but my second connected with a late holding bird. When that last bird of the day was delivered, I found to my delight that it also was a male.

The dogs were eager to continue the hunt but we were losing our brief winter daylight. Encircling pines had prevented my seeing the fleeing birds' flight paths. "Let's go home," I called my buddies to heel. "Time to see how the old man is making out with the "gospel birds." Father liked to call chickens "gospel birds." One of his standard jokes was "chickens were gospel birds because so many chickens had gone into the ministry."

Chapter 20 — *Nothing Could Be Finer*

Walking back toward the farmhouse as dusk crept in, we were treated to the whistles of quail reforming their covey. To me their call has always represented a truly distinctive voice of the rural south.

While visiting family in the Southern Pines and Pinehurst area, the addictive pursuit of training retrievers for field trial competition got me hooked. It started one day when I was driving the back roads looking for promising quail coverts and I noted a black Lab running across a grassy field. Curious, I pulled the station wagon over to watch. At a sharp whistle, the dog stopped at 100 plus yards out, sat, and looked back for directions. A lady wearing a white coat motioned to the right. The dog changed course and raced in that direction to pick up a white plastic bumper and return it to her handler. I introduced myself to the hander, a Mrs. Atkins. The dog she was handling was Penny, who in future years would become a Field Champion.

I had observed a retriever field trial on one occasion in the 1960s on Maryland's Eastern Shore. At that date, retriever field trials were still very much a social event. There I met some of Augie Belmont's famous field-trial champions and was also treated to a snack of boiled pheasant eggs.

My Labs at that time were trained only to the level of rough hunting dogs. They were wonderful at marking falls within reasonable hunting distance and would run relatively short land blinds (following handler's signals) if needed. I expressed my interest in training my dogs for more advanced handling to Mrs. Atkins, who was delighted. She informed me that she and her professional trainer, John Dahl, were always looking for "bird throwers."

A few days later I met John, a young, beginning professional retriever trainer. John's real life job at that time was that of college music professor. A friendship developed between us that has endured over the years. We have enjoyed training dogs together whenever our trails cross for many years and too many dog generations.

One time I asked John how a Yankee from the northern Midwest liked living in the sunny South. "I love it," he said. "But sometimes I wake up from a nightmare in a cold sweat dreaming that I'm living back in the North with the temperature 30 below and a blizzard raging outside."

John and I were sometimes competitive. During our first few training sessions together, I was embarrassed when my Labs failed to do long field-trial type multiple marks and water blinds. The tables were turned one day when John tried and failed to pick up one of my hunting marks with his field trial Labs. I set up the mark by launching a plastic dummy 60 yards into heavy timber and brush. To complete this retrieve, a dog had to watch the flight path of the object, run to the approximate location it fell, and then hunt extensively with no direction from the handler.

Eventually, John was to sell me the pup that became my first Field Champion and great hunting dog, Rock. I learned many advanced training techniques from John and we eventually ran a number of field trials together. We both kept in shape and often relieved the tension of training and the trials by running five or more miles together.

One evening John (who was then recently divorced) and I were in a Southern Pines bar seeking action. John is of Norwegian heredity and had just told one of his infamous Norwegian jokes. As we sipped on a second round of cold ones, John nodded across the smoke-filled room. Two women had just entered. "There's one for each of us." John reached in his pocket for a coin, "Call it. The winner gets first choice."

I reflected that John was usually exceedingly discriminating about dogs and women. Perhaps tonight the hour was too late, the drinks had been too numerous, or the smoke was affecting his vision.

"John with those two I don't think there would be any winner."

John looked more closely and sighed, "You're right. They would probably feel the same about us. It's long past time for us to head home."

One day while quail hunting across from my folk's country home, I came across an old sawdust pile from a long ago logging operation. The dogs put up an exceptionally large covey of quail. This became my "sawmill covey." I hunted this area on several subsequent occasions and could generally depend on finding quail nearby and take a bird or two.

On a several occasions while quail hunting, my rambling found me passing through some wet bottomland or bog. On one of those afternoons while in a bog, the dogs flushed a peculiar flying brown bird somewhat larger than a quail. The bird fell at my shot to be delivered by a mud-splattered retriever. I studied my first woodcock. On subsequent hunts, I sometimes took mixed bags of quail and woodcock.

One morning I decided to mount an expedition specifically for woodcock. The hunt area lay near a country school where mother taught. I dropped her off at the school and continued on with my hunt plans.

The area I had chosen to hunt was a large, wet woodland that lay along a good-sized creek. The woods were thick and included such water-loving tree species as gum, water oak, and cypress. These woods frequently flooded during high water and large water puddles were abundant and extensive the afternoon of my hunt. Wisely, I had worn hip boots.

A short time into our hunt found the dogs working along a water channel that ran through a stand of relatively open timber. They put up a woodcock, which fell to my single shot.

Chapter 20 — *Nothing Could Be Finer*

I thought to myself, "we are into the treasure lode of woodcock today. This timberdoodle shooting is not so difficult as stories would have it."

A couple of hours later, muddy from mucking through sometimes knee-deep water and scratched from bucking heavy cover and tangles of vines and with no more birds in the bag, we were frustrated to say the least. Three or four more birds had been jumped but they flushed wild or on the far side of trees. I consoled myself with the thought that woodcock were not nearly as good eating as bobwhites. My discouraged mood quickly improved when the dogs once again became birdy. A long-billed bird emitting that raspy call was airborne and twisting through the air. Somehow, my shot string intercepted his flight.

With a second bird in the bag and the sun disappearing into a large cloudbank lying to the west, we turned our steps back toward the highway. After a mile or so of zigzagging and picking my way through a maze of swamp, I heard highway noise not far ahead. There, directly ahead and blocking my route back to the car was a stand of immature trees and cane almost as thick as hair on a dog's back. I wearily started working and bulling my through this final obstacle. More than once a branch snapped back to slap me with a stinging smart across the face. Cursing under my breath, I continued forward.

Immediately ahead I heard the rasping call of a woodcock taking to wing. Intervening trees blocked my sight of the flush but the bird, climbing steeply to clear the 20-foot-high vegetation, passed above me. I snapped off a shot. My faithful dog companions conducted a quick but thorough search of the nearby brush and another bird was added to the day's take.

I broke open the double as we got clear of the brush and headed for the car. I praised my dirty yellow colored Labs. "You fellows have earned a place on a rug beside a hot air register tonight. Mother will never let you in the house as muddy as you are though. Let's go find some clean water for you to swim. I am very much looking forward to a hot shower and dry clothes tonight."

Genie Riis and Al Roggow look pleased indeed with the fine results of this South Dakota pheasant hunt in 1980.

You Bet

Wagers won and lost hunting South Dakota pheasants, 1980.

South Dakota in the fall is the Holy Grail for the North American bird hunter. In a good year, there are great opportunities to pursue abundant ducks, geese, sharp-tailed grouse, prairie chicken, and the ring-necked pheasant. Early one October, Al Roggow and I had exited Alaska by jet and truck respectively. Our trails merged at Watertown in South Dakota's northeast lake country. I had arrived with Rock, my canine companion on many an adventure. Jim Riis, a former Alaskan and close friend who had returned to his South Dakota roots, was our gracious host. In Alaska, we three had shared many hours training our retrievers for hunting and field trials and we had enjoyed memorable hunts to such locations as Alaska's famous Izembek Area.

South Dakota natives Al and Jim knew both the lay of the land and the ways of pheasants. As a South Dakota wildlife biologist, Jim was privy to the latest data on bird populations and hunting access areas. It also did not hurt that Jim's family owned a grain farm in the heart of pheasant country down around Winner.

Al, affectionately known to Jim's family as "Gramps," was well into his 60's but could still cover miles of rough hunting terrain. A young man was pushed to keep up with him. Al had hunted the Dakota plains back in the pheasant glory days before World War II. The problem he said he had in those days was a scarcity of shotgun shells.

Filling-in the fall days prior the pheasant opener was no problem for us. Initially, there had been hunts in the National Grasslands for sharp-tailed grouse and prairie chicken. Then duck and goose season rolled in and we connected on greenheads and giant Canada geese.

The night before pheasant season opened, our crew numbering five hunters strong arrived at Jim's family farm. The pheasant population was high, as evidenced by frequent sightings while driving gravel roads. As we waited for the noon opening the next day, we heard cock pheasants crowing in the brush back of the farmhouse.

Our group basically included five or six shooters and about as many dogs. Sometimes our ranks were swelled when other hunters joined to work a prime field of milo or corn stalks. When a field of many acres was pushed, the blockers were used to more effectively harvest birds. Action during that opening weekend was fast and furious. The dogs worked hard at finding, flushing and retrieving birds. Sometimes scores of pheasants were running and flushing from the fields, driving the dogs to distraction. By mid-afternoon each day, the warm, clear weather had us hunting in our shirt sleeves. Bag limits were quickly filled on most days.

After each hunt, the old farmhouse became the scene of festive activity as Jim's mother, aunt Agnas, and his wife (Genie) prepared wonderful, traditional pheasant dinners. Genie, who was a fine hand with a firearm, accounted for her share of the birds.

After opening weekend, we had headed back to the northern part of South Dakota. Our hosts had to work, so Al and I would hunt locally and be joined by Jim whenever he could tear himself away from work for hunting, which was often.

"Well, Jim, I am glad that you could join us today for a hunt," Al said to me a morning or so later. "We haven't seen much of you since the Ducks Unlimited banquet the other night. You must have found better quarters than Jim R. could provide. I have to admit that the little hostess you were taking a shine to was cute. I'm sure that she didn't have anything to do with your disappearance," he grinned.

Jim contributed to my discomfort; "You sure did miss out on a good snow goose shoot yesterday morning. I guess you were sleeping in."

I grinned as I came up with an excuse. A man could always make his best friend the scapegoat. "I thought that Rock needed a rest but now he is ready to chase birds again."

"Yeah right, blame your old buddy," Al allowed. "I've never seen Rock want to miss a hunt. Let's go find some pheasants."

We loaded the dogs into the back of Jim's truck. Our dog team that day included three retrievers. Al was hunting his Labrador FC AFC Cookies Annie Fanny and Jim had his Lab Tye. My Chesapeake was Rock Honeybear of the Yukon, who would in years ahead add the titles FC AFC to his name. We would be hunting areas of the state not considered to be prime pheasant country. But we were hunting during midweek. The crowds of opening weekend pheasant hunters were largely gone home. We would have no competition but we would have to earn our birds.

Our strategy would be to drive south along country roads. When we came across some good pheasant cover near the road, we would unload our dogs, grab our shotguns, and plunge in. The most productive cover was heavy cattail and tangled brush. This was impossible cover for a human to work effectively but the dogs put up birds. Our take mounted. No large numbers of birds flushed but we took a bird or two here and a bird or two there.

Chapter 21 — *You Bet*

Loading up and heading back after one such successful drive, Al remarked, "This is the kind of hunt I like. We are enjoying good dog work and good companionship but I think we could have even more fun. I think we need a bet."

Jim, a crack shot on sporting clays and game birds, was quick to agree. I hesitated for only a moment and considered the odds. I would be hunting against two of South Dakota's top bird hunters and pheasant dogs but I was confident. My shooting of late had been good and Rock was working well. "I'll get in on the action," I volunteered.

Having drawn us in, Al proposed that, "the man who bags the next rooster buys a jug." Something about this bet did not sound quite right but the odds of me losing were only one in three. Jim and I quickly accepted the terms. Al let it be known that he expected the looser to buy first class.

About then we arrived at a picture book perfect piece of pheasant cover. We unloaded the truck, loaded our weapons, and approached the cover, each from a different angle.

The released dogs worked the heavy cover frantically as they hit hot scent. Suddenly, a big, beautiful rooster was airborne, squawking angrily at being disturbed. The bird had been put up right in front of Al. The pheasant looked to be 4 feet long. Why didn't Al shoot? He looked to be daydreaming. The bird came on and would pass right over me. Could I pass him up? Jim, 40 yards to my right, was in position to make the interception. I swung my superimposed on the rooster. At my shot he crumpled to the cheers of my hunting partners. Rock made the retrieve.

"Guess who buys" Al chuckled

"Why didn't you shoot Al," I wanted to know.

"I must have had something in my eye."

"Well I owe you fellows a bottle. Let's go find a liquor store. Is Wild Turkey OK?" I will always wonder if Jim would have passed up that rooster if I had not shot. In my opinion he would have shot.

That night we stopped on the way home for dinner at a popular restaurant. Before going in, I unloaded and aired Rock. After a week of hunting birds in heavy cover and covering many miles he was showing some physical wear. An old pheasant hunter spotted us and observed, "that old dog looks like I feel."

Over breakfast the next morning, Jim reluctantly informed us, "I guess that I had better show up at the office today. I will give you fellers good directions to an area you can try for pheasant. As you know, birds are not as abundant locally as farther south but some can be found with a bit of work. The area I am sending you to is a public hunting area consisting mainly of a vast cattail marsh. There are roosters there but they have been hunted by now and are smart and very hard to drive out of the cattails. To make the hunt more interesting I will buy the next bottle if you come back with a rooster."

Al and I arrived at the marsh full of confidence, eager to bag some birds and collect from Jim. Al decided to rest Annie. She was getting up in years and the going promised to be brutal. The tangled masses of cattails and broken-off stalks could lacerate a dog's face and exposed belly. Rock plunged into the worst of the cover and went to work.

A couple of hours into the hunt, Al and I were losing confidence and tiring from busting cover. Frequently, the cattails were above our heads. As far as we knew we had flushed no birds. If birds were flushed, the cover would likely preclude shooting anyway. For the most part, Rock was out of sight but working reasonably close.

Then we broke into an opening where Rock put up a squawking rooster right ahead of me. This bird, very reluctant to leave friendly cover, barely skimmed above the densely packed and tangled cattails. Taken completely by surprise, I got off only a snap shot. As the bird came down, I knew I had hit him too far back. There was not time for a follow-up shot. We had a runner to deal with in this impossible cover. Rock plunged eagerly into the task. Al and I watched helplessly as he went crashing through the hostile vegetation. After several unsuccessful lunges, he finally connected and presented me with a big rooster.

"Gol dang it," exclaimed Al. "You really owe that old dog. He had to earn that bird twice; once when he had to find and flush it for you to shoot at and a second time when you almost missed and he had to run it down as a cripple. Now let's go and collect that jug from Riis."

Perro Grande

Dove hunting with Rock in Mexico, 1982.

We arrived at the blind in the cool of early morning. Shortly after our arrival, the sun broke over the horizon and bathed the eastern sky with a crimson glow. Another hot and dusty day was ahead. Our "blind" in the middle of a plowed field consisted of an unaesthetic two-foot-high pile of dirt clods. I viewed our cover skeptically as it would provide little concealment. My first dove hunt of this trip, 200 miles south, had yielded few shooting opportunities. I asked myself, "Will today be a repeat with the doves failing to show?"

A low and gray, undulating haze formed in the distance. The dark cloud fascinated me as it steadily approached. Sunlight illuminated the mass. I became aware of individual forms moving within and darting along its front. The rapidly approaching cloud was living and would descend upon us in waves. "*Dios mio*," I exclaimed in awe. "*Palomas*!"

My smiling Mexican guide handed me a loaded shotgun, "*Si, muchos palomas.*"

We crouched behind our blind to somewhat diminish our profiles. My faithful Chesapeake buddy, FC AFC Rock Honeybear of the Yukon, sat eagerly at my side. I put my hand on his head to steady him as I whispered, "get ready for much, much action old man."

As usual, the winter in Alaska had been dark and cold so that by late November most water was in the solid state or not far from it. All sensible ducks and geese had long since flown south. Bird hunting, for all intents and purposes, was over. For the hardy, there was the possibility of chasing ptarmigan in three to four feet of snow. Such hunts can be interesting and rewarding but do not provide wing shooting in the classical sense.

The idea of a winter break at some place tropical and sunny had great appeal to Alaskans by January. Mike (a fellow member of the Alaska Retriever Club) had mercilessly regaled us with stories of bird hunting in warm and sunny, winter-time Mexico. With his instigation, the idea of a Mexico expedition for retriever people and their dogs was born. Though hunting was the primary motivating factor for the trip, the promise of warm surf, beautiful beaches and great regional food did not make the trip any less appealing.

In late February, the six of us (Mike, Gene, Pete, Rose, Cathy and me) were accompanied by our three Chesapeakes as we escaped from frozen

Buddies Afield — Trips Outside Alaska

Alaska. Travel was made very easy by jet aircraft. Dog/hunter teams were Mike with Molly, Gene with Steed, and me with Rock.

Our itinerary required an early morning change of aircraft in San Diego. As I walked along a glassed-in corridor toward the departure gate, I noticed dog kennels sitting in a cart on the ramp. Two men of the loading crew were beating on a dog kennel. It was Rock's. The kennel was clearly vibrating as he tried to get at his antagonists. I was livid but I could not gain access to the runway. The kennels were finally loaded into the aircraft. My companions managed to calm me somewhat.

The 737 made a smooth touchdown at Mazatlan. We hurried to the baggage area where the dogs and baggage arrived OK.

We then approached customs. The dogs' rabies and health certificates were all up-to-date. Our baggage included legal limits of 12 gauge shotgun shells. But stories of shotguns seized and ransomed back to the American owners had come to our attention and I was not willing to take a chance on losing a fine shotgun. Our outfitters would supply the guns.. Our concerns were soon gone as we passed through customs with no problems.

Sunny skies, balmy air, and warm waters greeted the winter and travel weary in Mazatlan. During the next few days, we settled in and quickly got literally into the swim of things. Adapting to beach life and a laid-back lifestyle, we were somewhat distracted from hunting plans. Daily activities might include body surfing, walking, sunning, fishing, snorkeling, and also absorbing the beautiful scenery. Dining and refreshments were generally excellent and the prices agreeable.

Our dogs were well received by natives and tourists alike. Their enthusiasm for water sports and aptitude in the surf really impressed those unfamiliar with water dogs. We made the rounds of beachfront resorts and *cantinas* usually accompanied by our four-legged buddies. Guests of the El Sid, Holiday Inn, El Pescador, and other plush beachfront hotels accepted the dogs. Masters accompanied by dogs frequently appeared for verandah happy hours. But resort management did become disgruntled on occasion when a dog hurtled into their swimming pool along with the kids.

We finally got around to our main objective of hunting some *palomas*. We found in Mexico, as is true everywhere, that for good hunting success you must be at the right place at the right time.

After a late evening of festivities, we struggled awake for an early morning meeting with outfitter and guides. This was in particular difficult for those of us who had imbibed some local water or cocktails containing ice. Montezuma's revenge had struck us with a vengeance. Liberal doses of Pepto-Bismol were required to function away from an outhouse for any extended period of time.

Chapter 22 — *Perro Grande*

The local outfitter welcomed our *dinero* but he neglected to inform us that with local agricultural harvests completed, doves had largely moved out of the area. We took up our stands around the edge of a harvested corn field. Our stands were clumps of green corn stalks that had escaped the harvest and we concealed ourselves among them. I found my guide's method of calling doves by mouth most interesting. The call he made was a whistling sound, but very few birds flew for him to attract. We busted a few caps and brought down even fewer doves. The three dogs unhappily shared the few retrieves.

After lunch in a local *cantina*, we were dropped off at a shelter with some refreshments to wait out the siesta hours. We waited there in ever increasing frustration for a duck hunt that never materialized. During the afternoon, a troop of Federales packing assault weapons arrived. We had no clue as to their intent and I was glad that of none of us had firearms.

After a few more days of beach activities, I still wanted to have a go at palomas. I learned of an agricultural area 200 miles north of Mazatlan said to be holding large numbers of birds. I established communication with an area guide and outfitter there. After listening to my questions, he urged me to hurry there, "aqui muchas palomas."

Preparations for the trip were hastily made. Unfortunately, most of our Alaska crew had run out of holidays and could not make the hunt. And the organizer of our expedition, who had a lot of vacation time left, had not been content with the popular beach pastime of just watching senoritas go by him. He had become seriously involved in the active pursuit of a particularly fetching northern migrant, so *Palomas* were not on his current agenda. This was one of the hazards for bachelors traveling to Mexico without responsible female escort. Cathy, my attractive lady friend, helped me avoid such distractions. Though not a hunter she would make the trip north and help drive as we would see some new country.

The local Hertz agent had only a single, small rental unit left that I took. Rock was crowded into the small back seat with our gear. Somewhat reluctantly, we left the beautiful beaches of Mazatlan and hit the hot, dusty road north with a destination of Los Moches.

The roadside terrain on the drive north was initially rolling hills that were covered by brushy forest. An occasional small farm with a few scraggly palms providing shade changed the scenery. The air was hot and dry and the little car had no air conditioning. Large trucks claimed the right-of-way so defensive driving was a must for survival. The land along the road gradually changed to flat, uninspiring fields that were irrigated for intensive agriculture. The extensive fields of corn, sunflowers, and milo

Buddies Afield — Trips Outside Alaska

extended to the horizon and all were good dove food. *Palomas* flared up from the road where they sought gravel. Things were looking up.

We arrived in Los Moches, settled into a comfortable motel, and then indulged in the good Mexican tradition of *siesta*. Later, I reached our guide on the phone and a shoot was arranged for the early morning. Our guide would stop by before sunrise.

Late afternoon was passed in the nearby coastal fishing village of Topolabampo. Fishermen assured me that local waters contained many *pescados*. Too bad we did not have time to investigate. Deserted beaches beckoned and we donned swimsuits. Rock was ready to cool off and joined us in a prolonged dip.

Local children spied the big Chesapeake and rushed to pet him. His 90-pound size and water antics quickly earned him the title *perro grande*.
As a brilliant sunset reflected over the Gulf of California setting behind the rugged mountains of the Baja Peninsula, we hastened back to the village in search of food and refreshment. Much to our delight we found a restaurant that advertised and delivered fresh and very well prepared *camarones*.

In the predawn darkness next morning, the desert-like air was very cool. Light jacket and jeans felt good. My day-pack included a short sleeved shirt and short pants for late morning comfort.

The outfitter inquired, "*esta dia*, how many boxes of shells do you wish to shoot?"

"*Cinco*," I allowed. If I had opportunities to shoot five boxes of shells I would be more than satisfied. I opted to start with a superimposed, a mistake I soon found. An over-and-under requires some upkeep and care in use to function properly. The one available had seen much hard use with minimal care. Luckily, a Remington 870, an almost indestructible firearm, was available as a backup gun.

The *palomas* descending upon us were mostly white-winged doves with lesser numbers of mourning doves mixed in. Over the years I have shot good numbers of doves in the Carolinas, Florida, Maryland and Idaho, but the abundance of birds in the air at other locations hunted did not compare to the numbers here.

My first box of shells was quickly expended with few doves for Rock to pickup. I changed from the over-and-under to the Remington 870. By the time my second box of 25 shells was finished, I had settled down and my shooting was quite satisfactory and Rock was hustling. Shotguns in Mexico need not be plugged to limit capacity. The challenge became to try for runs of five birds bagged without a miss. This was possible if I picked my shots. Occasionally overconfident, I would have to try for a couple of

Chapter 22 — *Perro Grande*

birds passing high and wide. My average would then deteriorate. The shotgun barrel became hot to the touch as the birds passed in waves.

As the hunt progressed, my retriever/guide spent much of his time in plucking birds. He had never witnessed a trained dog retrieve. For all other clients he was the retriever. As Rock brought in a bird, frequently two or three more would rain down around him. Then, to expedite the hunt, the guide would demonstrate his human marking and retrieving abilities. For a while my lady companion filmed the action. Tiring of being a spectator, she wandered off to film shorebirds feeding along irrigation ditches.

As the morning warmed, so did Rock. After 20 or so retrieves, he would merely drop his latest bird on the growing pile of birds and hustle out for another. The nearby irrigation ditch was a lifesaver for him. Relieved to hear, "Rock, water," he would head for the ditch on a gallop. You could almost hear him sizzle when he hit the water. Occasionally, a lightly hit bird would continue flying, falling several hundred yards away. Normally, guides would make no attempt to retrieve these long fliers. Such lost birds would have been food for the coyotes. With Rock in operation, these birds were retrieved almost routinely as marks or as blinds.

By midmorning, bird numbers passing over our blind had decreased. The sun bore down mercilessly and I had expended my boxes of shells. Hunters as well as dog were hot. Time to call the hunt and head for the beach and water sports. There was tomorrow morning and another hunt to look forward to and rest for. Village children would clean, pluck and freeze the doves for five cents a bird. One wing would be left feathered to comply with U. S. regulations. I would take the frozen birds back north.

The second morning's hunt proved to be pretty much a rerun of the first. Maybe I shot well earlier. Rock continued performing eagerly, with the competence you would expect of a Field Champion. In conversations my outfitter said that local fishing for largemouth bass was excellent. This was another excuse for future trips to Mexico.

We made the hot, dusty drive back to Mazatlan in time for a final late afternoon dip in the surf. By the time Rock was fed, the cocktail hour was upon us. *Cervezas muy frio* went down very easily. Doves and a tip were delivered to the El Sid Hotel chef.

Later, as we sipped cocktails awaiting dinner on the El Sid's patio, we enjoyed the surf booming against nearby sea walls. Our romantic dinner was charcoal-broiled *palomas* with bacon strips festooning their breasts. Next day we would fly to the frozen north with many good memories.

Buddies Afield — Trips Outside Alaska

Near Los Moches, Mexico in 1983. Author Jim Mauney, Rock, and their local guide after a day of shooting mourning and white-winged doves.

Florida Outback

Winter retriever training and hunting in Florida, 1984

The trio of ring-necked ducks appeared from nowhere to strafe our decoys. "Take them," Tom yelled, swinging on and dropping the lead drake. Kyle and I jumped to our feet, caught unaware. We swung our shotguns futilely. We were too late to catch the rapidly escaping birds. Our shots disturbed only empty air. Clouds of blackbirds and coots flushed from the surrounding reeds at the noise. Tom's third shot brought down a second drake at the limit of shotgun range.

With two birds down, it was time for dog work. My old partner, Rock Honeybear, was an eager and impatient member of our hunt. Despite his 12 hard years afield, he whined eagerly to be off.

"Let old Rock have the close bird," decided Tom. "Looks like the far one is a cripple. I'll let Kimo try for that one."

"Keep your eyes peeled for gators fellows we don't want to lose a dog," I worried.

"If a gator appears, we are prepared to take the edge off his appetite," Kyle assured.

"Fetch Rock," I said as I released the big yellow Chesapeake. Rock jumped over the skiff's side to hit the water with a tremendous splash and briefly sank from sight. He surfaced close to the nearby drake. He then completed the retrieve and was quickly back at the boat with the duck in his mouth. Rock got his feet over the boat's transom as he surrendered the duck to Tom. Tom pushed down on Rock's big head while lifting up on his collar to pull him aboard in a spray of water. "Cripes, how much does this old dog weigh?" panted big Tom.

I heeled Rock to my stand in the bow of the skiff as Tom sent Kimo for the far bird. This far bird was now essentially a blind retrieve. Kimo had little advanced training on blind retrieves, but after numerous casts, Tom put him on the cripple and the fun began. The drake dove each time the big chocolate Lab closed on him. Kimo really got into the pursuit and followed the duck underwater. We watched as both duck and dog were submerged and out-of-sight. After long seconds, Kimo surfaced, snorting air with the ring-necked drake clasped firmly in his jaws.

"That was a spectacular retrieve," I exclaimed in admiration of the dog's work.

"That's why he is known as mobile Kimo," owner Tom enthused. "Good boy Kimo!"

We were hunting Florida's Lake Okeechobee in January. We had left the boat landing in predawn darkness to venture across what to me was a traceless water wilderness. Having spent most of my adult life in mountain country, I was used to having hills and peaks as references. Tom found his way unerringly through the Okeechobee environment of reeds, aquatics, water plants, and open water. From time to time, the boat prop became hopelessly entangled in floating plants. Tom would then be forced to tilt the motor and manually remove the tangle of plants.

Multitudes of coots squawked and splashed loudly among the reeds. As the eastern horizon brightened, we saw clouds of birds moving on the horizon. These birds brought us to attention. Ducks! Many ducks! "Ringnecks," Tom exclaimed.

As we dropped the last of our extensive spread of decoys in a fishhook pattern, the eastern horizon brightened into a pink glow. We hastily forced our boat into a dense spread of towering reeds and put final touches to our boat's camouflage by arranging palm fronds along its exposed bow and stern. A check of my watch showed that legal shooting hours had arrived. Shotguns were loaded as the dogs whined impatiently. We did not have long to wait for action.

As the morning passed, small flights of ring-necks buzzed our decoys almost continually. A number of these feathered visitors remained behind. My Browning over-and-under started to account for birds. I held up my first drake to admire the glossy, iridescent plumage of head and neck, which merged with the light gray side feathering. Kyle and I lagged behind Tom's success as he continued to demonstrate his wing shooting expertise. The dog work was efficient and no cripples were lost. The younger Kimo was allowed to make the bulk of the retrieves as old Rock was beginning to show his age.

The red globe of the sun rose to burn off all remaining wisps of the night's mist. We were enjoying another "bluebird" southern Florida day. Not exactly duck hunting weather but the ducks seemed not to have heard. As the temperature climbed, we discarded layers of clothes until we were gunning in shorts and shirtsleeves. Between flights we swapped tales of alligators and grizzlies. I provided the grizzly stories and Tom provided the gator stories.

"Have you ever had a gator come after a dog while hunting Lake Okeechobee, Tom?"

"Yes, but we discouraged him. Not too likely to see one today as air and water temperatures have been cool. They tend not to be very active

Chapter 23 — *Florida Outback*

until the water warms. I had a big 11-footer laying for and chasing my retrievers in the slough back of the house last summer. It was just a matter of time before he would have gotten a dog. Eventually, that gator found his interest in dogs as dinner not so rewarding."

"I have had my share of grizzly adventures in Alaska, including a hunt for a man killer, but I find alligators much more frightening for the safety of my dogs," I confessed. "In Alaska you can shoot a bear in defense of life or property. Here, with the gators now protected as threatened and endangered, you legally cannot defend yourself."

Tom responded, "Gators have their place in the National Parks like the Everglades and wildlife areas but not in people's backyards or golf course designer ponds. I admit that much of burgeoning development down here is taking place in their natural habitat, but it is no good to have them attacking people's animals and children. You saw that skull taken from a 12-footer collected from one of Joe's dog ponds. What a monster!"

"I basically agree with you about the alligators, Tom. The skull Joe has is quite an impressive trophy. As long as we are discussing dangerous activities, your sport of chasing after hounds trailing raccoons and wild hogs through the swamps at night, while wearing only tennis shoes and shorts, impresses me as extreme. I enjoy quite a variety of outdoor pursuits but I want no part of running through swamps at night. Strikes me as a very good way of having unwanted encounters. Gators, cottonmouths, diamondbacks, and copperheads may not choose to get out of your way. I recall a nighttime frog hunt I went on in the Dismal Swamp of Virginia. Cottonmouths were thick and aggressive. With flashlight dimming, I had to use the .22 rifle I was packing for bullfrogs to shoot my way out. My Chesapeake, Storm, was bitten one time but survived. I'll bet that swamp hunters loose a lot of hounds."

"Unfortunately, swamp dogs don't usually have a long life expectancy. Their lives are hazardous. When we catch up with a hog that the dogs are holding at bay—if it is a young one, we jump aboard, wrestle it down, and tie it up. The trussed-up hog is carried back and penned for fattening-up before butchering. Last winter, I misjudged the size of a hog I jumped. He would have gone 150 pounds or so. I don't know if I had him or he had me. Luckily, ole Bigfoot showed up and bailed me out."

I could just imagine the size of a man Tom (a 6 foot 4, 220-pound ex-Marine) called big. I later met Bigfoot. The old swamp hunter stood about 6 feet, 8 inches tall and weighed well over 300 pounds. His arms and legs exhibited numerous scars from up-close encounters with the sharp tusks of swamp hogs. He had a huge wild hog weighing several hundred pounds, and with very impressive tusks, penned up in back of his place.

Buddies Afield — Trips Outside Alaska

The whistle of wings again interrupted our stories as another brace of drakes checked out our decoys. Kyle and I each connected. The limits for this species in Florida in the early 1980s were conservative.

"OK, fellows, that does it," Tom concluded. "We have our limit, let's pick up the decoys. There will be some good eating tonight when Terry cooks us up a mess of ring-necks."

"Do you ever take any other duck species here?" I inquired.

"Occasionally a Florida mallard like you took the other day back on the homestead," informed Kyle.

As we picked up decoys, Kyle allowed he had worked up an appetite. "Let's hit the local fish house for lunch after we clean these birds. I am in the mood for a mess of fried catfish and hushpuppies."

We worked our way back across Okeechobee through the increasing heat of late morning, passing flotillas of crappie fishermen. Most were armed with locally popular fiberglass fishing poles 10 to 12 feet long.

"It was a great day afield; you are an outstanding guide," I told Tom sincerely. "If we had the time, I would like to try some Lake Okeechobee fishing. Before the week is up I must get back toward Tampa and get in some field-trial training with my Chessies. Bill should be down from New Jersey with his string of dogs in a few days. My Jay dog will be ready to run the Open and Amateur this year. Maybe I will hit the Englewood beach the next couple of days for some swimming and wildlife watching."

"Yeah," Kyle observed. "Too bad that your Norwegian girl friends had to fly home. Double-breasted mattress thrashers from up north are in full migration to our Florida beaches now. You might get lucky.

"Lots of palomas are working the homestead these days. We have had some good shoots there this winter. You might find it worthwhile to take a break from dog training and beach activities to join us for a shoot."

For the next several days my routine was to dog train early, then hit the beach with the dogs for a five or six mile jog and a dip in the Gulf. At times, Jay worried me by swimming offshore with the surfacing dolphins.

After the beach activities, it was lunch time and I headed to the famous Duke's Restaurant for a large bowl of seafood chowder and large ice tea served by a lovely waitress. In the late afternoon I found myself heading to the homestead to meet the fellows for a mourning dove shoot. As promised there were lots of birds. A bird missed brought derisive comments; when a difficult shot was made, "good shot" rang out. Kyle and Tom had picked their stands well and missed few shots. At the end of a warm afternoon's shoot, we dined on barbecued dove breasts and fresh garden salads with plenty of Cervezas to wash down the dust.

Chapter 23 — *Florida Outback*

I met Bill Thompson, a professional trainer of retrievers, when he arrived back on our training grounds on part of two large ranches in the lake country north of Tampa. Extensive surface water in this area was ideal for retriever training—numerous ponds connected by channels of water, with banks and bottoms of white sand. There were beautiful, huge spreading live oak trees and stands of pine providing shade. A dense stand of eucalyptus stood at the head of one pond. Extensive growths of water lilies and cattails covered the shallow areas. Fish, including sunfish and largemouth bass, found the habitat to their liking.

Unfortunately, this was also good alligator habitat that was not to the liking of dog men who loved their dog buddies. The entire water system eventually drained toward the north into a swamp covered with a tangled jungle of pine trees, bamboo, and vines. In Florida, such country abounds in wildlife and is a reservoir for alligators. The flat, intervening fields were heavily grazed but good areas for land training dogs.

One morning Bill headed to the Tampa airport to pick up his wife, Floran. She was flying down to get out of the cold northern winter and enjoy life in the sun as we trained dogs. Bill and wife were due back on the grounds before noon. I was cleaning and putting away the .30-06 as Bill drove up in his dog truck. Lovely blond Floran was still dressed for jet traveling and somewhat overwhelmed by the unaccustomed environment and heat. Bill made the introductions.

"Pleased to meet you," she gushed. "Good to be in some warm weather for a change. It seems so peaceful and quiet here. I was probably mistaken but I thought that I heard a shot as we drove up." As she said this, she eyed rifle.

Bill, standing near the truck, winked at me. "Oh, Jim likes to do some target practicing from time to time. Sometimes there are some quail hunters about."

Floran seemed doubtful that she had heard the entire story.

Bill hesitated and then admitted, "I guess that I should have told you about the alligators they have down here. We keep a rifle or two handy when the dogs in are swimming just as a safety precaution."

Floran was turning visibly paler. "You mean that there are alligators here where you train?"

"Not many," assured Bill. "They aren't very active this time of the year anyway."

"I think that maybe I spotted a gator across this pond a while ago," I said. "Doesn't seem to be moving much. Maybe it's sick." I handed Bill my binoculars. "Maybe one of the locals shot it. They have little love for gators."

"Help me get my car-topper off the dog trailer," urged Bill. "We will row across and have a look."

"I'll pack my little 35 mm pocket camera for some pictures." I helped him launch the skiff. Bill went to his truck and dug out a revolver.

"Please be careful," Floran urged, now on the verge of hysteria.

"We will. Don't worry," Bill reassured as we headed out.

With Bill manning the oars, we were soon across the pond and pulled up alongside the alligator. It lay unmoving in the shallows.

"That is a dead alligator," Bill observed. "A good bit of his skull is blown away."

"Not a bad shot if a man was shooting from a great distance. Not very big though, maybe 7 feet," I thought out loud.

"Plenty big enough to seriously hurt a dog though," Bill said emphatically. "Say I have an Idea. I will hold the gator up by his tail and you can take some pictures of me with the beast for my clients. Here, you hold the pistol."

Bill grabbed the gator's tail as I held the camera in readiness. Then our plans went awry. A major explosion and a geyser of water soaked us as the dead gator thrashed about. The boat rocked violently, threatening to tip us into the water with the gator. My camera went flying overboard.

"I sure wish someone would shoot but not hit me," Bill yelled.

Following a shot, quiet reigned until I fished a ruined camera from the pond. I then broke the quiet spell with enthusiastic curses. There would be no pictures.

Early one morning Bill and I were working our trial dogs on a difficult water blind. We were handling dogs the length of a 350 to 400 yard long pond. The dogs were sent into the pond, stopped by whistle as needed, and directed to the bird by hand signals. Arriving at the pond's far end, the dog would pick up the duck and return by water.

Bill was handling a string of Labs and had leaned his .30-30 against a nearby pine tree. I had run my Chesapeake, Jay, earlier and was sitting in the shade provided by the pines. My scoped .30-06 was close at hand on the truck seat.

As the morning progressed, we rehashed earlier misadventures in Florida. I started it off. "Remember the time I sat down on a pine straw covered fire ant nest while watching you run water blinds?"

Bill chuckled, "you sure came out of your pants in a hurry."

"Yeah, about 50 got me. Lucky you had some antihistamines handy. What nasty critters."

"Then there was the time we stopped at the Holiday Inn for happy hour. We had my Lab, Faa, and Rock in the cocktail lounge. After a couple

Chapter 23 — *Florida Outback*

of cold ones, we amazed the locals by sitting the dogs on stools at the bar. Things were going fine until old Rock wandered into the kitchen. The chef got irate for some reason and we got asked to leave."

"Old Rock's nose always did lead him to where the food was."

Our remembrances were interrupted as an official-looking green car drove up and stopped beside Bill's dog truck. Bill, concentrating on his dog, paid little attention to the man who walked up. The uniform, badges, and revolver identified our audience as a fish and wildlife enforcement officer. This officer was obviously very interested in our activities. He watched, at first puzzled and then amazed as the Lab Bill was handling picked up the distant bird and started swimming back.

The officer had noted our rifles with more than passing interest. He commented, "Amazing! I have never seen a dog do a retrieve like that before." He watched another dog go out and thought a bit. "What do you do if a gator turns up?"

"We maybe look for a rock to throw," I replied lamely. I realized as I spoke that there were no rocks within 100 miles.

Ignoring my reply the officer ventured. "I bet one of those dogs would make a wonderful hunting dog."

I assured him, "most of them could make very good hunters. However, many owners of these dogs use them for competition only. Some types of hunting like quartering; trailing, and flushing upland birds require independent thinking and this can take away from precision field trial training. My old Field Champion Chesapeake, Rock, has accompanied me on many hunts for many species of game birds and mammals."

"What is a dog like that worth?" The officer asked.

The Lab Bill was handling, now back at Bill's side, sat to hand deliver the duck. Taking the duck, Bill turned to the officer.. "Glad that you are enjoying the dog work. Some of these field-trial dogs, or a top hunting dog, can be worth $10,000 or more." He went on to confess, "to be truthful, if a gator shows up we will shoot around him to scare him off."

Bill had gotten out another Lab as he talked. The officer watched in fascination as Bill directed the retriever into and down the pond.

As the officer turned to go he commented. "I like your dogs and the way they work. Say, if I had a dog worth $10,000 and a gator went for him, I would grab my rifle and blow Hell out of the gator. Have fun and good luck. Keep your rifles handy. I have to go and see if I can find someone doing something wrong." He climbed into his car and quickly drove off. This officer was not born yesterday. He knew the score.

Buddies Afield — Trips Outside Alaska

Honeybear's Yukon Jay accepts compliments from rancher friend, Lewis, while owner Jim Mauney photographed the very successful end of a mixed bag hunt in Washington in 1988 that resulted in geese and a nice whitetail buck.

Washington Combination

After deer and geese in NE Washington State, 1988

Through the years, some of my most memorable times afield have been combination hunts for big and small game. There were duck hunting days on Alaska's Baranof Island when the ducks quit flying (or never flew) that I would then swap shotgun for rifle, heel my Labs, Kent and Big Ben, and head up a mountain in pursuit of blacktail bucks. There was a memorable morning on the Yukon that Rock and I bagged a brace of widgeon, and then by lunch, had added a record-class moose to the take. In Idaho, my Chesapeake, Jay, and I sometimes hunted the morning for deer or birds and then reversed the species we pursued in the afternoon.

The hunt on which I was now heading out would hopefully provide the opportunity for another mixed bag. While a resident of Alaska, I had the good fortunate to become acquainted with Pete and Rose, the owners of one of my Rock's pups. After I moved to Idaho, they whetted my interest with tales of many Canada geese and big whitetail bucks in nearby northeastern Washington State near the Canadian border. Rose's family operated a large farm along the northern bank of the Columbia River near Northport, Washington. Rose thoughtfully secured a gracious invitation from her parents for me to hunt on this ranch.

In phone conversations with Rose's father, he assured me that many geese were holding on the river bordering their ranch. Both mornings and evenings the geese lifted off the river to feed in nearby hay and grass fields. There was also a good deer population to hunt. Success in bagging the wily whitetail buck with limited time to hunt is never a sure thing. I decided to take the gamble. The week before Thanksgiving, I drove 200 miles north by northwest from Lewiston to Northport. A stop en route obtained a deer tag, along with general and waterfowl licenses.

Upon my arrival at the ranch in the late afternoon, I was greeted like a long lost member of the family and made to feel at home. During an outstanding home cooked meal prepared by Kay, we all discussed life and adventure in Alaska. I finally steered our conversation around to the local country and its wildlife. My wish was to absorb details of the ranch and outlying country.

"Snow is overdue. Might make the hunting better for you if we got a snowfall but there is none in the immediate forecast. The forecast is for cool, clear, and windy weather for the next few days," the knowledgeable rancher Lewis informed me. "I suggest that you spend your first day driving and hiking around and getting to know the country and the lay of the land."

"I agree with your assessment. Thanks for the wonderful meal Kay." I pushed back my chair and took my leave from the table. "I think it best that I turn in early tonight to get up and going at daylight in the morning."

"We rise early here. You can plan on breakfast," my gracious hostess insisted. "Do you need something to read? You are welcome to look through my book shelves."

"As a matter of fact I would love some good reading material. I forgot to bring a book with me. I often fall asleep while reading a good story."

The next day passed pleasantly. Rifle and shotgun stayed in the truck as I drove a winding highway that followed the Columbia's northwest bank. The pups and I went on short walks to get a feel for this very scenic northwestern corner of the United States. Heavily timbered mountain slopes rose sharply to surround the broad river valley. Here and there, the timbered slopes were laced by interesting rock outcroppings. Dense stands of tall cottonwood trees followed the river's banks. Immediately along the river, large cleared tracts of land were under cultivation for hay production and/or in pasture.

During the morning, several flocks of geese were seen moving from the river into grass fields. By midday, ducks and geese were splashing and resting along quiet river reaches. Excursions through the woods showed abundant deer tracks and droppings. Favored deer fodder species showed evidence of heavy browsing. As the bright day faded and a faint moon rose over mountains to the east, I headed my truck for the barn. In the gathering gloom, deer were out and moving. I cautiously hit my brakes to avoid two does that scampered across the gravel road. The outlook for tomorrow's hunts was increasingly bright.

I awoke to the blackness of four a.m. Dressed warmly for the frosty day ahead, I stumbled down the stairs. A most welcome cup of hot tea and a breakfast of homemade bread and jam got me charged up for a morning goose hunt.

The pickup cab and canopy were covered with a heavy, snow-like frost. But I did not find it necessary to scrape frost covered windows. We would walk to today's hunt. Jay eagerly bailed from the bed of the pickup. I lifted Old Rock, who was now pushing 15, gently down. His front shoulders were in bad shape with arthritis. I put a liberal supply of 12 gauge copper-plated BB's into my jacket pockets. A dog whistle and goose call dangled from lanyards around my neck. I slid the Beretta over-and-under from its case into my gloved hands. I had no decoys to pack. My

Chapter 24 — *Washington Combination*

strategy for this hunt would be to just locate myself in a strategic position along the riverbank. If lucky, I would intercept geese flying from the river to feed in the ranch's grass fields.

The condensing breath of hunter and dog companions intermingled as we covered the quarter-mile to the river in rapidly increasing daylight. But, exploring the riverbank, I searched in vain for cover. There was little to be found. A barbed wire fence followed along the riverbank. There were a few widely scattered, solitary pine and cottonwood trees. I could use a tree bole for cover, but a widespread canopy would obstruct overhead shots. I finally chose to sit beside two fence posts braced by a diagonal crosspiece. Two armloads of tall grass and weeds were added to my meager blind. The results were far from esthetically pleasing but would have to suffice. The geese I was hunting were fresh out of Canada and had been little hunted. Hopefully, they would not be very wary.

"The geese won't be moving around much until the sun melts the frost off their grass breakfast. We have a while to wait, boys," I told the eager dogs as we sat huddled together, sharing body heat.

Time seemed to drag as the sun slowly climbed to illuminate the frosty landscape. Our breaths were no longer visible. The grass began to show beads of moisture rather than frost. The music of geese talking was now heard over the river's murmur. As the minutes slid by, the goose talk increased in volume and also sounded increasingly restless. Excitement mounted to a peak when we heard heavy wings threshing the air on goose takeoff.

A flight of geese appeared over the riverbank but crossed just out of good gun range to my right. Then a flight of 10 or 12 birds materialized that were headed straight for our position.

"Sit! Quiet!" I ordered the dogs in hushed excitement. Then the birds were just overhead. I rose to my feet and fired twice. The sky seemed to be falling as two big birds plunged to the pasture. At my shots, geese took to wing with a great din from assorted points of the horizon.

"Fetch," I had no need to command further.

Soon father and son returned, each proudly packing a big bird. After a long and remarkable hunting career, this was to be Rock's last goose. I received his heavy bird almost reverently.

I patted the big, furry heads of my companions. Despite the relative simplicity of their retrieves, I was in a jovial mood and liberal with my praise. "It has been a good morning boys. Let's head to the barn. I need to draw and hang these geese. By the time lunch is over, it will be time to get my gear and rifle together for an afternoon deer hunt."

Buddies Afield — Trips Outside Alaska

I started that afternoon hunt still-hunting a thick band of timber along the river. The day was cool and gusty breezes whipped the landscape. The litter and fallen leaves were dry and crunchy under foot. Moving quietly through the woods under these conditions was difficult to impossible. There was little fresh deer sign. If deer were present, they would move out ahead of me. The deer hunting prospectus for today seemed poor.

My gaze turned up toward the high country. I decided to explore along those mountain slopes. The timber along the steep slopes would be more open than in the river bottoms. I would try to minimize the effect of the giveaway wind by hunting upwind and within sheltered coves.

As the afternoon slipped by, my hunt carried me slowly upward. The gusty wind and dry leaves continued to wreck my hopes for a successful still-hunt. More than once, I heard a deer snort that was followed by the crash of a heavy animal spooked through the brush. Approaching the upper slopes, I happened upon a clearing in the natural forest that was occupied by old, gnarled apple trees. The trees were heavily bent under a burden of red gleaming fruit. There was no sign of recent human activity here. The orchard was obviously abandoned. An apple plucked from a low branch proved to be firm, crisp, and juicy to the bite. Several additional apples found their way into my pack for munching later.

Studying the litter underneath the trees, I noted very abundant and very fresh deer spoor. Many apples had been partially eaten by browsing animals. I thought to myself. "Maybe I should be sitting, watching the orchard as the day wanes."

I still-hunted on for another half-hour or so, the hiking made easy along an old logging road. Finally, as the little used trail was nearing the mountain's summit, environmental conditions convinced me that further hunting involving movement was futile. My steps turned downhill as I hastened back to the orchard.

The intense sunlight of the fair day was beginning to fail as I selected an observation point at the orchard's upper edge where I sat with my back to the trunk of a large apple tree. Anticipation mounted as the sun rapidly slipped behind wooded mountain slopes. A dog's barking, cow's mooing, and blows of a woodsman's ax echoed from a mountain cove. Ravens called as they went to roost and announced the day's imminent end. A pair of great horned owls tuned up for a night of hunting.

The air temperature fell rapidly. My breath began to show white as condensation. The tension of waiting became almost unbearable. The time for a buck to show, and for me to have a successful deer hunt this day, was indeed now or never.

Chapter 24 — *Washington Combination*

Sharp snaps of twigs breaking in the brush above and behind me reached my ears. Then all was again quiet. "Surely a deer would not be so noisy," I tried to reason. "Perhaps my imagination has conjured up twigs cracking under heavy hooves."

Cautiously and slowly, I rotated my upper body and head so I could look uphill. A large and dark, shadowy form had emerged from the brush. I was looking at a large deer standing less than 30 yards away. The buck slowly raised his head. The last rays of daylight illuminated the silhouette of spreading antlers and many tines.

As I brought the 06 up to bring it to bear on the buck, I realized too late that I had failed to chamber a round before taking my stand. Safety conscious as per my usual practice while still-hunting, I had hunted with my rifle's chamber empty. Now I slowly, carefully, almost painfully, worked the bolt and a 180-grain hand-loaded Nosler slipped home. A faint metallic click rang out as I locked the bolt. It seemed to shatter the still of evening. Thirty yards away, the buck's head snapped to rigid attention. He stood gazing straight at me, on the verge of bolting.

The rifle roared and the streak of flame from the muzzle illuminated the darkness and temporarily took away my night vision. My last impression was of a leaping form frantically racing down the slope.

The darkness was now complete. Calming both my nerves and shaking fingers, I groped in my backpack for a flashlight. As a conscientious hunter, I now faced the difficult task of ascertaining the effect of my shot in the dark. Ten minutes of desperate searching later, I was wishing that I had a hunting dog buddy along to help out. I finally stumbled upon the buck where he had dropped some 70 yards down-slope.

I paused to admire the buck's immense size and 4x5 antlers. I quickly realized that it would not be possible for this man to pack this deer off this mountain tonight. I drew my Buck sheath knife and hastily set about the awkward task of dressing out a large animal while holding a flashlight. By the time the buck was opened-up and gutted to cool in the frigid air and the liver and heart stashed in my backpack, I was very late in starting the long hike back down the night-shrouded mountain.

Dog and human friends greeted my arrival back at the ranch. There was hot food to revive me and willing help with the deer. Piling in my rancher friend's 4-wheel drive pickup, we followed a circuitous, torturous way back to the kill site. The day's hunts had yielded unqualified success and winter meat for my freezer and that of my hosts.

Buddies Afield — Trips Outside Alaska

With the hard work over, Jay relaxes while his owner Jim Mauney records the end of this 1989 elk hunt on film

A Bull In The Brush

A most memorable Idaho trophy elk hunt, 1989

Loose rocks crashed down the draw's steep sides, first on my right and then on my left. Big antlers clanked against trees and brush. I sat frozen in place, hoping that I was concealed from suspicious eyes. Earlier, a branch-antlered bull elk had quickly trotted across the glade below me. Taken completely by surprise, I had reached for my rifle too late. Now cow elk began talking loudly up either slope. I had managed to sit down in the middle of a herd of elk!

The draw contained heavy cover except for the glade in which I sat. Visibility along the surrounding slopes was for the most part limited to 30 yards or less. I strained to see moving animals through the vegetation

The excitement was almost unbearable. Old Jay, my involuntary pack animal, had awakened to crashing brush. A roar rumbled deep in his chest. He was restrained by his lead tied to a big pine. I hastily grabbed and held his muzzle to quiet him, rubbing his head to keep him from barking.

Three big cows crossed the glade below me. An evening breeze had begun to eddy down the draw. Would the cows scent me and then spook? Dislodged rocks continued to crash down in the surrounding brush. There was nothing quiet about this herd of elk. Daylight was fading fast. I ruled out attempting a stalk of the elk as it was much too noisy under foot. In preparing my stand, I had cleared the ground where I stood of a thick carpet of dry leaves and twigs. Attempting to move from my stand would set up quite a commotion that would likely spook and stampede the elk. Would a second bull show while there was still shooting light?

I was hunting densely vegetated hill country. The base elevations were about 4,000 feet and the forested slopes climbed steeply to over 6,000 feet. Major timber species included Ponderosa pine, Douglas fir, and red cedar. The occasional tamarack or large cottonwood added variety to the tree landscape. Within the valleys, small streams supported a profusion of willow and other woody plant life. Occasionally, the timber yielded to a natural open area, "an elk meadow."

Much of the country had been heavily logged. Some of the cut areas were ancient and showed new growth while others were the sites of ongoing logging. A few remote tracts of old-growth timber still stood. A confusion of logging roads crisscrossed the country. The main roads were passable by four-wheel-drive truck. But most of the older roads had been overgrown by alder thicket "hells." Within these thickets, even foot passage was difficult.

I had been hunting elk since the season opened eight days earlier. I had yet to fire a shot. In fact, I had yet to see an elk. I had seen plenty of "where they had been" sign. Hunting conditions were generally poor. The weather was unseasonably warm for early October and a prolonged dry spell had parched the land. Afternoon temperatures climbed into the high 70's to low 80's F. The dry vegetation under foot made quiet walking almost impossible. There were too many hunters about. Most were hunting the road system by pickup truck or four-wheel ATV's, hoping to get lucky. The great human activity over the past week had made the elk extremely skittish. During daylight hours, elk were obviously holed-up in some cool, shady creek bottom that was inaccessible to most hunters.

My tent camp was in an old logging cut. Nearby, a nice, gurgling brook would be handy to refresh our water supply. A typical day started when I rolled out in the four a.m. pitch darkness. A hasty, usually cold, breakfast was quickly consumed. The backpack was loaded: a sandwich, water, candy, knives, saw, and emergency gear. My Chesapeake, Jay, sometimes accompanied as my pack animal. His father, Rock, was much too old for such demanding exertion and had to remain in camp. I was on the trail well before daylight.

The morning hunt usually started with a stakeout of a likely meadow. By midmorning, I was still-hunting along an old logging road or through open timber. After a lunch break, I explored, covering miles of country. By late afternoon, I would again be on a stand overlooking some likely spot.

After nightfall, I would hoof it back to camp by flashlight. My dog buddies, Rock and Jay, would welcome my return to the truck. A bonfire was hastily kindled to ward off the cold and the lantern was lit. The dogs were then fed and a cold beverage popped open to wash down dust and ease pain while a hot dinner warmed. Quality time was spent sitting by the fire, reminiscing under a glowing canopy of stars. By the time the fire had died down to coals, coyote howls echoed in the canyons and a great horned owl might be tuning up for the night's hunt. Then it was time to stagger to the tent, crawl into the sleeping bag, and pull up a dog or two for warmth. During the night, a heavy frost often formed. It would soon be four a.m. and time to start the fun again.

One morning while hunting, I heard the muffled bugle of a bull elk in the near distance. I figured him to be in the bottom of a draw a mile or so around a mountain to the west. Several times during the past week I had hunting the upper slopes of a draw in which I felt sure elk were holed-up. I recalled seeing almost steaming elk spoor on trails that dropped into the

Chapter 25 — *A Bull In The Brush*

draw's shady depths. And more than once I had found big tracks that were still filling with water, deeply imprinted in seep areas. I was well aware that a hunter did not want to down a big bull elk in the bottom of such a location known locally as a "hellhole." I had thus far made no attempt to descend into and hunt along these draw bottoms.

But about noon today, I arrived back at my camp located in a high saddle and prepared to pull out. My supplies were running low. I had one more day to hunt. I had been hunting down on the elk for the last several days. I would relocate my camp some 1,000 feet lower and then hunt up.

With camp once again set up, Jay and I headed out. I would try to find access to the suspected elk draw from an old logging road that branched off from the main road. The road followed a tiny stream for about a mile into the mountains. As we walked up the road, Jay hit hot scent and plunged into the brush. Grouse exploded into the air. Both ruffed and blue grouse were abundant in these woods.

"Heel up here, Jay, we are not after birds today," I commanded.

Forward progress seemed to be over. The road had terminated at an ancient logging dump. A careful search around the dump revealed an old, overgrown bulldozer track that continued steeply uphill. I took this trail, panting as we climbed upward. After a quarter-mile, the track petered out but a heavy game trail continued toward the draw that I wished to hunt.

Another quarter-mile in, I broke out of the brush into an open glade. There were pools of water here and heavily used game trails branched off into the surrounding timber. Vegetation showed signs of heavy browsing and there was fresh elk spoor. There was also fresh bear scat. I had walked far enough. I would make my last stand here.

Midway up the steeply inclined glade there were several large evergreen trees. I set up among the trees. Their boles would obscure me. Uphill I would be able to see about 60 yards and downhill 50 at most. To either side, my field of vision was much more restricted. I cleared debris from a patch of earth between a pine and a fir. I cut a few small tree limbs to open up shooting lanes. Jay's freedom of movement was restrained when I secured his lead. It was now mid-afternoon and I did not expect any action until late afternoon. We each downed water and waited.

A pileated woodpecker in search of dinner drummed on a standing dead tamarack. Chickadees flitted through the canopy. Red squirrels raised heck, chattering as they cut pine cones from spruce trees and scampered through the dry leaves. The afternoon dragged on. Occasionally rustling I heard in the brush seemed a little heavy for squirrels. Jay became very interested. Golden leaves fell from cottonwoods and rattled as they floated down in the still afternoon. The afternoon passed and waned and daylight was fading. The sun had passed behind the ridge to the west and the temperature was falling when I saw the first bull. Would there be another?

The minutes now sped by. Jay and I were on heightened alertness. Shooting light was fast running out. Suddenly, a big bull crashed from the brush on my left and totted across the upper draw. He was maybe 60 yards away. He was not going to stop in the open. I do not like shooting at moving big game but this was my last chance. I swung the 06 ahead of his shoulder and pulled the trigger. All hell seemed to break loose. A big, desperate bull elk came charging down the draw straight toward where Jay and I stood on the game trail. I stood transfixed, with my mouth open and forgetting to chamber another round. Jay was roaring and lunging on his lead. The knot gave and he was away! The bull turned and crashed into the brush with Jay closing.

I stood listening as noise of the bull's progress dimmed in the distance. I chambered another round and cursed at failing to get off a second shot.

Jay returned and I looked for the bull's trail. It was now dark in the heavy timber. I dug a flashlight out of my backpack. The light helped but little. There were too many elk tracks. I could not distinguish a blood trail. The only hope of finding the bull would be with the help of partner Jay.

Jay once again disappeared into the brush and I followed. A short time later, Jay came back for me again. I continued to follow him forward into a dense stand of alder. I found myself on a major elk highway. Then ahead in the dim light, there was Jay. He was standing over a big, very dead 5x5 bull elk! The 180-grain hand-load Nosler had passed through the lungs.

I had to bleed and gut the elk that night. Tomorrow would be another warm day. The meat would spoil if not gutted and gotten to refrigeration before the heat of tomorrow. I was prepared for night work with a Coleman lantern in my backpack. Very heavy, hard work followed for the next two hours as I struggled with the 600 to 700 pound carcass.

By flashlight, I stumbled back to camp, exhausted but jubilant. Old Rock, my companion of many a successful hunt, was awaiting our return. Tomorrow there would be fresh meat scraps for him. Tonight there would be a very late dinner for us and a cold beverage for me by the campfire.

Idaho Mixed Bag

A red-letter day for waterfowl and quail, 1989.

The day had started out a resounding success with decoying mallards. We were now stalking toward a flock of geese. The odds were looking good for compounding our luck.

I topped a bank fronting the Clearwater River, taking advantage of a last clump of brush. Reaching the cornfield edge, I could approach undetected no farther. The nervously shifting birds were only 30 to 40 yards away—plenty close enough! I stepped into the open. Thoroughly spooked geese sprang into the air with a great thrashing of wings and honks of alarm. I swung the Beretta Superimposed down the line of flying birds as I chose my shot.

My canine accomplices this day, as on many others, were my Chesapeake buddies National Master Hunter and derby star, Jay, and his sire, Field and Amateur Field Champion, Rock.. Jay was a 100-pound athlete toughened by a fall of hard hunting and he was primed for any adventure.

Rock had accompanied me on adventures afield the length and breadth of North America. While perusing *palomas* in Mexico one spring, Rock had become known to village children as the *perro grande*. Now 14, the years had taken their toll. Much to my great sorrow it had become necessary for me to limit his trips afield. No more hunting chukars in cliffs, pheasants in heavy cover, and breaking the ice for ducks, but today's hunt he could handle.

The previous night Tony, my rancher friend and neighbor, had stopped by with hot information about mallards. He had observed great numbers of ducks swarming into cut wheat fields near Lewiston. The ducks were flying from the Clearwater River to dine on waste wheat. Tony called the rancher friend (Don K.) and we quickly secured permission to hunt "his ducks." Tony and I discussed hunting strategy over a couple of cold ones. The plan was simple. We would arrive at the field before daylight and set out a few mallard decoys. High weeds and an old wagon along a fence-row would become our blind.

When I rolled-out in the predawn blackness, the temperature on the porch thermometer was in the mid 20's F. A light skiff of snow covered Clearwater Valley. Cloud cover was complete and more snow threatening. Tony arrived just as I finished getting myself into gear with a cup of hot tea. Tony was fortifying with coffee.

"I think those greenheads will be hungry this morning and will come in good," I greeted Tony.

"I believe you are right," agreed Tony. "We will give them what for. They are getting into Don's cow feed and he wants them thinned."

Grabbing my Beretta Superimposed, I suggested, "we are obligated to help a friend. Wouldn't want those cows to starve. Come on Jay; let's go! Rock, you stay here and protect the homestead; you can go next round."

Jay bounded out the front door and into the back of the pickup. Rock was not a happy camper and he let me know it in no uncertain terms, whining and pleading with his beautiful amber eyes. I relented. Retrieving a few greenheads on land would not be much work. With a boost from me, Rock was in the truck. Tony was in the cab, waiting with his Remington autoloader. The decoys had been loaded the night before.

Arriving at the field, we packed in and hastily set up. Only six decoys were deployed. We took seats in natural cover some 20 yards away. The sun weakly crested the eastern mountains heralding legal shooting time. The hiss of wings in the dawn drew our attention. Birds pitched into in our decoys.

I looked at Tony and nodded, "take them!"

As we sprang to our feet, ducks took to the air. Each of us managed a greenhead double! The retrieves were no challenge for the dogs, but steadiness was a challenge as impatient dogs waited their turn. With flyway duck populations down, the legal limit was only three ducks. Prospects for large numbers of birds in the bag were not why we were afield. Ducks continued to come for the feed. There was no need for more calling. We each had a chance to miss a bird or two. Missed bird provoked sarcastic comments and frustrated glances from the dogs.

Again, a pair of birds approached the decoys. Tony dropped a bird to fill his limit as I cheered, "good shot."

A few minutes later I collected the last bird. Shooting had been fast and furious. While most folks were rising for their first cup of coffee, Jay was retrieving the last bird of our double limit of greenheads.

We quickly loaded the truck. "Good outing Tony," I allowed. "It's too early to quit. Think I will ride up the river and look for some geese. Why don't you come along?"

"I better get back to the homestead. I have some cows that need attention," Tony said with regret.

After a brief stop by Tony's, I put the truck back on the road following the river upstream. It was just too early to call it quits. I approached a field of cut corn lying along the river. Geese had used this field within the past week. Maybe they would be at brunch this morning.

I drove slowly by the cornfield. About 30 big Canadas were busily feeding on scrap corn! I drove on and parked behind a rise. Permission to hunt was no problem; friend Don G. farmed this field. Jay, Rock, and I piled out of the

Chapter 26 — *Idaho Mixed Bag*

truck. This was before the days of steel shot regulations so I loaded the Beretta Custom 686 with copper-coated lead BB's. This shotgun, the most versatile I have ever hunted with, gave me confidence.

Keeping below a cut-bank formed by the river, we began an indirect approach, homing-in on the goose talk. Heart pounding and with the dogs impatiently at heel, the final approach was made from behind a hawthorn tree. Goose necks craned in suspicion. They spotted suspicious movement and then they were airborne. The Beretta swung naturally and I reflexively fired two quick shots. Two geese fell from the rapidly departing flock! I had acquitted myself well.

"Fetch Jay, fetch Rock," I sent the dogs to work. They bounded forward eagerly. Each found and quickly delivered his big bird. Jay did not tarry but headed-out again.

"What's this?" I asked myself. "Could there be another bird down?" Sure enough— Jay went straight to and picked up a third goose. "Good boy Jay. There are no lost birds when hunting with you. Let's go have some brunch."

The walk back to the truck was triumphant. I packed two big geese and Jay packed the third. As we approached the road, passersby spotting us with our burdens waved and honked horns.

Back at the truck, we enjoyed cold draughts of water. I broke out our brunch: a sandwich for me and biscuits for the dogs. "What a day," I reflected sitting on the truck tailgate. Again, I debated heading for the barn but it was still only midmorning. Today was the last day of quail season. The cloud cover was burning off. Any other adventures this day would be anticlimactic but I weakened.

"Let's go find us some quail, dogs." We loaded up and headed for quail cover. Locally, quail were the California or valley quail species, a handsome little game bird and a gourmet's delight.

As I drove upriver, I mused at spotting the new NO HUNTING signs. In years past, I seldom had difficulty getting permission to hunt a farmer's land. Now more and more land was posted and the NO HUNTING signs usually meant just what they said. All a farmer expected was respect for his land, livestock, and the wildlife. I had heard many horror stories about so-called sportsmen abusing hunting privileges. Too bad slob hunters were spoiling access for everyone.

The first stop in our quest for quail was a cut wheat field lying along the Potlatch Creek. Heavy brush and timber grew along the creek. Snow cover here was 2-3 inches, considerably deeper than along the river. Many, many tracks of pheasant and quail were evident in the snow. Pheasant season had passed, leaving good memories. We would pursue quail only.

Buddies Afield — Trips Outside Alaska

I slipped into my shooting vest and loaded pockets with an ample supply of no. 8's. I then uncased my little Ithaca side-by-side and unloaded the dogs. Their trailing and bird finding abilities were about to be tested. Scenting conditions proved good. The dogs started out working heavy brush along the field's edge. In short order, Jay held. Birds were hiding under the snow-covered brush. I moved in and quail erupted with thundering wings. I swung on a bird flying to the left and dropped him a shower of feathers. My swing continued on a bird escaping toward the timber on the right. I completed the double. I congratulated myself on a good start, thinking. "You are shooting well today."

As we worked the area, more birds flushed. Shooting opportunities were good as the birds flew across the open field heading for cover. There were some hits and some misses, with more of the former than the latter. But I did manage another double. Six birds out of a covey were enough. "Heel," I called the dogs in. "We will try another area. This sure is more fun than sitting around at some trial event," I was sure the dogs were in hearty agreement.

We reached the truck where I unloaded my shotgun and examined the birds. The take was largely bull (male) quail. The male birds seemed slightly larger than the hens. I could usually distinguish them in flight by their pronounced head plume and darker color. I prefer to harvest males and leave hens for future nesting. One bull quail will happily breed a number of hens.

The day's last stop was a heavily vegetated gulch that wound uphill through cut wheat field off Cottonwood Creek. As we worked upward, I struggled to hold the eager dogs back. Birds were running ahead of us as Jay made a hop into cover. A hen pheasant exploded from beneath his paws. A big cock followed, squawking angrily as he took to air. It would have been an easy shot!

"No bird," I cried. "We will leave those two to make more pheasants for next year." Needless to say, the dogs were not in agreement with my decision. They got a thrill out of flushing birds, but they always wanted to see birds hit the ground.

The dogs continued working eagerly up the draw. Quail were running well ahead of us. Their short legs were no match for Jay's long legs. As the birds neared the end of heavy cover, I was ready. The dogs closed and a covey of about 30 birds burst into the air. On the covey rise, I dropped one bird and missed an easy one straight away. The covey was now broken-up and we would have fun. Working our way up the draw into an abandoned apple orchard, we flushed singles and doubles. I took only easy shots at bull quail. A final shot connected and Rock retrieved the last of our day's limit of 10 and the season.

Deer tracks were plentiful in the snow that here lay heavy. The day had cleared and the tramp uphill and excitement of the chase made the air seem almost warm. I had time to pause for contemplation of the scenery and season. The apple trees provided frost-nipped apples for refreshment. Jay ate snow as Rock worked on an apple I had tossed him.

Chapter 26 — *Idaho Mixed Bag*

A little sparrow hawk, also taking a break from hunting, observed our activities from a nearby apple tree. He did not seem disturbed by the shooting. I have found through the years that raptors sometimes become conditioned to shooting and will follow the tolerant shooter as they look for an easy meal of flushed birds. I dressed out some birds and left him a few munchies.

Today we had lost no crippled quail; had taken a limit of birds; and I had made several nice doubles. In my years of chasing quail, I managed a limit of quail with an equal numbers of shells only once. On that day I had what I consider a bird hunter's equivalent of a basketball player's triple double. That was indeed another hunt to remember.

Across the valley, snow-covered hills rose steeply above the creek. Stands of pine intermixed with leafless deciduous trees clung to the hillsides, reflecting subdued greens, grays, and browns. Wood smoke curled up from farmhouse chimneys in the valley and cattle called to each other. The western sky turned rosy as the sun sank toward the horizon.

The time was at hand for three dusty, weary hunters to head home from the hill. Tomorrow I would have my hands full cleaning birds. Tonight we would enjoy our food and refreshment. Later relaxing by the old woodstove, we each would dream in our own way of this most memorable day.

Buddies Afield — Trips Outside Alaska

This 1995 hunt in Idaho resulted in filled limits of Canada geese for five hunters and three dogs, with later fine eating for the hunters.

Perfect Hunts

Idaho hunts of filled limits and no unretrieved cripples, 1989

There are many good or very good hunts. Almost any day a man gets afield with his dog and gun is a good day. By taking a couple of birds, a good day can become a very good day. It certainly is not necessary to take a limit of birds to have enjoyed a very good day afield. However, some poor shooting, or a crippled game animal left behind unretrieved in the field, or even poor dog work, can cast a pall over a day afield when a limit of game is taken. Depending upon the individual's outlook, such a day may or may not be remembered as a good day.

The definition to me of a perfect hunt would be somewhat analogous to the perfect baseball game—no hits, no runs, and no errors. The perfect hunt would better fit a bird hunt than one for big game. The perfect hunt would have to include a dog. Getting back to the baseball analogy, the perfect hunt could be defined as harvesting a bag limit involving multiple numbers of birds, no cripples left behind, and no shots missed. Most of us are fortunate to experience such a hunt. Through the years, I have been very fortunate to experience a handful of such days.

Rock and Jay were with Bill Conner and me when we used a late November day to hunt the upper Clearwater River for ducks. We were heading for a river stretch upstream of Kamiah, Idaho that included a number of islands and cutoff channels. Migrating mallards and geese utilized this area as a resting area during migrations. Nearby grass and cut wheat fields provided abundant waterfowl food.

We arrived at the trailhead in the black of very early morning. The rough trail followed along the river's east bank. A march of about a half-mile downriver would take us to our intended hunting area. Earlier, we had agreed we would not need many decoys; a dozen decoys should do fine. Waterfowl numbers in the late 1980s were depressed and bag limits were correspondingly low. With a limit of only three ducks apiece, we would not need to attract a great number of birds.

"I'll pack the decoys in, Bill," I volunteered as I shrugged into the decoy pack.

"All right, and I will pack them back out. Hopefully they will be heavier with six ducks."

"I see stars. Looks like we are in for a fair day."

"Doesn't bode well for a duck shoot, does it?"

Flashlights in hand, we stumbled through the woods and along the river's bank. Somewhere far off, a coyote's howl welcomed the new morning. Other welcome sounds reached our ears through the darkness. Mallards were talking and wings whistled as ducks moved restlessly along the river. Geese added to the clamor from a mid-river gravel bar. We arrived at our destination thoroughly warmed by our exertions just as the morning brightened. Individual trees stood out starkly. The slough's calm surface gleamed burnished silver. Down the slough a flock of mallards jumped, quacking angrily at being disturbed. Flashlights no longer needed were stashed and we hastily pitched-out decoys. Par for the course, six mallards swung over our spread, talking and wanting to come in. But spying us in the open, they swung away, thoroughly spooked.

Arranging an impromptu blind was our next project. A thicket of willows along the slough bank provided us our basic concealment and branches from a beaver-felled cottonwood added to our camouflage. A glance at our watches showed that shooting time was nigh but we would have to endure a short wait. The Chesapeakes sat in their designated places quivering with impatient excitement.

The vibrating hoots of a great horned owl announced the night's end. Across the slough a rooster pheasant greeted the morning with his rough crowing. Our decoys bobbed slightly from the wake thrown up by a busy nearby beaver.

"It's shooting time," Bill whispered.

I agreed. "Lock and load. The first bird is yours. We will take turns shooting and the dogs will take turns on the retrieve."

We did not have long to wait. A greenhead mallard swung over our decoys and started to settle in like he had found lost friends. Bill's vintage Browning automatic barked once and I sent old Rock for the retrieve.

Rock was pressing hard on 15 years of age. Hunting rough hillsides for pheasant and chukars was behind him but the stiff old Field Champion could still retrieve a duck. I was too well aware that this could be his last hunt. As it turned out he would not live to see a 16th season.

The early morning passed quickly and Bill and I had two greenhead mallards each. "Work that call Bill. Let's finish up on ducks." During our duck shoot, cock pheasants had continued to talk in surrounding brush. "We may pick up a pheasant on our way back to the truck."

Bill worked his call briefly and produced the desired result. A mallard swung in from right to left. Bill was standing to my left but it was his shot. As he connected, a second drake passed in front of Bill, flying from left to right. Feathers rained down and the two drakes lay bobbing gently on the water surface. Jay was sent for Bill's bird as Rock went for mine.

Chapter 27 — *Perfect Hunts*

The need to be quiet was over. "Way to go," Bill exclaimed in delight. "What a finish." We clasped hands. "We won't forget today's hunt for a while. Let's get in those decoys and see if we can flush a pheasant or two."

We picked up our decoys. On the way back to the truck, we did find a couple of pheasants. As best I recall, there were no missed shots that day and there were certainly no birds lost as cripples.

"What a lovely afternoon for a quail hunt," I thought to myself as I loaded Jay into the back of my pickup. I boosted Rock onto the front seat beside me.

The clear November day was unseasonably warm for northern Idaho and I was packing plenty of water. Briefly, I debated with myself which of my several farmer friends to call on. Rock, pushing 15, was not up to a long, hard hunt. I recalled spooking a large covey of valley quail at Don's during one early September dove hunt. The hunt would not be a long one. We would either find the covey quickly or not at all. If we found them and were lucky, the flushed covey might break up and hold up in relatively open terrain. With my hunting plans decided, I then steered the truck west toward Lewiston.

My shotgun of choice that day was my SKB 12 gauge side-by-side double. This shotgun in my mind was the ideal quail gun. New, it sported 26-inch barrels and was choked modified and improved-cylinder. Weighing only 6-1/4 pounds, it was lighter than most 20-gauge guns.

One winter day during hunting season I was chasing partridge down a steep, icy slope. My boots slipped and I fell, dropping my shotgun. As I recovered my footing, a partridge roared into the air and I shot quickly. Though an easy shot, I failed to connect. A bulge just at my shotgun's muzzle explained why. The fall had jammed the shotgun's muzzle with an icy plug. After a visit with Jim of Lolo Sporting Goods and some gunsmithing, I had my shotgun back. The bulged muzzle was gone from the slightly shortened barrels, both of which were now choked improved-cylinder. As requested, Jim had taken my measurements and shortened the shotgun's stock. The revamped shotgun was lightning quick to handle and reminded me very much of the double my hunting buddy, Hoyt, used very effectively for bobwhites in Carolina over his setters.

Don graciously granted me permission to chase some birds. I parked out back of the main house and I filled the pockets of my game vest with light loads of no. 8's. With shotgun broken open and dogs at heel, we passed through the gate to the cow lot we would have to cross to reach hunting cover. We crossed the lot, detouring wide of a small herd of cattle that eyed the dogs and shifted uneasily.

Buddies Afield — Trips Outside Alaska

The dogs hit hot bird scent a short distance beyond the feed lot and worked eagerly forward. Chambering two rounds, I followed them.

Approaching a wind-stacked pile of tumbleweed and sage, the dogs became rigid with attention. There was an unnerving roar as many wings and darting gray and brown bodies took to the air. I concentrated on a bird flying straight away for my first shot. The quail fell in an explosion of feathers. Continuing my swing, I connected with a bull quail flying sharply to the right. The dogs dashed forward and were quickly back, each proudly packing his bird. "We are off to a good start boys," I praised my buddies. "We acquitted ourselves well on the covey rise. If I am not mistaken, we are going find some more birds shortly."

I had observed that the covey appeared to have broken up and most of the 30 to 40 birds had flushed toward a deep draw that split a nearby hillside. The vegetation on the hillside and in the draw was a low, thick tangle of yellow thistle, tumbleweed, and sagebrush. The birds should hold close and there would be no brush to impede my shooting.

We worked slowly and methodically up the draw and then across the hillside. The dogs dug out quail, which held as singles and occasionally doubles. My shooting was good and the dog work approached the flawless. I collected a series of singles and two more doubles. Most of the quail taken were bull (or male) quail. The dogs retrieved each bird that fell. A couple of downed birds required short, intense hunts.

"Time to count birds, dogs." I conducted a quick inventory. "One more bird will give us our limit." Picking up my shotgun, I released Jay with a "hie on." Rock stayed close to my side now. The old dog panted loudly; he was very hot and tired. This would be his last quail hunt.

We hunted back downhill toward the feed lot. Soon, Jay pounced into some particularly high weeds and put up two quail. I dropped the darker bull quail to give us our limit.

Back at the truck, I filled the dogs' water pan for a second time. The hot animals almost sizzled as they drank. I unloaded our birds, examined them, and placed them into a cooler. There were eight males and two females. I shared my thoughts with my companions. "Today I fired 10 shots and you fellows brought 10 birds to hand. We have probably just shared the quail hunt of a lifetime. I can't think of better friends to have shared it with."

Bank Shot

Chasing chukars, the masked bandits of upland birds, 1990

"Send Jay down here to find this bird." Ed's voice reached me from far below. I cautiously edged my way to the cliff edge and peered down at Ed. He was walking along a rock-strewn bench some 300 vertical feet below my perch. The Salmon River gleamed in the canyon far below. The river's white sand beaches seemed to beckon with memories of summer and water sports.

"I'm not kidding you," Ed assured me. "Following your shot, a chukar came sailing over the cliff and fell down here. Seeka is having trouble finding it. Send Jay on down here."

The young Drahthaar, Seeka, was good at finding live birds but my Jay dog was our veteran for finding and retrieving downed birds. "Heel Jay. Let's get off the face of this cliff and see if we can find a place where you can work your way down to Ed."

We would have to find a slope where the cliffs gave way. We worked our way forward some 50 yards, finally finding a break where the cliffs were split by a steep, boulder-strewn chute. It would be possible for Jay to descend here, but with difficulty.

Jay was then an accomplished field trial Chesapeake as well as a very experienced hunting dog. Some years in the future he would be the oldest dog among an exclusive group of retrievers to qualify at the first AKC National Master Hunters event in Delaware. He was a veteran at taking lines and being handled for blind retrieves. I lined Jay up and then sent him downward with a command of "back."

Jay soon reached Ed's level, and following Ed's urging, he started searching among brush and rocks for the downed bird. After an extended hunt, he found the missing bird and headed back uphill to me. I examined the bird Jay returned to my hand. That bird had died either from heart failure or was the victim of a very unorthodox shot. The sequence of events that led up to this retrieve ran through my mind.

As we had hunted along the edge of a series of rimrock cliffs, Jay hit hot bird scent. He eagerly trailed moving birds, with me following him cautiously. I held him back by urging quietly, "easy, easy." We reached a point where the cliffs broke into tiers divided by a narrow shelf. Jay insisted that the trail continued out along the shelf. I hesitated briefly as I studied the unstable, threatening terrain. To hunt on would be an exercise in questionable judgment. But then a man who exercised good judgment would likely not be chukar hunting in the first place, so I followed Jay.

We continued along the rapidly narrowing shelf about 10 yards. The shelf's surface under foot was covered with loose, unstable rocks. Vertical rock walls rose above and fell off into the void below. A few feet ahead of us the shelf ended. We had reached a dead end. I called to Jay and started to turn back. About that time a chukar exploded from under Jay's nose, screaming insults at us. I lifted my shotgun in frustration for a snap shot but I lost my balance and began to fall. Desperate to keep from following the bird over the cliff, I made a grab for the rock wall with my left hand and seized rock. My Beretta was clenched in my right hand. I reflexively shot in the direction of the escaping chukar. Puffs of rock dust appeared where most of the shot charge impacted the cliff's face. Shakily, I started to retreat from the dangerous ledge, offering thanks that Jay was cliff wise. An excited young or inexperienced dog just might have pursued that bird over the cliff. It was about that time that I heard Ed calling me.

The midday winter sun seemed warm and Jay was panting heavily from his recent exertions. I got out my water bottle and we shared a refreshing, calming water break. The lightly hit chukar joined others in my increasingly heavy hunting vest. The unlucky bird had been the victim of my "bank shot."

During the early 1990s, chukar populations residing in the cliffs overlooking Idaho's Snake and Salmon River country were at very high levels. A hunter with strong legs, good lungs, and a good dog could move 300-400 birds in a day. If he did not bring home a limit of birds, the fault likely was his shooting. However, when hunting chukars in their preferred cliff habitat, for most of us poor shooting seems to be the rule rather than the exception. A hunt on which a limit of eight of the big birds had to be packed down from the cliffs was an occasion to live in memories.

Ed liked to say; "at the end of the hunt you counted your empty shells to find out how much fun you had." Usually, the number of empties in your vest greatly exceeded the number of birds in your vest.

Though this white meat bird is excellent eating, on par with that of the ring-necked pheasant, I think most chukar hunters got hooked on the sport for the pursuit and challenge of bringing these birds to bag. Ed felt that each chukar brought to bag under fair pursuit was a true trophy bird. I know of upland bird hunters who would never dream of ground sluicing a pheasant or quail. But this same restriction did not hold true for them in the case of the "masked bandit."

As an old mountain sheep and mountain goat hunter, I took naturally to chukar hunting. I really enjoyed an excuse to be in the spectacularly

Chapter 28 — *Bank Shot*

beautiful country that chukar choose to inhabit. Falls by the hunter seem to be a part of hunts for this bird and scarred stocks usually distinguish the shotguns used in chukar hunts.

Some years down the road I would take a serious fall and break ribs while hunting the masked bird. On that same trip my partner Clay fell and lost his Tritronics Electronic Collar control. The replacement cost was $300. Team chukar won that day. After recovering from those broken ribs, I still pursued chukars, hoping for but seldom getting revenge.

In my best years, I had a season take of 20 to 30 chukars over maybe six to eight hunts. A hunt resulting in three or four birds brought to bag was considered very successful. Before a tragic car crash rendered Ed unable to hike rocky cliffs, we made a successful team. We would locate a covey of birds and shoot over them, breaking up the covey. Once they scattered, the birds often held in cover as small groups or as singles. They could then be hunted effectively.

One winter morning in early December, Ed and I were guided by Seeka and Jay as we ascended again into the chukar cliffs. The clear, pale blue sky promised a fair day as the sun peeped over White Bird Ridge. The weather would be unseasonably warm in the brief winter afternoon. Our trek had been under way scarcely a half-hour when the dogs started hitting fresh bird scent. The slope was green with a new growth of cheat grass, a favorite chukar food. The ground below the grass was littered with chukar spoor. The dogs were wind-scenting birds as they hunted into the wind and they wanted to surge forward.

We permitted Seeka to hunt ahead, hoping the birds would hold for a point. Jay was restrained impatiently at heel. Often chukar coveys will not hold well for a point. These birds were of that variety and they exploded into the air some 60 yards in front of us.

At my shot, a chukar folded and Jay scrambled to make the retrieve. "Maybe this would be an omen for my shooting success," I thought.

"No way should I have connected on that shot," I exclaimed.

"Hey don't complain about good luck in chukar hunting. We need all the good luck we can get. Some of the covey pitched into that brushy draw." Ed indicated a deep ravine some 200 yards below our present level. "As much as I hate to descend. I think that we should follow them up."

"I'll work along the draw's far side if you want to work this side, Ed."

The drive in to White Bird chukar country along a narrow, gravel ranch road was always a thrill. The road had been carved out of the mountain's face. Sheer cliffs fall abruptly to the swirling Salmon River below. The mountain's face rose along the road's inside as a solid rock wall. The road had no shoulders and a driver had no room for error.

During the early morning trip in, the road's surface was frozen. The afternoon sun thawed and turned that surface into slick, treacherous slurry. Getting out to pavement was hairy, even in a four-wheel drive.

Back on the mountain, we descended, picking our way very carefully along and down the unstable slopes. The dogs went into and worked brush along the draw's bottom. Jay found a seep of water and paused for a drink. Many mule deer and bird tracks marked the muddy ground around that little seep.

My first hunt in the White Bird country had been for mule deer. On that hunt in the late 1980s, deer were plentiful and were frequently seen in small herds. Forkhorn and 3x3 bucks were commonly seen. One day I saw a coyote pass right by a herd of does. The does paid very little attention to the wild dog.

As the years passed, fewer deer and fewer chukars seemed to occupy the country, much of which belongs to the Bureau of Land Management. The land was managed as leases for sheep production. As sheep numbers increased, ground cover decreased. In areas of heavy usage, there was no longer any grass. The ground was literally layered with a cover of sheep droppings. There appeared to me to be an obvious correlation between high numbers of sheep and low numbers of deer and game birds.

As our dogs worked the draw, birds flushed as singles and pairs. We added another bird or two each to our take. The morning had progressed and the sun was now uncomfortably warm on our laboring bodies. We stopped for a water break in the shade of a towering, isolated ponderosa pine that crowned the bleak landscape.

"As much as I'm not looking forward to the climb, I guess that we will have to climb back up to find more birds. I think that we should hunt the ridge's top and then hunt the east slope," I concluded.

Ed added to our strategy, "Let's spread apart 50 yards or so and work upward at an angle."

As the morning passed, we continued to put up birds and occasionally one was downed. The thunder of shotguns echoed from slopes west of the river. Evidently, several hunters were working that area and finding birds.

Ed checked his watch and observed, "About noon." We had reached a somewhat level break in the steep slopes. "What do you say we pause for a well earned lunch break."

"Good to rest the feet," I sighed, reclining on the grassy slope. "We had quite a morning. For me, collecting a double from that last bunch of birds was an exceptional accomplishment on masked bandits."

"A double on chukars is an accomplishment for anyone," Ed flattered. "My shooting success has been good today but yours has approached the

Chapter 28 — *Bank Shot*

sensational. I predict that we are going home with two limits of chukars today. That happens about once in a coon's age."

There was a mid-afternoon lull in the action. With several miles of rough terrain behind us, tired hunters and dogs hunted with diminished enthusiasm. The sun was slipping toward mountain summits that towered on the western horizon. Finally, my shooting vest hung heavily from my shoulders with a limit of birds.

Ed suggested "what do you say we start working our way back down to the truck. Maybe I'll pick up another bird or two as we hunt down."

We picked our way along rocky outcroppings with Ed working up the slope from me. A chill evening breeze eddied downward. Jay picked up the scent of birds above us. A sheer rock wall blocked his ascent but Seeka was locked on point. Ed worked forward and kicked up a single bandit. At his shot, the bird folded to fall at the foot of the cliff where Jay and I stood. Jay returned to me with Ed's bird.

We worked slowly, angling gradually down the ridge. We had covered perhaps another quarter-mile when Jay gazed intently upward, focusing on a jumble of scree and boulders. Following the eddying breeze with great interest, he scrambled 20 feet up the unstable slope. I watched for a flush. Ed stood watching the action from above. Jay worked the jumbled area thoroughly but no bird moved.

"Come on Jay," I called. "Let's go. That bird has left,"

I tiredly slogged on, following a faint, narrow game trail. I soon realized that Jay had not followed. He was still hung up on that rock pile. Maybe a dead bird had fallen under a rock there. I would have to back him and go up there.

Jay was sniffing and scratching at the base of a good sized boulder when I reached his level. I noticed a small tunnel extending back under the rock. The opening was too small for Jay's big head. Getting on my hands and knees, I peered up into the tunnel. I could see blue daylight beyond its upper end. Silhouetted against that blue was the dark form of a chukar. I reached in, trying to grasp the bird. The bird bailed out of his refuge, making his escape by way of the "back door."

I heard the boom of Ed's shotgun and his holler of delight. "Another masked bandit bites the dust." That was followed by, "You can give me that bird, Jay."

I grinned as I expressed my feelings. "Let's head for the barn, Ed. The chukars took a beating today. That is 16 between us. Today's hunt will be the standard by which we will judge all future chukar hunts. Most will pale in comparison."

Jim Mauney's favorite retriever was Honeybear's Yukon Simba MH, shown here with a mixed bag of birds. A very likely outstanding career in field trials was cut short when Simba died early after needed surgery.

Special Memories of Simba

Sharing life with my most outstanding dog, 1991-2001.

Simba means lion in Swahili. My Simba was born in Alaska. You are right, we do not have lions in Alaska. My Alaska Simba was a Chesapeake Bay retriever. His full handle was Honeybear's Yukon Simba MH (the MH signifies the AKC Master Hunter).

My life has been blessed with a number of great dog buddies. Simba was outstanding among them. He was many talented but perhaps his greatest forte was tracking down wounded game. Mark Sternhagen, an old-time professional dog trainer and personal friend, was Simba's breeder. Simba was line-bred on my old Field Champion, Rock, who was both his grandfather on the sire side and great grandfather on the dam side.

For man's best friend, years always pass much too quickly. I suppose I had clues early on that Simba and I would have fewer years together than was our right to expect.

One fall Bill Petrovich flew down for a pre-Christmas bird hunt with Jay and me. Bill arrived accompanied by his Field Champion Labrador, Brute, and a tiny yellow puppy. As is always true of pups that will grow into big dogs, his outsized feet and long legs made him appear to be walking on stilts.

"It's going to take a lot of chow before this pup reaches his adult weight of 100 pounds," I commented.

Bill, as the boys in Jersey would say, "was a piece of work." You did not want to engage him in a serious game of billiards. If you did, you had better hope to win the toss and score on the break. Failing to sink an initial ball, you were unlikely to get additional shots. Bill's unusually good coordination was not limited to inside sports. From what I saw, he was a fine shot with his Ruger Red Label shotgun. Bill had also taken most of Alaska's big game species with bow and arrow.

After several days hunting together, I had to put my nose back to the grindstone. Horror of horrors—I had to work during hunting season. My route to work took me across the Clearwater River. En route, I passed a big field of alfalfa. A flock of about 40 big Canadas had pitched in and were busily feeding away. I high-tailed it back to inform my guest of the possibilities.

When I arrived home that evening a limit of big geese was hanging above my door stoop. Bill was absent but he showed up about dark. "I see you got lucky," I greeted him.

"Geese ain't all," Bill grinned. "There's a limit of roosters in the back of the truck."

"Damn!" I exclaimed. "You sure had quite a day. I have never managed that combo. We had better drink a cold one or two to your success."

"I appreciate the offer. I'll stick to one. After I clean these birds, I'm heading into town for some pool. I need to pick up some pocket money for more shells."

On a December mid-afternoon, Gene Agee, Craig Johnson, and I were sitting around on the tailgates of our trucks, hot, dusty and beat. Jay hit the waters of the nearby Salmon River to cool off. We had been chasing chukars among the cliffs since early morning. Each of us had three or four birds to show for the expenditure of a great deal of ammunition.

"Did you see Bill on your way down?" Gene asked anxiously.

"Yeah. He and Brute were still up there working across a shale slope, and hot after birds. Fifteen years ago I would still be up there myself," I replied.

"Fifteen years ago I have to believe that we were all more coordinated and would have been back down long ago with our eight bird limit," ventured Craig.

A half-hour passed. Shadows were lengthening rapidly as darkness approached. Then Bill showed up, happy as a lark. He took in our bedraggled appearance and exclaimed, "now we're having fun. How about a cold one?"

"Get your limit?" Gene asked the question for the rest of us.

"No but I came close. I bagged six or seven."

Bill arrived at my place one December evening with a six-week old Chesapeake pup in tow, courtesy of his breeder, Mark Sternhagen. Rudely separated from his family and suffering from his recent jet flight, the yellow puppy was none too happy with his new surroundings. He was unsure what to make of Jay, his big uncle. Jay quickly taught him that pups were not permitted to steal a big dog's food.

For several days I tried throwing him a ball and then a duck wing to retrieve. He showed no interest and I was becoming frustrated. Mark had assured me that the pup was a precocious retriever. Finally one evening I picked up a rubber squeaky mouse toy and squeezed it a couple of times. Pup was immediately all attention. At the toss, he dashed out, picked up the mouse and returned it to me. From that point there was no looking

Chapter 29 — *Special Memories of Simba*

back. His proud little growl as he packed a thrown object and his yellow color earned him the name Simba.

Arriving home at the end of a hunt, I would toss Simba a bird. It might be quail, chukar, partridge, pheasant, or duck. He was quick to pounce and retrieve. With increasing size, he graduated to goose wings.

The pup liked to prance around with something he had retrieved, a playful growl rumbling in his throat. That habit, combined with his lion-cub like looks, took me back to my days watching and filming big cats in Kenya and Tanzania. The name Simba came naturally.

Simba topped out as a tremendously strong 95-pound adult. Strangers meeting him generally described him as gorgeous or magnificent. I had to thank them and concur.

One of his first outings was a truck ride into the mountains with Jay and me. The objective was venison. At 4,500 feet, snow lay deep. I let the pup out of the back of the pickup to air. I still have memories of him romping and disappearing in deep snowdrifts between bounds.

At the tender age of three months, the small pup was accompanying me and Jay on bird hunts. During his first venture afield, he could not quite put everything together. Jay was working tall wheat stubble when a big cock pheasant flushed with an indignant cackle. The 12 gauge boomed and Jay rushed to make the retrieve, with Simba hard at his heels, pestering him for the bird. Jay delivered. I took and admired the beautiful bird. The Clearwater River gleamed far below, the day was beautiful, and life was very promising.

One December day I tossed a few decoys in a Potlatch River marsh with shore ice forming along the river. The weather was so clear that few birds were flying. Most had probably retreated to bigger water along the Clearwater River.

I blew on my duck call with decreasing enthusiasm. The day suddenly improved when a single mallard buzzed the decoys. At my shot, the duck fell into thick, high grass interlaced with channels of spring water. I sent Jay for the retrieve. Veteran though he was, it was soon evident he was having trouble finding the bird. Simba and I joined the search. The pup promptly fell into a water channel concealed by grass. To my amazement he came out with our missing duck. He had just completed his first retrieve of wild game in the field and in doing so had wiped veteran Jay's eye.

Early on I realized Simba's unusual ability to watch downed birds or to mark and remember multiple retriever field trial marks. With the help of a couple of local friends who also had pups to train, I got back into the trial training business. I also acquired an additional promising pup, another son of Jay that I named Tip, for training.

Buddies Afield — Trips Outside Alaska

Simba had considerable success as a derby dog in field trials. He wound up with a total of 22 points. One of his wins was over a large field of 43 dogs in Jackson Hole, Wyoming. Most of his competition was from Labradors handled by professional trainers. The end of his derby career listed him as number 22 on the National Derby list of 80 plus dogs. The preponderance of dogs making the list were Labs. His accumulated point total was the highest of any Chesapeake running derbies during the 1990s.

After advanced training, Simba quickly earned the title of Master Hunter. He went on to earn 15 ribbons in Master Hunter stakes. We managed to win some all-age points in trial competition. My interest level in trials eventually waned. A great deal of time is required to attain the demanding level of training necessary to win. Attending trials took just too much time away from hunting and fishing.

Simba's half-brother, Tip, showed great promise as a hunting and derby dog. With very limited campaigning, he had two derby JAMS. My field dogs also become house dogs. In time, I came to the reluctant conclusion that three big male Chesapeakes were too many for one house. There would eventually be serious conflicts. I found Tip a new home with Gene Agee and his wonderful family.

Gene, Joan, and their son Dave and I were hunting Idaho's pheasant opener. Michelle, then a very young lady, was just along for the walk. Our dog companions were my dog, Simba, Tip who had become a part of the Agee family, and Jake, Dave's black Lab.

The Agees had only recently come down from their home in Alaska and their dogs were accustomed to waterfowl hunting. In Alaska they had limited opportunity to hunt upland birds. Their upland hunts in the 49th State had been for ptarmigan. Simba was then a four-year-old veteran of many hunts for most major upland bird species.

Friendship between the Agee family and me went back to our early years in Alaska. I have memories of Gene heading out with shotgun or rifle and backpacking a very young Dave. Early on, Dave developed a fascination for flying birds and feathers. Years later it was Joan who packed Michelle. I had seen her drop more than one quail while hiking a steep hillsides with 30 pounds of excited daughter strapped on her back. The general consensus among us men was that she was an excellent hand with a shotgun.

There was a bright fall day when Gene and I were hunting wildfowl in Alaska's Goose Bay. Our companions were my then young Rock and Gene's Chesapeake, Strider. As the morning wore on, we slogged across miles of marshland as snipe flushed from under our feet in seeming

Chapter 29 — *Special Memories of Simba*

multitudes. We had no light shot along, so they were ignored but noted. On another day we would return with light snipe fodder loads of 7-1/2 shot.

As the morning passed, our success had been limited to a duck or two. Just short of timber line, which lay along the western end of the marsh, we blundered into a great flock of Canadas. The dogs flushed the first birds from deep marsh grass where they had been feeding on small plants in concealed pockets of low-lying terrain. At the report of our shotguns, two birds fell. Sounds of the shots echoed off the surrounding hills as many more honking geese lifted into the air. The air was filled with seeming hundreds of milling, confused geese. Waves of birds flew low over our heads as we stood concealed by high grass. Twelve-gauge guns boomed again and several birds were down. Our canine buddies worked the grass for downed birds while waves of geese continued to fly overhead.

"Gene, is the limit two or three each?" I shouted frantically.

Gene hesitated, "You know I'm not sure. You're supposed to know these things."

"We had better hold up and make a body count then," I cautioned. We shouldered our shotguns as the last flights of geese passed overhead. By the time the dogs had thoroughly scoured the cover, we had five geese in hand. Later we confirmed the limit was three geese each. We could have taken an additional bird. No matter, the pack back to the truck was a long one with those big geese.

But back to our Idaho hunt with Simba. The hunting party had bagged a couple of roosters early that morning as we worked a strip of wheat missed by the harvest. The still standing wheat lay along a tangle of yellow star thistle. The wheat field climbed sharply to our left, extending to the horizon and covering many acres. Tall wheat stubble had been left behind.

In the bottom of the draw below us, tall walnut trees towered over the dilapidated ruins of an old farmhouse and outbuildings. A tangled jungle of hawthorn, blackberry, and thistle covered the hillside and the draw above the farmhouse. The dogs hit hot bird scent there and began working frantically. A big rooster flushed in front of Tip. It was a long down hill shot but Gene connected. The bird fell into wheat stubble only to streak down and out of the field. That rooster disappeared into a stand of sumac whose leaves glowed like flames in the brilliant sun.

Gene sent his young dogs, Tip and Jake, out for the retrieve. The pair worked the wheat stubble in the area of the marked fall thoroughly. They eventually broadened their hunt but would not exit the field. They lacked the field experience to track the blood trail into cover.

Gene heeled his panting, overheated dogs. "I hate to lose that bird. Why don't you let Simba have a try."

"Fetch, Simba," I commanded. Simba quickly reached the area of the fall, checked a couple of times in the general area, found the cripple's escape trail, and took up the trail at a dead run. With his long legs, he covered ground in great bounds. Passing rapidly through the sumac in a shower of leaves, he disappeared into the dense tangle in the draw's bottom. The minutes dragged slowly by as I waited impatiently. I had learned by experience that once a dog was on a cripple, he was pretty much trailing on his own. Calling him in could amount to calling him off that cripple. You had to trust your four-footed buddy.

Finally, Simba appeared, coming back up the hill to me. His fur was a tangle of burs but he was packing the cripple. He gratefully surrendered the bird to me and stood panting from exertion. His face was flecked with blood from the bird as well as his own from thorns and briars.

"Good job, Simba," shouted the Agee family. "What a performance!"

"I don't care if I shoot another bird today," I admitted. "That retrieve made my day."

On a windy day, Simba and I were hunting a field of high native grass. Natural grass cover has, unfortunately, become most unusual locally. Most ground suitable for supporting wild grass was either heavily grazed by cattle and trampled flat by their many hooves or was under cultivation. A few grasslands have been set aside as game habitat under the Agricultural Conservation Reserve Program. Such areas are a treat for hunters.

Simba's yellow coat blended well with the yellow grass tossing in the lashing wind. The grass was so thick it made forward progress a task. The grass towered over six feet high in the more fertile areas. This dense cover gave pheasant and partridge a warm, snug refuge during the cold winter nights. Getting a clear shot at a flushing bird would prove difficult for me in the high cover. Despite sometimes impaired shooting, I found hunting the high grass a pleasure. Dogs love to work such cover.

We worked our way into a depression surrounded by higher ground where the wind was less severe. "This is a likely spot for birds to hold," I told myself. About that time Simba got a whiff of warm scent. "Easy Simba," I cautioned.

Thundering wings sounded over the wind. Two hens and a big cock pheasant barely cleared the threshing grass as they sailed over it and away on the wind. I made a snap shot through grass towering head-high. The rooster came down too far out and obviously too lightly hit. But Simba was immediately off in pursuit.

I stood alone in the moaning wind and swaying grass, awaiting my buddies' return. I was at a loss to help. The roaring wind rendered verbal shouts, or even a come-in whistle, inaudible beyond 50 yards or so. I held

Chapter 29 — *Special Memories of Simba*

little hope Simba could run down a wing-tipped pheasant under the present conditions. As the minutes passed, I became anxious just wanting my dog back. My anxiety was relieved when the grass parted and Simba appeared with an unhappy ringneck. His direction on return was off 90 degrees from his line of departure. He had once again made an impossible retrieve.

"Good boy Simba." I killed and then put the rooster into my vest and brought out the water Bota. "Sit. I'll give you a shot of water." Simba intercepted the water stream, drinking thirstily.

After almost 40 years of hunting big game animals, I have come to believe that effectively finding and retrieving big mammals is just as important to sound conservation and wildlife management as is the retrieving of downed wildfowl. Unfortunately, a fairly high percentage of big mammals hit lethally by bullet or arrow do not die in place. Fatally-hit animals frequently are lost to the hunter. I have for years used retrievers as pack animals. They have often led me to a variety of mortally-hit big game that could have been trailed by few if any human eyes. This situation frequently arises during early fall deer or elk seasons when an animal is lung shot and runs into heavy brush. Often, game is shot with night fast approaching. If the animal is not found promptly that night and gutted, the meat will spoil even before the next day's heat sets in.

It was late one bull elk season when my desire for some fresh red meat overcame unpleasant memories of packing heavy loads of meat from the bush on a back no longer so sound. The weather was unusually fine for late October. It would be good to get away with the dogs for a few days in the hills. Whether we took an elk or not was really not that important to the success of the trip. I would throw in the shotgun in case some ruffed grouse decided to attack us. I planned to spend early mornings and late afternoons sitting near my elk honey-hole where I had taken three bulls over the years. Evenings we would spend sitting under the stars by a crackling campfire. I would roast a sausage or two for dinner while sipping a cold one and reflecting on memories.

As had come true for his sire (the great hunting dog, Rock), Jay's time to wait in camp had arrived. Old Jay's serious days afield were over. In his time, Jay had been in on many harvests of game great and small. His spirit was more than willing; but as he approached 14, his body let him down.

After setting up camp with shadows lengthening, Simba and I headed up an old logging road to check out the trail to my stand. The road followed a small, gurgling stream into a V-shaped mountain valley. Steep, heavily wooded slopes rose on either side. Steller's jays fussed among cedars and white pines. Two ruffed grouse roared from brush to perch in nearby trees. At my insistence, Simba let the grouse go and walked reluctantly at heel. I reflected on the quietness of the surroundings. I was thoroughly enjoying the absence of human competition. Most hunters afield during the early part of the season had long since gone home.

After we had covered about a half-mile, the valley widened and we approached the site of an old logging dump. Suddenly, a huge, shadowy form trotted from the wooded slope on my left and paused in the road. I stood gaping at a big bull elk standing not 100 yards away. Simba quivered eagerly at my side as if experiencing a severe chill.

Coming to my senses, I chambered a round and dropped into a sitting position. I looped into the rifle's sling for additional support. The scope's cross hairs came to rest just behind the bull's right front shoulder. The elk did not fall at the impact of the 180-grain Nosler as I had expected. He leaped the creek to dash up the far open slope for heavy cover. In the excitement, Simba broke from my side and caught up with the bull, which turned on the dog with antlers lowered. Simba wisely backed off. Seeing my chance, I slammed another round into the bull's shoulder. The bull staggered, lost his footing, and finally fell.

"Oh no, not in the creek!" I pleaded.

Cautiously approaching the spot where the bull disappeared, with Simba back at my side, we found the dead bull. He carried a symmetrical pair of nice 4x4 point antlers and yes, he was lying in the creek.

The next couple of hours were agony. I struggled to maneuver and dress out the heavy animal. The stream banks on either side were a perpendicular six feet. Under foot, stream-polished rocks were moss covered and slick. By the time my task was accomplished, night had descended. I trudged wearily but elated back to the truck, with my path illuminated by flashlight. Tomorrow there would be much backbreaking work packing meat but tonight we would celebrate. By the time I reached the truck, I had come up with a new plan. I would drive back home for the night and draft old buddy Don into helping with the butchering and packing. He would be more than happy to share in some prime elk meet.

Simba had several wildlife encounters in which he remarkably came out none-the-worse-for-wear. Twice during walks in Idaho I saw him go up to and practically touch noses with big coyotes. The encounters were during the coyote's mating season and I believe that they were curious males. On observing his considerable size up close, they decided discretion was better than valor and retreated.

Late one summer evening at my Indian, Alaska homestead I settled down to enjoy a much-anticipated dinner of fresh-caught Arctic Grayling, coleslaw, and rice. The 10 p.m. sun had set behind Indian Mountain, which towered to the west. Late rays of light filtered dimly through towering

Chapter 29 — *Special Memories of Simba*

Sitka spruce. White trunks of birch showed stark white against a dense, dark forest background. Rain fell gently and the evening was cool. A low fire crackled in the woodstove, warding off the chill. My big blond Chesapeakes, Simba and his son Wily, had disposed of their evening meal and dozed in front of the woodstove.

Suddenly a deafening din of barks and growls rudely interrupted my dinner. The dogs rushed the door while I glanced curiously out the window overlooking my table. There I saw a large, black animal mounting the front porch. My first thought was that a neighborhood Lab had come for a visit. Just then the swipe of a huge paw and a crashing sound claimed a cooler of ice and fish I had carelessly left on the porch. I spoke my thoughts aloud, "There is no Lab that damn big!"

Dinner forgotten, I stumbled to the door. What to do? On the spur of the moment I opened the door and released my Chesapeake buddies, by now berserk with excitement. Their ancestor Rock had been notorious for his bear routing abilities. I would give his offspring a chance.

As the bear retreated under their onslaught, I scrambled for a shotgun. Back at the open door I witnessed an astounding sight. The bear had come to a stop about 30 yards away, just short of dense forest. Simba and the bear were standing practically nose-to-nose.

My screams for Simba to heel had no effect on either him or the bear. Very much aware that this could turn ugly for old Simba any second, I ran to the bedroom for my Remington 870 shotgun. My standard practice is to always have a loaded shotgun or rifle handy in the house in case of threatening visitors in the night. Checking the chamber, I realized that somehow I had neglected to load the shotgun. I scrambled to find shells and quickly dashed to the door. Bear and dog were still in a standoff. Simba was even slowly wagging his tail. I put an end to what could become a fatal encounter. A load of birdshot fired into the air broke up the standoff and sent the bear hastily on his way.

As the years passed, Simba's retrieves of birds ran into the hundreds. He had often helped at the conclusion of hunts for antlered game. He also loved to go fishing and to catch fish. He often entertained fishermen on Alaska's Bird Creek and Kenai Rivers by landing silver and red salmon that I had reeled near the bank. A typical comment from a fisher watching Simba's performance was "I guess that you don't need a landing net."

True, I did not use a landing net. I have to admit that on some occasions Simba tried to land a fish that was still too strong. Then, the thoroughly spooked fish would sometimes break off.

We fished inland lakes as a pair and amazed lake fishers with our performance. Simba would ride in the bow of my little 10-foot car-topper

Buddies Afield — Trips Outside Alaska

boat. I manned the stern alternately with paddle and fly rod. After fighting a trout or sunfish to the boat's side, I would give Simba the go ahead. He would grab a fish in his powerful jaws and lift it into the boat. Generally he held the fish until I took it from his mouth. The big Chesapeake was remarkably soft-mouthed and seldom left tooth marks on a fish.

Simba's last pheasant hunt was a classic. Dimitri, J.T., and I were hunting South Dakota birds. We had enjoyed some good shoots over Simba's sons, Hap and Wily, north of Pierre. I made contact with a distant relative who had a ranch south of interstate 90. He invited us down with the cautionary note that the spring's pheasant hatch had been a disaster. Conditions were just too dry for chick survival.

Arriving at the ranch, we found the land bone dry and crumbling under foot. The soil lay shattered and cracked. Cover everywhere was sparse. We chose to hunt a large, relatively flat field across from some standing milo.

J.T. unloaded Hap from the truck. and I started to unload the expectant Wily. Simba's pleading eyes locked on mine. I weakened and lifted Simba from the back of the truck; "You will have to sit this one out, Wily. Come on, Simba. Let's go."

We hunted with the scant cover crackling against our pants. Pheasants were forewarned of our progress. Having played and survived this game before, birds started flushing wildly a hundred or so yards ahead. There was no shooting. Maybe we should have set up a blocker. Finally, we came across some good holding cover where along the foot of a low hill a strip of yellow, waist high grass lay. Simba headed for the cover with Dimitri and I following. John chose to hunt the field's border.

Simba began working the cover like the veteran he was. Soon, he was into hot scent. As expected, pheasants had sought refuge in the dense cover. Working a scent trail, Simba froze, studied the cover at his feet, and pounced as I came up. A beautiful, yard-long rooster cackled angrily into the air. Sunlight glittered off his beautiful plumage as I shot. This scene was repeated three times. Later, and from another field, we collected a fourth rooster. The examination of spurs showed that all four birds were adults older than a year. The lack of young birds was evidence of a poor spring hatch.

Toward the end, Simba showed me the character of genuine courage. Spinal disks pinching in on his spinal column paralyzed his hind legs. Two agonizing spinal surgeries were of no avail. I would assist him to the truck and boost him to the front seat when Wily and I headed out for a hunt. He was happy to be with his friends. Returning to the truck after a hunt, I would sometimes weaken and throw Simba a bird. Operating purely on heart and determination, he would pull himself forward with his still

Chapter 29 — *Special Memories of Simba*

powerful shoulders to retrieve. At the end he still wagged his tail feebly in gratitude for the smallest kindness.

A famous dog man once said that the best place to bury a good dog is in your heart. I basically agree. For my dogs I have also chosen some outstanding physical surroundings. My departed buddies' physical remains lie in a lofty stand of timber or atop a high mountain.

I packed Simba's remains to the top of a famous Alaska hiking ridge where he joined those of his ancestors. They rest where the eagles soar, ptarmigan cluck, and Dall's sheep and bear occasionally walk. The view of snow-studded peaks, cloud patterns over the Inlet, and the shifting tides is breathtaking. Spring, summer, and fall, the voices of summit-seeking hikers echo over nearby slopes. In late summer, clumps of forget-me-nots dot the slopes. I will continue to visit there for as many years as my old legs permit me to navigate the steep ascent. Then, one year in the not too distant future, our physical remains will intermingle there.

Buddies Afield — Trips Outside Alaska

Her formal name is Beezer's Yukon Abbie Cakes SH and her everyday name is "Lil-bit." She weighs only 70 pounds but she uses them all in hunting such as this good day in 2003 in Idaho.

Chukar The Hard Way

Earning a "game bird from Hell," 2001.

A raucous, angry-sounding squawking and the roar of wings threshing the air destroyed the quiet. A large covey of chukars exploded from the cliff, just out of shooting range. Most chukars in the remote Snake River country probably die of old age, never having seen a hunter. That day, I was hunting public land not many miles from town. This country had been hunted and foolish birds were no longer among the survivors. The spooked birds sailed off the cliff and out of sight around the slope. Time for hunting was rapidly running out but I would pursue these birds a little farther.

It was the last day of chukar season in Idaho and eastern Washington. Since the dove opener in September, I had been fortunate to spend many days afield pursuing birds with my canines and a few select human companions. We had hunted the states of Idaho, Washington, and South Dakota. Numbers of quail, pheasant, and waterfowl taken during the season had been very satisfactory. Dog work, such an important a part of the wildfowl hunting experience to me, had been good and quite often memorable. However this fall, Mr. Chukar, the masked bandit of the upland bird world, had largely thwarted my best efforts. I had come to realize long ago that the number of birds brought to bag afield does not best judge the quality of a day, but of course some harvest is intrinsic to the hunting experience and satisfies table needs.

Local populations of the chukar are down drastically from highs in the early 1990s. Catching the chukar in his favored habitat above the Snake and Salmon Rivers is never easy. But in the high population years, a hunter with a good dog could find and flush plenty of birds during a day's hunt. Bagging the birds once found was another problem. It is difficult to shoot well when one is worried about—or in the process of—falling off a cliff. In most wildfowl shooting the hunter is firing at birds flushing upward or passing overhead. Chukars frequently flush downhill and the hunter finds himself shooting at a sharp downward angle.

Hunting acquaintances that would not consider shooting most game birds species unless they are in flight, admit that they would readily ground-sluice chukars. I admit that at times I have been tempted.

My current canine companions that day were Master Hunter Honeybear's Yukon Simba and his son, Simba's Wily Cub. Wily is the fifth generation of dogs in this line that have hunted with me. Their ancestors include the legendary Field and Amateur Field Champion Rock Honeybear of the Yukon and National Master Hunter Honeybear's Yukon Jay who hunt with me now only in memories.

Recently, our outings had been limited by weather to the pursuit of waterfowl over decoys. Old Simba's last retrieve on one of these waterfowl hunts was a memorable 200-yards plus retrieve of a winged but diving greenhead. Such feats, at the limit of canine ability, had over the years become almost commonplace for Simba but then his unusual abilities had been evident since early in his life.

Today, with rain and snow threatening, seemed to be best suited for another waterfowl hunt but there was still a week left in that season. After today, my next chance for upland game hunting, barring another long trip to a southern locale such as Arizona, would be some eight months away.

During the last several days, midday temperatures had climbed well above freezing. Rains were frequent and snow, once extending to valley level, receded up the canyon walls.

There is danger enough from falls when pursuing chukars under the best of conditions. Two years earlier while chukar hunting, I took a bad spill and broke some ribs. The terrain had been dry but a loose, round rock got me. Snow on cliffs and the unstable slopes preferred by the masked bandit upgrades the sport from hazardous to very hazardous.

Hunting cliff-dwelling chukars is what I consider a good sport for dogs under three and men under 30. Those were ages Simba and I had long since passed. However, the excitement, exercise, scenic habitat, and physical challenge of hunting birds in such country are addictive. It also does not diminish motivation that this is a superior table bird. Of the few hunters I have encountered in chukar country, a surprisingly percentage have been old-timers. The hunter who was once addicted to hunting mountain sheep and goats is in particular risk for chukar hunting addiction.

The physical risk to the hunter from most North American upland bird hunting is due largely to carelessness with firearms. In chukar hunting, the main risks are heat stroke in the early season and falls throughout the season. The risk of injury by falls is also inherent to spring hunting for the male blue grouse (the "hooter") on southeastern Alaska's forested and cliff-studded mountain slopes. Hooter hunting became my spring passion for several years when as a young man I lived in Sitka, Alaska.

My strategy for today was to hunt eastern Washington. I would hunt terrain along the Snake River. I was likely to find California quail and Hungarian partridge there. Today was also the last day during the Millennium season for hunting these species. There always was the odd

Chapter 30 — *Chukar The Hard Way*

chance that I would find some foolish chukars that had wondered down to lower elevations.

Last night, a mixture of snow and rain showering the house's roof awakened me. Remembering the e-mail a hunting buddy sent me about the recent death by a fall of a chukar hunter increases my skepticism about chukar hunting today. The smart thing would be to sit this one out at home.

I rolled out about 5 a.m. to check the conditions. A skiff of snow covered the ground. Though threatening, it was no longer snowing. Hunting the local Idaho terrain was out of the question. Nearby land along Washington's portion of the upper Snake River is generally warmer and was still a possibility. I put the hunt on hold to await further weather developments. By midmorning, the sky was brightening. Just maybe I could take the boat and check out some hunting areas along the river.

The boat was still hitched to my truck from a recent duck hunt. I got busy cleaning snow out of the boat and also off the truck. By 9 a.m. the gear was loaded with Wily in the back of the truck and Simba on the front seat with his big old head resting sleepily in my lap. Off to a late start, we headed out.

Arriving at the reservoir and driving downstream, I am encouraged to observe that the snow line had receded to 400 or 500 feet. There would be plenty of snow-free country to hunt. I decided to pack only my Ithaca side-by-side for the hunt. Weighing in at only 6 pounds and extremely quick handling, this is my quail specialty shotgun. The over-and-unders I usually pack for chukar are equipped with slings. The sling makes it possible to have both hands free when needed to hold onto a cliff face or slippery slope. The side-by-side was not so equipped, but then I did not plan to get into the steep country.

Running down the river in the boat, I arrive at the initial jump-off point for today's hunting. As I motored into the cove for anchorage, some big gray shapes along the beach catch my eye. Geese! I am close! I hastily shut off the motor and scramble for the cased shotgun and some large steel shot but I am too late. These geese had played the game before. They are airborne and over me. I stand there frustrated, with my still cased shotgun in my hands. Not a good start. I run into the beach and anchor. I plan to hunt up the draw to the west along a small, gurgling creek. After a few hundred yards, we will cross the creek and hunt a steep, brushy slope just above the river. I had previously found coveys of quail in both areas.

Within a couple of hundred yards the dogs become birdy. I hear quail talking in the nearby brush and tree cover. I decide to hit the cover with the dogs. A mistake! I should have stayed on the cover fringe for shooting and sent the dogs in for the flush. As I enter the canopy, birds from a small

Buddies Afield — Trips Outside Alaska

covey began to flush. Overhanging limbs obscure the flushing birds. I took no shots. Oh well, on to the next opportunity.

We hunt around the edge of the lake, gaining elevation. The lakeshore is studded in places with boulders tumbled in profusion and it rises directly from deep water as cliffs. The shore is impassable in these places. I choose to hunt a strip of brush immediately above the shore. There is a 30 to 60 foot drop-off to the lakeshore. Once again, we hear quail talking. They are running ahead in heavy brush. I choose to stick to the open, grass-covered slopes where I will be in the clear for shooting. The quail will not willingly leave heavy cover. There is no choice but to send the dogs in for the flush. Birds from a sizable covey begin to flush. The window of opportunity for shooting through the brush is extremely limited. I get off two quick shots but I see no birds drop.

We hunt around the drop-off in the direction most of the birds headed. As we hunt, additional birds flush from the brush. I take one hasty shot but again no bird falls. My shooting opportunities continue to be blocked by brush. Finally, we arrive at a deep draw where serious cliffs start. This is a must-turn-around point. Wily, in the bottom of the draw, is into heavy bird scent. I anticipate and am ready for a flush. To my surprise, he retrieves a bird. I admire the handsome bull quail that must have succumbed unknown to me by my last shot.

We hunt back toward the boat. There are more flushes in heavy cover, or in the open when I am in cover. I take no more shots. We cover a few hundred yards and Wily does it again. He delivers another handsome bull quail. This bird was likely downed by one of my two first shots. Thanks to Wily, we will not go home skunked on the season's last day!

We arrive back at the boat and pause there for our lunch. Lunch is a sandwich and jug of water for me and a dog biscuit each for the dogs. The afternoon is nice now, with sunny breaks. Temperatures have risen above freezing and there is little wind. The water surface is flat calm. A nice flock of mallards enters the cove flying our way. From about 60 yards out they spot us. I had no designs on them, but we are not to their liking and they head back the way they came.

There is still time to try to another area before dark. A short, brisk ride in the open boat brings us to an extensive flat. This will be the last area we have time to hunt on this last day of the season. I had had a good shoot over a large covey of quail here earlier in the fall. The dogs had found birds in light cover and I had acquitted myself well with the Beretta Superimposed I was packing. During past hunts of this area, I had heard chukars talking from the steep slopes and cliffs above this flat.

Chapter 30 — *Chukar The Hard Way*

We hunt for a distance across the flats. Is that chukar talk I hear that is coming from steep country above? We hunt farther but locate no quail. By now I know that the noise coming from above is definitely chukar talk and not too high up the mountain. The temptation is too great to resist. We head up. I will not go above snow line, I promise myself. The time is now 2:30 p.m. and it would be dark by 5 p.m. The sun is already behind the bluffs in the west and light is flat. There will be very little time for hunting. A hunter would not wish to be caught in the cliffs after nightfall.

We continue uphill with the chukar talk drawing us on. We need to get above them or at least reach their level to have a chance. The slopes we are traversing are increasingly steep, in places exceeding a 45 percent grade. Now we are getting into serious rocks and cliffs. Going is very slow and laborious and I follow game trails whenever possible. Trails make footing across the steep slopes and above the cliffs somewhat less hazardous. In really bad spots, I used the three-point contact method, holding on for support with a hand and placing both feet carefully on bare ground or rock. In some spots there is no bare ground or grass, with snow turned to slush, overlying frozen ground that makes footing about as bad as it gets. I again discover a great advantage of hunting with big Chesapeakes as hunting companions. I bring one dog or the other to heel at my side and lean on his shoulders. Their four-point stability on those overlarge, claw-studded paws is much greater than mine. We are now about 400 vertical feet above the river. The dogs are wind-scenting birds and droppings litter the slope. We are very close. I head across a draw toward a sharp, rimrock outcropping.

Wily, an extremely eager and birdy hunter, is working the cliff edge. He is hunting terrain that would put a mountain sheep or cougar at risk. He has learned caution when in the cliffs but maybe not enough—he is not yet three years of age. If there are birds around, he will find them with his exceptional nose. This is his game. He has learned well the ins and outs of bird finding from his father, Simba.

Wily's actions show birds to be along the cliff face or maybe at its base. The drop-off is 80 to 100 feet but he seeks a way down. He is an extremely strong 100 pounds and toughened by a fall of hard hunting. However, the physical risk is too great. I call him back. We will hunt on around the rimrock. I urge the dogs, "easy, hunt close."

More elevation is gained. We are 500 feet above river level now and bird spoor is increasingly apparent. The birds are feeding on their winter dietary staple, the newly sprouted cheat grass. I will learn later that they were also consuming large quantities of a very minute burr.

Cresting the next ridge, I admire the view. But I am made uneasy by the reflected colors of the rapidly setting sun in the western sky. We will

Buddies Afield — Trips Outside Alaska

hunt around this ridge and then turn back. The terrain is a series of rock shelves and drop-offs, interspersed with some grassy slopes. Wily is eagerly following a hot trail. Just above us the snow cover is solid. Simba makes a sudden lunge upward to a rock ledge on my right. A single huge chukar explodes, flushing uphill. The escaping bird is plenty close but terrain permits only a fleeting shot. The little side-by-side is responsive and the bird is down. Simba now has the chukar and is returning to me.

I pat Simba's big head. I am pleased he was able to "wipe the pup's eye" so to speak and make the last retrieve of the upland season. Today was another very good day afield and a fitting season closure. Now for the long and tedious trip back down the mountain and then across the flats to the waiting boat.

During our descent, chukars are talking. They hurl chukar taunts at us from the cliffs and rockslides above. Wily wants to go up but I call him to heel. As my old hunting partner Ed used to say, "every chukar taken by fair chase from the cliffs is a trophy bird." Today we have our trophy.

The chukars will be safe from human hunters for another nine months. I hope that the spring is kind to them and they have fun and success in making many little ones.

Tonight, looking back on a very good season afield and its successful conclusion, there will be a cold one or two for me. For my two tired dogs, there will be extra helpings of chow. Tomorrow I will decide which recipe to use for baking a trophy chukar.

The Devil's Backbone

Hunting upland birds and waterfowl in Snake River country, 2002

As I huffed and puffed up a steep logging road, Wily ran ahead. After hoofing it for a half-mile we finally reached the ridge summit. I called a halt there for a breather. The ridge summit fell gradually away in the south as an extensive meadow. Native bunch grass grew over the meadow in profusion, with patches rising midthigh high to provide food and cover for upland birds. On three sides the meadow was bordered by rimrock, with lower lying slopes descending precipitously.

We were hunting the Wapshilla Ridge area of Idaho. My old chukar-hunting partner Ed and I first stumbled on this bird-rich area during a period of very high chukar populations. During our first expedition to the area, our mixed bag included chukars, partridge, blue, and ruffed grouse. On several ensuing years I had returned to this ridge in the early fall.

With chukar populations down, I had not hunted the ridge for several years. In the intervening years the State of Idaho had acquired thousands of acres of land in this area and set it aside for wildlife management.

The area is one of the most spectacular pieces of bird real estate I had hunted anywhere. The scenery is of National Park quality. A portion of the terrain consists of a spectacular long and sharp rock ridge that eventually falls to Salmon River flowing 4,000 feet below. Walking this ridge gave glimpses of the gleaming river. Ed named this ridge the Devil's Backbone.

The high terrain is largely open but broken here and there by stands of timber. Mountains and ridges include seemingly endless slopes of natural grasses. Some can be hunted with little elevation loss but most drop precipitously thousands of feet to the Salmon River lying to southeast and to Eagle Creek to the east and Snake River canyon to the west.

The Salmon River and Snake River canyons and associated mountains are prime big game habitat with populations of whitetail and mule deer, elk, bighorn sheep, black bear, and cougar. During bird hunts, we have frequently seen or jumped a variety of big critters. During one chukar hunt, Jay spooked a huge Boone and Crockett class mule deer from a brushy draw. These days hunting this area for elk and mule deer is generally limited to a few lucky hunters who have drawn permits.

Today, the countryside was parched. Rainfall had been scarce for the past several months. Surface water was restricted to a few scattered springs. Afternoon heat in the early fall could prove lethal for a dog. It would be necessary to complete my hunt and get out by noon. I departed the homestead about 5 a.m. and arrived at my jump-off point about 8 a.m. The distance driven was only about 50 miles but the road was not exactly up to freeway standards.

Reaching this area is always a challenge. The last 30 miles are by a bad single lane road with 1,000 foot drop-offs or more on either side. For the final few miles, the road consists largely of sharp, blind curves, and exceedingly steep up and down grades. Undercarriage-threatening rocks often project from the surface. The road frequently follows a knife-edged strip of land connecting peaks. The driver has no room for error in such stretches. This final stretch of road is best assaulted in a four-wheel-drive vehicle. Once there is a significant serious snowfall, the area is not reachable by any wheeled vehicles. The first snows of fall usually blow in by late October or early November.

My initial hunting strategy this day was to prospect along a sparse stand of large Ponderosa pines for blue grouse. As I walked among the pines, Wily worked ahead but within shotgun range. Soon he found hot scent and became animated. Birds were close.

The tranquil landscape was suddenly filled with motion. About 100 yards ahead a band of mule deer spotted us and panicked in clouds of dust. The stampeding deer flushed a cloud of birds. My first impulse was that the birds were a migration of robins. When their chatter reached my ears, I made positive identification. We had happened upon a vast covey of Hungarian partridge! There had to be more than 50 birds in the covey.

Partridge sometimes provide the shot gunner with great sport. If a covey can be broken up in heavy cover, they will often hold tight for a hunting dog and can be flushed for good shots. Wily and I took up the chase with enthusiasm.

Part of the covey had flown to the left and into the bottom of a deep valley. If we chased these, we would lose much elevation. I elected to follow birds that had flown down the main ridge. We worked methodically down the ridge and approached rimrock that marked an abrupt drop-off.

"Easy, easy," I urged Wily who was wind-scenting birds and wanted to surge ahead. Thirty or so birds took to the air in a chattering bunch with a thrashing of wings. I managed a nice double. Most of the covey flew back up the main ridge. We started back up in pursuit as I remembered some earlier hunts.

One fall my dear mother, at that time a spry octogenarian from North Carolina, rode along with Ed and me on one of our chukar expeditions. Accustomed to the somewhat gentler terrain of the southern Appalachians, she found the steep, narrow road and sheer drop-offs more than a little

Chapter 31 — *The Devil's Backbone*

frightening. "Oh James be careful!" and "I can't bear to look down," were her frequent comments as I inched along some particularly bad stretch of road in low gear. When we finally reached the top of a broad ridge, I parked the truck for an early picnic lunch. Mother stood there enjoying the spectacular vistas. The day turned warm and mother was content to stay around the truck spending the hours reading, working crossword puzzles, and absorbing the scenery while Ed and I chased birds. As Ed and his Drahthaar (Seeka) and Jay and I headed out she urged, "you have fun but please, please be careful."

That day, as the sun sank low and glowing red in the western sky, Ed and I arrived back at the truck. We wearily shrugged out of heavy game vests and began unloading birds. Mother was amazed at our success, and exclaimed, "gracious, you surely had good luck."

Ed admitted, "Jim and I usually hunt well together Mrs. Mauney. You will have plenty of birds to eat. I hope you are cooking your son some desserts so he can keep his strength up for bird hunting."

I responded with, "don't worry about the desserts Ed. She insists on cooking two different kinds almost every day. Tonight we will dine on elk roast, tossed salad, potatoes with gravy, and pumpkin pie topped with Cool Whip. Tomorrow we will feast on baked chukar, wild rice, and steamed broccoli. We will have blackberry cobbler topped with French vanilla ice cream for desert. I'm sure that she has some other side dishes prepared I don't know about. We do not go hungry."

And I remembered a September that I shot unusually well on the first day of dove season. Usually on opening day, my first box of shells accounts for few birds. That morning, my limit of palomas and the number of empty shotgun shells were similar. The birds were taken in the first hour or so after the dawn opening. But Lee, my young buddy and hunting partner, was having trouble connecting and he was more than a little frustrated. This was his first dove shoot.

I assured him, "it's no disgrace to miss a dove. Often a hunter will not connect very often until he has run through a box of shells. I have been there myself. Today I shot exceptionally well. Just keep shooting." Lee's shooting did improve and shortly two limits of birds were in the bag. I was back home with birds cleaned and brunch eaten before noon.

That September, two women friends visited me from Florida and they needed to be entertained. It just so happened that September 1 was also the opener for forest grouse hunting in Idaho. This day's afternoon would be beautiful, sunny and warm. Plenty of daylight remained in the long afternoon. There were grouse in the high mountains and the scenery unparalleled. I would kill two birds with one stone, so to speak.

"Ladies how would you like to go for a little ride and take in some of the most spectacular country in North America?"

"That would be wonderful," enthused Sue.

The ladies packed a picnic lunch and dogs and a shotgun were loaded. We covered a couple of miles of the final approach to Wapshilla Ridge, had crossed a knife edge, and were passing through a grove of Ponderosa pines when I spotted a big gray bird in the road. It was a blue grouse! I hastily edged the truck onto a narrow grassy shoulder, grabbed the shotgun, and unloaded old Rock and Jay. During the next hour, I had one of the few wing-shooting opportunities at flushing blue grouse it has been my luck to experience. The dogs worked brush around the pines, finding and flushing several of the huge grouse. I acquitted myself well with my Beretta and soon had my limit of three grouse. The last grouse downed fell far down-slope into a dense stand of small trees and brush. Jay was up to the challenge and made the difficult find. He puffed back up the hill and surrendered the bird to me. All good memories but back to today.

For today's hunt, Wily and I worked along the west part of the high meadow looking for partridge. Following a half-mile or so of tramping, Wily was once more into hot scent. I demanded repeatedly that he stay in gun range. Carelessly, I let him surge forward too far ahead. I was caught unprepared when he unexpectedly put up another covey of Huns at the fringe of gun range. I managed to fire twice.

The covey flew to the east and dropped over the ridge edge a hundred yards away. Just as the covey disappeared over a fringe of timber, one bird appeared to separate and fall from the flock. I walked over to the timber and sent Wily in. Wily hunted ahead working the cover and then came out with the missing partridge.

We continued south along the broken rock of knife-edged Devil's Backbone. I knew from past hunts that chukars liked this ridge. Today, with the time approaching midmorning, the ridge was too exposed to the intensely warm sun. Wily did find some scent but no birds. We worked down the ridge for a half-mile or so, losing 500 feet. An old cowboy road along the east slope provided a relatively quick but steep path back to the top. We took a water break in the sparse shade of a scrubby pine there.

Back at the summit, I studied the country lying below and to the west. Immediately below my feet rimrock cliffs threw deep shadows. A cool breeze eddied up the cliffs. Wily inhaled the breeze with keen interest.

"Do I really want to bite the bullet and descend?" I asked myself. The sun was high and moving toward the west. The temperature was climbing. I decided to hunt below the cliffs.

Chapter 31 — *The Devil's Backbone*

A search turned up a break in the rimrock. We descend very slowly and carefully on my part. I did not wish to take a serious fall. Wily darted into some green brush lying at the rimrock's base. Wouldn't you know it? Four chukars flushed, screaming insults. As usual, I was unprepared and I shot twice but missed.

We continued to descend. Approaching the bottom of the draw, a covey of Huns flushed. One fell to the gun and Wily made the retrieve a hundred yards down-slope. The hunt continued unproductively down the ridge covering another half-mile and losing 500 or 600 additional feet. The sun was straight overhead and bearing down intently. It was past time for the long, hot, dusty climb back to the truck.

Back at the truck, Simba greeted us happily. We swallowed great quantities of water and took a lunch break. I dined on a peanut butter sandwich while my four-legged partners snacked on dog biscuits. While we rested in shade thrown by the truck, I studied the distant slopes. A mile away, a green stand of brush stood out against the parched brown slopes. I knew from past hunts that green vegetation usually grew on the site of a spring. Maybe some chukars were like us, watering and resting in the shade. We loaded up.

As we prepared for a new assault, the sun was bearing down. I was determined that this would be an easy, short hunt that old Simba could join in. As we approached the vegetation, Simba and Wily wanted to surge ahead. Were they scenting birds already? I studied the vegetation to determine the best approach for shooting opportunities.

Chukars seldom wait around to give a hunter the advantage. As I neared the brush, a covey burst out, hurling insults. I was unprepared. Two long shots brought one masked bandit to the end of his career. I watched the dogs rush down to make the retrieve. At that moment, another bunch of chukars exited the cover. These birds were in good range but caught me unprepared again. I had failed to reload! Fumbling, I managed to chamber one shell and get off a parting shot that this time was too late. But we had our trophy bird, which Wily delivered to hand.

Using poor judgment, I worked down-slope. We would hunt up the draw the birds seemed to disappear into. Reaching my planned turnaround point with no birds located, we faced another 500 feet of vertical ascent. As Simba and I struggled upward, the sun bore down. Simba and I were both hurting. Whenever my pulse rate reached a thundering crescendo, I called a breather. Young Wily ran ahead, occasionally stopping to look impatiently back and down at the struggling old-timers.

Back at the truck we seriously hit the water. A gallon jug of frozen water stored in the cooler had partially thawed. No wine ever tasted better.

I was all in and so was Simba. There were five nice birds in the cooler. We had enjoyed enough bird hunting for one day.

I headed the truck back up the bumpy road on the slow trip north, with anticipation of a cold beverage or two awaiting me back at the homestead. Driving slowly, I planned a new recipe. I would baste a couple of birds with orange marmalade, put them in a brown-in bag and then into the oven for slow baking. They would be served along with rice cooked with some celery and okra.

On that trip home, I pulled up to two ruffed grouse that were sitting on the roadside. Unlike their eastern cousins, western ruffed grouse are not willing fliers. I did not care to take sitting birds. At eight feet, they scurried off the roadside into the brush.

Each year's visits to the ridge seem to result in the unexpected. This year's early October visit was no different. The trip got off to a late start. By our 7 a.m. departure from the homestead, the sun was well up. Driving along the road, which ascended steeply along the ridges immediately south of Wapshilla, an occasional ruffed grouse was spotted scratching for gravel. These birds were passed up. Wily rode on the seat by my side, impatient for action.

As the 4,000-foot level was passed, frost lay heavy on the landscape. Several camps of big game hunters were noted along the route. Chances were that today I would be the only hunter after feathered quarry.

My first stop was in the vicinity of an above timberline spring. Green vegetation marking the spring contrasted starkly with the generally brown, parched landscape. Determined not to be surprised by wild-flushing chukars, I approached the spring stealthily with Wily close at heel. We passed through the heavily vegetated area but flushed only a couple of robins. Large birds had left ample spoor in the mud surrounding the spring.

Another spring was only a quarter mile on around the mountain. I walked on, careful to avoid stepping on loose rocks. We neared the second extensive patch of green, which I decided to hit about midway down from its upper reaches.

When I sent Wily in, he surged ahead and worked through the brush. To my surprise, he insisted in searching upward out of the green into the dry brown grass and rocks. I was about to order him down when a covey of Huns exploded and sailed downward. They were a bit far out and I missed with both barrels. Standing there, cursing silently to myself, I watched the birds sail down the precipitous draw. They seemed to pitch in near another patch of green vegetation a quarter mile and 400 feet below. Wily continued working the unstable slopes above me. I figured that he was into the scent of the recently departed partridges. Suddenly, more

Chapter 31 — *The Devil's Backbone*

birds jumped, cursing in bird language, and they flew in the direction in which the partridges had disappeared. Wouldn't you know it. Wily had put up a covey of chukars and I had not reloaded.

I had planned the spring excursion to be only a short one and I had packed no water. The sun was now bearing down and temperatures were rapidly climbing. But the temptation of all those birds was too great. I heeled Wily and picked my way slowly downward.

We reached a small side draw in the area of the birds' disappearance. The draw opened upward, revealing more previously hidden greenery. I was surprised to spot a trickle of water in the draw's bottom. Chukars were talking from among the rocks up the slopes above me.

The birds became uneasy and started taking to wing far out and above us. I dropped a bird with my first shot. Wily rushed for the retrieve. Birds continued to flush from above and sail downhill in power dives. I was unused to having passing shots at chukars. My shots were ineffective.

An inspection of the bird delivered to hand showed it was immature. Recalling the size the flushing birds, I realized that most were the product of this spring's hatch. We had a trophy bird. The young chukars would be tender eating. I would pursue the birds no farther. I turned back uphill and panted my way back to the truck.

We next hunted the meadow at the Wapshilla Ridge's summit. One covey of 10 to 12 partridges was located. A single bird fell to my two shots. We continued to hunt in the direction the Huns had flown but to no avail. We made a brief excursion of the Devil's Backbone and its upper western facing cliffs. Wily found little scent to get excited about and still no more birds.

As the noon hour approached, we headed back to the truck. The shade of the truck gave us a temporary reprieve from the glaring sun. I dined on bread and cheese. After gulping down most of a gallon bowl of water, Wily enjoyed a couple of dog biscuits. We were both tired and hot. A brief, fitful siesta revived us somewhat. I decide to make a final hunt along a nearby old logging road. This road swung back around the mountain to the south and passed through some good blue grouse cover before it then dropped steeply toward Eagle Creek.

A steel gate blocked access to the road by wheeled vehicles. Idaho Fish and Game was trying to reduce the impact of motorized vehicles on big game herds and reserve some country for the quality hunter willing to use non-mechanized transportation. I was looking forward to not having to compete with road hunters. Passing the gate, tracks showed that an ATV had circumvented the barrier. Despite clearly posted signs prohibiting their use, some so-called sportsmen insisted on hunting from vehicles.

Wily and I walked the road. Escape cover along the road was excellent and plants bearing grouse food were abundant. Occasionally, Wily hit some scent and left the road to search the steep, brushy hillsides but we found no birds.

After covering the better part of a mile, I was ready to head back to the truck. The road made a sharp turn to the north and crossed the head of a draw. Pine and tamarack grew on the opposite slope. My eye caught movement at the base of a large boulder about 300 yards away and just short of the stand of timber. A mule deer buck was bedded down at the foot of the boulder. The 3x3 point buck looked restlessly around and then rose to his feet peering toward the timber. Evidently he had picked up some sound we had made but he was unsure of its source. He finally spooked along a game trail through the towering trees, hoofs throwing up clouds of dust.

The roar of wings reached my ears and I watched a large bird the deer had flushed settle onto a broken limb midway up an old-growth moss-covered pine. That big bird had to be a blue grouse. "Heel Wily," I demanded quietly.

We skirted around the mountainside, hoping to approach our grouse from uphill. The last 50 yards we covered very carefully and slowly. I methodically scanned each individual tree below. Finally, I spotted the dim outline of the grouse against the bole of a large spruce about 40 yards below. Surrounding brush and trees precluded any opportunity for a wing shoot. The bird was watching us and would not hold for a closer approach.

Memories of spring hooter hunts in Alaska came to mind. I was not above collecting a blue grouse from a tree. I raised the shotgun and its boom echoed from the surrounding ridges. Wily dashed down the hill to find and retrieve his first blue grouse.

I admired the big bird delivered to my hands. The grouse was a very large and handsome male. In my judgment, his weight was equal to that of a big male ring-necked pheasant. A most unusual "bird dog" had provided us with unexpected success.

Afield In The New Century

Late season hunts for upland birds and waterfowl, 2001-2002.

Wily and I had shared anther excellent season afield. Old Simba, with his back deteriorating, got to hunt only a limited number of days. His presence on our hunts was sorely missed. I do not judge the success of a season by the number of birds taken. More important is the number of days hunted and the quality of dog work, my hunting companions, and my shooting proficiency. My records for the past season showed that out of over 60 days hunting birds, fully 20 percent produced no kills.

This past fall I had spent a total of about two weeks big game hunting that reduced our days for chasing birds. However, I enjoy tramping the hills and woods with a rifle, seeing big critters, and having the opportunity to put some red meat in the freezer.

Wily cut a front foot twice during the fall, with ensuing vet bills and time off from the chase. Upland hunting locally is very hard on a dog. Physical stress on hunting dogs can be compared in human equivalents to the stress encountered by a professional football player.

My harvest of upland birds in recent years included few chukars. The lack of chukars bagged was not due to lack of effort. Populations were down from levels of the early 1990s. A basic problem in chukar hunting is that once they flush, you must be able to hit the damn things if you wish to bring them home. You are frequently shooting at a downward flushing bird. I believe that the tendency may be to miss by shooting too high.

In my experience, it takes three to four years of experience afield and training for a dog to learn most aspects of hunting. The complete hunting retriever must learn to handle on blind retrieves, where to look for birds, to trail cripples, and to work with the hunter. There seems to be no limit to what the hunting retriever can and must learn. If the dog is to help in big game hunting, there is another big chunk of learning for him. He must learn to pack and trail.

My dogs tend to be big, "ace-high," pack-leader type retrievers. Wily is certainly one of these. Maybe, I have to admit, at 100 pounds, one of these dogs is sometimes too much for an old man.

Mike Vogel flew down from Alaska with his two Chesapeakes (Bandit and Katmai) to join us for some hunting. We had several good hunts. One day hunting in an old orchard above Lenore, we really got into California quail in a classic hunt. We took 10 quail and Mike bagged a bonus pheasant. The dogs worked well, pushing birds out of the tangled grapevines. There were more than a few misses but I felt I shot well. Mike admitted that he needed some more practice on upland birds.

During several hunts for chukars on ensuing days, we tramped for miles around canyon walls, skirting the cliffs and rockslides. But only two birds fell to our shots. There were too many misses and too many missed opportunities for us to be satisfied with the hunts. Of course chukar hunts are always good exercise, providing you do not break your body. Chukar hunting, for me at least, is largely an excuse to enjoy the spectacular terrain they inhabit. On these hunts, we did pick up the odd Hungarian partridge and quail.

While we were hunting a ranch west of Clarkston, Washington, Wily robbed Mike of the opportunity at a rooster. On that day the dogs were working a heavy grass strip that bisected fields of wheat stubble. Wily paused and then lunged into the grass, coming up with a wild rooster. One of our last hunts was up Coyote Draw where we moved two coveys of quail out of blackberry thickets. The coveys broke up, holding as singles and multiples. The dogs did a good job of finding and retrieving and Mike's shooting was quite satisfactory. I think that he took seven birds. I took fewer.

On another afternoon hunting up Mission Creek, Mike got into a band of ruffed grouse. It sounded like a war was in progress. Mike brought three birds to bag. By the time I could move in to back him up, it was pretty much all over.

Another day we hunted Pine Creek for deer and we both took nice whitetail bucks. Mike dropped his with a difficult offhand shot within a quarter-mile of the truck. Later in the morning, I dropped a nice buck some 400 plus yards up an almost vertical, snow-covered slope. I should have known better than to take that shot. Getting the buck down proved to be a dangerous ordeal after Wily was brought to the kill site to find the downed deer. Thankfully, Mike—a glutton for self-abuse as evidenced by packing out a big Alaska bull moose 12 miles that fall—was along to help me get the buck off the treacherous hillside.

Just before Christmas, John Terry flew up from Park City. Pheasant had become generally very spooky by this late in the season and their ranks were thinned considerably by two months of harvest. There were still plenty of quail but John had only four days to hunt. The weather did not cooperate for our hunts. Temperatures fell to 20 degrees F, the lowest of the fall on a couple of nights. A skiff of snow had accumulated at about the 500-foot level on the surrounding canyon walls, making hunting the canyon walls hazardous to hunter health. With the ground frozen and snow

Chapter 32 — *Afield In The New Century*

covering it, quail consequently were slow to leave their blackberry castles. But finally the weather moderated and we took advantage.

The highlight of our hunts was a mid-morning venture up Coyote Draw. Strategy was for me to walk through a cow lot, sans shotgun and dog, where birds were holding in their sanctuary of the surrounding blackberry bushes. Like a good guide I produced, flushing 60 or so birds up the draw. Now the birds were where we could work them.

As the morning progressed, John acquitted himself very well with his Browning pump. Wily was a very busy dog, finding, flushing, and then retrieving the downed birds. We could have used a backup dog. Some searches for downed birds in the thick cover of overlying, steep creek banks were physically very brutal.

As Wily hunted for downed quail, he pushed a rooster up in front of John. We were using only light quail loads of 7-1/2 shot but the range was not great. John took the shot as I backed him up. By the time I shot, the bird was too far out for our light loads. Wily, working the creek bottom, had not seen the pheasant come down. The tough bird had flown across the creek, across a road, and finally two fences, to come down some 150 yards up the bare east canyon wall and he then hit the ground running upward. No human could have retrieved that bird.

I brought Wily to heel. This could not be a picture book field-trial type blind retrieve. A dog could not reach the bird by running a straight line. Wily took my line, crossed the creek, squeezed through the first fence, crossed the road, and then passed through the second fence. A hundred or so yards up the steep hillside, he was wide to the right of the fall and was hunting short. Stopping on my whistles and taking my casts, he crossed the pheasant's scent trail. Slowly at first and then running flat-out, he followed the trail up and up, looping and curving in pursuit. He had by now covered 300 or more yards. I had my doubts that the pheasant could be overtaken. John and I saw the bird bounce into the air trying to escape. Then Wily had him and was coming back down. We stood in awe. Finally John exclaimed, "fantastic!"

After taking delivery of the rooster, we counted our quail. We were five birds short of our combined 20 bird limit. John was out of shells. I offered to re-supply him at a dollar per shell. But, he seemed to believe this was too steep a price. I relented and agreed to re-supply him. We hoofed the road to the truck for more shells and also a drink of water. The day was warming fast. Hitting the brush again, John shot well and quickly dropped a couple more quail.

Wily did his job retrieving. As he delivered the second bird, I noticed blood on his leg, too much blood for a bird. Fearing the worst, I checked his left front foot. He had a deep and ugly gash between the pads and was bleeding profusely. Needing just a couple of more birds to limit out, and perhaps using poor judgment, I decided we would hunt on.

We quickly limited-out. John's good shooting on quail did not at all deflate his ego that was already sky high after the nice elk bull he had taken with a bow in Utah three days earlier. I sought to bring John some what back to earth. "How about that easy rooster you failed to bring down up Mission Creek the other day. Seems impossible for someone to miss such a big bird doesn't it."

Unfortunately, John had recently witnessed me missing a pheasant. "Seems to me that I remember Jim Bob doing some poor shooting that afternoon. Wily bailed you out with an impossible save on the second bird or you would have gone home skunked."

Later, over a couple of cold ones, John and I reconstructed the hunt. Our bag consisted mainly of bull (male) quail. Come spring, one bull quail would delight in servicing numerous cow quail. Our day's harvest would therefore little affect the next spring's breeding success. We agreed that a dog, besides being essential to find quail for shooting, was essential to find downed birds. Without a dog, the 20 quail we had dropped would have been reduced to four or five that we could find.

After home doctoring, Wily was restricted to short hunts for the rest of John's stay. The young dog hunted gallantly with his foot either heavily bandaged or in a rubber booty. I stopped our hunts when he started to limp badly. Hunting success dropped off sharply. I had no doubt this second cut of the season was due to a broken beer bottle some slob had thrown from his vehicle.

One windy morning I awoke determined to chase birds despite the adverse weather. I decided to try the vast Lloyd Ranch that includes a huge chunk of land extending from the Camas Prairie at 3,000 feet plus to the Snake River 2,000 feet below. I called Mrs. Lloyd who assured me that there were lots of pheasant and that I was welcome to hunt. She told me that hunters had harvested few birds of late.

By the time I arrived at the ranch the air temperature was in the mid 30's. But a fiercely gusting wind pushed the chill factor down drastically. I decided to hunt the steeply walled but somewhat sheltered canyons. We started out working the bottom of a draw that climbed steeply upward.

The draw topped out in an extensive field of cut wheat where there was a fence to cross. As I opened a gate in the fence, two Huns jumped just out of range. They did not fly far. We worked around the head of the draw, eventually flushing and taking four Huns. One bird was hit as it flew over a rock cliff and fell into the draw. Wily went down for the retrieve,

Chapter 32 — *Afield In The New Century*

and I followed, navigating down the drop-off carefully. Suddenly, Wily turned, climbed back up the steep canyon wall, then disappeared toward the field above. I continued to descend to the draw's bottom. In a short time, my big dog showed up above and then descended with a bird. I have yet to figure this retrieve out.

While chasing the Huns, we had jumped a nice covey of quail. The little quail had real difficulty getting airborne against the wind and could fly only a foot or so above ground. Most took refuge under abandoned farm equipment. I called my partner off; we would not pursue them.

Another morning I decided to hunt Pine Creek Canyon. During my November deer hunts, I had frequently seen very large coveys of quail there. Wily and I would try to locate these birds.

We did find birds. We flushed three or four coveys that totaled more than 80 birds. However, the birds were spooky or always flushed on the far side of heavy cover. Precipitous canyon walls covered with a light skiff of snow and heavy brush were their ultimate refuges. I sent Wily up to flush birds out and hopefully down. I followed him a short way up. A few birds did flush downward but I was always in the wrong place. Climbing further up the slope for better shots would invite a disastrous fall. I called Wily in and leaned on him to make it safely back to the canyon's bottom. I had to ask myself what a man would do if he were hunting a pointing dog here today and the dog locked on point in heavy brush up the unassailable slopes. I am glad I did not have to find out.

Finally I scratched down a single hen quail. "This is futile exercise Wily. Let's take ourselves to the barn."

December 31 was the last day of the 2001 pheasant season. It dawned cloudy with about 2 inches of snow on the ground but air temperature was moderate. Wily and I were on our own that day. Wily's foot had pretty much healed. This would be the last chance at pheasant for almost 10 months, a long time in a man's life and a long, long time in a dog's. I doubted we would do much on pheasant but at least we would get some fresh air and exercise. I could probably find quail.

I thought of Eddy James, a 90-year-old Nez Perce tribal elder. We would be hunting a draw above his place. Observing preparations for a hunt, Simba dragged himself to the front door and he gazed at me longingly. I helped him across the porch, down the steps and onto the truck seat. He would ride along with us.

Wily quickly loaded up. I was packing my Beretta Silverside. Though I perceived that my shooting on upland birds with this shotgun sometimes was none too good, I had no wish to expose my old classic 686 to the threatening elements. I had convinced myself that there probably would not be much shooting. I could not have been more wrong. Passing through the small village of Lapwai, I stopped by the local deli for a morning snack and shared my breakfast with Simba. We reached our destination where we pulled into the edge of a field of new winter wheat. The ground under foot was frozen and there was an inch or so of snow cover. Walking on the frozen ground would not harm the new crop.

A hundred yards or so across the way lay a steep hillside covered by thick brush. A bunch of birds were feeding beneath a big, gnarled apple tree at the bottom edge of the brush. The birds were quail, many quail. They were feeding on the fallen apples.

The quail quickly dispersed uphill into the brush as Wily and I crossed the open field. I restrained Wily with difficulty. We reached the brush line together I sent Wily in and he worked the hillside, flushing birds above me almost continuously. The shooting was largely pass shooting and I shot very well. During the next half-hour or so, Wily delivered six quail to my hand. I could have pursued a limit but the morning was getting on. I told my companion, "time to look for big birds, Wily."

I followed a brushy draw that projected upward into a field of planted winter wheat. About 100 yards into the climb I let Wily go into the brush. He flushed a very angry, squawking rooster that had mistakenly held tight. The rooster fell to the shot and Wily was on him. Onward and upward, the snow-slick slope grew increasingly steep. I kept Wily at heel as the plan was to reach the top of the draw without spooking birds out of range. How ever, by this late date these birds were educated. While we were still 200 yards from the top of the draw, pheasants stated flushing. We continued upward and birds continued to boil from the draw. At the draw's top, pheasant tracks and spoor in the snow were reminiscent of a chicken coop. Wily was released and he worked the brush. He drove out another half dozen or so hens.

I knew about a heavily wooded draw most of these birds had headed toward. Past experiences had shown me the probability of bagging birds in its heavy brush and timber was remote. Anyway, it was good to see that there were seed birds left for next year. With all those hens, the surviving roosters would have big grins on their faces come spring. I would pursue easier game.

We started down the hill, with me slipping and sliding. A covey of about 30 quail flushed wild and flew upward. Back up we headed but this covey eluded us. We started back down the hill once more. Reaching the bottom, I passed the old apple tree. A few quail flushed there, and I shot one. It was time to head to new covers.

Chapter 32 — *Afield In The New Century*

I headed the truck up Mission Creek Road with pheasants on my mind. Thirty or more quail were picking gravel along the road in front of a farmhouse. These were passed up. A quarter-mile farther up the road, 40 or more quail were feeding along a cow pasture that was bisected by Mission Creek. We would have a go here. As we tried to figure a way across a difficult barbed wire fence, many quail flushed from blackberry bushes that grew thickly along the creek. I dropped one that unfortunately fell into blackberry bushes. I worked past the bushes, with quail flushing continuously and crossing the creek. I took no more shots. I did not wish to drop more quail into the blackberries. I refrained from sending my dog into blackberry bushes. There was too great a chance of losing an eye. But Wily went in anyway. After a prolonged and brutal hunt I called him out.

I then sent Wily across the creek, ice covered in some reaches. It was too high for me to cross. This effort produced no birds. Wily re-crossed the creek and went back into the blackberry bushes looking for a missing bird. This time he was successful. "Good boy Wily," I complimented him.

Driving on up Mission Creek Road, I slowed in front of the old Mission to avoid a huge covey of 60 or so quail picking gravel along the road. There would be no room for shooting here; I had enough quail.

I turned west along a gravel road to park after a couple of miles in the edge of a cut wheat field. After crossing a quarter-mile of plowed ground, we reached a hidden draw containing heavy brush. We worked up the draw and Wily became birdy. He pushed a cackling rooster into the air that fell to my shot. Continuing up the draw, he flushed another rooster. This bird was a bit far out. In the now failing daylight, I missed the opportunity to fill my limit.

On the way back to the truck, we walked through tall wheat stubble. I noted abundant pheasant spoor littering the snow among the stubble. Wily worked the stubble hard but could not come up with a bird. He finally was about to enter a strip of heavy brush. He forced his way into a particularly thick patch of brush and I prepared for the flush. There was no flush, but I filled my limit with a rooster Wily caught. This was a second wild rooster he caught during that fall.

Our take for the day included a limit of roosters and eight quail. We had flushed over 200 quail and maybe 100 pheasant. It had been a very good last day to close out the Idaho pheasant and quail season.

All excuses to be afield were not over. Hungarian partridge and chukar seasons remained open. This day was unseasonably mild for January and the chukar ridges called. I decided to give Chukar Ridge another go. Hopefully the trip would be more productive than most chukar hunts of late. Besides, I needed the exercise and the hunting terrain gave some magnificent views.

Within a half-hour after leaving the truck, chukars were talking on the ridge above us. Wily hit hot scent and tuned in on their talking. He wanted to surge ahead. No way could I keep up if I released him. I had to insist he remain at heel. Then a hundred yards or so ahead I spotted numerous birds sitting on rocks overlooking the Clearwater River lying far below—the chukars were watching us. As we moved up, so did they, easily staying out of shooting range. Finally, they tired of the game and sailed off the cliff, making good their escape on the inaccessible rocky slopes below.

We continued up the ridge, climbing steadily. Then, Wily became animated. A steady breeze blew off the ridge rising to the right. He was wind-scenting birds. We worked in the direction he indicated, with me cautioning, "easy, easy."

A covey of around 30 chukars burst into the air some 40 yards out and not in good shooting range. One fell to my first shot but my second shot missed. The downed bird was a runner. Wily disappeared over the ridge in pursuit. After a long absence, he returned with a nice mature chukar.

We hunted the rest of the morning along the steep sheltered slopes that overlook Potlatch Creek. Several bunches of birds were flushed but none fell to the gun. A couple of missed chances I could blame on my overeager canine hunting partner. However, I had to admit that most of the missed opportunities were due to missed shots. The turn-around point, maybe two miles along the ridge, was attained. I found a dry rock and paused for a quick lunch of cheese and bread. Drinking ice cold water did little to make me warmer but was welcome. There was a dog biscuit for my partner. He refused my offer of water, preferring to eat snow.

Heading back around the mountain, a tremendous covey of between 40 and 60 birds flushed far out. The birds flew up and around the mountain and then dropped down in a distant brush patch. We started in pursuit by angling upward. The precarious slopes of unstable rock had me struggling to stay on my feet. Finally having had enough of the ascent, I sent Wily on up. Hopefully, he would flush birds down within shooting range. My 11th and last shot of the day connected. Wily picked up the bird far down-slope. Not a memorable day's shooting but a good day afield. We must have had upward of 120 flushes for the two trophy birds in the bag.

Another promising morning dawned with me planning to haul the boat to Lower Granite Reservoir to chase birds. Most upland bird seasons were still open in Washington State. During my earlier hunts, I had flushed good coveys of birds along the western shore of the reservoir. At some reservoir locations there were extensive tracts of public hunting land. Flats rose

Chapter 32 — *Afield In The New Century*

steeply to precipitous canyon walls inhabited by chukars. Quail occupied the flats and sometimes fed upwards into the steep bluffs.

My boat carried us to the first prospective hunting area. We were maybe a mile from the landing. I found quiet anchorage behind a barrier island. The firearm of choice today was my SKB side-by-side.

We started out along the lake's shore where Wily picked up hot scent almost immediately. Suddenly, the air was full of quail and one fell at my shot. Continuing on, Wily homed-in on a large clump of blackberry bushes. As he tried to find a way in, quail came boiling out. The shooting was fast and furious and my take mounted. Suddenly, a big, beautiful rooster jumped squawking from the bushes 20 feet away. I could not help swinging on him but there was no shot. The season was out on his kind. I consoled myself that my take of pheasant had been ample this year.

Reaching the end of the flat, we began working upward and around the rock cliffs. Birds had scattered and taken refuge there. Wily occasionally found and flushed a bird that fell to the gun. Two birds flushed and I completed the double. One bull quail fell below us into the lake. A hen bird dropped into heavy grass cover slightly above me on the steep slope. Wily was coming uphill after picking up the bull quail.

Another nice bull quail flushed below me and flew over water. At my shot he veered farther out to sea. The lake was nearly a mile across here. I found it hard to believe how far out from shore this quail flew. Finally, several hundred yards out and down river, he came down. Wily was still looking for the quail in the nearby grass. A light breeze stirred offshore. "Forget the easy bird, Wily, let's try for the lake bird right now."

Wily hit the water below in a shower of spray. This was not the line we needed. This was not the time for an honest, field-trial type water retrieve. The bird was much too far out and moving away, pushed by wind and current. Swimming to the fall would take too much time. We needed to walk the bank a few hundred yards. Then, Wily could make the swim straight out. I called Wily back.

We headed around the bank for a couple of hundred yards. I then sent him out on what would be a 300-yard blind retrieve. I handled him to what I thought was the quail. It turned out to be a stick. More futile handling and swimming ensued. The bird was not to be found; it had either sunk or been blown entirely out of the area. I called Wily in once more. This was to be our only bird lost this day and the dog could not be blamed. He had given his all.

We walked back around the bluffs and Wily came up with the hen lost earlier. Moving on, another bird fell and was retrieved. A pair of birds roared into the air and I made my second double of the day. As Wily completed his job, I took off my vest. It was time to count birds. A quick inventory showed we had our 10-bird limit. "That's it for the day Wily, let's head for the barn." As we made our way back to the flat, Wily could not resist flushing a few more birds holding in our path. We could have had some easy birds.

A final inventory of our take was made at the boat: seven bull quail and three cows. An inventory of my shells showed 14 shells expended for 10 quail brought to bag. My shooting had been exceptionally. No cripples were left in the bushes. It had been an outstanding hunt even if over almost too quickly.

An almost spring-like January winter day dawned when I was tempted to try Chukar Ridge again. By 10 a.m., we were in the truck and on our way. En route, we passed the Gibbs' cornfield patch along the Clearwater River where a flock of geese was feeding in the corn! Chukars would have to wait. I would try a sneak on the big birds.

We made a slow, stealthy approach through the standing corn. The birds became agitated and hit the air with a din of honks. They were a bit too far out. But our luck soon improved.

"Down Wily, they are circling back around." Two birds passed over head and in range. One came down cleanly to my shots. A second goose flew out and across the river, losing altitude. Wily came back with the first bird and we hastened back to the truck. A drive upriver to the bridge crossing brought me to the old road that followed down the river's south bank. After an hour's search along the bank, glassing with binoculars, the goose was finally spotted. I made a head shot and Wily packed him up the steep bank.

The clock had crept past the noon hour. There were not enough hours of daylight left to climb Chukar Ridge, but it was too nice an afternoon to go home. I decided to drive to Upper Catholic Canyon to hunt the Zenner Ranch. After the hike in, we worked the upper extent of brushy draws for chukars. The canyon floor lay several hundred steep feet below. We found no large numbers of birds but I had a couple of chances. A single chukar was added to the day's bag as Wily and I had shared another outstanding day together.

When Simba's time with us had ended, I needed to escape the house. Three more days were left in the waterfowl season. I called Clayton Evens, Wily's breeder. He agreed to drive down to join me for some waterfowling along Lower Granite Reservoir. Using my skiff for transportation and as a makeshift blind, we hunted two days with good success.

The first day we were a little late getting ready. Lots of ducks pitched in while we were setting out our decoys. The morning turned fair and

Chapter 32 — *Afield In The New Century*

clouds dissipated. We cursed about early missed opportunities. In view of the fair weather, we did not expect many more shots. As the midmorning approached, we were pleasantly surprised. Large numbers of ducks started moving. Quite a few checked out our decoys. Some greenheads remained behind. The dogs reluctantly waited their turn making the retrieves. A flock of geese swam into our decoys and two stayed behind.

"I'm surprised you fired only once Clayton."

Clayton chuckled ironically, "I had forgotten to reload my magazine after that last duck."

As the morning progressed, Clayton impressively called two geese right into the decoys. We each took a bird. Later, two mallards lit among our decoys. One shot boomed and one duck fell. The drake mallard I was swinging on flew away unscathed. Wily looked at me accusingly as my curses warmed the air. My firing pin had fallen on an empty chamber. I had forgotten to reload.

A wing-tipped mallard came down far beyond the decoys. With the breeze pushing it, the bird rapidly moved downstream 200-300 yards out. Wily broke and was on his way. From past, bitter experiences I knew the probability of a dog swimming down such a bird was remote. We hastened to pull anchors. I cranked the big motor and started maneuvering out through the decoys. Looking out, we saw Wily closing in on the bird that was now 400 yards out. The bird dove repeatedly. Wily stuck with the chase and with a final lunge had him.

After chasing down another cripple with the boat, we headed for Rooster's Landing for a lunch break. A steaming bowl of clam chowder was most welcome. Returning to our spread, we spooked several mallards from among the decoys. We hunted through the afternoon. Few birds were flying. Although a couple of birds short of our combined limit of 14 birds, we decided to forego the evening shoot and call it a good day.

On Sunday morning, we were in place with our decoys out early and our boat blind set up. Few birds were flying and those that were ignored our decoys and calls. I should have known better than to hunt the same spot two days running.

Two hunters passed our spread as they motored downstream. They set up 300 yards below us. As the morning passed, they started doing a lot of shooting. They were intercepting most of the ducks moving back upriver. We were having almost no action. Clayton dropped a single greenhead. By 10:30 a.m. we had enough. We pulled our spread of decoys and made preparations to head in.

Out of curiosity, I decided to check out a sleeper spot about a mile downstream. As we passed our hunter neighbors, a mallard lit among their decoys. They "ground-sluiced" the bird on the water. They had no dog.

Clayton observed, "they were not much for sportsmen."

We arrived at the downstream spot I had in mind as some 60 to 100 mallards flushed out of the cove. We forgot about lunch and went in and quickly set up. Again we had a good midday shoot, taking an additional nine mallards over the next couple of hours. There was little or no shooting by the "gentlemen" upstream. Two can play that cutoff game.

With another couple of hours of shooting light left and 10 birds in the bag, we called it a day. Clayton had a long drive home and the chance of snow was threatening.

Passage Of The Seasons

Recent hunting is bittersweet with aging friends, 2001-2003.

I have been most fortunate to share outstanding seasons afield with two and four-footed buddies. Simba's untimely passage early in 2002 was a stark reminder of our mortality and that each day spent afield with a buddy is one of a very limited and precious allotment. Wisdom would seem to dictate that we savor each day afield to its fullest. No friend can ever be truly replaced. But if we are very lucky, life will permit us new friends to help fill the void.

Simba's son, Wily, was left with very big paw prints to fill. In his fourth year of life this field season, he eagerly stepped up to the challenge. His ability to locate quarry in the field, be it live or dead, often borders on the unreal. The athleticism of his hard, lanky body is often demonstrated by awesome and frightening leaps on dangerous terrain. I am personal witness that even a Dall's sheep sometimes misjudges a leap. Wily is still his own dog, as his breed and sex dictate, but he is very outgoing in his affection for human buddies.

It was March when we arrived in southern Georgia. My buddy, Bill Thompson, a professional retriever trainer, welcomed me to the sunny south. As was his custom, he had moved his Blue Springs Kennel operation from New Jersey to the south for late winter training. "You should have been here last week. The bass were biting. A cold front is rolling in and temperatures are forecast to fall below freezing tonight. We will still get in some dog training and drink a couple of cold ones though. You can try for bass tomorrow if you like."

The cold front was protracted. One morning, with time for my visit running out, I decided to try some fishing anyway. By midmorning I was paddling my car-topper boat along the shores of a 50-acre farm pond. The temperature was in the 50's F and wind gusted fitfully. My casts with fly tackle were largely in vain. I had connected with, landed and then released, only three or four small bass.

In mid-lake, two fishermen were beating the water with much more success. Using light spinning tackle, they were landing fish after fish. I finally rowed over and inquired as to their success.

"We are catching a lot of white perch. Some of them go a pound or so. How about you-all?"

"I'm not doing much good."

"Try some small white lures. Good luck. We're about to pull out."

I dug a white beaded nymph out of my fly assortment. Over the next couple of hours, strong fighting bluegills and crappie often bent my fly rod. I noticed that the fish known as crappie over much of the country was known here as white perch. Back on shore, I busily filleted fish until dark. Rolled in cornmeal and deep-fried, the fillets later provided the basic ingredients of a number of wonderful meals.

The cold front finally weakened so that by mid-afternoons, the temperature was pushing 80 degrees F. Late one such afternoon, I was afloat in my car-topper boat after bass. The southern sky was midnight black and ominous, while flashes of lightning played among the ascending clouds. Stalking the shallows, I noted with excitement some explosive action as bass actively fed on scattered minnows, fracturing the pond's placid surface. During the next hour, I hooked several nice bass but failed to bring them to net as my tackle was marginally light. Then the storm descended. Overhead, the lightning flashed and thunder rumbled. In the near distance there was the deep explosion of a lightning strike. Rain came down in torrents as I scrambled to stash my boat and find refuge in my nearby van.

During April, I joined John, Amy, and their children at Oak Hill Kennels in North Carolina's Pinehurst area. When not dog training, I flyrod fished with poppers on local ponds. Waters were very low locally due to extreme drought. I landed and released a few small bass. But when I resorted to beaded nymphs fished wet, the action picked up. I caught and released many wonderfully game and large black bream. Wily eagerly participated, serving as my landing net.

My travels took me to North Carolina's outer banks and Topsail Island where, at Robin's invitation, I was looking forward to fishing from his Jolly Roger Pier. "Do you want the good news or the bad news first?" he asked when I got there.

"Hit me with the bad." I had come to expect, "you should have here yesterday" when arriving at an anticipated fishing hot spot.

"You should have been here last week. It was spring break. The local weather was hot. The coeds were abundant and the scenery was wonderful. The weather forecast is for unseasonable cold the next few days. The girls have gone back to school. But the fishing is wonderful."

"When do we start?" was my reply.

"This is a busy time for me. I probably will not be able to get away much. You can go with my favorite guides. Their mother will drop them off here shortly."

Chapter 33 — *Passage Of The Seasons*

Within two hours I became reacquainted with Robin's sons Rob (age 9) and Jake (age 7). Over the next three days, we passed many fun hours fishing together. Their enthusiasm was contagious and they were not to be easily out-fished by any adult. Most impressive was their expertise with tackle and fishing techniques. When large schools of bluefish moved in along the pier and angler's rods were constantly bent, Rob's favor saying was "it's blues city out there."

Later, I arrived at my mother's western North Carolina home with a cooler full of filleted and frozen blues and whiting. Mother, a spry 91 years old, very much enjoyed the fresh fish for dinners.

Late one afternoon, Cousin Fred and I packed my car-topper down to Banner Elk's Wildcat Lake. Its clear, placid waters reflected nearby peaks of the Appalachians. Fred then wandered off and finally showed up a half-hour later.

I greeted him, "I was beginning to wonder if you would ever tear yourself away from that co-ed volley ball game so we could go fishing. I see the attraction. Some of the ball handlers are spectacular."

"A man must have his priorities," Fred philosophized.

I manned a fly rod while Fred cast with a light spinning outfit. As we crossed through a patch of water lilies, I caught glimpses of flashing gold beneath our keel. Fred exclaimed, "Did you see those big gold fish?"

As the sun began setting behind nearby ridges, I noted many dimples as fish surface fed along the lake's inlet shores. We paddled quietly among the feeding circles but my dry flies and Fred's spinner failed to trigger any strikes. I tied on a beaded nymph and immediately hooked into a nice fish. Fred manned the net. Soon a golden fish flopped in the boat. The fish was definitely not a goldfish. A crimson lateral line stripe showed it was a color phase of rainbow trout. With their weakness discovered, we took fish on almost every cast until darkness drove us off the water.

One afternoon Wily and I descended into the Watauga River Gorge. The river reach we fished was restricted to catch-and-release fly-fishing. Above, the gorge traffic for the busy Boone-to-Linville highway roared by. But in the gorge I was lulled by the sound of whitewater rushing over boulders while a male cardinal claimed his territory with lovely song.

I began casting a no. 12 caddis fly. During the next hour, I caught and released four very nice and vividly colored wild fish. Included in my catch were rainbow, brook, and brown trout.

Later in the year, on a warm June Idaho afternoon, I got a hankering for a fresh fish dinner. I loaded the car-topper onto my van's roof and Wily and I headed out of the Clearwater Valley for higher and cooler country. We arrived at Spring Valley Reservoir where college students fished and

Buddies Afield — Trips Outside Alaska

sunned on piers. The shrieks of young children splashing in the cool water rang over the lake. I quickly launched the boat to escape the crowd. Big Wily held down the bow while I paddled. My white popping bug then accounted for bluegills, rainbow, and an occasional crappie. By sunset, the basic ingredients for a big fish fry were in the cooler.

Late June found us on the banks of the North Fork Clearwater River. The North Fork Clearwater, with Kelly Creek as its headwaters, is listed among Idaho's blue ribbon wild trout waters. Fishing restrictions in the North Fork permit the retention of only two cutthroats. Fish retained must be a minimum of 14 inches. The spring before, with old Simba as my fishing partner, we had fished the North Fork very successfully. We caught and released a number of beautiful cutthroats but did keep two wonderful specimens for dining.

When we arrived this spring the river was in a raging flood due to an unusually heavy snow pack and a late, cool spring resulting in late and high runoff. White water enthusiasts were enjoying the torrential water but fishers were few and far between. I made a few half-hearted casts over the frigid water with the expected negative results. We passed the night in the camper beside the roaring river. Early the next morning we headed home with our tails between our collective legs.

As the hot days of an Idaho July approached, I telephoned long-time fishing partner Ann in Alaska. "How's fishing for Kenai reds?"

"I don't think so good thus far but come on up. There are other fun things a man and woman can do together."

With that assurance, I was no longer hesitant "I'll be up!"

August found me exploring Alaska's beautiful wilderness of Twenty-Mile River valley for silver salmon. One morning Mike and I arrived at the river in midmorning to find the launch site crowded with boats. Finally, we were launched and Mike headed his jet boat up the glacial river. Mike's Chesapeake, Bandit, accompanied us on the outing. Two hours later with only two of our permitted four salmon in the cooler, Mike decided to take the boat up Glacier Creek toward Carmen Lake.

Alaska's cold, branched glacier rivers can be very unforgiving of boaters' mistakes. Through the years a number of boats have been lost in the Glacier Creek tributary. One fall a partner and I successfully ascended this tributary by jet boat all the way to spectacularly beautiful Carmen Lake. But trouble developed on the return trip. The stream broke up into numerous braided channels but only a single channel was the correct one to follow. We were swept rapidly along by the speeding current and it was necessary to keep the jet boat in mid-stream. At the tiller, I made a couple of wrong decisions. My screw-up resulted in a hole in the bottom of our

Chapter 33 — *Passage Of The Seasons*

boat that we plugged with a glove. My partner then took over the controls. Soon we hit hard and were minus a lower jet unit. We spent the next several hours paddling and drifting downstream back to the boat landing.

Today, Mike steered the 18-foot skiff up a deep channel that hooked sharply to the left. Manning the bow, I spied a logjam around a sharp bend ahead and frantically hollered and motioned for Mike to abort. He tried to turn the boat back downstream. The channel proved to be too narrow. We were swept downstream to crash against the logs and the stumps. The boat tipped dangerously, taking on many gallons of water, but somehow rode out the collision. Bandit was almost thrown overboard. He would likely have been pulled down by the raging current and trapped under the logjam. I climbed out on logs and ran the bow line to shore.

As we caught our breath, I suggested, "that was a close one Mike. We could have lost the boat."

Mike, visibly shaken, agreed. "We could have lost a lot more than the boat." His boat's electric water pump proved a lifesaver and soon the great weight of water trapped in the boat was diminished. We managed to hand line the boat downstream to quiet water and safety.

"From now on, I'm sticking to the main river for my fish," Mike made a resolve.

A few days later our courage had mostly recovered. Mike invited me to join him and Joe, a friend from Oregon, for another trip up the Twenty Mile. "No more Glacier Creek," he promised.

We were on the water shortly after Alaska's early summer sunrise made river running safe. We were ahead of most competition. A few miles up the river we arrived at a large, clear-water slough. Lee Miller, my neighbor in Indian, had built a trapping cabin on the slough years before. Sometimes, this slough was a holding area for migrating salmon. We decided to check it out.

As we made our approach over the spit of silt and gravel to reach the slough, many swirls and the sight of large, silvery, glittering bodies greeted us. We dashed back to the boat where we hastily strung up rods with trembling hands. The next hour's fishing was memorable. The silvers were large and bright and they hit willingly. They were full of fight and frequently went airborne. Several heavy fish broke free from our light tackle. More fishing boats arrived. As the water become crowded, hits become few and far between but our keeper fish were in the cooler. We had fresh fish for frying, baking, and to put into the smoker. (Mike's recipe for smoked salmon proved to be wonderful.)

My last trip up the Twenty Mile that summer was in a 12-foot skiff I borrowed from my neighbor Lee Miller. I had only my four-horse kicker

Buddies Afield — Trips Outside Alaska

for power. Wily was along to hold down the bow and share the excitement. We were on the water just after sunrise. A high flood tide followed us, helping to boost us over obstacles and upriver. The flood tide also permitted fresh salmon to enter the river. It took the better part of an hour to cover the three miles to our fishing hole of choice. As we chugged slowly upstream, I consoled myself that our progress, though slow, beat the heck out of walking. Walking would have involved miles of bucking alder Hells, flooded tide channels, and the assault of hoards of bloodthirsty insects—it would have been a true ordeal.

As I beached our transportation, a mammoth swirl in midstream sent my pulse racing. I fumbled together my light-weight Fenwick spinning rod. My first lure of choice was a small brass spinner. On my first cast, I hooked into a big, air-seeking silver missile. Wily was very excited and had to be calmed—he wanted to retrieve. The silver was finally overcome by relentless rod pressure and slid into the net. It was a good salmon for smoking. His final struggles ceased after a couple of raps on the head with my fish club. I held up the bright silver fish to admire it. Sea lice still clung to his body in front of the anal fin. The heavy male would weigh well over 10 pounds.

Subsequent casts into this pool produced no more action. I decided to check the next pool down. Soon after moving downstream, I tied into and finally landed a very large female silver. She proved to be even heavier than the male. I was having too much fun to quit so early. It was time to play catch-and-release. I experienced almost no lull in the action during the next hour. I hooked and lost many fish. Five more silvers were brought to net and then released.

The last silver I hooked to end my season was huge. He took the lure with a slam, followed by repeated leaps clear of the water. Then he went deep. Finally thinking that he was ready to give up, I tried unsuccessfully to net him for release. I repeatedly led him to the net only for him to surge away and fight again. Finally, I had him netted and unhooked. The long fight had left him exhausted. The minutes crept by as I steadied and held him in the current, hoping desperately for his survival. Eventually, I came to realize that my efforts were to no avail. I faced the moral dilemma of an extra fish. I personally have no tolerance for and I would never willingly waste fish and game resources. But fish recycled back into the river are part of the natural food chain and may feed bears, birds, small fish, and insects, and in turn all these will become food for juvenile salmon. That was the end of catch-and-release for me.

September first found me in Idaho and in place just before sunrise for the season dove hunting opener. For the first hour after sunrise, Wily and I

Chapter 33 — *Passage Of The Seasons*

were frustrated. Few birds flew within range and I had expended very few shells. My shooting success had not been impressive. Wily had retrieved just a single bird.

Additional hunters arrived. Some of the newly arrived stretched their shotgun barrels sky-busting and spooking out-of-range birds. A young, untrained black Lab accompanied one member of the newly arrived. The Lab's loud whines and barks of excitement assured that no doves would approach within shooting range of hunters in his vicinity.

Studying flights of doves I had detected some interesting flight patterns. I made my move and set up at a new location. A couple of closely spaced fence posts were my only cover. I was soon shooting frequently and my success rate was good. Wily made a couple of very difficult finds on crippled birds that had dropped into a deep, boulder-strewn draw. We collected bird 10 before 8 a.m. With my limit in the bag, I invited another hunter to shoot in my spot. As we sat and chatted about hunting, he was able to occasionally drop a bird. I handled Wily for the retrieves. The air temperature was climbing rapidly upward by the time I called it a day.

Usually, I spend 10 days to two weeks each fall hunting big game. My quarry is most often a whitetail buck, but sometimes I opt for a mule deer buck. Though venison is an important part of my diet, I am most motivated by big game hunting as an excuse to hike the hills and woods and observe wildlife. My hunts are also motivated by the chance of bagging an outstanding trophy. Ideally, the hunter has the opportunity to look over and decline to take a number of animals.

Following opening day in mid-October, my deer season ended quickly this fall. My third day afield was actually more an early reconnaissance than a hunt. Hunting open country in midmorning, I came across a nice mule deer buck. He was overseeing a harem of five does. They stood alert on a canyon wall some 400 to 500 yards away. My success with a similar shot the previous fall gave me false confidence.

A stand of hawthorn bushes provided me with cover and a stout bush gave me a quick rifle rest. At my shot, the deer herd scattered. The buck was among the deer dashing downward. I found myself desperately hoping that my shot had missed but his stride did not appear normal. I spent the next hour climbing and examining the steep rocky terrain for signs of blood or a distinctive trail. An extended drought had rendered the soil and vegetation bone dry. There was no hope for a human to successfully trail an animal under such conditions. Assistance from a four-footed buddy was the only hope for not losing a fine animal. I had such a buddy in Wily.

The buck was found bedded down in the draw's bottom in a brushy thicket. He had traveled almost a half-mile. My over-hold had not been sufficient. The bullet had dropped over the ultra long distance and taken out a front leg. I resolved to never again try at such extreme range.

As I dressed out the buck, I noted with amazement his excellent condition. The body's cavity contained a tremendous quantity of fat. The backstrap and hindquarters were covered with over an inch of tallow. My supply of excellent venison was assured for the winter.

Then Joe flew in from tidewater Virginia to sample some western bird hunting. I was glad to have him join me for a few hunts. I had known Joe since he was knee-high to a cottontail rabbit. He had become quite an accomplished SCUBA diver and had made dives in many exotic places. Though in good physical condition, Joe was astounded at the vertical nature of much of northern Idaho's bird habitat. He was not physically or mentally ready to pursue chukars in their preferred cliff habitats. We would stick to hunting quail and pheasant.

Quail population levels were down considerably in the old south. As a result, Joe had little opportunity to hunt upland birds in recent years. We sat around the kitchen the evening he arrived telling war stories. His account of Virginia dove shoots assured me that he was more than a little competent with a shotgun. For our outings, he would be shooting one of my Berettas.

As we sipped a couple of cold ones, he admired some of my whitetail racks. Joe was quite a successful deer hunter.

"Sure enjoyed that fishing trip we made on Chesapeake Bay a couple of springs back," I told him. "I still cannot believe how bluefish some times bite the tail fin right off hooked sea trout. Our catch sure made for a lot of good eating."

"I have a bigger boat now. You'll have to come down next spring," Joe invited. "I have been taking some nice rockfish this fall."

"I still get a kick thinking about of our trip through Chesapeake City. When you pulled up beside that little white sports car convertible I could not help gazing at the two babes who were the driver and passenger. They were exposing much skin to the hot spring sun. The girl driving looked straight at me, stuck out her tongue and touched the tip of her nose."

"She sure blew your mind," Joe remembered, chuckling.

Our first day's bird hunt took place just up the road from my home. The draw we hunted was home to a large quail covey. We started the hunt by some large, impenetrable black berry bushes, "quail castles." The strategy was to toss a couple of rocks into the bushes. If we were lucky, the quail were at home and they spooked up the draw. Wily could then work them for us.

Chapter 33 — *Passage Of The Seasons*

Our plan worked well. Many quail flushed from the blackberry bushes and flew up the draw. The coveys flushed and the birds scattered to pitch into cover along hillsides and into the creek bottom. Wily worked ahead with enthusiasm and soon was finding tight-holding quail. Joe was in the lead when Wily started kicking quail out of a particularly attractive patch of cover. I stood watching Joe's shooting exhibition in amazement. While standing in one place, he dropped five or six quail, including one double. During Joe's shoot-out, I managed to drop a couple of birds that escaped him and flew my way. When the smoke cleared, I muttered, "Wily has his work ahead of him now, Joe. We have seven or eight quail down. I hope you are good at marking falls."

"I have a good idea where most of the falls were," Joe assured me.

It turned out that Joe was very good at marking falls. With him indicating where we should search, and Wily performing spectacularly, we soon had retrieved a half-dozen birds. I caught a glimpse of one cripple darting into an inaccessible patch of brush and blackberry.

"I have one of your birds marked down across the road." Joe directed Wily and me across the road where Wily put on a long search in vain.

I finally gave up. "Let's work on up the draw. We will look for the lost bird again on our way back to the truck."

We progressed up the draw, flushing singles and sometimes multiples. By the time we found no more birds to flush, our take neared the limit.

On the way back to the truck I gave Wily his head. He began a search for the cripple that had eluded him on the far side of the road. He hit scent and ran swiftly, coming up with the bird.

"Wily was hot today," Joe admired.

"He doesn't lose many birds," I admitted proudly. "Let's head to the house for some lunch. We will try for pheasant this afternoon."

Over lunch, we discussed the prospects for pheasants and some of the finer aspects of quail management. I started it off. "Lots of hunters keep pounding a covey weekend after weekend. They leave few birds for seed or drive them out of the area. I do not like to hunt the same coverts more often than once in two or three weeks. Though one bull quail can service several cows, I do not like to see any covey hunted down to less than 50 percent. I spread my harvest out over 12 or 15 coveys during a season. Habitat loss to commercial and suburban development has decimated some local areas of quail and pheasant abundance and decreased hunting possibilities. Most of the serious local bird hunters agree that pheasant and chukar populations are way down this year. These species are arid and desert country birds. We have had back-to-back wet and cold springs. Under such conditions the chicks die of hypothermia."

I continued. "A number of years back, one farmer friend presented me with a different theory of pheasant population declines. He blamed low game bird numbers on 'All them grizzly bears the Government is stocking.' I am personally familiar with only one area where grizzly and pheasant habitat overlap. That is Nine Pipes Area of Montana's Mission Valley. I have observed many pheasant there. But I wished to hunt the farmer's land again so I agreed that 'maybe you have a point there.' This farmer and I have become fast friends through the ensuing years despite some differences in political and wildlife management theories. He likes to hunt birds, is a participant in Conservation Reserve Programs, and seeds a portion of his land for wildlife food."

Later, while driving along canyon roads, we spotted a golden eagle. I was stimulated to relate some of my eagle stories. "I used to see a lot more goldens here. These days, I often see a bald eagle but seldom a golden. I believe they may be suffering from habitat loss and illegal shooting. One afternoon I watched a golden hunting a field inside the Lewiston city limits. The field is now occupied by a major shopping center. I once saw a golden take a rabbit from land now occupied by the Nez Perce Casino."

"They are magnificent birds but they must take some pheasants," Joe observed.

"They add much to the environment and as far as I am concerned, they are entitled to their fair share of game birds. Their main food is rodents but I have seen raptors take snakes. Too many rodents or snakes may also impact bird populations."

I continued. "My most unusual eagle sighting occurred one fall up Coyote Canyon. Rock, Jay, and I were pheasant hunting along high canyon walls. At the head of an almost vertical draw, Jay dashed into some brush. Out came two hen pheasants. He also spooked a nice 4x4 whitetail buck. The buck trotted across the draw and stood looking curiously back at us, 40 yards away. The quiet was suddenly shattered by air screaming over giant pinions. I stood awe-struck, with my mouth open in amazement, as the golden stooped on the buck, narrowly missing his antlered head. The buck was thoroughly spooked and dashed for protection into a thicket. The eagle went in after him and drove him out. The buck then ran flat-out around the hillside with the eagle in hot pursuit. They both disappeared in the distance."

"That is an amazing story," Joe admitted.

"I only wish that I had been packing a camera instead of a shotgun. In his book, Horns in the High Country, Andy Russell gave two accounts of goldens stooping on adult mountain goats. The theory is that the eagle

Chapter 33 — *Passage Of The Seasons*

hopes to spook or knock a large animal off a steep drop-off to its death. The eagle can then dine at his leisure."

The next day we sought birds. Although we hunted several coverts I felt certain would be productive, we found no birds home. We hunted the abandoned apple orchard and vineyard above Lenore that Jay and I had first hunted with smoke-jumper Don. Even in this ideal habitat we could find no quail. Clusters of frost-shriveled, sugar-sweet grapes provided us with a welcome excuse for a break. Driving downhill away from the orchard, we heard quail calls and saw numerous birds working in thick brush. It was a relief for me to see that the covey was not extinct. But this day our quarry was much too close to human habitation for hunting.

Late one afternoon Joe and I followed Wily up a brushy draw in the Mission Creek area. A covey of Hungarian partridge exploded just ahead of us and Joe and I each collected a partridge. Joe paused to admire his first bird of this species.

After some discussion, we decided to follow the partridge. They had disappeared over a vast, steep field of newly sprouted winter wheat. We loaded and closed our 12 bores with light bird loads. The ridge's top, too rocky for the plow, was covered with high grass and brush. Joe elected to continue on up and across the hill. I skirted along plowed ground just below its summit. Wily worked between us.

On the hill's far side, we approached a draw with a bottom containing a dense stand of four-foot-high grass. Wily was in front, working excitedly and obviously trailing a pheasant.

Suddenly, a beautiful cock, feathers gleaming iridescently in the late afternoon sun, took to the air cackling indignantly. I shot twice. Joe followed my efforts with two shots from the hillside high above me. To my eyes the bird gave no indication of being hit and disappeared from sight over the next hill, gaining altitude.

"That bird was out maybe 60 yards. No way we were going to down him with the light loads we are using," I shared my thoughts with Joe

Above me Joe was staring intently into the distance. "That bird just fell dead."

"You have to be kidding."

"I ain't lying. He's way up there, near a big pine. He suddenly flew straight up to spiral down dead."

By now I had become very impressed with Joe's ability to mark falls. His description fitted a bird that had been heart or lung shot.

"I'll take Wily over. You stand on the hillside and direct us." I struggled up the steep incline, spotting a lone pine tree a hundred or so yards away and hastened in that direction. Upon reaching the pine, I started to search.

"Not that pine. The tall one way on back." Joe's voice reached me from afar. I stared in the direction Joe was pointing. Several tall pines towered a good 300 yards away from the hillside where Joe was standing. I thought to myself, "Joe has to be mistaken this time." But I had to humor my guest and put on a show of hunting for a dead bird. We trudged on.

Wily and I hunted futilely through dense thickets surrounding the patch of Ponderosa pines. The odds of finding the bird were impossible. We were hunting for the needle in a haystack.

Joe had deserted his high observation post and shouted encouragement and directions from below. Beyond the pines, the country fell abruptly into a chasm. Wily disappeared in that direction and soon reappeared with a big and very dead rooster.

"You and Wily earned that bird Joe," I praised their partnership as we hiked back to the truck. "That was a bird we will remember for a while. That reminds me of a retrieve Wily made a couple of years back in South Dakota. During a week of hunting pheasants, Dimitri, John T., and I had some memorable days. Each of us had bagged about 12 birds. John took off for home and family. Dimitri and I had one more day afield to hopefully take three more birds each to round out our 15 bird possession limit. My third bird of the last day was heart shot similarly to the one we took today. The South Dakota bird attempted to fly across an arm of Oahe Lake but died some 200 yards offshore. Wily made that long, cold swim to complete the retrieve."

On a day in early November, with a weather front predicted to roll into northern Idaho, I decided to enjoy a day in the sun by hiking up a nearby chukar-looking ridge. As Wily and I ascended the steep, switchback trail, my old and stiff joints seemed to protest every vertical foot gained. By the time the 2,000-foot ascent was completed, I was sweating heavily. Wily and I paused to share a limited water supply.

At the ridge's summit, a covey of about 12 partridge flushed, taking us completely by surprise. As I mounted my shotgun, the sling caught on my vest. By the time I recovered, the birds were too far out and I missed with both of my shots.

Three hours later we were navigating a sunny, southwest-facing slope. I noted with more than passing interest the large, fairly fresh tracks pressed in muddy spots along the trail. Either a small black bear or a large cougar had preceded us.

By now, I was tired and neglected to pay attention to my dog as he worked bird scent, moving ahead and down. A covey of maybe 15 chukars

Chapter 33 — *Passage Of The Seasons*

jumped into the air, screaming curses. My shots were again too late. Two big mule deer does were spooked by my shots and crashed out of a patch of brush below. Despite all the commotion, two chukars had held through it all. Wily now put them up. For once, I was operating efficiently and I had reloaded immediately after the earlier misses. One bird fell to my first shot. Wily made the pickup far below.

Buoyed by our success, a few days later we persisted in our pursuit of the wily chukar. With chores to run in town, it was late morning when I parked the van at a Snake River landing west of Clarkston. The morning was overcast and a cruel and chilly wind blew upriver. I hastened to get the hunt under way and generate some body heat. Initial plans were to gain access into the chukar cliffs by an old cattle road. The road's surface was covered with sandspurs. Wily began limping. I hastily and repeatedly de-spurred him. Finally, with Wily's paws bloody from repeated spur injuries, I turned back. After a fall of hard hunting, his paws were tough and hardened but any dog would need booties to use that road.

After turning back, I debated calling off the day's hunt. I finally decided to try ascending a brushy draw for access to the high country. As we entered the draw the sun overcame the thick clouds and peeped through. About 100 yards into the draw we found shelter from the wind among small, stunted trees. I called a lunch break there. Wily found and lapped water in the draw's bottom. We snacked while I studied the surrounding slopes. We might work our way upward between rock cliffs by following game and cattle trails.

We headed upward, "switch-backing" methodically to gain elevation. In a half-hour, the steep cliffs and rimrock had been negotiated and we were some 400 to 500 feet above the river. Ascending along the steep ridgeline, we reached a grassy slope where last summer's wild sunflowers grew in profusion among a predominant cover of bunch and cheat grass. The high vegetation was dry but within the dry grass, new green cheat grass sprouted. Sunflower seeds and new cheat grass are favorite chukar foods. The prospect for finding birds changed from discouraging to good. Wily soon picked up bird scent. We advanced and four chukars sprang into the air. A chukar dropped at my first shot. The second bird flew low, then dropped over the horizon. I fired but missed my chance at a double.

We ascended a few hundred more vertical feet. Wily began wind-scenting birds. I cautioned him, "easy, easy." I slowly trailed him to an abrupt drop-off where six to eight chukars hit the air, fussing furiously. I dropped a bird veering to the left and then swung on and dropped a second bird swinging to the right. Wily picked up the first bird and then hustled to save our double. The second bird came down crippled and Wily caught it only after a 150-yard chase down the mountain.

A power line access road crossed the mountain slopes a half-mile and 500 vertical feet above me. I decided to hunt up to the road and follow it across to an adjacent slope. We would hunt the second slope back down to the river. There would be time to descend through the cliffs before dark if we hurried—but just barely. We reached and started to descend the far slope when Wily was again on bird scent. A single bird flushed some 40 yards out and downhill. The Beretta came up for what should have been a futile shot. The bird was 60 yards or more out. Wily and I watched as the bird sailed far down the mountain. Three hundred or so yards out, the chukar veered for 100 yards sharply to the left. He then flew straight up and came down with a crash. Wily had marked the distant fall. He quickly ran the long slope downhill, picked up the bird and started back to me. I had just witnessed the longest mark I have ever been privileged to observe outside an all-age field-trial event. As Wily ascended, I worked along slowly and carefully down the steep rocky terrain to him.

I paused to admire the handsome bird Wily delivered. This was a true trophy chukar. It was as least as heavy as a hen pheasant or sharp-tailed grouse. I later weighed it as over 2 pounds. The bandit's mask was broad and the legs were a vivid red. It would be a wonderful taxidermy mount.

My vest was now heavy with big birds. The sun was descending behind the ridges across the river to the west. Wily picked up scent again and again but I called him off. I had no desire to try and find a way down through the cliffs after dark. Wily carefully picked his way around and through patches of small cactus, which covered the slope in some places.

Descending rapidly with shotgun slung over shoulder, I was taken completely off-guard when a covey of 12 to 15 birds spooked below us. I hastened their departure with a shot in vain. After a final, careful descent through the cliffs, we reached the river just at dark. A most successful chukar hunt was over.

Mike arrived from Alaska with his Chesapeakes Katmai and Bandit. Bandit had matured from a puppy into a nice looking male. My frank appraisal of the low bird abundance gave Mike little encouragement.

"I have limited out on pheasant only a couple of times this fall. But on most hunts I have felt lucky to bag one or two birds. I wound up skunked opening day in Washington State. On opening day in Idaho I brought home only one bird. A few years back, both Idaho and Washington traditionally opened pheasant season on the same day. I remember well an opener when Simba and I took a limit of roosters in Idaho in the morning and then, after lunch, drove to Washington State where we also took a

Chapter 33 — *Passage Of The Seasons*

limit. This fall, some landowners have decided not to open some of my favorite pheasant country for hunting because of low bird numbers. There are, however, pockets of habitat where birds are plentiful."

As a chukar hunter bordering on the fanatic, Mike was cranked-up about my recent successes with the masked bandits. He was more than ready to assault Mr. Chukar's cliff strongholds.

An Italian hunting buddy (Carlo) had turned me onto Beretta Superimposed shotguns during my Annapolis days. Now Mike and I were both sporting new 20 gauge Beretta over-and-under shotguns. Mike had opted for an Onyx model. Mine was a Silver Pigeon. We were still trying to figure out the best choke combinations and the shot loads for species pursued.

I urged caution. "Let's start on quail and pheasants and work our way up to the more challenging bandit bird. There are plenty of birds in isolated habitats but we will have to work hard for them. Lots of walking will give you and the pups the opportunity to toughen up."

Mike was no slacker when it came to walking. On some days the birds eluded us. But overall during the next week we hunted pheasants and quail with good success.

Mike was good at approaching new landowners for permission to hunt their land. "It's too bad that you are not as persuasive with the young women as you are with farmers," I teased him. "You would be dangerous."

One memorable day Mike was standing in the right place at the right time when the dogs put up roosters. Mike was shooting well and took his limit of three, firing his 20 gauge only three or four times. I told him, "I guess that you are ready for a chukar hunt now, Mike. You and Bandit are becoming a good team."

We started putting in long days of hunting and miles tramping chukar covers. The Chesapeakes did their part of finding birds much better than their masters acquitted their shotguns. The birds seems to lead a charmed life. We had our shotguns over our shoulders and failed to shoot, or we could not get our guns off safety or we just plain missed birds.

One morning, despite adverse weather forecasts and high wind warnings, I decided this was the day to take on Chukar Ridge. Following an uphill hike of 1-1/2 hours, we reached the ridge summit in a raging gale. Just to stay upright and on one's feet was a challenge. Firing a shotgun and connecting with a flying bird would have been an impossible challenge. We were not to be presented with bird-taking opportunities. We saw and flushed no birds. Our quarry was not to be found on the exposed ridge. All the birds were dug into heavy cover, holding tight and seeking shelter from the storm. At one point we escaped a deluge of rain and snow

Buddies Afield — Trips Outside Alaska

under a stand of Douglas fir. When the precipitation slacked, we retreated, defeated, back down the ridge.

As the days afield passed with many hard miles tramped and no birds brought to bag, both hunters and dogs became discouraged. The dogs seemed to look at us with disdain when we picked up our shotguns before heading out to hunt.

One evening, over pre-dinner cocktails, I discussed bird-hunting strategy. "I keep detailed records of each year's hunts. Since moving to Idaho 15 years back, my average annual bird harvest has been over 100 birds. I am fortunate to be able to put in many more days hunting each year than the average hunter. The last three years I have averaged over 70 days hunting wildfowl each fall. My records show that fully 20 percent of my days hunted yield no harvest. I suspect for chukars the zero harvest rate is much higher."

"The chukar is in no danger of becoming extinct in this rugged mountain country. The sportsman certainly does not threaten their future. Most birds probably die without ever seeing a hunter. My friend Craig Johnson is something of a chukar expert for the BLM. It is his contention that because of the tremendous chunks of land involved, it takes a really dense chukar population to give the hunter a reasonable chance for harvest. Our chukar hunts are hardly the same sport as the formal driven shoots of European gunners. Their sport is in the shooting. Ours is in the walking, communication with nature, and dog work."

Mike added, "we should start calling our chukar hunts nature walks. The non-hunting ladies would be much impressed with our activity. We would not need shotguns on most of our nature walks."

Mike rolled out of his camper early the next morning and showed up in the kitchen as I was getting a lunch together for a day for bird hunting. "Looks a fair morning. If you want to kill something today we can go pheasant or quail hunting. If you want to go for a 'nature walk' we will try for chukars. You make the call."

Between chukars and chukar hunters there is a love-hate relationship.

"Let's give the chukars another go," Mike decided unenthusiastically. "How about trying the area above the Snake River where you shot the big Canada when you were boating across. It was foggy on top that day but you said that you jumped a lot of chukars before finally bagging one."

"We will need the boat then. Give me a hand hitching up the trailer and we are off. It will be a long strenuous day. Most of the birds are concentrated around the gorge's summit. We face about two miles of stiff hiking up the ridge to reach hunting territory. The hike in will take upward of two hours."

Chapter 33 — *Passage Of The Seasons*

After carefully anchoring the boat, men and dogs slowly made their way up the steeply inclined slope. The three dogs were impatient with the slow progress of their human buddies. The morning was overcast and a cool wind blew from up the Reservoir. Movement served to keep bodies warm. Recent rains had brought forth a new growth of cheat grass that gave the slope a greenish hue. As the first rocky outcroppings were reached and passed, bird droppings littered the ridge top. The dogs discovered hot scent and sought to surge ahead. We were near chukars or partridge, quite possibly both. As we continued upward but found no birds, it became obvious that the birds were running ahead of us. It would do no good to give the dogs their head for the flush. We could not keep up and the flush would be out of range.

My pocket watch showed noon as we reached rimrock at the ridge's summit. We elected to take a quick lunch break before starting the serious part of our walk. Finding shelter from the chilling breeze was not easy but Wily and I found some protection at the foot of a rock bluff. Far below Lower Granite Reservoir glimmered as fishing boats trolled for steelhead. At our lofty perch, the only sound was that of the moaning wind.

After the brief pause I walked the few yards upward and joined Mike at the ridge's summit. Patches of bunch grass and sagebrush ran to cliff edges. Flat wheat fields in various stages of cultivation lay west of the river breaks. Just as I arrived, Mike's dogs ran into a patch of sagebrush and a huge covey of chukars exploded angrily in all directions. Mike started the afternoon off with a bang by downing a bird. Taken completely by surprise and out of position I did not shoot.

"Good shot Mike," I offered my congratulations.

Mike tried to mask his thrill at success with, "I should have had a double."

We hunted around the summit to the southwest, skirting along steep bluffs. Just at the head of a rocky draw we flushed a small pod of birds. Mike collected a bird heading downhill. I collected a bird that chose to escape uphill. During the next hour or so more birds were flushed. There were more misses.

Mike wished "I sure would like to know how to lead a bird dropping sharply downhill."

"The downhill shot is where we make most of our misses. The birds do not descend at a constant angle. I expect we are usually overshooting them."

As the afternoon waned, I decided to retrace my route and hunt back down the ridge we originally ascended. Mike elected to hunt down the adjacent ridge.

Buddies Afield — Trips Outside Alaska

As I hunted downward, a number of shots echoed from Mike's direction. He was into birds. I shot several times myself but added no birds to my bag. As Wily and I made our way down the ridge of our ascent, Wily picked up strong bird scent wafting down from above. I was too tired to head back up. Besides, the rapidly setting sun would not give time. I gambled and gave Wily his head. He dashed upward to disappear far upslope among the rimrock. Two large chukars flushed downward in my direction. The birds passed me high and 40 yards out. I swung my 686 and one bird did not escape. Wily presented me with a huge trophy bird that would easily top 2 pounds.

As Mike and I arrived back at boat twilight was rapidly deepening. I popped the question "Did you get your limit?"

"No, I should have. I wound up with four trophy birds." He tried to suppress his grin. "Today was my best chukar hunt ever. I think that I will drink a beer or two tonight."

"Missed limits is the usual story with chukars. We had quite a day though. I know that we moved well over 100 birds. Wily and I also jumped a covey of 30 plus partridge on our way down. There will be plenty of seeds left for next spring's nesting."

Wily and I took a break from pursuing birds in the cliffs and had a classic pheasant hunt. We hunted along the edges of vast fields where high wheat stubble gave way to draws filled with native grass and brush. During the hunt we put up 60 to 70 pheasants, but for the most part the birds were spooky and flushed wild and far out. Working beautifully and hard, Wily managed to dig out two tight-holding roosters, which I then packed home.

Watching Wily work brought back memories of other hunts over years long gone. There were many hunts shared with his great, great grandfather, my FC AFC Rock. While I was spending a Thanksgiving season with the Parkers at their Sunshine Kennels in eastern Idaho, Steve and I embarked on a pheasant hunt. Steve encouraged me to hunt over his FC AFC Meg, Wily's great, great grandmother. Meg put up a big, beautiful rooster, which she then delivered to me for us to take home.

Buoyed by recent successes Mike and I decided to conduct an assault on the chukar population in their mountain fastness above the Salmon River. A period of promising fair weather arrived. So early one morning we departed the homestead full of hope and high spirits. En route we stopped by Cottonwood to talk over strategy and chukar lore with Craig Johnson. We decided to hunt Bureau of Land Management holdings in the White Bird area.

Chapter 33 — *Passage Of The Seasons*

Reaching the village of White Bird, I steered the truck up a dirt road that followed the banks of the Salmon River. The road was rough but had been considerably improved since my last visit several years before. To our left, the river ran low and clear along the foot of cliffs abruptly below us. Farther along, cliffs gave way to brilliant white sand beaches that in the summer support a population of swimmers. Today, several steelhead fishers cast from choice spots. On our right, the high, rugged cliffs rose abruptly to mountainous summits. The morning was clearing and brightening and looking very promising for the day's enterprise.

After following the road for a mile or so, I edged off and parked along a shoulder. The three dogs were released to investigate what to them was new terrain. Mike and I studied the cliffs that dominated the horizon towering to the east. Our enthusiasm had become somewhat subdued.

"I used to gain access into the high country up that draw," I pointed out terrain features. "I haven't hunted this ridge in years. I had conveniently forgotten how steep it is."

"I have hunted goat country that was not nearly as sheer and challenging as this," Mike observed.

"I can't believe that once upon a time I packed a mule deer buck off the ridge's summit. Fifteen years make a lot of difference in what a man is willing to tackle."

Mike allowed, "I'll take my hat off to any man who packs a limit of chukars down from that country."

"I did once but that was some years back. Not many men eligible for social security would be standing here contemplating climbing among those cliffs for a bird."

We ascended slowly and carefully. At a point some 500 feet above the road we halted for a breather and to discuss the hunting terrain above. Our dogs sat patiently at heel. Our conversation was interrupted when a covey of chukars flushed 50 yards above us, screaming what sure sounded like "f*** you, f*** you!" I threw up my shotgun and shot in frustration. Of course no bird fell. "If we hadn't stopped to talk we would have been right on top of them," I lamented.

The rest of the day passed with much the same result. We put up birds but were never in good shooting position or just plain missed the few good shots we did have. With the sun dropping toward the snow-streaked ridges to the west, it was time to head down from the cliffs.

At my suggestion, Mike and I split up for the descent hoping that by covering more country one of us might get lucky and put a bird in the bag. I elected to work down through some foreboding cliffs to the south. Mike's descent would be basically along our route of ascent. I soon found out that in selecting my route I had made a big mistake. I should have ascended another couple of hundred feet and two rimrock ledges higher before starting around.

A game trail I was following soon ran out. Cliffs closed in below and above me. I found myself studying the loose rocks under foot carefully and each step was made with studied deliberation. In places the benches I followed fell away sharply into the void. I found myself seeking handholds on the uphill rock wall for support. A single misstep or stumble and this hunt would be my last. Wily worked out the trail ahead or stayed close at heel. Hunting birds was no longer the objective. With the sun now sliding behind the western horizon and snow threatening, the objective was to get safely down from the cliffs.

Mike and I arrived back at the truck considerably discouraged, weary, and birdless. The dogs hastened down to a nearby sandy beach for a cooling swim and long draughts of water.

"Same old story," Mike sighed. "Lots of hard miles covered and missed opportunities."

"At this point I'm just glad to be down in one piece," I confessed. "We have won a few battles with chukars this fall but Mr. Chukar won the war.

Later, Bill and Micki, accompanied by their black Lab, Brute, and chocolate Lab, Sadie, stopped by for a too short visit and bird hunt. Several years had elapsed since our last hunt together. Brute, a Field Champion of some renown, was pushing 13. Sadie, who had made a good field trial showing, was also a senior citizen. Both dogs visibly showed the effects of advanced age. Their hearts were still eager for the chase but their bodies would obviously not stand up to hard upland hunting.

It was well into the afternoon when Bill and Micki arrived. The short winter day was rapidly waning but Bill was eager for a short hunt. Micki had errands to run in town. Mike was preparing for departure west and also had errands in town.

"We'll take Brute and Wily and try a short hunt up the draw. We will have only an hour or so but we should find some birds."

"Good luck," Micki wished as we headed out.

As we made the short drive to some local quail "castles," I explained our strategy to Bill. Sans shotgun, he would initially follow the draw by a neighboring house and try flushing birds from blackberry brambles on up the draw where they could be hunted. I drove up the road and then pulled over to check Bill's progress.

As I walked away from the truck, a single large bird thundered from blackberry bushes. I watched in disbelief as a chukar flew and landed in

Chapter 33 — *Passage Of The Seasons*

cover along the creek bottom. Plans were suddenly in bad need of revision. I trotted down the road to head Bill off.

"Let's get our shotguns and dogs out in a hurry. A chukar is waiting in the wings. He made one mistake today in being here. He just might make another mistake and stick around."

"Which side of the creek do you want Brute and me to take?" asked Bill who was now excited.

"You take the far side. Wily and I will stick to this side."

We walked slowly up the creek bottom with the dogs at heel. As we approached the area where the chukar disappeared, Wily picked up scent and wanted to cross. Then a commotion arose across the creek, followed by a shot. The chukar had flushed from the hill above Bill. He fell to Bill's single shot. "Fetch him up, Brute."

We met at the creek. Bill proudly displayed his trophy, happy at success but sad at an ending. "This will be Brute's last chukar."

"Congratulations Bill and Brute. I can't wait to see the look on Mike's face."

We hunted up the draw but found no more birds. The quail had learned from past mistakes and were holding tight in very heavy blackberry thickets. However, the afternoon had been a resounding success. When Mike and Micki showed up from shopping a short time later, Bill and I were sipping on cold brews.

"Bill bagged a strange looking bird" I told Mike with a straight face. "Bill, show Mike your bird and see if he can identify it."

Mike looked in disbelief at the chukar.

"Jim saves the easy chukars for his real friends," Bill joshed.

After a light breakfast next morning, Bill and I organized a serious quail expedition. I planned to start the hunt up Potlatch Creek. Micki would join Bill and me. With only two days available for hunting, she had opted to not purchase a nonresident license. She went along just for the walk and outing and proved a most delightful companion. Our canine crew included Brute, Sadie, and Wily.

We began the day's hunt by working through willows and weeds along Potlatch Creek. The dogs soon put up a nice covey of birds. Bill and I, with Micki's enthusiastic coaching, downed a couple of birds. As we hunted on, each of the dogs had birds to retrieve. The old timers found their birds gratefully. Wily accepted his opportunity to retrieve as his due.

Micki was good at marking down birds. "A couple of quail pitched in that patch of cover to our left," she directed.

Gunners and dogs approached cover to be alerted by her excited shouts as a quail flushed "there goes one."

Buddies Afield — Trips Outside Alaska

We worked the edge of an old pasture now gone to seed. It was now broken by water channels and supported high weed cover. Wily working bird scent suddenly locked up and froze in a classic point. He was staring into the grass immediately in front of his feet.

"He has birds. Close up," I hollered.

Sensing our approach, Wily made a little hop into the cover. The air exploded as a large covey of quail took wing. Our shooting was terrible. Our four shots tumbled only a single bull quail.

As the morning progressed, our hunt moved into an area lying beside an abandoned vineyard. Here we put up a nice covey. The birds scattered and flew toward a series of deep draws containing heavy cover. Micki joined the dogs in the deep draws, flushing birds for our guns. Back at the truck we unloaded our game vests and I took inventory. Our morning's take totaled eight quail. The elder dog members of our party were obviously tired and tuckered out from their exertions. Bill lifted them into the back of the truck.

"We had a good morning. But the shooting was not impressive. We should have downed several more quail." Bill declared.

"Let's head for the house and take a break for brunch. I have another area in mind for the afternoon hunt."

Micki prepared a delicious lunch. We each dined on a three-egg omelet filled with mushrooms, onions, green peppers, and cheese. A pound of crisp bacon and stack of toast quickly disappeared.

As Bill and I gathered up gear, Micki declined the proposed afternoon outing. "I really enjoyed this morning's hunt but I have projects in town this afternoon. You fellows have fun. Sadie has had enough exercise for one day. She can stay with me."

"Brute has had a very good morning. I am happy for him. He also has had enough exercise for one day. From your description of the next area I don't think he needs to hurt himself by overdoing it. Let's just take Wily this afternoon," Bill suggested.

We crossed the Clearwater River and headed the truck up a long private drive. I knew from an earlier hunt that a very large covey of quail and numerous pheasants occupied the farm's coverts. Much to my disappointment on the drive in we passed another hunter's truck.

The friendly landowner welcomed us to hunt. He cautioned, "a couple of young fellows are already hunting today."

"I think they are hunting down below. We will hunt the upper coverts."

Bill and I hastily donned hunting vests and shouldered shotguns. We began the afternoon's hunt by working heavy cover along a steep hillside.

Chapter 33 — *Passage Of The Seasons*

I was startled by an immense covey of quail flushing on my left. They caught us unaware and escaped unscathed to settle among low trees, brush, and weeds up the hill.

As we hunted in that direction, two hunters and a black dog seemed to materialize out of nowhere. We watched in great disappointment as the trio worked around the hillside firing a broadside of shots.

"What do we do now, guide," Bill asked unhappily.

"Well, I don't know. It's too late in the day to drive somewhere else and find another covey. But you call it."

"Let's hunt on here," Bill decided. "The young fellows worked the cover pretty fast. They may have missed some birds."

Just downhill of where the departed trio passed, Wily picked up scent and started flushing birds. Bill's shooting returned to his accustomed high success rate. I held my own with my little 20 gauge Beretta.

Wily worked quickly and proficiently, leaving no fallen birds unfound. As we entered a new piece of cover, Wily retrieved a bird evidently killed by the earlier hunters and missed by their dog.

Less than an hour after the shooting began I called for a bird count. We were two birds short of our combined 20-bird limit.

"We get one more bird each," I announced.

A short hunt followed. Bill connected and then it was my turn and I took the day's final bird. Wily dredged that last bird from dense cover.

"What a wonderful day's hunt," enthused Bill. "Brute and Sadie and I thank you."

"We did some good shooting this afternoon. This morning, two lightly hit birds made it into impenetrable quail castles. But overall today was outstanding. This afternoon Wily gave us a performance approaching perfection. Our day's take was 75 percent bull quail which will little effect on spring reproduction."

The second week in January brought the Idaho general upland bird season to a close and the Washington State season was also rapidly drawing to a close, with pheasant season already closed. Wily and I would spend a couple of final days beating the bird coverts. Our hunting area this day was a large cattle ranch. We had expended the morning working the lower reaches of several draws for quail with no success.

I found Sam loading cows at a lower corral and asked about hunting chukars on a different section of ranch.

Sam offered some advice. "Sure haven't seen many chukars this year. I saw a small bunch the other day when riding the hills to the west. My impression is that they are still very high. You are welcome to have a look if you are ready for a long walk."

Buddies Afield — Trips Outside Alaska

At our jump-off point, I munched on a sandwich and weighed possibilities. Sam's opinion that the birds were still high meshed with mine. Wily and I would head for the top.

We hastened uphill and quickly surmounted a steep, grassy hillside. I was surprised to find the uphill climb somehow easier than expected. The many miles of hiking during the fall were paying off. I was in pretty good physical shape. The treeless and arid country we tramped seemed stark and hostile in late winter. Cows grazed on the hill below us. Their blacks and browns contrasted against the green of new growth. Patches of bunch grass clung to some less rocky slopes. My attention was still locked on the highest ridges as our ultimate objective when a very large covey of Huns flushed ahead of us and winged down the slope, chirping away.

The temptation to follow this covey was too great to pass up. I heeled Wily and we angled downhill. We quickly lost 300 or 400 feet in elevation to reach and hunt a bench that supported a heavy stand of bunch grass. The dead, bleached grass moved in the wind as our path led us into a deep, v-shaped draw. In the draw's bottom, Wily hit hot bird scent and surged upward. I followed him, urging caution. I noted numerous bird droppings under foot. As the draw rose ever more steeply, shooting would be considerably restricted. I pulled Wily off the fresh spoor and climbed up and out to the right. We would try to circle and come in on the birds from the side.

Wily's head went up as he took in great breaths of scent eddying down from just up the slope. I released him to hunt slowly forward. I followed right at his heels into a particularly high grass stand. Wily pawed the grass at his feet and the broken covey started boiling out. I dropped a partridge that fell across the draw. They disappeared over rimrock and I missed my chance at a double. As I fumbled with an empty shotgun, a second covey flushed down the draw in front of me.

We worked on and around the hillside. After covering another quarter mile, we encountered another draw. As we descended into the draw to cross it, partridge took to wing giving me another chance for a double. I rose to the occasion and both shots connected.

As we worked the steep slopes, I thrilled to the way Wily worked the wind and triangulated in on birds. He soon found another bunch of birds, which flew sharply downward to the hill's base. We followed and at the hill's base, we found and followed a streambed that held scattered pools of water. Wily drank deeply. Droppings, tracks, and—as was evident by Wily's behavior—bird scent were plentiful.

Wily pushed a cottontail rabbit from a tangle of cattails and tumbleweed. He pursued the rabbit only a few yards and quickly lost

Chapter 33 — *Passage Of The Seasons*

interest. I had never shot rabbit for him to retrieve. The rabbit and Wily's short pursuit turned my thoughts back to the many Alaska snowshoe rabbits I had bagged with my little lever action Browning .22. Big Ben, Kent, and later Rock had delighted in hunting and retrieving snowshoes. As many another subsistence hunter had found, I learned that one does not grow fat eating rabbits.

Daylight was waning and I was tired. I found myself hunting too fast. I was permitting Wily to flush birds too far out. "Time to head for the truck," I thought. "Maybe we will pick up another bird or two on the way back." We did.

Back at the truck, our tally was four partridge. I estimated that we had flushed 80 birds during the short afternoon hunt. Wily and I had stumbled upon a mother lode of Hungarian partridge.

Two days later I returned to the partridge slopes. The new 20 had acquitted itself well by the day's end. The day was off to a good start when I connected with my first shot. I then went really cold and missed six or seven shots straight. I think that both Wily and I were ready to quit and go home in frustration. We stopped for lunch in the bottom of a draw. After lunch, my shooting settled down. Wily soon found birds and I connected on a double. I went on to fill my limit, taking three of the next four birds shot at. As we headed back to the truck, my game vest bulged with six big birds. I let Wily have his head and roam. He continued to put up birds. One covey of 15 flushed immediately in front of me. The birds wheeled away with the last rays of setting sun gleaming from rufous wing feathers. The day's outing had accounted for around 150 flushes.

With upland bird seasons over, Wily and I turned to waterfowl as an excuse for our outings. Late one afternoon we hiked in a half-mile to a pool on Potlatch River. The pool was sometimes frequented by large numbers of mallards but not so that day. Seven birds were flushed as we approached. The next two hours were spent waiting in vain for their return. I was entertained by the activities of the natural world.

I was amazed to observe a heavy hatch of a small, dark stonefly. The unseasonably moderate 50-degree temperatures had triggered the mid-January hatch. I was also entertained by a water ouzel. I am constantly amazed at their feeding antics, which involve submerging in torrential whitewater riffles. The bird would disappear, then re-emerge, not the least bit wet from all appearances. As the day drew to a close, I was enthralled when a pair of otter entered the large pool to fish for dinner. I observed them devour a couple of fish. In appearance the fish were either squawfish or suckers.

Buddies Afield — Trips Outside Alaska

Clayton and Jim Barker came down for a few days of duck hunting. Our hunting area of choice was the mallard-rich area of the upper Snake River below Clarkston. Our hunting craft was Clayton's camouflaged boat. Sunrise would find us tossing out a large spread of mallard and a few goose decoys for confidence builders. Wily and Clayton's little Chesapeake bitch, Annie, took turns retrieving. Ducks were abundant but they were educated and the weather was generally too nice for effective decoying. We spent the time between often widespread opportunities at ducks swapping old war stories. Such camaraderie is so often an important part of waterfowl hunting. As we shared a lunch of snacks, I recalled a goose hunt near Fort Collins, Colorado. Joe, my host, prepared a breakfast of bacon and eggs with toast as we waited for geese to check out our decoys. I found Jim's accounting of a mountain rescue attempt he was in on while in the military especially interesting. Two military helicopters had gone down in the high mountains above Lake Chelan, Washington.

During the four days of our Snake River waterfowl hunt, we made some hard shots but we missed some easy shots. The dog work was good. The retrieves were generally routine, requiring swims of up to a couple of hundred yards. Wily completed one spectacular retrieve that had us all applauding. He caught up with a crippled drake after a long, long swim. The drake temporarily succeeded in eluding the determined Chesapeake by diving. Wily dove after the submerged duck to finally came up with him in a shower of spray. We also found it necessary to run down a couple of wing-tipped ducks with the outboard.

"I have heard fellows claim that their dogs never failed to swim down a cripple." My voice revealed my skepticism. "Through the years I have seen a number of ducks and geese elude pursuit by a power boat. Fellows making such claims have never hunted big water, have not shot many ducks and geese, or else are darned liars," I concluded. "Likewise hunters who claim that their dogs never lost a crippled pheasant or quail haven't shot many birds, don't hunt heavy cover, or are better wing shots than any of the great ones I have hunted with. Again, more than likely these claims are out and out fabrication."

I continued. "One January hunt Ted and I were set up on an alfalfa field near the Clearwater River for geese. We wounded a big Canada. The goose made it to the Clearwater River Refuge. We were experiencing a period of frigid Arctic air and the river was running high and bank-to-bank with ice flows. I sent Simba on a blind retrieve for the goose. Simba, well past middle age in dog years, tried valiantly to reach the wing-tipped bird. Every time Simba reached him, the goose would flap over the ice floes and upstream. There is no way a dog can fight successfully upstream against

Chapter 33 — *Passage Of The Seasons*

the six-miles-per-hour current and ice. Finally exercising some wisdom, I called the tired, cold, old dog in. No bird is worth losing a dog for."

"I have personally bagged over 150 wild birds over Wily this fall. Counting birds picked up for hunting buddies, he retrieved over 180 birds. He flushed literally hundreds of birds. I admit that we lost a few birds but very few. Without a good dog, I believe that a hunter would loose two-thirds of the birds knocked down in heavy cover. But then without a dog, I would have lost no birds because I would not have gone bird hunting."

Jim agreed. "You are right about dog owner's exaggerations. As you well know, many hunters like to stretch the truth a bit about their dog's abilities. With your dog's accomplishments there is no need to stretch the truth." Jim added, "I always enjoy getting out. Most of us old timers have long since passed the time when the kill is the main reason for hunting. I have enjoyed our duck outings of the last few days. We had plenty of opportunities and our harvest was adequate. I enjoyed the company and dog work. Too bad we didn't have some geese visit our decoys though. When you decide to mount that trophy chukar, look me up and I will give you a hand."

Earlier, I had expressed my desire to mount one of my trophy chukars. As a teenager I had dabbled in taxidermy. Jim and Clayton had developed their skills to the level of art.

Buddies Afield — Trips Outside Alaska

Yukon Simba's Wily Cub (Wily) had a full day of retrieving on this 2007 hunt for diving and puddle ducks in Idaho with Bill Conner (l) and owner Jim Mauney(r).

Some Fall Firsts

A young dog and a senior hunter share some hunting firsts, 2003

Years flow rapidly down the river of life. In recent years the flow seems to me to have become a torrent. Most of the days I have been allotted to be afield are now memories. November of 2003 brought the sad news of yet another untimely passage. Larry, my dear cousin and college roommate, was added to the list of those I sorely miss. As time takes its toll, I am determined to miss fewer opportunities to be afield with buddies. Numbers of fish caught or animals brought to bag become increasingly less important. Good timing with the shotgun, good dog work, exercise, a hard-fighting fish, the fresh air, and the opportunity to communicate with nature make the day. Of course, a day afield can be made more memorable by some harvest to enrich later menus.

Sometimes a man's thoughts turn to the questions about the hereafter. I personally find the Native American version of a "Happy Hunting Ground" one of the most appealing. Surely a Happy Hunting Ground would have to include dogs and those wild mammals, birds, and fish I have pursued, protected, and come to love in this life.

The opening day of fall dove season was shared with my dog, Wily, and friends Bill and Dave. It was a pleasure to watch Wily, a veteran of many hunts, complete his work with great enthusiasm and confidence. Dave had matured as a fine young sportsman and was fun to be with afield. I had had the pleasure of watching young Dave, son of friend Gene, develop over the years.

Dave completed a difficult pass shot to my enthusiastic "good shot, Dave." Bill's shooting with a vintage Browning automatic was awesome. He quickly limited out. Dave's shooting success was erratic, as was mine. With his limit of "palomas" bagged, Bill then took advantage to sit in judgment of our shooting. He used very choice comments and chuckled disconcertingly over misses.

"You need to borrow some shells, Jim. Think I shot 13 times for my 10 birds. I still have a good part of a box left. Be glad to loan you some."

"Seems that I recall some opening days when your shooting was not nearly so sterling," I prodded back.

Abbie-Cakes, a little dark brown Chesapeake female and my latest pupil in training, had spent most of the opening morning unhappy in the back of the truck while her old buddy, Wily, was designated to pick up most of today's birds.

Abbie earned her official name by stealing a fresh-baked lemon chiffon cake from my mother's table. She managed to eat a large portion of her plunder before retribution descended upon her. To me, being used to 100-pound male dogs, Abbie at 65 pounds also became Lil'Bit (short for Little Bit). Abbie had always shown a great enthusiasm for birds. I had witnessed her retrieve a live, but protesting, full-grown bantam hen when she was just a pup.

With one bird to go of the 30 birds our group could legally take today, I retired Wily to the truck and released Abbie. Lil'Bit's first birthday was coming up later in the week. This would be her early birthday present. Dave dropped a last bird that fell far out and into a rock pit. The fall was too far out for her to mark. With the pup at my heel, I headed to the pit to began a search.

We searched the pit's bottom without success. With the most obvious possibilities exhausted, Abbie insisted on scaling the pit's east wall. She found the downed bird just at the pit's lip in a thick tangle of yellow star thistle. Her descent to deliver the bird was spectacular and frightening. Operating on adrenaline she chose the shortest path, which was down an almost vertical rocky fall. Somehow, she survived the tumbling boulders dislodged by her downward progress and delivered the bird to me. I hastily examined her for broken bones. She was trembling violently but OK.

"Dove hunting isn't supposed to be a dangerous sport you crazy little bitch. The dangerous sport locally is chukar hunting. You are obviously not ready for that sport. You would follow birds over a cliff for sure."

In October's progression, additional Idaho bird seasons open. Abbie accompanied Wily and me on hunts with increasing frequency. She learned quickly and showed an increasing talent in rooting birds from the brush.

I interrupted my fall season in late October to expand my social horizons. Tearing myself away from my dog family and hunting and fishing opportunities, I spent two very interesting weeks on my first tour of Eastern Europe.

Shortly after my November return, Mike from Alaska showed up in Idaho accompanied by his two Chesapeakes, Katmai and her son Bandit. Most days found us afield with dogs and shotguns. Our success judged by the weight of game bags was mixed. But at a day's end there was generally a bounty and variety of birds to keep the designated chef happy.

For several years I had regaled Mike with tales about expeditions to the Wapshilla Mountain Wilderness where the scenery was breath taking

Chapter 34 — *Some Fall Firsts*

and hunting success was usually good. By November, early winter snows usually render access into Idaho's mountains impossible. But this fall with moderate temperatures and a generally extended drought, there had yet to be a major snowfall in the high country.

Following an afternoon chasing quail, we had enjoyed a wonderful evening meal of pheasant prepared South Dakota country style. I was the evening's cook. For those unfamiliar with this recipe it runs as follows. Onions are sautéed in a large frying pan; a cut-up pheasant is dusted in flour and browned; water, white wine, mushrooms, and fresh garlic are then added. The dish is allowed to simmer slowly with constant stirring for a couple of hours. Milk may be added late in the cooking process to give richer gravy. The cooked pheasant is complemented with wild rice and a vegetable such as green peas. One pheasant easily satisfies two diners and can be stretched to satisfy three light eaters.

After the meal, we made plans. "I hate to interrupt you while you are absorbed in dish washing but what do you want to try tomorrow, Mike."

"How about Wapshilla Ridge for chukars and partridge. I really want to see that country. The forecast for tomorrow is for good weather."

"You and I are pretty beat up and limping with knee problems. I don't know when you will learn to quit shooting big Alaska critters that must be packed out miles to a road. But if you insist, we will give the high country and chukars a go. I am pretty sure that the road will be passable. I always enjoy seeing that country. We need to get an early start in the morning. It's a long, slow drive to our jump-off point. With some luck, we might just pick up some grouse on the drive in. We should put together our lunches tonight and pack plenty of water."

Driving into the mountains in the pale predawn light we passed several camps of deer and elk hunters. The winding gravel road was generally in good shape, but in some shaded spots snow-covered. Progress with a four-wheel-drive truck was no problem. As we gained altitude, the road became increasingly hemmed-in by heavy timber broken by an occasional open grassy park. Finally, we reached the prominent and southwest running Wapshilla Ridge. Along this ridge the country opens to grasslands broken by scattered fingers of pine and fir. The views were spectacular—steep walled canyons dropping to the Snake River lying thousands of feet below.

Mike absorbed and admired the views. "Some country. Now all we need are some chukars." A couple of miles farther along, his wish was granted. A covey of 8 to 10 brown birds scurried across the road in front of the truck. "Stop! Chukars!" Mike exclaimed.

We fumbled for shotguns and shells and hastily exited the truck. Four Chesapeakes in the back of the truck sensed the impeding action. A couple gave voice to their excitement.

Shotguns at the ready, we made our approach. Much to our mutual disappointment, the chukars did not wait for our visit. Just out of gun range, they dropped into the void with screams of derision. Mike and I unloaded our shotguns and climbed back into the truck.

"Par for the course for hunting the masked bandit," Mike sighed with exasperated resignation.

Another half-hour of bumpy riding brought us to the area of an old roadside corral. As we approached the corral, another large covey of birds hustled across the road. This time Mike was ready and he bailed out of the truck with shotgun at ready. Two shots rang out and the Kat had two partridge to retrieve.

It was midmorning when we arrived at road's end and our jumping-off point. To our great disappointment, two rigs were already there. Their equipment showed that one vehicle had carried in deer hunters. The second vehicle was a rented rig and had two dog kennels in back. We had some competition.

"Guess we will play sucking the hind tit for today's hunt, Mike."

We hunted along alpine meadows and grasslands for the next hour. The dogs found some scent but put up no birds. About noon we arrived at a point where the ridge dropped off sharply.

"Let's take our lunch break among these boulders. They will protect us from the cool wind. We need to consider the situation and plan our next strategy. I am very surprised and disappointed we are not finding birds."

"Beautiful day and spectacular country for our nature walk," Mike observed. "Sure would add to the trip if we could find some more of them chukars."

As we finished our sandwiches, our dogs' excited barking announced the arrival of two spaniels and their human companion.

"How's hunting?" Mike inquired.

The new arrival's reply made us feel more than a little shortchanged. "Good. We jumped 30 or 40 birds. We have bagged four partridge and two chukars."

"Where are you from?" Mike wanted to know.

"Anchorage," our new acquaintance revealed. "I flew down with my dogs for some bird hunting."

"Wouldn't you know it." Mike spoke for two somewhat frustrated hunters. "I come all the way down here from Alaska, hunt one of the most

Chapter 34 — *Some Fall Firsts*

remote areas in North America in the winter, during the middle of the week, only to have another Alaskan beat me to the birds."

Mike and the newcomer were soon exchanging addresses and agreeing to swap hunting stories back in Alaska. Having already had a very good day, our competition took his leave and headed for his truck.

"What is our strategy now?" Mike wanted to know. "Maybe we should head back to the corral area and try to find that big bunch of Huns."

"Let's do that. We will take a different route back and work around the mountain. We should find some birds."

The next hour passed as we followed game trails carefully along the precipitous mountainsides. Finally, as we reached and descended a steep slope, the dogs hit hot scent. Despite their frantic searching, no birds were found. Discouraged, Mike and I relaxed our vigil and then continued our way down. As we descended, Wily changed tactics and circled back up the slope above us. He seemed to be hunting ground we had just covered. We more or less ignored him. Then, wouldn't you know it, he found birds. A large covey of partridge flushed and sailed screaming over our heads. But, none fell to our shots.

"I want to know how we managed to walk right by those birds," Mike asked the dogs.

"Too late to cry over spilled milk. Let's head on down. I'm reasonably sure the birds pitched into heavy brush and grass in the draw's bottom or in brush up the opposite slope."

We arrived in the draw's bottom and began our search. An old access road ran up the draw's bottom. Working through the brush and up the draw's far slope produced no birds.

"I think that I will drop back down and follow the old road. I believe that a half-mile hike will take me back up to the truck."

"Let's split up then and increase both the area covered and also the probability one of us will come across birds. I will hunt on up this slope." Mike concluded.

My walk up the old road brought me to an extensive stand of forest fire damaged timber. I noted with interest the tangle of berry and seed bearing vegetation along the roadside. There was ample bird food here. There should be birds.

Wily supported my belief as he became animated by bird scent and took to the brush. The thunder of wings frantically thrashing air broke the mountain stillness. I swung on a grouse fleeing through the brush on an angle to the right. The bird fell in a shower of feathers. The brown form of a second grouse fleeing through fire blackened tree trunks to my left caught my eye. The Beretta 20 gauge roared a second time. With shooting over, Wily completed the action by picking up my first double ever on ruffed grouse. The day had suddenly become a resounding success.

As I admired our grouse, I heard the distant report of Mike's 20 gauge. "Mike is into birds," I thought.

Plodding upward, two tired hunters reached the truck. I cranked up and headed out to intercept Mike. I found him hunting grassy slopes along the roadside.

"I really got into the partridge," Mike enthused. "I took four more. Should have had my limit."

A short time later we agreed to call it a day. The sun was rapidly dropping toward jagged mountain peaks lying to the west in eastern Oregon. I had no wish to drive the ridge road in the dark.

"We have had another outstanding day. Let's head for the barn. All we need now is for a nice whitetail buck to show along the road. I am not a road hunter and I do prefer a real hunt, but I would not pass up a big, easy whitetail buck."

As late afternoon shadows lengthened, blue grouse frequently hit roads for gravel. Today was no exception. One very large blue grouse made the mistake of blocking our right of way. Mike added him to our now bulging cooler.

With nightfall imminent, I brought the pickup to a halt and shut off the motor. Two deer were browsing among the trees some 50 yards ahead. One was a nice buck. I groped for the binoculars and brought the buck into focus. My rifle was cased beside me. "That buck is well worth taking. A 5x5. But he is a mule deer. This area is open to mule deer by permit drawing only. I have no such permit. Take a look." I handed Mike the binoculars.

When cleaning the grouse the next day, I found that their crops were full of purple berries. They had been dining on either blueberries or huckleberries. With such a diet, they were sure to be prime eating.

One afternoon Mike and I hunted quail along Potlatch Creek. Four eager Chesapeakes accompanied us. You might say that we were "over dogged" for the game pursued. Initially we put up two coveys of birds and succeeded in relocating some as singles. Few birds fell to our shots.

As we worked up the creek in search of another covey Wily jumped a small tributary stream to work a patch of high grass. Wings thundered. I glimpsed a rapidly departing cock pheasant through intervening branches of a cottonwood tree. I had no shot.

"Damn," exclaimed Mike. "Did you see the long tail on that bird. I could not shoot as you were in my line of fire. Hope we can find him."

Chapter 34 — *Some Fall Firsts*

I was not optimistic. "Don't think we will find that bird again. He is headed for the swamps. I have tried hunting there. The going is very rough and vegetation is generally too thick for shooting."

Further efforts as the afternoon passed resulted in only a few quail flushed. Just before sunset, we headed back to the truck along an old, abandoned railroad bed paralleling the highway. With the traffic hazard the dogs were kept at heel.

Bandit was insistent on checking out scent emanating from a nearby brush. "Heel," overruled Mike. "With a busy highway on our right and the swamps on our left, you don't need to hunt here."

Cackling and wings threshing the air to our rear startled us. We had walked right by a rooster crouched among blackberry bushes at the swamp's edge. Bandit ignored his master's orders and had dropped back and flushed him. I managed get the 20 gauge Beretta off my shoulder and bring it to bear. The rooster was now at extreme gun range and my load was only 7/8 ounce of no. 7-1/2 shot; but at my shot, he crumpled. Three dogs rushed to make the retrieve.

"That bird is going nowhere," Mike bet.

When the bird was delivered to hand, I was astonished at the length of his tail. "This must have been your pheasant we flushed down the creek. He landed in the swamps and worked his way through to high ground. I bet we won't find many shot in him."

Mike took the bird for examination. "You had better have this bird mounted."

Back at the ranch, a yardstick showed that the pheasant sported tail feathers over 24 inches in length. His was the most spectacular plumage of any pheasant I had ever taken. With his unusual genetics and also some environmental breaks, he had become the one bird in a thousand.

Another late evening found Mike and me butchering a big whitetail buck a mile or so up a steep-walled canyon off the Clearwater River. We had gotten a late start with our task and there had been two bucks down to cut up and pack out. The weather was rapidly deteriorating and the air temperatures were falling. The wind roared down the canyon in violent gusts that threatened to hurl us off our feet and down the steep, rocky canyon wall. The bucks had died almost 100 vertical yards above the canyon's bottom. To get the meat out necessitated boning the deer where they lay, loading backpacks with meat and then shouldering the heavy packs and staggering along a narrow game trail that gradually descended into the canyon. The pack out was about 1-1/2 miles. Accomplishing all the butchering and getting all the meat packed out before nightfall rapidly became impossible.

"We had better settle for getting out only this buck today," Mike cautioned. "I am afraid that with heavy packs on our backs and the wind approaching gale force, a man could be knocked off his feet for a rather bumpy and maybe fatal landing. This big buck is a nice animal. He is an old timer with heavy 5x4 antlers. His antlers would have been bigger a year or so back. Why don't you pose for a couple of pictures before we break out the knives? The background here is spectacular."

"I think you are right about our limitations. No way can we finish butchering both animals today. The smaller animal is gutted out. Wendell is in his 80's and sure is not up to doing any packing. I will come back for Wendell's buck first thing in the morning. It is plenty cold enough so the meat will hold overnight. I just hope that the predators don't bother the carcass."

Wily and Kat had accompanied us to the kill site as possible pack animals. Wily and I posed for pictures. Wily then enjoyed an occasional snack of raw scraps as butchering progressed. Kat did not seem interested in such crude dining. When we started down, Mike elected her to carry the meat-loaded dog pack.

Loose volcanic rocks littered the slopes and the game trail we followed out. Stepping carefully, we stumbled down the trail with heavy backpack straps biting into our shoulders. Mike and I each packed a single ski pole. He had suggested that a pole would be a great asset in maintaining our balance during the walk and climb down and also take some weight off abused old knees. In recent years I had observed that many backpackers and alpine hiker in Alaska carry such poles. My friend Bill Hart of North Carolina used poles during his hike from Georgia to Maine along the Appalachian Trail.

Back at the truck we shrugged off our heavy packs with relief.

"Glad we packed the ski poles, Mike. They came in handy. We got down with no falls. My right knee doesn't feel bad. My winter meat supply is assured. Let's head for the house and a cold one or two I can look forward to a repeat of this packing ordeal tomorrow. Hopefully, the wind will die down tonight."

"One of these years we will learn not to put ourselves in situations requiring such hard, risky work," Mike observed. "You need a woman to persuade you to forego such foolishness. My knee is really acting up. Think I will sleep in tomorrow and let you and Wily have all the fun."

"Your advice is sensible. But seeing as how you packed a big Alaska caribou bull 12 miles this fall, it's kind of like 'the pot calling the kettle black.' Maybe we each need a sensible woman to cut us back on our hunting excesses."

Chapter 34 — *Some Fall Firsts*

Early morning found me approaching the area of the second kill. Wily surged ahead to pause and examine scent some 30 yards below where the buck had fallen. I could see no deer. Something was wrong. I arrived at the scene to find only scattered, gnawed bones and a bedraggled hide. Even the deer's skull was missing. Sometime during the night some critter or critters had devoured over 100 pounds of meat. From available evidence I could not determine what type of critter had done the eating. Locally there were lots of coyotes, an occasional black bear, and cougar. Recently there were even rumors of wolves.

Sometimes, hunters of black-tailed deer in Alaska's brown bear country lose deer to grizzly. But for me this was a first. I personally had been lucky. I had on several occasions left animals in the field overnight with little loss of meat except for scavenging birds.

I sighed in disappointment. The three-mile walk had been in vain. I resolved to never again leave meat in the field overnight. "Let's go home old fellow. At least you and I can be relieved that we will not have to pack meat today. We will pick up Mike and your dog buddies and maybe look for some quail after lunch."

A few mornings later, Mike checked in about eight to find me finishing up some correspondence on the computer.

"You want to use this machine to check your e-mail," I inquired. "Please don't get hung up all morning playing the stock market. After that dinner of liver and onions last night, I'm all charged up to chase some pheasants today. We will hunt a tract I have yet to hunt this year."

Our hunt started in an extensive field near Sweetwater Creek, which was being managed under the Conservation Reserve Program. Abbie was assigned to stay home. The terrain we would hunt today would be very steep. Mike's dog, Bandit, was suffering from a chronic front leg injury and would remain unhappily kenneled in the truck. Our hunting companions were the veterans Katmai and Wily.

We began hunting up a steeply pitched slope. To maximize the terrain covered and maybe spook a bird to each other, our paths were separated by 40 to 60 yards. In some areas, the native wheat grass grew head high. The heavy going quickly warmed us. Sweat popped out on human brows and dogs panted. Layers of unneeded clothing were shucked and stored in our backpacks.

Less than a quarter-mile from the truck, a shot rang out from Mike's direction. A quick check showed that he had bagged the day's first rooster, a very nice, heavy bird. We continued up the slope, seeming to gain about as many feet vertically as horizontally. Though the dogs hit some hot bird scent, no additional birds were found during the next half-mile of our tramping.

The hunt took us by a stock-watering tank in a brushy draw. I quickly suggested, "Let's take a short break and water these dogs and ourselves." But just then Wily hit hot bird scent and lost interest in water.

"Maybe we should work on up," Mike suggested.

"I know from past bad experience that the climb up this draw is a workout. My hunting strategy is to hunt the grass fields extending on around the hill. I will let Wily do his thing. Maybe he can flush a bird down to us. Flushed on terrain this steep, a pheasant will usually flush downhill."

Wily plunged into the brush and disappeared up the draw. Breaking brush and tumbling rocks followed his upward progress. No bird could outrun long-legged Wily. Soon, there was raucous cackling as a rooster was forced into the air.

"Get ready," I shouted.

Mike was ready but this time I had the first shot. I swung the Beretta 12 gauge as a rooster dropped past, his air speed increased by gravity.

"Nice pass shot," Mike called. Kat completed the retrieve of another nice, heavy rooster. Wily appeared, panting. Now he was ready for water and he lapped noisily and long.

"The day is already a success even if we get no more birds," I declared. "But I believe that we will have additional opportunities."

The next half-mile of tramping put up only hens. Arriving at the ridge's summit, we exited the CRP plot and faced a vast agricultural area. This past spring the land had produced peas.

"We will cross about 500 yards of field and hunt south along the ridge's far side. Along the northeast-facing slope there is thick brush and tangles of wild rose. In past years, this slope has been a good refuge for pheasants in the late season. You can hunt along the slope and I will walk the field edge with Wily. You should have the most opportunities."

It turned out from Mike's standpoint that my strategy was wrong. He flushed only a couple of hens in the next hour of hard walking. Wily, on the other hand, dug out a rooster that fell when I executed a difficult shot. As I walked on around the field I was feeling good about my shot.

"Two for two," I thought. "The way I'm shooting I could have a perfect day. Find me another bird, Wily. I'm on a roll."

About that time Wily tensed up at the field's edge. He sat down on my whistle with his eyes locked on brush at his feet. I closed in and Wily pounced. I emptied the double with two quick shots. The rooster flew away cackling derisively.

Chapter 34 — *Some Fall Firsts*

Expletives about a perfect game lost filled the air as Mike inquired from below, "how did you miss that easy shot?"

"Sun must have gotten into my eyes," was my lame excuse.

At noon, we rested in winter bleached grass. The high cover was swayed by a cool breeze as we took a lunch break.

"We still have a lot of country to hunt this afternoon. We should get some more opportunities."

"Bring on the opportunities."

Another couple of hours tramping resulted in a number of classic flushes, with several seeming from right under our feet. Trouble was that they were all hens and no shots were fired. The dogs put up one cock bird just out of shooting range. No shots were fired.

Given the short November day, the sun was already steadily sinking toward the western horizon while coloring the few clouds with bands of pink. Our steps turned downhill toward the truck. As usual at the end of a day's hunt, the human contingent was tired and no longer hunting alertly.

An old cow path took us along the top of a steep, brush-choked, rock-filled draw. The dogs went on alert as Mike wondered, "Maybe we should hunt down that draw."

"My knee is starting to act up. We have our five miles in and another mile to go to the truck. Think I will decline. Hold my gun while I cross this barbed wire fence."

In the meantime, independent-thinking Wily, who just loved to flush birds, decided to conduct a sortie on his own. As I crossed the fence, he dropped down the draw to find and push a hen pheasant out of tangled brush and weeds. Then, to my amazement, he put up a rooster. The rooster sprang into the air and flew angling uphill. His initial flight pattern was safely wide of where we stood. Then he mistakenly veered toward us and came within marginal range. I had no shotgun. My 12 gauge lay at Mike's feet. Besides I was hung up on the barbed wire fence.

Mike came through and made a spectacular shot with his Beretta 20. Kat completed the action by delivering Mike his second hard-earned bird.

"Spectacular shot, Mike."

"Note that bird flew uphill not down."

"There is always a exception for every rule. Wily is really earning his Purina today. Sometimes the strategy of letting dogs flush far-out birds to you works; sometimes it doesn't. Anyhow it has worked twice today."

We approached the truck with the sun setting behind bluffs in the west. The dogs were pretty much given their head. We had enjoyed a good day and were looking forward to water and heading for the barn. The dogs worked high cover ahead and startled us by pushing up a rooster. My reaction time was slow but at my shot he fell. Wily made the retrieve. Today's take was five extra large, fine roosters.

During an aborted duck hunt, Mike suffered lower back problems and a reversal in his hunting plans. He opted to gather his pups and fly home to Anchorage for recuperation. There would be opportunities afield for him in later seasons.

I awakened one morning with chukars on my mind. A weather check showed that conditions for hiking into their preferred high country were marginal. Outside, a moderate wind rattled limbs of large locust trees and the sky was overcast. An option was to try some local draws. I could cancel operations early if conditions continued to deteriorate. Wily would be my companion. I still lacked the control over Lil'Bit necessary for effective and safe chukar hunting.

Access into the country I wished to hunt was complicated by the necessity of crossing a four-lane highway busy with morning traffic. I left the van in a sportsman's access area beside the Clearwater River. With Wily on lead and at heel, we made it safely across this obstacle.

We hunted methodically up a steep draw. In the draw's bottom, brush and weeds provided cover and abundant seeds for a bird's dining pleasure. New cheat grass, one of the chukar's favorite salads, showed green growth. About a mile up the draw we reached a stretch of water seeps and puddles. In years past I had taken chukar here. Today, Wily found little scent to get excited about.

If the birds were not in the draw's bottom, maybe they were on the ridge tops. We would check this possibility. Our steps turned steeply upward. Going upward, we reached a stock tank. After a brief pause for Wily to hop in and cool off and also slack his thirst, we continued puffing up a cattle trail to the ridge's summit. An unpleasantly cool wind blew down the river valley and gusted along the exposed ridge. The Clearwater River gleamed in the weak, late-morning light far below. There was no spoor of our quarry. There was little reason for optimism but we would continue to hunt on the way back to the van.

Descending, we finally reached a point about a quarter-mile and 100 vertical yards above the river. Below, steelhead-seeking fishermen worked their jet boats hopefully along river riffles. To avoid the cliffs fronting the highway, it was necessary to leave the ridge to descend into and follow the draw we had hiked up earlier to the highway.

As we began going down, Wily finally found fresh bird scent and then began frantically hunting the steep slope. No birds were to be found. Our quarry must have "flown the coop," so to speak.

Chapter 34 — *Some Fall Firsts*

By the time we reached the draw's bottom, I had given up on birds and was looking forward to brunch. About a hundred yards from our escape from the canyon Wily again found hot scent. He worked the main draw and then headed up a steep, brushy side draw. His upward progress dislodged loose rocks.

"I am tired Wily," I thought. "We have already gotten in our three-mile hike. Besides, we hunted through this area earlier this morning. Have yourself a look. I'm not following you up."

Some 60 yards up the draw, the air exploded in a thrashing of wings. A covey of 15 to 20 birds sailed downward. I swung my Beretta 20 on a bird descending to my right. The bird dropped at my shot. As the covey's flight ascended the far slope to my left, I continued my swing and then completed a classic double.

Wily delivered the first bird, a nice masked bandit, to hand and then was off in search of the second bird. I was very surprised when the second bird he handed me was a Hungarian partridge. We had found a mixed covey and bagged a mixed double!

"Let's go have brunch Wily. This was our first mixed double of chukars and partridge. I do not know how often they hang out together but I don't think it is often. You just made the day."

A few days later Wily and I were high up a steep, rocky bluff overlooking the Snake River. My armament was the Beretta 20. The previous year, the ridge we had just hunted produced chukars. Today, after two hours of hiking, no birds had been found.

A quarter-mile below the ridge's summit, the cackling of chukars reached our ears over the whispering wind. Birds were holding somewhere in the rocks and cliffs up ahead. We ascended to the suspected chukar hideout area to work back and fourth across unstable and dangerous slopes. Wily found plenty of scent but no birds. They were no longer talking. Finally, I was ready to throw in the towel. I told Wily, "we have worked this area pretty thoroughly, considering the terrain. The birds must have flown. I'm ready for a lunch and water break."

I carefully picked my way upward to an old power line access road. The road ran just below the merger of ridge and prairie farmland. Here I found boulders that provided me a seat and some protection from the cool wind. Wily wished to hunt on but I overruled him.

"Let's take a break while we are in a good spot. There will be plenty of time to hunt after lunch. Sit!" I got out my water jug and directed a stream of water into his panting mouth. I then enjoyed a drink myself. While munching my sandwich, I offered Wily a dog biscuit. He crunched his snack down and again started out. I called him back, "Wait a minute. I have another snack for you."

Getting under way, I donned my shooting vest, then shouldered my shotgun and called Wily to heel. He directed us to the edge of a drop-off and started picking his way down a very unstable, boulder-studded slope. He was obviously following bird scent. I watched his progress doubtfully. His four-footed drive was a definite advantage here. I did not very much wish to chance this slope.

I missed my chance. Thirty yards below, a band of masked bandits flushed screaming from their lair behind a boulder and disappeared into distant valleys. Hard pressed, they had decided not to await my approach. I saluted their departure in vain. I had chosen to hunt with open chokes and light loads today.

"Amazing those birds sat there quietly so close by while we had lunch. Pays for a man to always believe and follow his dog."

At the day's end, we arrived back at the truck tired, thirsty, dusty, and birdless. I hope that with each hunt a man grows somewhat wiser.

Wily took a plunge in the Snake River to cool off. "Got warm and dusty climbing in the mountains today didn't it, old man. It is about that time of the year to set out some duck and geese decoys. Then you can hunt in a proper environment for water dogs."

As we loaded up, the sun slipped behind the western mountains and illuminated the river in its last rays. I muttered to myself. "Sometimes the hunter wins when chukaring, but more often the chukar wins. In any event we had another good nature walk."

After November had given way to December, pale-light dawn found Wily and me watching our goose decoys. The decoys had been set out in new and green winter wheat. The Clearwater River glistened in the back ground as a mild, sunny bluebird day dawned. As the hands of my pocket watch approached 8:30 a.m., we watched as hundreds of mallards left the river to fly in search of grain available from feedlots and wheat stubble in the surrounding hills. My goose decoys attracted no ducks. But I suddenly picked up the gabble of talking geese. Wily was frozen in attention and gazing down the river. I turned my head cautiously and sighted wavering lines of geese approaching. They decided to join the decoys in an assault on the farmer's wheat. A large bird fell at the thunder of my under barrel. I swung on a second goose confident of scoring a double. My finger then tightened but resulted in only a very frustrating and infuriating click. The firing pen of the Beretta's over barrel had fallen with insufficient strength to fire the primer. This scene was repeated again and again. I was

Chapter 34 — *Some Fall Firsts*

effectively hunting with a single shot shotgun today and would have to bear down and make every shot count.

The day approached perfection as flight after flight of greater Canada geese came to visit. Before the morning had passed, our limit of geese remained behind. Packing two dozen decoys and a bag of large geese, the quarter-mile or so back to the truck proved to be heavy going.

A couple of weeks later Wily and I shared the fall's first perfect pheasant hunt—three shells fired and three roosters retrieved. This was also my first limit taken with my new Beretta 20 gauge. The birds were taken with a skeet choke and 1 ounce of copper plated no. 6 shot. The day was marred when back at the truck I discovered that Wily had injured his left front leg. A big, hard-going dog facing rough terrain much too often results in injury. Wily faced sitting out the action for a few days.

One Sabbath morning found me hammering away on the computer. By midmorning, I was restless with my assigned indoor task and I resolved to spend the rest of the day afield. Before heading out, I did prepare and enjoy a fancy pheasant omelet for brunch.

We arrived at a tract of wheat stubble and brushy draws. Wily was aired and assigned to remain in the van. "You need to rest up that shoulder old fellow. You can protect the homestead today." Left behind, Wily's cries of distress were heart rending.

Today, Abbie would have her first solo hunt. An hour into the hunt Abbie had put up a number of hens but no roosters. Occasionally, she would stop between coverts and gaze into the distance searching for her big blond friend.

Stealthily, we covered a last few yards of plowed ground and approached a small patch of excellent pheasant cover. The patch contained dense grass tangles and piles of tumbleweed. Abbie plunged in eagerly. Wings thundered as several pheasant took to the air. At my first shot a rooster fell far down the slope. My second shot at a second cock bird was wide. Abbie completed her retrieve like a veteran.

A short time later we were working up a large, brushy draw. Abbey came to a sudden halt, tested the air currents with a quivering nose, and then headed for the draw's far side. Catching sight of a number of songbirds flitting through the brush beyond her, I whistled her in. "Come in here Lil'Bit. We don't want to bother those little birds." About the time she started back and I turned to walk away, a covey of 30 or more quail took to the air. I sighed in frustration. I had been wrong and Abbie right.

Our hunt carried us into the draw's upper reaches where a few quail were found and flushed. Most of the quail had apparently found refuge in a very extensive quail castle of blackberry bushes. I had just added a single hen quail to the bag when a bull quail exploded practically under my feet. At my shot it fell in a shower of feathers. Abbie, out of sight working in dense brush, did not see the fall. At my urging, she put on an extensive and determined search for the downed quail. She finally made the find and proudly delivered me the handsome bird.

"Enough fun for today, Abbie-Cakes. You have performed admirably. Let's head down and let your unhappy boyfriend loose. We will try for some more birds tomorrow."

The next afternoon, I made a stand within a patch of brush as Abbie pushed quail out of heavy cover. I had some decent shots and downed three birds before we began picking up. The first find, a bull had fallen into short grass and was easy. Then the real work began. Abbie worked and reworked through heavy brush and thorns. Panting from exertion, she finally found and delivered a hen bird. The third and final bird was proving to be an impossible find. As the sun set behind pine-covered bluffs to the west, I began to consider calling the persistent pup to heel. About that time Abbie started lunging and jumping into the limbs of a large elderberry bush: crash, crash, crash.

Abbie's attempts to climb the bush met with little success. All the while she was whining and yapping in excited frustration. I painfully made my way through clinging branches to where she sat gazing upward. Sure enough, a dead quail was trapped in branches about seven feet above the ground. I secured the quail and tossed it for the frustrated pup to retrieve.

"Good going, Abbie-Cakes. You are becoming quite the hunting dog."

Some retrieves are above and beyond the course of ordinary retriever duty and expectations. The truly gifted retriever will sometimes make saves on game that will forever live in the minds of human companions.

One sunny December day Wily and I were hunting quail along the Potlatch River. Wily was finding plenty of birds and my shooting was pretty fair. Approaching our limit, we were heading back to the truck, when Wily put up a quail from a brushy slope above me. I took a snapshot as the quail passed, twisting and turning through saplings. The bird fell and disappeared down a 60-degree slope. Just above the river, the slope fell off in a 20-foot cliff. Wily, in hot pursuit, disappeared. I heard the loud ker-splash of a heavy body hitting water. Wily had either leaped or fallen from the cliff! From my vantage point, much of the stream was obscured. I dashed forward, very distressed over the possible fate of my faithful companion. The watery V of a heavy body moving downstream came into view. I blew continuously on my whistle, hoping to direct Wily to a break in the cliffs where he could land. Finally, and much to my relief, the big

Chapter 34 — *Some Fall Firsts*

yellow dog was scrambling upward to me and shaking off a rain of icy water as he deliver a wet and bedraggled quail.

Another morning dawn showed promise of a fine bluebird day. It was with misgivings that Clayton, Josh, and I boarded Clayton's duck boat for a day of waterfowling along the Snake River. Finally, we were under way for a late (8 a.m.) banker's hours duck hunt. Our four-footed companions were Clayton's Annie and my Abbie. This would be Abbie's first duck hunt. A surprising number of ducks visited our decoys and several greenheads remained behind as the day passed. The two bitches were unhappy when restricted to alternate retrieves, but when sent they both acquitted themselves well. Much credit for the day's successful duck hunt I attribute to the expertise of Josh with a duck call. The young Arkansas man did an outstanding job of talking ducks into shotgun range.

Weather patterns in northwestern Idaho had shifted to unseasonably cold and snowy by late December and December 30 arrived with only two days of pheasant season left. Pheasant hunting was planned as Mike had come down from Alaska to join me.

Early morning light revealed snow covering the hills and the valleys. "Let's give eastern Washington a try today," I said to Mike. "Hopefully, the snow cover will be lighter there."

Our hopes for improved weather proved futile. As we drove the few miles to eastern Washington, the snow cover actually became heavier. A cold, cruel wind kept us sitting and procrastinating in the warm truck. The day was getting on and there was no time to alter hunting sites. We finally decided to bite the bullet and get some exercise.

We hunted up and down steep draws transacting fields of wheat stubble. Within one deep draw we found tangles of weeds along with some trapped tumbleweeds and cattails. This vegetative combination made for an ideal bird refuge. A blanket of snow overlaid the cover and many pheasant tracks zigzagged between the cut wheat and the cover.

Wily found hot scent and enthusiastically led his female companions in pursuit. They found and flushed numerous hen pheasants from their secure refuges in the heavy cover. A few roosters exploded, cackling angrily in eruptions of snow. Two of them fell to hunter's guns.

After the New Year, snow continued to accumulate. Restless hunters and dogs finally took to the field despite the challenging weather conditions. Snow cover would make hiking steep hillsides extremely hazardous so we would hunt heavy, woody cover in draw bottoms.

One late morning found me parking the truck at the mouth of a brushy draw in eastern Washington. As we exited the truck, a large covey of chukars flushed screaming from roadside brush. They had not waited for us to arm ourselves. We watched them land and scurry along and up a hillside 100 yards away. They seemed to chuckle at us in derision. The steep, snow-covered and rock-studded hillside precluded our pursuit.

As the morning passed, we moved up the draw bucking a severely cold wind. We found and flushed a covey of partridge. Again we were caught unprepared and they took wing just out of range.

Finally, the dogs found and put up a small covey of quail. This time, we connected. We continued to work up the draw after the broken covey and several fell to our guns for the dogs to retrieve.

Earlier in the fall we had hunted this tract for pheasants but had found few. Today, with pheasant season over, the dogs flushed many pheasants including several gaudy roosters. The birds were holding tight. They would flush only when the dogs pushed them out, sometimes practically under our feet. When no shots were fired and the birds flew away, our canine companions looked at us askance.

The short winter day was winding down as we drove to another tract. Two miles down the softly-packed gravel road I braked sharply. I had spied large gray birds in cover along a cut wheat field.

"Chukars, Mike! We have finally found some bandits on flat terrain. They are vulnerable."

We hastily exited the truck. For once, masked bandits were at a definite disadvantage. Mike took the first shot as the covey flushed at extreme range and he hit a bird hard. The hard-hit chukar sailed down in midfield wheat stubble, then scampered toward a hillside and heavy cover. The balance of the covey had pitched onto the hill's lower, more gentle slopes. We marked the covey down in the area of a small, lone tree. The dogs were heeled until we drew within shotgun range.

We reached the hillside cover to find many bird tracks. Two birds were spotted scampering up the slope from us. Wily was suddenly digging into snow at our feet. I figured that he was after the lost cripple and would make the catch. I was unprepared to shoot when it escaped him to take wing. Mike shot twice, but too quickly and missed the departing bird. At his shots, the snow around us exploded as several chukars flushed from their hides under the snow cover. We had walked right into the middle of the covey! I got off two shots.

Mike's jinx on chukars had continued. "Wouldn't you know it. Those lowly birds flushed and caught me with an empty shotgun."

Wily and I hunted down and added a lightly hit bird to our bag. Dogs and hunters then worked the heavy cover along a small stream at the field's base. Within the next hour, Mike and I added two more chukars to the day's take.

Chapter 34 — *Some Fall Firsts*

We met back by the truck in the day's rapidly diminishing light where I summed up the day. "We finally caught the masked bandit in some flat country. Doesn't happen often. Added to our quail, we have a good take of birds. The dogs had a good day flushing and retrieving birds."

"We should have killed more of them chukars while we had a chance," muttered Mike. He had a long-running score to settle with this species. "It was sure encouraging to see all the potential brood stock for next spring's nesting."

"When shooting upland birds I always try to select for male birds. The surviving males seem to have a grin on their faces when hunting season goes out. There will be lots of hens to go around for spring servicing. I just hope that we don't get a freezing rain on top of all this snow. An ice crust would kill many birds."

Tony, my rancher neighbor, had given me the interesting information about lots of ducks coming into waste grain on a ranch near Lewiston. A scouting trip verified the truth of his information. Mike and I secured permission for a duck hunt. As the date of our scheduled hunt approached, Dr. Bill from Orofino was invited down to join in the shoot.

The weather deteriorated seriously on the night before our scheduled duck hunt. Air temperature dropped into the single digits and snow came down thickly. Before I turned in early for a before-dawn start, Mike elected to forego waterfowl. "Won't be any fun sitting around waiting for ducks in this weather. I don't have my cold weather gear along. Besides my vacation is coming to an end. Think that I will drive up Joseph Creek tomorrow and try to catch chukars at a disadvantage. The heavy snowfall may have forced them down into flat terrain."

Bill and I trudged up a snow-covered hill by flashlight. Our dog buddy this a.m. was Lil'Bit. Her dark brown would better blend into our planned cover than would blond Wily. We planned to have a dozen duck and four goose decoys in place by a half-hour before shooting time. The landscape was unnaturally illuminated by snow-reflected light. Snow fell thickly as squalls passed. As we approached the hilltop, much duck talk reached us through the mist. Many dark bodies and whistling wings were passing over our heads as ducks rushed to join the multitudes at breakfast.

We reached an area where the terrain under foot turned black and squishy. Waste cattle food stood out in stark contrast to the surrounding snow. Our approach flushed literally hundreds of mallards and widgeon into the air. Hopefully, as the day progressed, they would return to feed.

"We have really found the honey-hole for ducks, Bill. Not much cover on this barren hilltop. We can set up along the fence. That pile of rocks and fence posts will help break up our outline."

"It's well worth the trip just to see all those birds," Bill allowed. "They should come back in good."

We did not have the hill to ourselves this morning. Another party of two occupied a somewhat better "blind" nearby. As we settled in after setting out decoys, ducks pitched boldly into our spread. The minute hand of my watch seemed to stand still, frozen as time, before legal shooting time arrived. Young Abbie, secured by a lead, waited impatiently.

Many, many wings whistled as large flight of mallards descended to join ducks already sitting among our decoys. Birds were also pitching into our neighbors' spread.

A salvo of shotgun blasts from our neighbors announced the arrival of shooting hours. Bill and I each unlimbered our 12 gauges. Two greenheads remained behind. Abbie rushed to make the pick ups.

As the morning passed, flights of ducks returned to check out the scene. The easy shooting was largely over, however. These birds had been hunter educated and were wary. Given the scant cover we had for concealment, they were very suspicious, easily spooked, and would not light. Bill succeeded in dropping a couple of birds that fell far out. Abbie did a first-class job of running down and retrieving these cripples.

Multitudes of mourning doves worked the feed. Two approached and attempted to light on our hat-covered heads. One dove lit shivering in the cold and began feed within two feet of my seat.

"I believe that I could pick that dove up," I quietly observed.

I watched in fascination as birds landed within inches of Abbie. Curled in a ball so tight she seemed to squeak she seemed to ignore the little birds. When a shotgun went off, however, she was instantly on the alert.

"I can't believe that Abbie is ignoring those doves. I guess that since we are not shooting them she is waiting for bigger game. I don't believe Wily would be so patient. He would be up spotting birds. He spots incoming birds better than I do."

With few birds now decoying, our neighbors gave up the game and picked up their decoys.

By midmorning, large flocks of geese flew tantalizingly along the Clearwater River below. Most were drawn into a frenzy of geese feeding in a new wheat field a quarter-mile away.

Chapter 34 — *Some Fall Firsts*

A medium size, swept-wing falcon materialized to strafe the doves. The "palomas" took frantically to wing.

"I do believe that was a peregrine falcon, Bill. This year's Audubon Christmas Bird Count included one sighting in this area."

"I think that you are right," Bill agreed. "Mark! Geese coming!"

Four large birds were rapidly approaching our spread. Bill tuned up his goose call. There was no time to dump the duck loads from our shotguns and reload with goose fodder. We would have to make do.

At our shots, two geese fell far out. Little Abbie would have her first chance at geese. Her job would not be easy. She would have to chase down and retrieve big and fighting birds. They were both cripples.

Bill and I stood watching in amazement as she chased down the first and then the second goose. Each of the 10 to 12-pound birds was delivered to hand.

"I am very pleased and more than a little surprised that she could pack these big birds on land. I think this will prove to be the day's highlight. It's almost noon. I am cold and I have errands to run in town. I think I will head for the truck."

"I'm here for the duration and am more than happy sitting over the decoys watching birds fly. You go ahead," Bill declared. "Maybe we will have an evening shoot."

"I agree the ducks will start coming in again about dark."

Three hours later, Bill and I were waiting as the darkness rapidly approached. Snow was now coming down thickly and in a serious way.

"Here come the ducks," Bill warned. He began working a flight of birds with his call.

The birds were now serious about feeding and approached our decoys with no hesitation. Bill dropped a bird as I missed with my first shot, only to have my Remington 870 jam as I tried for a second. "This damn shotgun is jammed again; bad this time. Don't know if I can fix it out here or not. This is my second duck gun to go out this fall."

Ducks continued to come in and flare as I nosily attempted to eject the spent shell. With fingers numb, I finally resorted to using a rock in its extraction. Bill patiently endured my efforts. Finally my gun was once again functional.

"This weather is hard on guns," I concluded. Little did we know that Bill would face attempting to shoot ducks with a frozen Browning the next morning.

Buddies Afield — Trips Outside Alaska

With only minutes of shooting time left, the ducks started coming in like Kamikaze pilots. We picked our shots. And with shooting hours over, birds were still dropping in from what was now a genuine snowstorm.

"We shared another very good day today." Bill concluded. "Most birds I have seen since hunting in Montana years ago."

"We took all the birds we need. We are just short of a double limit of 7 mallards each and we have a goose each as a bonus. We have shared some good hunts through the years. We will remember today for a while. Abbie had quite a day. Wily missed out on the action today and will be mad with me. He will have other days though. The torch is passed on."

"With this storm you had better plan to sleep over at my place. We can hear about Mike's further adventures with chukars while we drink a cold one or two. This past year had been a great one for sports afield and the New Year shows much promise."

Season's End Waterfowl

The best waterfowling arrives with the New Year, 2004.

A trio of baldpate twisted erratically away from the decoys that had deceived them. I swung the Beretta Superimposed, playing catch-up. I was determined to shoot no hen ducks today but feather shadings were subdued against the dark bluffs across the river and light reflected from lead gray clouds and water. As the birds passed from left to right, I could finally determine that two of them were drakes. I made my selection and pressed the trigger. A bird plunged downward with the boom of the 12 gauge. The duck's impact generated ripples that rocked the decoys gently. Stray feathers drifted on an otherwise glassy calm surface.

My two canine companions whined eager for release. Earlier, Abbie had started the morning's retrieves by fetching a mallard drake. It was Wily's turn. "You're up Wily. Back!" Released, he leaped from boat to the bank in a rush to navigate the circuitous route required reach the river. His spectacular plunge exploded the frigid, mid-January Snake River water.

Following his delivery, I had Wily hold by the boat while I received the drake and ordered him to "Shake." A spray of icy water filled the air. "Good boy Wily," I told him as I smoothed and admired the drake's plumage. Clouds of mallards were moving on the horizon. The whistling of many wings reached our ears as flocks of goldeneye passed, following the middle river channel.

When I said, "Kennel," Wily complied by leaping back into the boat. Whether we took additional birds or not, the morning's outing been a success on a day that had started out unpromising.

With the end of Washington State's 2003-2004 waterfowl season in sight, next fall seemed far away. The wildfowl season had been an outstanding one for the dogs and me but I wanted more memories—a final good duck hunt.

Yesterday evening I had hooked up the boat, which was loaded with decoys and blind materials. We would hit the Snake River in the early morning, hoping some nasty weather would roll in to give us an edge over our duck quarry. I turned in early as there was a possibility of awakening to a snowy or at least a foggy day. This hope was dashed when I peeped out the front door into four a.m. blackness. Stars winked through a broken cloud cover. The early morning air seemed almost balmy. The outside thermometer showed temperatures above freezing. There would be no snow today.

I tried to justify our hunt strategy by addressing Wily. "This is not a promising day for ducks. With only a couple of days left in upland bird seasons, we should probably hunt chukars and partridge today. But since the boat is hooked up and loaded for waterfowl, we will give ducks a go."

The plan was to have decoys out and a blind up before shooting hours. I steered the boat slowly and carefully down the Snake River in predawn blackness. Too much haste down the night-shrouded river could lead to unwanted encounters with logs.

As we made progress west along the river's north shore, some blacker shapes materialized on the black waters off our bow and to our starboard. The quacking and honking of nervous ducks and geese disturbed by our sudden appearance filled the air. There were many birds! Ducks were in!

Progress toward our hunting site took us by a grain barge lying at anchor. As we passed, wings of many spooked ducks and geese thrashed as they took to the air.

The questions now were: would birds return and if they did return, would they decoy?

Decoys were carefully set out with each anchored in place. The river bank fell off steeply and the slight current would carry away decoys not well secured. Local regulations prohibited shooting from the bank at this location. Our boat blind would be beneath the overhanging bushes. Half of my duck decoys were placed just upstream and half just downstream of the brush patch. The goose decoys were anchored downstream of the duck decoys. My spread of 12 duck and 6 goose decoys seemed sparse for hunting such big water.

With decoys out, I hastened to anchor and begin the process of making the boat into a blind. First, I covered the boat's structure with camouflage cloth and canvas. Then tumbleweeds and other weeds were added to break up the boat's outline. Preparations for the hunt took much longer than I expected. Clouds covering the eastern horizon glowed from the rising sun and I was no longer working with a flashlight. As I gathered plant cover, I perspired heavily. My clothing was too heavy for the day's moderate temperatures. It would be necessary to shed a layer. A glance at the watch showed that legal shooting time had already arrived.

A quacking drake mallard dropped into the decoys, tarried for a few moments, and then spooked. With my shotgun left behind in the boat, I could only watch in frustration as the drake flew off. "Might be my only opportunity today," I morosely thought.

Chapter 35 — *Season's End Waterfowl*

A glance upstream showed that, much to my dismay, a large log had drifted into the upstream decoys. Without disrupting my boat blind, I headed up the rocky bank hoping to dislodge the log before decoys were carried away. I was puffing from the effort as the log was cleared from the decoys and anchored along shore. This logging operation scared off six more decoying mallards.

Finally, the dogs and I were settled in the blind. "At long last we are ready to begin hunting. I am not expecting much shooting. The weather is too nice. Maybe I can at least bag you each a duck to retrieve," I told them.

A short while later a drake mallard caught me in an inattentive mode. By the time I shouldered the shotgun, he was heading out and at marginal effective killing range. I tried one shot but missed behind cleanly.

The dogs whined in frustration and looked at me accusingly. I, too, was very frustrated. I was expecting very few opportunities this day and these missed chances hurt.

During the next hour, a few birds flew by at marginal range but I attempted no shots. I had no wish to cripple a bird. Often a dog cannot out-swim a wing-tipped bird. Such a cripple would have to be chased down by boat, necessitating dismantling my "blind." Chasing a cripple by the boat always costs valuable hunting time and usually results in some missed opportunities at ducks over the decoys.

The day was not boring. Bands of goldeneye continued to move up and down the river on whistling wings. Cormorants flew by, mere feet above the river's surface. Upstream toward Clarkston, and downstream toward Chief Timothy Park, flocks of geese in the hundreds moved inland over the hills in search of food. A mature bald eagle soared far overhead. The dogs became attentive as mourning doves and pigeons seeking spilled grain darted over and behind us. I knew that my blind was OK when a band of coots swam to within arm's reach.

A few hundred yards up the stream a grain barge was being actively loaded. A scum of chaff spilled from the barge floated slowly in midstream. Pods of mallards began to appear and land for brunch.

Finally, a big, beautiful northern drake mallard approached, responded to my short and low feeding call, and then came into our decoys. I stood and took him as he sprang from the water.

Much to Wily's disgust and frustration, I sent Abbie for the easy retrieve. The young bitch returned proudly with her bird to leap from the bank into the boat and sit for delivery. She had perfected her system. She generously shared her cold swim by shaking water vigorously.

Buddies Afield — Trips Outside Alaska

"Thanks a lot Lil'Bit. I did not really want a shower this morning. It's good that I am wearing hip boots. Flawless job of retrieving though. I have to admit you are well trained even if I did the job myself."

Across the river geese continued to move over the hills in search of feed. I thought that I knew where many of them were headed.

After the day's second duck, a baldpate, was bagged, the morning seemed to drag. Few mallards were flying and those that were joined the gangs of birds feeding in mid-river. A few ducks swam tantalizingly just beyond shotgun range.

My hope was that the ducks would move in mid to late morning. We waited impatiently. The dogs munched on biscuits and I shared a bite of delicious Christmas raisin-oatmeal cookies baked by my brother back in Carolina with them.

At last, about ten o'clock, ducks began to move. Despite the almost bluebird day and the glowing sun circling to the west, a number of ducks chose to visit our decoys. Picking my shots, I selected only drake mallards and a second baldpate drake. The 1-3/8 ounce loads of no. 2 steel shot I was shooting were effective. My secret to effective duck shooting with steel shot is to take only close birds. As the hour hand approached eleven o'clock, I was feeling very good about my shooting. I had six birds in the bag with seven shots fired. There had been no cripples for the dogs to chase. For me, this was phenomenal duck-shooting success.

When a pair of mallard drakes strafed the decoys, I raised to my feet to shoot my final bird of a limit. I had waited too long and impatiently violated the day's rule of taking only close shots. My shot was behind the duck. My swelling ego was temporarily bruised but a short while later I redeemed myself when a final shot brought down the last bird of the daily bag limit. Wily made the day's last retrieve.

"We have had an outstanding day dogs. Never even fired the second barrel," I mused. "Let's pick up the decoys and head in. I have lots of birds to clean. Time for lunch. I think that I will stop by Rooster's Restaurant. A steaming bowl of clam chowder will go down good."

Mallards continued to check-out the decoys as I disassembled the blind. With the aid of the four-horse kicker, I quickly rounded up decoys. With decoys in the boat, the big jet outboard was cranked up to quickly push us back to the landing.

Two days later all local upland bird seasons were over and we were into the final week of waterfowl season. I called up Clayton Evans to regale him with tales about good waterfowl hunting on the Snake River. "Come on down and help me out with all these ducks and geese. They are about to take over."

Chapter 35 — *Season's End Waterfowl*

Clayton talked Barb into taking over kennel duties. Leaving the snowy landscape of northern Washington behind, he arrived in the valley with his Chesapeakes, Bandit and Tess.

"Good to see that there is no snow on the ground down here," he said when arriving. After Clayton and the pups were settled in, we discussed the pros and cons of trying for ducks or geese. We finally opted for ducks the next morning, hoping to duplicate my last duck outing.

Morning again rolled in fair. We arrived at the launching area an hour before sunrise. A second party of waterfowl hunters was on hand to buck the fair weather odds.

As the morning passed, few puddle ducks moved and even fewer of these chose to decoy. There was little shooting. As per usual, there were some blotched opportunities. By noon, Tess and Wily had each retrieved just a single mallard.

"This is the slowest day hunting I have ever had here," Clayton noted. Normally Clayton was hard to discourage but I had to agree with him.

"Prospects don't look good for shooting to improve this afternoon. The grain barge is gone. Must have been moved last night. There is no food to draw the birds in and the weather is too nice. This late in the season, the birds have seen lots of decoys and the survivors have wised-up considerably. We need some bad weather to give us a chance. Probably most ducks are feeding safely in the refuge along the Port of Lewiston. Hindsight is best but I guess we should have gone for geese this morning."

"Maybe we should pull the decoys and head in. The young dogs are no doubt tired of sitting in trucks. We could salvage the afternoon by taking them training. Our training ponds in the Spokane area have been frozen for some time now. "

"I personally elect to hunt with retrievers trained as generalists not specialists. But if we're going to run field-trial derbies with Bandit and Abbie this spring, they sure could use a lot of brushing-up on their training. Our competition is not hunting their dogs. They are training for the trials. I know of an open pond in Lewiston where we could set up a nice field-trial type double mark." We took apart the blind and began to pull decoys.

Following a good training session, we sat over pre-dinner cocktails back at the homestead. "Hope you enjoy Cajun-type beans with venison and rice. That is this evening's menu. I think I will also bake a batch of cornbread. Unfortunately there will be no homemade chocolate cake like Barb serves you for desert."

Buddies Afield — Trips Outside Alaska

"The dogs were sure hungry after our water training. Dinner sounds fine. Prospects for a productive duck hunt in the morning are not good. Tell me about the geese you located."

"During an unproductive quail hunt three days ago, I came across hundreds of big Canadas feeding in a large field above Clarkston. Heck, there may well have been a couple of a thousand. Wheat was harvested from the field last summer and it has been replanted. The field is rectangular in shape and covers an area of about one mile by two miles. The property is part of a land trust. Hunters are welcome but vehicles are not permitted to drive into fields or along access roads."

"There is little cover to hide hunters in or around the field but I think I have a plan. The bad news is that we will have to pack decoys and blind materials about a half-mile on our backs. We need to be in and set up by shooting time at 7:05 a.m. That means rolling out about 4:00 a.m. Let's get decoys and camouflage into packs and loaded in my truck while dinner is cooking. I'm planning to hit the hay right after eating."

"I'm up for it. How about hunting the young dogs in the morning? Bandit has never had a goose."

Shortly after 6 a.m. the next morning we were parked at the field's east end. Another hunter's truck was ahead of us in the parking area. We might have competition but it was a big field. We shouldered heavy packs and grabbed shotguns and headed out. The young dogs romped excitedly. Full of energy, they heeled reluctantly. Coyotes chorused in the distance as Wily howled mournfully in protest of being left behind. The access road's mud surface had frozen during the night. Walking in would prove easy. Later, surface thawing would make packing-out slippery, heavy going.

A barbed wire fence followed the access road. At infrequent intervals locust posts were set close together to brace the fence. Following a 20-minute pack, we reached a series of four such posts that could be incorporated into our blind. A 10-inch rise of ground would contribute somewhat to our concealment. Camouflage cloth was hung over the fence to our north. Another section of camouflage material was strung from the fence to circle between us and the open field. The material was propped up in back by an extended camera pod. We added a few bedraggled clumps of tumbleweed to break-up the blind's outline. The resulting concealment was makeshift but it would have to suffice.

Our goose decoys were quickly put 30 or so yards out in the field. Our spread was severely limited by the long pack in but it included 18 shells and 6 silhouettes.

Streaks of red and blue in the east promised a fair day. Sunrise was heralded by goose music. Birds were up and moving! Strings and V's of

Chapter 35 — Season's End Waterfowl

birds came into view, converging on our field. Above Lewiston-Clarkston, the Snake River flows from south to north. Below the towns the river makes a great bend to flow from east to west. Geese were leaving the river from several directions and they seemed to be moving from all points of the compass.

Much to our frustration, several flocks moved over the field just wide of us and set up camp and loud conversation in midfield.

Clayton ventured, "Must have been a couple hundred birds in those flocks. With all that competition we are going to have a tough time drawing geese to our decoys."

"Maybe if we both work a call we can get their attention and pull some here," I speculated.

Additional flocks of geese continued to appear in the distance. The birds in one flock loomed larger and larger. They were heading our way. We crouched in anticipation as their course held. They were overhead. Clayton hit a bird that came down as a cripple. But my curses warmed the surrounding air. The firing pins of my over-and-under had clicked on empty chambers. I had neglected to load my shotgun.

For experienced dog trainers and hunters, we then made another bad mistake. Bandit was sent for his first goose. The big young dog faced a challenge as the crippled bird proved to be very mad and defiant.

Clayton, none too happy, was returning to the blind with a subdued dog and goose when, as usually happens when a hunter leaves his blind, a flock of geese approached with wings set. I watched in frustration as they saw hunter and dog and spooked.

"It's back to another round of force breaking for Bandit."

"I am sure that as a professional retriever trainer you have found that with dogs you can always expect the unexpected to happen. My old friend, Al Roggow, was born and bred to South Dakota bird hunting. I consider him a retriever guru extraordinary and Alaska's finest. When a training problem cropped up, he liked to say, 'Just keep on training. One of these days that dog will make you proud'."

But this seemed to be our hunt to make mistakes. A short while later a flock of geese checked-out our spread as I waited for Clayton to call, "take them." He was waiting for a second, closer, band to come in. Locked on the first flock passing in marginal range, I had not seen the second bunch. Finally loosing patience, I jumped to my feet and dropped a bird from the escaping flock. The birds Clayton was watching flared out of range.

"We really messed up there. Should have a couple of birds apiece."

"Back Abbie." Abbie dashed out to make the retrieve and returned toting her big goose and prancing proudly.

"Lil'Bit thinks that she is a veteran goose dog now. Though only a year-and-a-half old, she is very precocious. I first saw her when she was a very small pup. Peter Brown (her breeder) threw a live, full-size chicken. She ran it down and retrieved it to hand. At that moment I knew that she had unusual potential for training."

We watched from our blind as a flock of 30 to 40 geese pitched down 400 yards to our east. Three shots rang out as birds scrambled frantically into the air. The unknown hunter was revealed as he walked out into his decoys to pick up a bird.

"We'll get more birds," Clayton assured me.

"Mark to our right." Geese were approaching. Their wings were set. As they neared, I couldn't resist and made one short, off-pitch call. The birds flared and veered away.

It was now Clayton's time to express frustration. "Never call geese when they have wings set and are coming in."

"Mistakes continue," I lamented. "Can't complain about not having opportunities today though."

Action slowed down as goose movements fell off. Most of the birds using this field were feeding by now. Finally, another flock materialized and flew within range. I dropped a single and Clayton bagged two with his autoloader.

The third hunter pulled his decoys and stopped by for a brief conversation. He had not done much shooting.

Just after 9 a.m. we had a final chance as another flock of birds approached within marginal range. Two birds were hit hard and appeared to be coming down. Much to our dismay, the birds somehow recovered and flew off as cripples.

"Damn steel shot, anyway," Clayton muttered for us. "If lead BB's were still legal, those birds would have been dead."

"Let's take the dogs and search across the field to the south. May have come down far out." A half-hour of tramping produced no birds. The field's surface was thawing and walking became difficult. The wounded geese had likely flown over cliffs and into the canyon bottom to the south. We called off the chase.

"Some happy coyote will feast tonight," I ventured.

By 10 a.m., no birds were moving and we were ready to call it quits. We gathered up decoys and loaded our packs. With 30 pounds of big geese and 20 to 30 pounds of decoys and camouflage, I figured my pack topped out at 50 to 60 pounds. Furthermore, the heavy packs were very awkward and hit the packer behind the knees at every step.

Chapter 35 — *Season's End Waterfowl*

"With the slick, muddy hike ahead, I have all the geese I really want to pack. Any more and we would have to make two trips."

"Our shooting was sure not outstanding this morning," Clayton lamented. "I hate crippling and loosing birds. We each should have our limits of four."

"I agree our shooting wasn't memorable. I do not much mind missing some shots and not bagging a limit of geese, but I do sorely hate to lose a cripple. We will long remember those hundreds of geese flying all around us. Abbie had fun and Bandit started learning the finer points of retrieving geese. It has already been a good day and it's not over yet. We are to have a go at diving ducks this afternoon."

After lunch at the Rooster's Restaurant and Marina, we were to join Mike McCarthy who was bringing his boat and diving duck decoys down from Orofino. Clayton and I were anxious to check-out Mike's spread and techniques for hunting divers. Though I had hunted diving species in such diverse locations as Alaska, Maryland, Florida, and South Carolina, these hunts had been years ago.

Mike had been a sport-fishing guide as a young man. Now retired, he was a very serious waterfowler. Visits to his home showed decor heavily into collectable decoys, artistically mounted waterfowl, and waterfowl art. As we loaded Mike's roomy boat, the afternoon weather promised to be similar to the morning: high clouds, subdued sunlight, and air temperatures in the low 40's. A stiff down-river breeze had sprung up.

Additional layers of clothing were added to ward-off the cold. We would be shooting from a boat anchored away from the bank and would be totally exposed to the elements. It was decided to include only one dog in our crew and Tess was designated.

As Mike steered upriver, Clayton and I admired Mike's hand-carved and painted strings of goldeneye and bufflehead decoys.

"My son, Jimmer, made those decoys for me. As a serious taxidermist, he really learned waterfowl color patterns. Just wait until you see these deceivers at work. When bookings permit him to tear himself away from his profession as a fishing guide, he is one serious waterfowl hunter."

In a short while, Mike had four strings of diver decoys out. For good measure we then tossed six widgeon decoys just downstream of the diver spread. The boat was hastily secured.

Decoys moved by wind and wave bobbed very realistically. "Those are sure handsome decoys. They should fool some ducks if any come by," I observed.

"If divers come by, they will decoy," Mike assured us. "I have had divers set right in my boat's wake while setting out decoys. Diver shooting can be fast and furious. I don't usually bother with camouflage for diver hunting. They think that we are just another boat of steelhead fishermen. Contrary to popular opinion, goldeneye and bufflehead can be excellent eating. You will have to come up to the house sometime for dinner. I'll cook up some divers that will rival the best puddle ducks for gourmet dining."

A few days later I took him up on his offer and found the goldeneye he prepared delicious.

As the afternoon waned, few ducks of any species were moving, so we swapped stories to enliven the time.

"We three are fortunate to be able to spend so much of our time and resources training and afield with dogs. You and I are the only hunters I personally know who have flown with their dogs to Mexico to hunt for palomas, Mike. You have chased ducks across North America. Clayton has shot Saskatchewan for geese."

"That Canadian goose hunt was an experience but it was almost an overkill," Clayton remembered "Only so many geese a man can eat and give away."

"I don't know too many men who left Idaho during October bird season for a social flight to Eastern Europe," Mike ribbed me.

"A man can get into a rut and occasionally needs to expand his horizons. There is nothing like a visit to another culture to make you appreciate what you have at home. Besides having been afield with shotgun or rifle some 75 days this fall I have gotten in my share of hunting. Two-legged dear hunting in Europe can be most interesting and rewarding."

"Tell us about those European women. I'm surprised you didn't bring a trophy home with you."

"A man could do a lot worse than to do just that."

Clayton and I had put in a long day exposed to the elements. I do not mind cold weather hunting as long as I am moving. However, by late afternoon, sitting around all day waiting for birds had taken its toll. When three lesser Canadas came over, I was caught napping. Clayton downed one giving him his bag limit of four dark geese for the day.

A whistle of wings aroused us again. A goldeneye drake buzzed our decoys. I was slow bringing my over-and-under into play. Mike was prepared and acquitted himself well with his side-by-side 12 gauge. He dropped the drake with a long going-away shot.

"Back," Clayton ordered Tess. She dived overboard and swam to where the duck had splashed down. No duck was to be found where

Chapter 35 — *Season's End Waterfowl*

expected. Wind and current had carried it downstream. She would have to find her quarry as a blind.

Clayton stopped Tess with a blast of his whistle and gave her an "over" cast to the left. Tess took the cast beautifully, swam to the duck, and made the pickup.

"Nice job, Tess," Mike and I agreed as she returned to the boat.

I examined the handsome drake as I passed it forward to Mike. There was one small speck of blood on his head. "Looks like you made a head shot, Mike."

Mike was not one to be overly modest, "Sure. That's where I was aiming."

Clayton added to our afternoon's bag by dropping a handsome ring-necked duck. Not much later, he took advantage of his position in the boat's bow and caught up with an incoming drake lesser scaup as two birds dropped into the decoys. Mike and I each missed going-away shots at the survivor. Tess was overboard for another retrieve just as a pair of redhead ducks pitched into the decoys. Clayton was ready again and dropped them both with his autoloader.

"Good shooting Clayton! You are on a roll," Mike enthused. "Don't you ever miss?"

"Good thing you weren't along this morning. You would have seen me miss my share of geese," Clayton chuckled.

"Shooting time is over in five minutes. Tess has her work cut out for her. Those last two ducks are drifting away fast. What say we give her help with the boat? It's time to pick up the decoys and head back anyway."

As we headed for the dock, I summed up our day, "Another interesting day on the river. Much more rewarding than a day spent in the office or watching TV. I really enjoyed seeing the variety of ducks we saw this afternoon. Five species of waterfowl were brought to bag. We saw at least four additional species. I recall seeing mallard, widgeon, greater Canadas, wood duck, and bufflehead. There are probably a few pintail and green-winged teal around we didn't see. Good dog work topped the day off. Dog work is the main attraction bird hunting holds for me."

"The ring-necked drake and pair of redheads I took today were my first. I'm going to have a couple of ducks I took today mounted for addition to my collection," Clayton decided.

All too soon Saturday and the next-to-last day in the 2003-2004 season for Washington waterfowl arrived. The dogs and I headed out early for high goose pastures. Hopefully, the field we hunted earlier in the week had not been hunted since. Maybe we would have a chance at a goose or two.

The hunter met during our last outing was at the jumping-off point again. He had brought along a friend. "Have you hunted here during the last couple of days?" he wanted to know.

"No. How about you?"

"Negative. Hopefully geese are still using this field. Not much obvious food in the field for them but that many birds are sure putting away many pounds during a day. Hard to decoy with no cover though. Good luck."

"I'm not expecting to do much. Good luck to you fellows."

My faithful Wily was my companion for the day's hunt. As I shrugged into my heavy pack of decoys, I found myself wishing he could help me pack but goose decoys do not readily fit into a dog pack. With no help, I had to cut back on the amount of camouflage for my blind and the number of decoys I would set out. As we hiked away from the truck, Abbie barked with indignation at being left behind.

The other hunters disappeared in the darkness ahead. We cautiously approached and skirted four bulls breakfasting on hay left in the middle of the access road. Three of the critters were big and black; the fourth was a genuine longhorn that sported a trophy set of antlers. Fortunately, the bulls were not aggressive.

I elected to set up at the same location we had gunned three days earlier even though the geese would be spooky of that spot. With my blind up, I hastened to set decoys out. A low-flying flock of geese containing many birds approached quietly, spotting me and then spooking. The geese headed a few hundred yards deeper into the field and settled in with much honking. The time was 6:55 a.m. and legal shooting time was five minutes away. Birds were not supposed to be flying this early!

During the next half-hour, flock after flock of geese approached the field and joined the feeding hordes. My attempts to draw them closer by calling were completely ineffective. Several flocks of geese passed over my head in marginal shotgun range but unmolested by me. I still had hopes that some birds would decoy into sure killing range.

Birds continued to pay no attention to my decoys. As the day turned brighter, one flock leader flared 100 yards out and turned his charges to pass into the field a safe hundred yards away. My blind had obviously spooked the wise old bird.

Wily was rapidly loosing patience with all the geese going over and none falling for him to retrieve. He was whining by now. Seeking to calm him, I stroked his big head. I bet he was thinking like me that the decoys were not working any too well.

Chapter 35 — *Season's End Waterfowl*

A band of maybe 10 birds approached. "If we are going to go home with a goose today, I guess that I will have to try some pass shooting," I thought. "If this flock comes into range I will give them a try."

The birds continued to come on, crossing a little high and to my left. At the roar of my Beretta, a big bird crashed down. "Fetch Wily."

The weather was deteriorating fast. Clouds had lowered and light snow was falling. A short time later I connected on a second bird out of a flock passing to my right. I took the bird Wily delivered to hand. "Two shots fired, Wily, and two birds in the bag. I am shooting well. The 1-1/8 ounce loads of steel BB's I am firing seem to be effective. We have already had better success than I expected for today. This snow might force the birds to fly lower. If our luck holds, we may get a third."

We did not have long to wait. A flock of 25 or 30 geese crossed in range to my left. I swung on a bird midway down the nearer leg of the flight V. The 12 gauge crashed once. I stood with my mouth open. The bird I shot at and a trailing one both tumbled down.

Wily dashed to pick up a bird. After making the first delivery, he hastened back for the second bird.

"It's only 8 a.m. And we have our limit of four big Canadas with only three shots fired. I never even fired the second barrel this morning. This has been a hunting season to remember and today's hunt caps it off."

As we headed out, three shots rang out down the way. Two geese fell from a low flying flock. My fellow hunters had scored. The birds were thoroughly spooked and flew toward and crossed within easy shooting range of me. I watched them pass. Snow fell very thickly now.

The real work was ahead. It took me two trips to pack gear and four geese to the truck. Each round trip was over one mile of now slick, muddy roadway. Abbie ran along with us on the second trip for exercise.

At last, the truck became visible through falling snow as the final pack ended. I told the dogs, "Let's head home, stoke up the woodstove, hang some geese, and have some brunch. This hunting season is over. We have a lot of memories to fall back on. We can look forward to some spring fishing. In the seasons to come, we will retrace some old trails and hopefully explore some new ones."

Successful field trial experiences start with emphasizing the basics of handler and dog communication. Shown here with author Jim Mauney are Abbie (dark color) and Wily.

Appendix

Prepping Buddies For The Field

Proper preparation means greater enjoyment afield

    I realize more and more as the years go by how essential a good dog is to my thorough enjoyment of a day afield. Watching good dog work and sharing the day with an enthusiastic companion amounts to at least 75 percent of the day's experience for me. My needs in a hunting companion seem best satisfied by a versatile hunting retriever. Most often over the years my hunting and fishing companions have been Chesapeake Bay and Labrador retrievers. There is no doubt that a dog knowledgeable in the habits of game can use keen scenting ability to give his human hunting companion many more shooting opportunities than the dog-less human hunter. However, I believe the main contribution of the hunting dog to the day's success, and to the conservation of game, is in finding downed game that would otherwise be lost. Game such as ducks falling into heavy cover, or a crippled and running pheasant, can be impossible for the hunter with no dog to find.
    Retrievers with little natural instinct for retrieving birds can, with force training by a professional trainer, become adept at retrieving easy-to-find birds. But to work heavy, hostile cover or enter repeatedly into frigid water to chase down difficult cripples a dog must have tremendous natural drive and desire for birds. Given a start with a quality pup that finishes as an all around good companion afield, the sportsman must instill in the pup at least a minimum level of obedience and field training. An out-of-control flushing dog can have a grand old time clearing a field of roosters flushed far out of good shotgun range. I personally consider a retriever that cannot complete 100-yard land and water blinds as incompletely trained for tasks he may encounter in the field. Most of us have witnessed a frustrated

owner throwing rocks, or even shotgun shells, in the direction of a floating bird in the hope of getting a clueless pup to make a blind retrieve. A field-trial trained dog that can accurately mark four birds thrown by the fellows wearing white coats hundreds of yards out, but cannot trail and run down a cripple, has no place in a pheasant field with me.

I make no attempt here at detailing the training of a hunting retriever. There are numerous good books on how to train retrievers—very specific books for training hunting dogs, field-trial dogs, and companion dogs. A word of caution is needed here that some of these books must be read with a grain of salt. Not all dogs mature at the same rate and therefore may not be ready to do test X on day Y. Insistence on perfection or an absolutely rigid training regime can cause dog burnout. Likewise, the misuse of electronic control devices such as the electric collar can result in a thoroughly confused dog. Owners encountering problems in training their pups are advised to consult a hunting or field trial group or to seek the services of a professional trainer.

For the dog owner who lacks training assistance there is now hope in a number of helpful electronic devices such as bird and dummy launchers on the market. None of these devices can really replace a knowledgeable human assistant in the field.

My dogs are maintained in top physical condition year round. During the fall, they usually hunt three or four days a week and may run for miles or swim hundreds of yards daily. During the non-hunting seasons they accompany me on runs or walks. We cover around 20 miles a week under this program. In addition, they get intense exercise from running and swimming training marks and blinds.

When I started training Storm, my first retriever, I had no knowledge of the techniques for training a retriever. I took pride in and impressed observers with Storm's tremendous physical strength shown in retrieving logs from the Chesapeake Bay surf. This inadvertently led to the development of "hard-mouth."

York, my first Lab, was allowed and encouraged to retrieve beer cans. He also delighted in retrieving box turtles from the woods behind the house. The chagrined turtles were released unharmed to make their way back into the woodland. One morning York trotted over to me and proudly delivered his latest acquisition. In disbelief I accepted from his mouth a set mousetrap. This was a demonstration of the ultimate soft-mouth. The hunting dog owner who permits his dog to retrieve objects indiscriminately will at some time find himself very chagrined. His pup, failing to find a difficult fall during a hunt or trial, may return proudly packing some inanimate object.

Chapter 36 — *Prepping Buddies For The Field*

Until my ex-wife Judy lost patience and found me some dog training books, my dogs and I continued to learn together the hard way through trial and error. Then, visiting my parents in the Southern Pines area of North Carolina, I crossed paths with Mrs. Atkins, a successful Amateur owner and trainer of field trial dogs. She subsequently introduced me to her new professional dog trainer, a young John Dahl. My knowledge of advanced retriever training techniques such as handling for blind retrieves benefited greatly from this association. Later, as I became a field trial enthusiast, I had the privilege of getting to know and training with additional professional trainers including: Bill Thompson of New Jersey, Tommy Sorenson of Arkansas, and Chuck Crook, Jr. of California. I also trained with several very successful amateur trainers including, among others: Al Roggow and Roy McFall of Alaska; Linda Harger, Dr. John Lundy, Dr. Steve Parker, and Dr. Ben Baker of Idaho; Lance Brown of Montana; Ken Johnson of Louisiana; and Dick Cook of Virginia.

My retrievers have always loved fish, both to eat and to catch. One March afternoon I took Rock "hooligan dipping" along Alaska's Turnigan Arm. I had promised friend Nancy that I would show up in Girdwood that evening with a mess of hooligan to fry up for dinner. Dipping success was slow. Finally, the cold glacier water of Twenty-Mile River got to me. When I quit, my pail contained only a dozen or so of the small, oily fish. I judged the sun was long over the yardarm, time for drinking a cold one or two. I loaded wet dog and pail of fish into the back of the truck and headed up the road for the 10-mile drive to Girdwood.

When I arrived at Nancy's, I was handed a cold beer. "Fishing wasn't so good," I admitted. "I have only a few hooligan."

Nancy soothed my concern, "Doesn't matter. There is plenty of beer and hooligan are mainly to make you thirsty."

I opened the back of the truck to find Rock licking his chops. The fish bucket was empty. Rock had enjoyed a fresh fish dinner.

The tides in the Cook Inlet area of Alaska are some of the highest in the world. Tide fluctuation from low to maximum flood can be 20 feet to almost 40 feet a day. During migrations, salmon trying to enter a spawning stream are sometimes caught by a falling tide and stranded.

One day Jay and I were walking the beach at low tide just off a major salmon stream. Jay suddenly plunged into a large tidal pool and after considerable chasing succeeded in beaching a 30-pound king. I accepted the fish, telling him, "so that is how wolves fish, Jay. You know it just so happens that we could use some fresh salmon for dinner."

Some authorities have asserted that field trial retrievers do not make good hunting dogs. This has not proved to be true in my experience. It is true that a few trial dogs have too much drive for the average hunter to control in the field. But I believe that most trial dogs can make good hunting dogs if given the chance and experience. I personally have had a degree of success in running retrievers in field trials and hunt tests that have also hunted a wide variety of game in the field.

The dog that has become accomplished at flushing and thinking for himself in the upland field will lack the precise control exhibited by the exclusive field-trial dog. An outstanding upland hunting dog having learned to think independently may thus not make a good trial dog.

My first trial dog, FC AFC Rock Honeybear of the Yukon, got off to a late start in his trial career. His (and my) main interests were in hunting or fishing. The fall of his second year I foolishly returned early from a successful hunt for Dall's sheep to run a field trial derby. The weather in the high Wrangells had been beautiful, our meat supply was abundant, and the mountain quiet had been interrupted only by the murmur of sighing wind, the tinkle of flowing water, the whistle of a marmot or the scream of an eagle. Life there was good. Rock and I and Linda, our delightful human companion of the hunt, were not ready for and should not have made our hasty return to civilization.

To make a long story short, we arrived at the trial just in time for Rock to break on the first bird thrown in the first series and be disqualified. In later years, Rock went on to become a Field Champion. He had an uncanny ability to complete impossibly complex marks. His marking ability was probably in the top 5 percent of field-trial retrievers. Judges generally set up the first series of marks for 90 to 100 dog trials of such complexity that many dogs fail. If five or six dogs could pass such a test with flying colors, Rock was usually among them.

For learning bird sense and finding, trailing, and flushing birds there is no substitute for a lot of field experience. I have found that a young dog can learn much about these skills by hunting with an accomplished older dog. It is common for my dogs to freeze and come to a brief point when tracking down and coming eyeball-to-eyeball with birds. If the trainer so wishes, the young dog can be encouraged to be a pointing retriever.

I learned the value of dogs as pack animals by reading adventurous accounts of wilderness explorers, trappers, and Indians. Charles Sheldon's book, The Wilderness of Denali, is a classic that relates this technique. I purchased my first dog pack from an Indian family in the Kluane Lake Village of the Yukon Territories. This first pack was a heavy, awkward affair made from moose hair and canvas. These days, many dog supply houses can equip the dog packer with a nylon pack in a choice of colors. Some of the old timers packed a dog with up to 50 percent of the dog's

Chapter 36 — *Prepping Buddies For The Field*

weight. As a rule, I ask a dog to pack no more than 30 percent of his or her weight. A husky, long-legged animal is best suited for packing. My pack dogs have been in the 90 to 100 pound range or more. In brushy country small dogs tend to frequently entangle their packs in brush. Dogs used for backpacking must be physically very sound. The extra weight of a loaded pack will quickly aggravate any physical problems such as weak hips.

I have used my dogs on outings for big game as pack animals and to track down wounded game that would otherwise be lost. When hunting with your dog in big game country, a pup must be under absolute control at all times. His place is at your side unless released to perform a task.

During my years of walking Alaska streams that teamed with salmon and hunting the southeast rain forests, I had my share of close-up encounters with grizzly bear. I do firmly believe that my constant canine companions often saved me from stumbling over and being surprised by bear. Since time immemorial, packs of wolves have successfully routed bear. Bear do not like to be around barking and darting canines. The dog is more agile than the bear and, if wise, does not close with the bear. But few modern hunters need their dogs for bear protection. There is no safe way I know for a retriever to learn the art of bear herding.

A dog accompanying his master into big game country, particularly in bear country, should be trained to always walk at heel unless released. He may be released to forge ahead through thickets of heavy bear use to rout any bears. Whether in the mountains of Alaska or the pheasant fields of Idaho, a dog that breaks away to chase big game on his own is nothing but a nuisance. If the dog is wearing a dog pack when he takes chase, the pack and gear may wind up scattered over the countryside.

A sport fishery biologist friend of mine was attacked by a sow grizzly while working on Alaska's Admiralty Island. The bear severely mauled and left him for dead. Following a second grizzly encounter, he ordered a pup from a litter born to my Labs (Brandy and Kent). To my knowledge, he had no bear encounters when accompanied by a dog companion.

My young dog, Rock, learned to herd bear from a master of the art, Anvik River Brute. The pair of them delighted in sending bears, black or grizzly, on down the trail.

Mixing dogs and bear does not always result in the expected or wanted outcome, although most times the outcome is as desired. Sometimes our canine buddies come out on the short end when confronting big wild mammals. Jay Massey came home from work to his Eagle River, Alaska home one evening to find that his black Lab had been eaten by wolves. Gene Agee's Chesapeake, Strider, in his old age evidently ran afoul a pack of coyotes near their Peters Creek Alaska home. Strider never recovered from his severe wounds.

Early one morning a few years back, my brother Gene and I were cleaning limits of silver salmon harvested just at dawn from Alaska's Bird Creek. We had chosen a clear, cold pool of a neighborhood stream as the site for our task. As the cleaning progressed, Simba and Wily were occupied with munching on salmon heads. Suddenly Wily lost interest in his snack, becoming alert, and frozen in rigid attention. A deep rumble sound developed from his chest.

Gene observed unnecessarily "I think that Wily is onto something." He walked cautiously in the direction of Wily's gaze, then he stopped and gestured for me to come up, pointing to a huge old cottonwood tree. A large black bear was sitting in a tree crotch, watching our every move. He undoubtedly was eager for a breakfast of salmon but he was not too eager to take on two big dogs to secure it.

"Damn," I exclaimed. "I didn't bring a shotgun with me today. Let's finish up with these fish and head out. Hopefully the dogs will keep Mr. Bear at bay."

"Sure wish I had my camera," Gene sighed in regret. "That big bear in the big cottonwood would make some picture."

On a summer morning, Gene Augustine and I were fishing Alaska's Kenai River below the Russian River ferry crossing for red salmon. With record levels of reds returning, fishing was hot. Given the thousands of butchered carcasses fishermen left behind on the stream banks, some bear activity was expected. Gene and I were sharing a long gravel bar with three parties of drift boat fishermen brought there by professional guides. Each boat contained three or four fishermen, all enthusiastically working on taking their limits of salmon.

The morning was clear, sunny, and warm for Alaska. As we landed salmon, Gene and I stashed our catch on the riverbank in a patch of brush shaded grass. Wading out some 30 yards into the river enabled us to intercept migrating fish with fly rod and flies. Both Gene and I had 12 gauge shotguns slung over our shoulders.

Suddenly, all eyes turned upstream. A splashing too loud for a hooked and leaping salmon was very apparent. A young black bear was working his way downstream along the gravel bar with a salmon lunch in mind.

The bear rapidly neared our stash of fish. I sure hated to lose our hard-earned catch, but I would not shoot a bear over fish. I knew one of the boat guides from past years' fishing excursions. As the drama unfolded, my guide acquaintance loudly remarked for everyone's benefit. "I bet that big

Chapter 36 — *Prepping Buddies For The Field*

Chesapeake can take that black bear." The fishermen temporally ceased fishing to watch the action.

About that time Wily spotted the bear. Wily was not about to share his fish with any black bear. He let out a deep roar of anger and a series of challenging barks. I struggled to restrain the powerful dog as he plunged against his lead.

The bear hesitated, gazing intently our way. He quickly reached the decision that Wily was too much dog and that there were easier fish to come by and made tracks for the hills.

The hunter's days are richer and life's experiences are sure to be more rewarding when he or she is accompanied by four-footed buddies.

His good bloodlines show as Rock Honeybear of the Yukon begins a retrieve with a mighty leap into the water.

The Cast Of Canine Characters

Great dog buddies, listed by name, with descriptions by their owners

Acadia Artemisia Diver, 1986-1995.
Don Polanski, owner. Chesapeake female, brown color and 80 pounds. Don's first dog, she hunted as a team member and she learned to excel at tracking crippled pheasants.

Alaska's Big Ben, "Benny," 1975-1977.
Jim Riis, owner. Labrador male, black color, and 80 pounds weight. Benny was a very promising young hunting and field-trial dog. He came into his own during a Cold Bay hunt for brant. He departed this life much too early when he died from heart trauma that was probably induced by running into sharp-pointed brush while he was retrieving.

WR Aleutian's Water Strider JH. 1981-1992.
Gene Agee, owner. Male Chesapeake, dark brown color, tall, lanky frame and weight of 90 pounds. An excellent retriever of ducks and geese in Alaska. NAHRA listed. He died of wounds from a pack of Alaska coyotes.

Anvik River Brute, "Brute," 1973-1987.
Jerry Lavoie, owner. Jerry's legendary sled dog, an Alaska malamute male of solid white color, a very large body, and weight of 120 pounds. Brute was an "ace-high" pack leader and master of bears who also loved to fight. He completed the Iditarod Trail Race in 1982. He passed away in Anvik Village, Alaska at a very old age for a sled dog.

Beezer's Yukon Abbie-Cakes SH, WDQ, "Little Bit," 2002-present.
James L. Mauney and Jane Brown, owners. Chesapeake female, dark brown color and petite but solid 70-pound body. She has earned AKC Derby points. At the age of two, she was an accomplished hunting dog that could handle 12-pound geese easily.

Blue Skies Cinder Chip JH, "Chip." 1995-2008.
Clayton Evans, owner. Chesapeake male, dark brown color, 85 pounds.

Blue Skies Contessa SH, "Tess," 1996-2008.
Clayton Evans, owner. Chesapeake female, light brown color and a 60-pound body. Tess was a very good boat dog. She had a special enjoyment of pheasant hunting and also had no problem in handling the largest geese.

Blue Skies Duggans Mailman JH, "Duggan," 1996-present.
Clayton Evans, owner. Chesapeake male, light brown color and a massive, tall frame, and weight of 120 pounds, especially enjoys pheasants.

Blue Skies North Street Anne SH, "Annie." 1999-present.
Clayton Evans, owner. Chesapeake female, dark brown color and 65 pounds. Annie is a good size for retrieving ducks from a boat.

Brandy Sniffer, "Brandy," 1966-1970.
James L. Mauney, owner. Labrador female, black color, a very large body, and weight of 95 pounds. Brandy was my toughest cold-water and cold-weather dog. She delighted in swimming southeast Alaska's frigid waters and was an accomplished waterfowl retriever. She drowned in the Indian River of Baranof Island, AK when strong current swept her over a dam.

FC AFC Brutus of Widgeon Creek, "Brute," 1990-2003.
Bill Petrovish, owner. A Labrador male, black color, tall frame and 90 pounds. A versatile hunting and field trial dog, Brute qualified for five AKC Open/Amateur National Trials. His first hunt was for Idaho chukars at age 10 months; his last hunting retrieve was an Idaho chukar at age 13. He and Bill spent many days hunting and training for field trials in Alaska. His big heart finally failed at an advanced age for a big field dog.

Charismatic Chui of the Yukon, "Chu Chu," 2007 to present.
James L. Mauney, owner. Chesapeake male, dead-grass color, and a rangy 90-pound frame. Chui is a brilliant young dog with a great deal of natural instinct for hunting and retrieving.

Columbia's Cottonwood Gal MH, "Chilo," 1995-2008.
Sandy Flowers owner. Labrador female, black color and a 65-pound body. Described by Sandy as a great dog.

FC AFC Cookies Annie Fanny, "Annie," 1972-1984.
Albert Roggow, owner. Labrador female, black color, compact body and 70 pounds. Annie was Al's versatile hunting partner and also his field trial companion. She loved to handle on blinds, learning to do so by treats of cookies. Annie was Al's last personal dog and she died of cancer.

Chapter 37 — *The Cast Of Canine Characters*

Gant the Blue Ridge Brown Bear, "Gant," 1982-1995.
Bob Quinlan, owner. Chesapeake male, dark brown color and a blocky 85-pound frame. Gant earned Field Trial Derby ribbons. Gant was a son of Rock and sire of my Simba. He was Bob's personal companion and also the protector of the homestead. He disappeared from home one winter day and never returned.

Golden Kent, "Kent," 1967-1976.
James L. Mauney, owner. Labrador male, yellow color and 85 pounds. Kent was a friendly, outgoing family dog and also a versatile hunting dog. Death followed complications from heartworm infection.

Grandpa's Shot of Brandy JH, "Brandy," 1995-2008.
Clayton Evans, owner. Chesapeake male, sedge color and a weight of 115 pounds. Brandy was a fine duck dog.

Happy, "Hap," 1996-present.
John Terry, owner. Chesapeake male, light dead-grass color, stocky body, and weight of 85 pounds. Hap is John's family and upland bird dog.

Highland Storm, "Storm," 1962-1966.
James L. Mauney, owner. A light brown Chesapeake male, a rangy, raw-boned frame and 85 pounds weight. Storm was my first retriever and a loyal companion He lived up to his name, loving to fight. He was killed by heat stroke on a humid 95 degree day on Chesapeake Bay, Maryland.

Honeybear's Yukon Jay MH, "Jay Bird," 1981-1995.
James L. Mauney, owner. Chesapeake male, dead-grass color, a rangy frame, and 90 pounds weight. A fine field trial competitor and versatile field dog. Jay was on the National Field Trial Derby list. He came out of retirement at age 10-1/2 to qualify in first Master National in Delaware in 1991. He died at 14 when his heart failed during a July Idaho heat wave.

Honeybear's Yukon Simba MH, "Simba," 1992-2000.
James L Mauney, owner. Chesapeake male, light dead-grass color, a rangy frame and 95 pounds weight. His 22 derby points was the highest earned by Field Trial Derby Chesapeakes during the 1990s. He was a wonderful, loyal companion whether occupying the homestead or retrieving birds in the field. His passage was premature and his loss haunts my dreams. Death came after two surgeries on his spine for injuries during retrieving.

Irondale's Susie Q MH, "Susie," 1989-2000.
Tom McGlaughlan, owner. Labrador female, black color, and 75 pounds. She retrieved as many as five limits of ring-necked ducks on a single morning in Florida and also worked well on pheasants in her later years.

Ivan, "Lufer Boy," 1969-1975.
C. Eugene Mauney, owner. Norwegian elkhound male, silver-gray color and a husky, 65 pound body. Ivan had very strong hunting and trailing instincts that sometimes found him in difficult situations. During a visit to Gene and Jim's parents, Ivan wandered off and was never found.

Jess, "Jess," 1992-1999.
Lee Halbrook, owner. Labrador male, yellow color and 75 pounds. Jess became an accomplished midwestern hunting dog. He was used as a pickup dog on large preserve shoots and passed away at too early an age from epileptic seizures.

JJ's Gambling Chugach Bandit MH, "Bandit," 1999-present.
Mike Vogel, owner. Chesapeake male, dark dead-grass color and 95 pounds. A good-natured, enthusiastic hunter and a great nose.

CH Katmai Chugach Splendor MH, "Kat," 1996-present.
Mike Vogel, owner. Chesapeake female, sedge to reddish-brown color and 70 pounds. Mike describes her as a great temperament and a versatile huntress. Kat is adept at finding crippled ducks and hunting the uplands.

Mallardtone's Kimosaubi, "Mobile Kimo," 1980-1992.
Tom McGlaughlan, owner. Labrador male, chocolate color, rangy frame and weight of 75 pounds. An outstanding retriever of crippled divers, Tom calls him the best diving duck dog he has ever seen.

FC Oak Hill Exponent, "Pudge," 1977-1993.
John Dahl, owner. Labrador female, black color and 75 pounds. Pudge was a laid-back house dog that came alive for stylish performances in field trials and waterfowl hunts. She enjoyed a long life until her heart gave out.

Pacer's Ruff and Ready Lady, "Ruffy," 1983-1985.
Dimitri Bader, owner. Labrador female, black color and a blocky, 80 plus pounds body. Dimitri's family and "dream dog." Retrieved first goose at five months. A promising young field-trial dog with early qualifying trials. She drowned on a goose hunt when a storm capsized the boat at Knik Arm, Cook Inlet, AK.

Chapter 37 — *The Cast Of Canine Characters*

FC AFC Rock Honeybear of the Yukon, "Rocky Raccoon," 1975-1990.
James L. Mauney, owner. Chesapeake male, light dead-grass color and a husky 85-pound body. Born on Valentine's Day in 1975. A most versatile hunting and field-trial dog, he competed in the National Amateur Field Championship held in Maine, 1980. During his long lifetime Rock perhaps hunted more species of game than any other dog in modern North America. Our little campfires brightened many a wilderness setting. He died at the age of 15-1/2 swimming the Snake River in Idaho. Rock was the foundation dog of my line of Chesapeakes.

Sadie May of the Ranch, "Sadie," 1989-1999.
Dr. Bill Connor, owner. Springer spaniel female, liver-and-white color. Sadie was a very good companion and had an excellent nose for birds.

Seeka, "Seeka," 1988-1997.
Ed Larson, owner. Drahthaar female, brown and white color and a 65-pound body. Seeka was Ed's upland bird partner and had a superior nose. Her specialty was chukar in the years before an auto accident injured Ed's spine and curtailed their ventures into the cliffs.

FC AFC S&S's Sunshine Meg, "Meg," 1978-1992.
Steve and Sharon Parker, owners. Chesapeake female, reddish-brown color and a 72 pounds. As a stylish field-trial dog, Meg earned over 80 all-age points in an extended, 12-year career. Steve's best memories of her include her sweet personality and value as a hunting companion.

Tricrown Turlock Steed, "Steed," 1977-1988.
Gene Augustine, owner. Chesapeake male, dark dead grass color and 85 pounds. Gene's partner for ducks. Kidney failure ended his life. He was a part of the 1983 Alaska Chesapeake Expedition to Mexico.

Tsunami Ben of Baranof, "Big Ben," 1969-73.
James L. Mauney, owner. A Labrador male, yellow color and a massive, tall frame and weight of 105 pounds. Ben was an enormously strong and versatile hunting dog and a companion that had no peer. An accomplished pack dog, he was taken from me much too soon when a speeding car hit him as we were unloading for a day of hunting.

Willowmount Alfa Black Indigo, "Faa," 1976-1983.
Bill Thompson, owner. Labrador female, black color, stocky frame and weight of 65 pounds. One of Bill's early trial dogs and his personal duck hunting companion.

Yukon Jay's Silver Tip WDX, "Tip," 1992-2002.
Gene Agee, owner. A dark brown Chesapeake male, stocky frame and 85 pounds. Tip had some AKC Derby completions and was both a hunting and family dog. He was a very tough, dog that specialized in digging quail out of blackberry bushes. Spinal disk failure brought about his death.

Yukon Simba's Wily Cub WDQ, "Sunny Wily," 1998-present.
James L. Mauney, owner. Chesapeake male, light dead-grass color, a very large and rangy frame and 100 pounds weight. Wily earned his field-trial ribbons from very limited campaigning. He is a versatile and accomplished hunting retriever and a faithful, affectionate companion.

Title abbreviations listed for Canine Characters

CH	Conformation Champion, American Kennel Club
FC	Field Trial Champion, American Kennel Club
AFC	Amateur Field Trial Champion, American Kennel Club
JH	Junior Hunter, American Kennel Club
SH	Senior Hunter, American Kennel Club
MH	Master Hunter, American Kennel Club
WDX	Working Dog Excellent, American Chesapeake Club
WDQ	Working Dog Qualified, American Chesapeake Club
WR	Working Retriever, N.A. Hunting Retriever Association